Our Veterans Remember

Sarah A. Larsen and Jennifer M. Miller

Introduction by Jeremi Suri

Foreword by Kenneth B. Black, Secretary, Department of Veterans Affairs

Wisconsin Historical Society Press

Published by the Wisconsin Historical Society Press
Publishers since 1855

© 2010 by the State Historical Society of Wisconsin

Wisconsin Vietnam War Stories is a partnership of the Wisconsin Historical Society and Wisconsin Public Television, in association with the Wisconsin Department of Veteran's Affairs.

wisconsin**history**.org

Photographs identified with WHi or WHS are from the Society's collections; address requests to reproduce these photos to the Visual Materials Archivist at the Wisconsin Historical Society, 816 State Street, Madison, WI 53706.

Front cover photo courtesy of Tom Schober
Back cover photo courtesy of Bruce Jensen

Printed in the United States of America
Designed and composed by Jane Tenenbaum
14   13   12   11   10   1   2   3   4   5

Library of Congress Cataloging-in-Publication Data

Wisconsin Vietnam War stories : our veterans remember / [compiled by] Sarah A. Larsen and Jennifer M. Miller ; introduction by Jeremi Suri ; foreword by Kenneth B. Black.
　　p. cm.
　　Companion book to the Wisconsin Public Television three-part documentary of the same name.
　　Includes bibliographical references and index.
　　ISBN 978-0-87020-448-7 (pbk. : alk. paper) 1. Vietnam War, 1961–1975—Personal narratives, American. 2. Vietnam War, 1961–1975—Veterans—Wisconsin—Biography. 3. Vietnam War, 1961–1975—Wisconsin. I. Larsen, Sarah A. II. Miller, Jennifer M.
　　DS559.5W578 2010
　　959.704'30922775—dc22
　　　　　　　　　　　　2009043737

WISCONSIN
VIETNAM
WAR
STORIES

Bruce Jensen

Wisconsin Vietnam War Stories *was made possible in part by gifts from Don and Roxanne Weber, Associated Bank, The Onieda Nation, The Ho Chunk Nation, Kwik Trip, Wisconsin Public Service Foundation, Ron and Colleen Weyers, Lowell Peterson, and the Evjue Foundation.*

For all of those who served in Vietnam, thank you.

Contents

Acknowledgments

First, I would like to thank my editor at the Wisconsin Historical Society Press, Sara Phillips, without whose help my work on this book would not have been possible. You were there to offer guidance and support whenever I needed you. Thanks also to editorial assistants Mallory Kirby and Kate Carey and to production editor Diane Drexler who put many hours into getting the details right. Thank you also to Wisconsin Public Television producer Mik Derks. The tireless commitment you bring to the Wisconsin War Stories programs served an inspiration to me.

One of the things that struck me in working with these transcripts was how so many of the veterans recounted their memories in the present tense. It seemed, as they spoke, that they were still there, sending a dispatch back. I hope this project can shine a light home for the men and women who witnessed so much, and have born the weight of the experience ever since, fighting in the service of our country. Thank you. — S. L.

I would first like to thank the veterans for sharing their stories. Working on this book has both deepened and fundamentally changed my understanding of the Vietnam War, an experience that I am sure will be shared by many readers. I would also like to express my gratitude to the Wisconsin Historical Society Press for the opportunity to work on this wonderful project, particularly my editor, Sara Phillips, who was an absolute joy to work with. I want to extend my appreciation to Vanessa Walker Gordon, Margaret Lee, and Christine Lamberson for helping to find materials and for reading many of my chapter introductions; they improved them considerably by paring down unneeded sentences and clarifying confusing prose. Any errors that remain are, of course, my own. I would also like thank my advisor at the University of Wisconsin, Professor Jeremi Suri, who offered support and suggestions throughout the writing process. Finally, thanks to my family and my partner, Udi Greenberg, for offering love and support, suggestions, and for checking out, copying, and returning library books as I endeavored to finish writing the introductions. — J. M.

Foreword

Occurring between 1959 and 1975, the Vietnam War was the longest and most divisive conflict the United States has ever taken part in. In no place was the division more evident than right here in Wisconsin. While thousands protested the war on the University of Wisconsin campus, many thousands more from the Badger State served with honor in Vietnam. Approximately 165,400 servicemen and -women from Wisconsin served during the Vietnam War, 57,000 in Southeast Asia. Of those, 1,241 lost their lives "in country," another 79 died elsewhere in Asia, and 30 are still listed as missing; 71 of Wisconsin's 72 counties lost a son in the war. Whether they served, sent a loved one off to war, or spoke out against it, every citizen of Wisconsin was affected by the Vietnam War.

The Wisconsin Department of Veterans Affairs is honored to be associated with the production of the television documentary and its companion volume, *Wisconsin Vietnam War Stories*, produced by its valued partners, Wisconsin Public Television and the Wisconsin Historical Society. Promoting the role of our state in the Vietnam War and the experiences of Wisconsin veterans is an important part of our department's mission to improve public understanding of this multifaceted conflict.

The stories contained within these pages are a reminder that each veteran's experience was unique—no single story tells the whole story of this long war. Whether the veteran was a truck driver or a company commander, every story matters. Two Marines may have both been at Khe Sanh, but the way each remembers it can differ greatly. Put two helicopter pilots in the same room and you will discover that one might have flown slicks in the Delta, while the other flew a Cobra attacking Vietcong strongholds. Despite these differences, a connection exists between these men and women. Thirty-five years after the conflict, the collective remembrance of war has created a bond that will never be broken.

It is now time to move beyond the politics of the Vietnam War and focus on the veterans of this conflict. Reaching out to this group of veterans, neglected for so long, is paramount. Each time the Department of Veterans

Affairs holds an outreach event, more and more Vietnam veterans discover how we can assist them with health care, counseling, and other benefits. Collecting their stories is one way we can help them to heal. For some veterans, it has taken nearly four decades to fully understand the significance of Vietnam, make sense of it, and move forward. To those still struggling to find their way, we hope these stories will open the door to healing.

When the United States left Vietnam, it left behind more than abandoned base camps and empty ammunition crates. The ruins of Hue City are still there. So are the jagged cliffs and isolated perches of the Rockpile. Ghosts still hover in the forests of My Lai. When the war ended, veterans returned without fanfare or thanks, unsure of their place in the world. Now, through this project and the additional outreach efforts of our agency and our partner institutions we, as citizens of this state, are proud to say "WELCOME HOME."

Kenneth B. Black, *Secretary*
Wisconsin Department of Veterans Affairs

Introduction

Vietnam: America's Misguided War

The Vietnam War was not a war that anyone in the United States, including the combatants from Wisconsin, wanted to fight. More than 160,000 men and women from Wisconsin served in Southeast Asia between 1959 and 1975. Their experiences varied considerably, but they all shared two things in common: they entered a foreign society they knew little about, and they had only a vague understanding of their mission. They saw themselves as peacemakers and nation builders, not imperialists or plunderers or warmongers. For most soldiers, the Vietnam War was an act of American duty, ordered by politically elected leaders. The non-American allied combatants, especially the Hmong, also shared a sense of duty in their actions.

A number of commentators have focused on the atrocities committed by American military units in Vietnam—defoliation with Agent Orange, the My Lai massacre, and the napalm bombings, among others. Many commentators have also emphasized American excesses: simple-minded anti-Communism, overambitious efforts to "modernize" Vietnamese society, and widespread drug use and debauchery among soldiers. These portraits are not without some basis in fact, but they are caricatures of the real war experience. The vast majority of American servicemen and -women in Vietnam did not commit atrocities, and they did not succumb to the excesses of the "Ugly American." Quite the contrary. As this volume shows, most Americans and their allies were driven to survive and make Vietnam a better country in some small way, if at all possible. Many, but not all soldiers, lost faith in their ability to effect positive change, but most of them remained true to their calling as men and women in the service of their nation. For all of their diversity, these soldiers were patriots who deserve our respect and understanding.

The Vietnam War remains difficult for Americans to discuss because patriotism did not produce the intended results. In this sense, the Vietnam

War stands apart from the "great wars" of our history: the revolutionary struggle against Great Britain, the war between the states, the global battle against fascism, and, in Korea, the war to deny Communist control of East Asia. In Vietnam, the United States fought against a brutal Communist adversary with extensive foreign support, but the United States also defended a corrupt and incompetent ally that often looked worse than the enemy. In the best moments of the war, American forces prevented political collapse in South Vietnam and assured some semblance of social order. In the worst moments, American soldiers found themselves defending the indefensible against an organized, committed, and sometimes popular Communist military. Reading through these oral histories it is quite sad to see how good soldiers recognized the futility of their efforts on behalf of an ineffective local government. The problem was not the American anti-Communist cause in Vietnam, but the South Vietnamese regime that Americans supported. The North Vietnamese Communists fought to unify their country; the South Vietnamese forces sought to protect their families, often at odds with the political needs of their state. Deployed to defend what the South Vietnamese would not themselves defend, Americans were caught in between.

Vietnam was not the last time the United States found itself in these circumstances. One of the enduring questions raised by the experiences of American soldiers is how the United States should use military force abroad when confronting a dangerous enemy without viable local alternatives. Threats to American interests often emerge from distant regions where established powers are weak, where the United States has few direct connections, and where the terrain and culture prohibit easy penetration. In theory, policy makers in Washington could simply avoid any serious intervention in forbidding settings like these, but the breadth of American trade, resource needs, and alliance commitments makes separation unrealistic in many cases. One need not believe in a rigid "domino theory" to acknowledge that Vietnam's proximity to Japan and China meant that it would in the 1960s, like today, play an important role in the future of Asia.

The oral histories in this volume encourage us to think not about *whether* to become involved in other societies, but about *how* to do so. Is there a place for legitimate nation building in American foreign policy? What role should young men and women, like those featured in this book, play in this process? One must come away from the experiences recounted here with a sense that the United States often misapplies its best human resources. Why weren't more of the talented and well-intentioned Wisconsin citizens in Vietnam working to improve the politics and social conditions of Southeast Asia? Why weren't they helping local villagers live the kinds of lives they wanted to live, free from Communist and other tyrannical intrusions? Why weren't they better prepared for the challenges they faced?

The United States could have done much more without imposing itself on Vietnamese citizens. There were many avenues the United States could have pursued that defy the misleading categories of American liberal capitalism and Soviet authoritarian Communism. Working with local interests, addressing global concerns in ways respectful of tradition, and negotiating innovative solutions to common problems—these are the areas where Americans are best suited to work with peoples of other societies. The Midwestern voices in this volume capture that pragmatism and discipline; they also capture how those attributes were misused at the time.

The Vietnam War was part of a broader Cold War struggle against Communism that forced Americans to reimagine how they could protect and improve distant parts of the world, without becoming a global empire. Again, this was not altruism but basic self-interest. Southeast Asia is one region where Americans did not find a path to success. Their goals were laudable, their efforts sincere. The sacrifices—American and Vietnamese, Hmong and Cambodian—were tragic in their futility. The voices of anguish in this volume could have become voices of achievement if the leaders who sent these men and women to war thought more effectively about how they could accomplish their aims. Was the United States fighting the right kind of war, strategically and tactically? Did the United States do enough to appeal to local villagers in Southeast Asia? Had Washington done enough to promote appropriate and effective allies?

These are not easy questions for leaders. They are not, however, impossible to address. Successful wars require successful politics. Presidents Lincoln, Roosevelt, and Truman were effective commanders-in-chief because they understood that maxim and consistently worked to make the political compromises necessary to give the fighting forces the best opportunity for victory. In Vietnam, overwhelming American power—and overwhelming confidence about that power—tempted men like General William Westmoreland, Presidents Lyndon Johnson and Richard Nixon, and their many intelligent advisers, to use the military as a substitute for difficult political bargaining with allies and adversaries. Their successors might have made the same mistake a generation later.

The central lesson of the Vietnam War is that American virtue—as displayed in these revealing oral histories—will only find full expression with sophisticated and strategic leadership. Our state and our society produce able-bodied and ethically grounded citizens in abundance. Effective leaders are, however, few and far between. The soldiers who fought in Vietnam were not well served by their commanders, their politicians, and the public intellectuals of their day. Our society must strive to do better next time.

Jeremi Suri
E. Gordon Fox Professor of History
University of Wisconsin–Madison

A Note on the Text

More than 125 veterans—men and women from all ranks and orders of the military—were interviewed for *Wisconsin Vietnam War Stories*. Of these, 40 appear in this volume; many more were chosen for a television documentary by the same name, produced by Wisconsin Public Television in 2010. The interviews were conducted by Mik Derks, producer at Wisconsin Public Television, and edited for this volume by Sarah Larsen. Jennifer Miller provided the historical chapter introductions.

The transcripts of oral interviews conducted between 2007 and 2009 form the basis of the text printed here. We have tried to create a clean, readable text without sacrificing the original language of the interviews. Words added to clarify the text or to amend inaccurate dates or place names appear in brackets. The transcripts omit false starts as well as filler words, such as "you know" or "um." We made no attempt to preserve dialect or pronunciation.

In each chapter, we join together interviews from several veterans and weave their stories together into a cohesive narrative. As much as possible, we stay with the order of events as presented by the interviewee, though in some cases, stories are rearranged so that the narrative is easier to follow. For consistency, we listed either the hometown or the town each veteran lived in before or just after their term of service rather than the town they live in currently. In the chapter introductions we referred most commonly to NLF (National Liberation Front) rather than VC (Vietcong) to indicate pro-North Vietnam fighters, although we recognize both terms as valid.

We have contacted the interviewees and asked them to review the text selected for inclusion in this book. In several cases they requested (and we made) minor changes that corrected inaccuracies or clarified statements. We hope by presenting these oral testimonies of the Vietnam War that we honor the veterans' experiences and broaden our readers' understanding.

Sarah A. Larsen and Jennifer M. Miller

Advise and Assist

"In retrospect, the roots of our involvement didn't take place simply in [1961] when Kennedy sent the Green Berets in. We were there with a lot of money [and] a few hundred people.... We were putting on a real effort."— *John Brogan*

Though American memories of the Vietnam War are indelibly associated with the upheavals of the 1960s, U.S. involvement in Vietnam dates from 1950, when the United States first offered aid to the French Army in Southeast Asia. In the aftermath of World War II, France sought to reestablish its colonial presence in what was then called Indochina (Vietnam, Cambodia, and Laos), whose borders the Japanese military had invaded during the war. The Vietnamese people, however, who had fought the Japanese invasion during World War II, sought their own independence and resisted a return to colonial rule. On September 2, 1945, the Viet Minh independence movement, under the leadership of Ho Chi Minh, proclaimed Vietnamese independence and established the Democratic Republic of Vietnam (DRV). A nationalist and a Communist, Ho was driven by a strong belief in the independence of a unified, self-determined Vietnam. Despite Ho's declaration, France was unwilling to renounce its colonial control, and in a time of postwar upheaval, Ho's government was not internationally recognized. Tensions between the French Army and the Vietnamese thus continued to rise as France sought to regain control over Vietnam. With the establishment of the Communist People's Republic of China in 1949, the colonial conflict between the French and the Vietnamese took on a heightened significance within the context of the Cold War. In 1950, the new Communist Chinese government recognized Ho's government in Vietnam; this, shortly after the "loss" of China to Communism, heightened U.S. fears that Communism was on the march in Asia, with Vietnam as the next battlefield. The United States thus granted France's aid request, offering $15 million in aid in March 1950. This small grant was the beginning of a multidecade U.S. commitment in Vietnam.

Patti Isaacs, Parrot Graphics

U.S. concerns about the spread of Communism in Asia escalated further with the outbreak of the Korean War in June 1950. Communist North Korea's invasion of South Korea confirmed U.S. fears that the Communist countries sought to militarily dominate Asia. Along with sending troops to defend South Korea, the United States expanded its aid program in Vietnam and the first direct U.S. military assistance — planes — arrived in Saigon only a few days after the outbreak of the Korean War. In September 1950, to assist the French military more fully, the United States sent an official Military Assistance Advisory Group (MAAG) to Vietnam. Though MAAG assistance was initially comprised of small amounts of aid, material, and personnel, historian Katherine Statler notes that "American intervention each day became more tangible and visible."[1] The United States' role soon expanded into instruction, pilot training, and supervision of the French war effort.

Despite U.S. assistance, the French effort against the Viet Minh and DRV forces was failing. The devastating defeat at Dien Bien Phu in May 1954 ended France's hopes of regaining control over its former colony. In reaction to France's difficulties in Vietnam, President Dwight D. Eisenhower first articulated the now-famous domino theory describing U.S. fears that the region might fall to Communism: once the first domino fell, "you could have the beginning of a disintegration that would have the most profound influence."[2] This logic committed the United States more fully to Southeast Asia even as the French prepared to withdraw. Agreements signed at the Geneva Conference held in the late spring of 1954 ended French control over its colonies and divided Vietnam at the 17th parallel into two regions of control: one under the DRV in the north and one as the newly established "South Vietnam" (soon named the Republic of Vietnam). These agreements also planned for an election in July 1956 to reunite the country under one unified government. The Geneva Accords, however, were between the French and the Viet Minh and were not signed by either the United States or South Vietnam, leading to questions about their future viability. Indeed, the 1956 elections never took place, and in the years following the Geneva Accords, the United States continued to commit aid, material, and advisors to South Vietnam. Though the Geneva Accords limited MAAG's strength to 342 troops, the United States exceeded this limit through the use of military technician programs, civilian specialists, and other advisory personnel throughout the 1950s.[3]

The United States' objective of stopping the spread of Communism in

Southeast Asia now hinged on the creation of a strong, viable South Vietnamese government. In the words of Secretary of State John Foster Dulles, the United States hoped to build up the South as a "dike against Communism."[4] MAAG played a central role in this process. In January 1955, the French relinquished authority over the South Vietnamese military; the next month, MAAG began directly training the newly named Army of the Republic of Vietnam (ARVN), a program that would continue through the rest of the 1950s. ARVN quickly took on the trappings of its U.S. advisors, adopting U.S.-style uniforms and an American military salute as the United States also expanded its training facilities in South Vietnam.[5] By this point, MAAG was part of a broader U.S. commitment to Vietnam that included economic and developmental aid, psychological and cultural programming, political activities, and covert operations. MAAG represented a deepening U.S. presence in Vietnam, one that would become more entrenched throughout the decade, and lay the groundwork for direct U.S. military intervention in the years to come.

John Brogan, De Pere* (Army, MAAG-Cambodia)
John Mielke, Appleton (Army, Medical Corps)

JOHN BROGAN I was drafted in 1954 and served until 1956. I [spent] the better part of 1955 assigned to Phnom Penh, Cambodia. I was in the Agent General's Corps in Washington, D.C., as a private after I got out of basic training. I got assigned to be a clerk typist. I saw this thing come across my desk in the Pentagon where I was punching a typewriter. It was establishing new units, and I thought, "Well, since I've got another year and a half in here and that sounds like a pretty interesting place, I'll go up and volunteer for it." It turned out that the general in charge of supplying these people in the Pentagon said that this was a hardship post and was having a hell of a time getting any officers to go there.

Our involvement in the area really actively started right after World War II. We were giving military assistance and advice to Jiang Jieshī [Chiang Kai-shek] in his battle against Mao Zedong. When he lost to Mao in 1950, the nationalists pulled out and went to Taiwan. The American military mission in China was, to a large extent, switched in 1950 to Saigon. We were pro-

---

French soldiers rush into battle at Dien Bien Phu. *National Archives (306-PS-54-7595)*

viding military assistance, supplies, arms, and training to the French Army in their attempt to get back the colonies that they lost to the Japanese.

In 1950, the French were already at war with the Communists in the North, against the Viet Minh and Ho Chi Minh. By 1954, they were good and truly whipped in Dien Bien Phu. So, the whole French Army was rolled up and defeated and the war came to a standstill. The United Nations made a treatise telling the French, "OK, you get out," and the French agreed. Then the United Nations supervised free elections in the three constituent nations that made up French Indochina: Vietnam, Laos, and Cambodia. I got there in 1955 when these elections were going on. I saw the American government establishing Military Assistance Advisory Groups in Phnom Pehn, Cambodia. It was an interesting time. It was interesting for a twenty-year-old kid from De Pere, Wisconsin, that's for sure.

In [1953] Nixon came out to Vietnam and was so enthralled by the French effort that he tried to convince Eisenhower to put active troops in and even use the atomic bomb. Eisenhower was bright enough to tell the kid from Yorba Linda, California, to sit down and shut up for a while. We kept pouring in more and more military and economic aid and assistance. I was part of that effort. In retrospect, the roots of our involvement didn't take place simply in [1961] when Kennedy sent the Green Berets in. We were there with a lot of money [and] a few hundred people in the Military Assistance Advisory Group mission. We were putting on a real effort. We picked our people to support and we were putting money and talent into getting them elected and so forth.

JOHN MIELKE I'm part of a medical family. My dad was a physician here in Appleton, but he was in World War I. I can remember as a little boy talking about the flu and about how they stacked the dead bodies up like cords of wood, there were so many of them. I never forgot that. My father-in-law was in World War II, as a physician. Being from a medical family, I wanted to be a physician. I personally became involved with the military in 1952.

I was in the reserve military rather than the regular Army as a physician. You went in a captain. What did I know about leading anybody? Gosh, I was just out of my internship. I was twenty-seven or twenty-eight years old but I was a captain. They sent me down to Fort Sam Houston in August. We spent two weeks down there — two weeks to learn how to be a soldier. It took me six years to learn how to be a doctor but two weeks how to be a soldier.

One day I got the information that I was going to Vietnam and I was going to take care of helicopter pilots. They were warrant officers. Had I had any experience with aviation or anything like that? None whatsoever. They assigned me to nine enlisted [men]. I got on a plane at Louisville and flew out to San Francisco. I remember they said I would hook up with the warrant officers out there. I asked somebody where I could find the warrant officers. I was told, "The ones that are making all that noise in that bar, that's your crew." They were wild, but they were good, and they were good to me.

JOHN BROGAN I was assigned to the [MAAG] in Phnom Penh, which at the time was an absolutely bucolic, beautiful, French-colonial tropical town. It just couldn't have been nicer. The people couldn't have been more pleasant, less antagonistic.

A Vietnamese palace in Saigon. *John Brogan*

I got in and out of Saigon regularly, carrying messages and communications. Saigon was an entirely different deal. I could see the deterioration at that time. It wasn't laid-back. It was hurly-burly, hustle-bustle. Everything that happened was done by the overseas Chinese. They were the main merchants and traders.

JOHN MIELKE We got to Subic Bay and anchored. We sat there for two days. Didn't go anywhere. I know now the reason for that was that our government really wasn't sure they wanted to do what they were going to do. We didn't have any military over in Vietnam at that time other than the MAAG units. They decided that we'd go ahead. That was probably one of the government's first major decisions — going beyond the MAAG units. We took over when the French were defeated.

We went up the Saigon River, through the Mekong Delta. We hit Saigon about six o'clock at night. I'll never forget the view. We're up high on the ship looking down on downtown Saigon. It was a French city with wide boulevards. The lights were coming on, and it was beautiful. It was absolutely gorgeous. To add to the beauty of it was the Vietnam women. They came to the ship in very beautiful costume[s]. Chiffon, the upper portion was form fitting and then it flowed down to their feet. The skirt was split all the way up. As they walked along, it would just be floating in the breeze with brilliant colors. I'll tell you who knew what to do. It wasn't the soldiers; it was those girls down there. They had it all figured out. We were sitting ducks for them. They just cleaned us out of our money. These guys came back drunk and every other which way. I thought that was kind of sad. How are we supposed to act in a country that we didn't know anything about?

That was my introduction to Vietnam. . . . It was my first experience with the military not knowing what they're doing. A military person had come on ship for one hour to introduce us to Vietnam. What can you tell a group of people in one hour about the history of Vietnam, what they [are] going to get into, what they should be looking for, the customs, in one hour? These guys had been on this ship for twenty-four days. [The military] gave them seventy-five dollars and let them go. What was I supposed to do as a physician to take care of these people? My training in the Mayo Clinic wasn't really heavy on tropical medicine. But I was suspicious that we were going to go to the tropics, so I got a textbook on tropical medicine. They certainly didn't teach us that at Fort Sam.

JOHN BROGAN [Vietnam] was incredibly different from the climate that I lived in. There was one air-conditioned room in the whole country and that was the code room of the American Embassy. You shortly learned what fans were all about and how those lizards on the wall were really your friends and not your enemies. They eat the bugs.

Saigon was a tropical chaos: the streets, the bicycles, the mixture of the Chinese culture and the Vietnamese that always rubbed against each other. It was not a laid-back, colonial place. It was one busy, herky-jerky spot. It was when I was in Saigon that I would have an evening out on the town and I got to meet some of the most colorful people I've ever seen in my life.

We were out one night to this nightclub and everybody was sitting around. Tua Tua beer was served in a rather large brown bottle. As I recall, it was frighteningly bad beer. There was a scuffle on the dance floor with some Senegalese Foreign Legionnaires. When the place erupted it was like a movie set: boom, bang, dancing, argument, wham! First thing I see, somebody takes one of these Tua Tuas, smashes it on a table, and slices the guy across from the upper shoulder to the lower hip, just lays him open with a beer bottle. The only guy at our table who knew exactly what to do was this Alsatian. He said, "Run!" He jumped up, smashed a beer bottle to get himself armed, and whipped a jacket around his other arm and we ran through a window. I mean we just retreated as fast as we could because ugly things were going on in that crowd. But that was Saigon. That's how it was. There was a mélange of people and cultures and it was crazy.

JOHN MIELKE We [were] in a French-type motel; it was called the Rex, R-E-X. It was about eight stories; it was a modern motel. The military took it over for our group and the helicopter pilots and some other support services that were there. Our job was to transport Vietnamese soldiers out into the field or wherever they were going to fight. These helicopters, the pilots said, weren't the safest helicopter in the world at that time. They had absolutely no guns, of any sort, on those helicopters. They were completely defenseless.

The warrant officers that flew these helicopters were very good to me, and I liked them, but they were wild. They loved to drink, and they'd party. A sheltered kid from Appleton, Wisconsin, they'd say, "Come [on,] Captain, let's go to the bar." It sure wasn't Appleton, Wisconsin.

[We] were very worried. We had no machine guns. They got smart, the Vietcong, and they were taking a few hits, but [we] didn't shoot them down at that point in time. Then our government said, "We'll get [our soldiers] some machine guns and put them in the open door to try to protect themselves." The order was you shot back only if someone shot at you and you weren't the aggressor. This sort of worried me. So I asked them, "If something happens, if you get shot down, do you have any medical supplies?

Do you have any morphine, do you have any antibiotics, do you have any bandages, do you have anything?" They had nothing, not a thing. I didn't have anything. I did have morphine and some antibiotics, but nothing to put them in. We had twenty or thirty helicopters. I went to the PX and bought some soap dishes and packed them full of stuff, particularly morphine, some antibiotics, and more morphine, and gave it to them.

Why was it done that way? As I look back on it now, if the rest of the war was run that way...I was running my show, purifying my water, using the medications, with no knowledge of tropical diseases. Maybe that's a reason that the men got frustrated and used drugs and drank and things were undisciplined, with no objective.

Helicopters were used during early U.S. involvement in Vietnam to transport ARVN soldiers and medical supplies. *John Mielke*

JOHN BROGAN [The battle at] Dien Bien Phu was more than just a major defeat. It was a major wake-up call to the West. The occurrences in '53 and '54 around Dien Bien Phu received lots of publicity. The French had this idea that the way to handle native insurgency, armed peasants and so forth, was to put heavy military concentration in various parts of the country, draw the peasants out, and machine-gun them down. One of the things they forgot is that the bases at Dien Bien Phu up the Red River were right squat in the middle of a valley and ringed by mountains. When the North Vietnamese got on the mountaintops it was just like duck soup, firing down on your soup plate.

The Peace Treaty of Paris brought the end of fighting in '54. After Dien Bien Phu they separated Vietnam into North and South. Actually the country of Vietnam is about seven provinces. Ho Chi Minh was running the North and [Ngo Dinh] Diem was running the South and we were backing

MAAG units trained South Vietnamese soldiers in helicopter deployment and other tactical skills. *WHi Image ID 11527*

North Vietnamese leader Ho Chi Minh. *National Archives (306-NT-94A-10)*

[Diem]. So it was set up for a real conflict. Ho was a Vietnamese nationalist. Diem was one of a select group of local folks whose parents and grandparents spoke French and were educated in France. They were Catholic in a country that's 97 percent Buddhist. They were the elite of the elite. Basically, the whole system was run by this group of elite Vietnamese who were acculturated to the West. They didn't have very deep roots in their own society.

Just after Dien Bien Phu, the French petulantly dropped everything and said to the U.S., "That's it. It's all yours, you can take it over." So, that was our mission. That morphed into more and more active training in Vietnam, after I left. MAAG Saigon and MAAG Vietnam became more operational in nature with thousands and thousands of people over there. The American hubris was based on the assumption that we were so powerful and had so much muscle and that we could do any damn thing we wanted to do.

2 Naval Presence

"We were very young. God, I was only twenty-one. After you have been flying there for a year, you feel like an old man. I guess I never thought about it that way, but you did get old in a hurry."— Dan Schaller

Although the Geneva Accords (1954) called for 1956 elections to reunite Vietnam, these elections never took place, and throughout the rest of the decade Vietnam remained divided along the 17th parallel, with Ho Chi Minh in power in the North. Hoping to create a viable base of political power in the South, the United States — including the CIA — threw its support behind Ngo Dinh Diem. Diem, a Catholic with experience in the French government, was strongly nationalist, pro-Western, and vehemently anti-Communist. The United States had originally hoped that Diem would facilitate a strong South Vietnam, but Diem's rule quickly proved to be authoritarian and repressive. As a Catholic leading a predominantly Buddhist country, Diem ruled from a narrow power base, supported by Catholic elites and nepotistic followers, and relied on terror to sustain his control. Failing to create a broad coalition of political support, Diem's government fueled a growing insurgency and fostered instability in the South. In 1958, Communist Party members in South Vietnam coalesced into an armed resistance that Diem dubbed the Vietcong (VC), and by the end of the decade, attacks on government military targets, including U.S. military establishments, were becoming increasingly common. In 1960, the Communist Party joined with other anti-Diem figures to form the National Liberation Front (NLF)* in Saigon. The NLF called for an overthrow of the Diem regime, the end of U.S. military presence in Vietnam, and ultimately, the reunification of the North and the South, as stipulated by the Geneva Accords. Although the NLF was a nationalist organization, its members

---

* U.S. troops commonly referred to NLF soldiers as Vietcong or VC.

included Communists and it maintained a close relationship with Ho Chi Minh's leadership in the North in a shared struggle for Vietnamese independence. The United States' plan to build up the South as an anti-Communist bulwark had thus far failed to create a politically viable regime.

Nevertheless, the U.S. government remained committed to South Vietnam. After he became president, John F. Kennedy expanded the U.S. presence in Vietnam, sending more military advisors and authorizing increased covert and counterinsurgency missions in the North. Despite this expanded U.S. presence, resistance and violence continued to spread through the South. In May 1963, in response to Diem's attacks on Buddhism and jailing of Buddhist monks, sixty-six-year-old Buddhist monk Quang Duc set himself on fire in the middle of Saigon, vividly demonstrating the depth of the resistance to Diem's rule. Diem's actions against Buddhists, combined with his attempts to make contact with the Democratic Republic of Vietnam in the North, led to a widening rift between the Kennedy administration and the Diem government. With U.S. assurances that it would not interfere, a group of Vietnamese generals assassinated Diem on November 2, 1963. After Kennedy himself was assassinated three weeks later, new president Lyndon B. Johnson continued to back the South Vietnamese government, believing that an ongoing show of U.S. support was necessary despite, or perhaps due to, South Vietnam's extreme political instability. By the summer of 1964, Johnson had increased U.S. military advisors from 16,000 (under Kennedy) to 22,000, and more than 90 percent of ARVN's weapons came from the United States.[1] The United States was spending $1.5 million a day in Vietnam.[2] The Johnson administration also expanded covert missions, which included increasing both Naval Desoto destroyer patrols in the Gulf of Tonkin off the coast of North Vietnam and raids by South Vietnamese guerrillas into the North. Still, the goal of a politically stable South Vietnam remained elusive and as international discussions arose about the possibility of another Geneva Convention — something the Johnson administration sought strenuously to avoid — Johnson and his staff debated the possibilities of direct U.S. action in Vietnam.

The Gulf of Tonkin Incident, which took place off the coast of North Vietnam in August 1964, served as the turning point in this debate about U.S. involvement in Vietnam. On August 2, 1964, while engaged in eavesdropping in the Gulf of Tonkin, the U.S. destroyer *Maddox* was attacked by three North Vietnamese patrol boats. Though the United States issued a warning to the attackers, after a reported second attack two days later the United States responded with air strikes against North Vietnam. Historians now believe that the second attack never took place.[3] Nevertheless, the Johnson administration used these attacks as a justification for a new level of U.S. military commitment in Vietnam, quickly informing Congress that the United States had undertaken retaliatory measures and utilizing the sense of crisis to pass a congressional resolution supporting U.S. military action in Southeast Asia. The Johnson administration had actually drafted this resolution in July; the Gulf of Tonkin Incident merely provided the context to issue it. According to historian Fredrik Logevall, the Gulf of Tonkin Incident allowed Johnson to accomplish several objectives: it demonstrated that he was not "soft" on Communism prior to the 1964 presidential election; it proved the United States' commitment to South Vietnam, which the United States hoped would strengthen the South's resolve against the North; and it prevented the South from seeking a separate agreement with the North.[4] The United States was now officially, openly, and militarily committed to the preservation of South Vietnam.

The fact that naval activities sparked the conflict leading to an expanded U.S. commitment to South Vietnam highlights the diverse roles fulfilled by the Navy throughout the Vietnam War. Indeed, the U.S. Navy first arrived in Vietnam in 1950, when it supplied French forces with aircraft and vessels, and it remained in Vietnam until 1975, when it helped to evacuate U.S. personnel from Saigon. All told, more than two million naval personnel served in Southeast Asia, including Vietnam, Laos, and Cambodia, during the Vietnam conflict.[5] Prior to the Gulf of Tonkin resolution, the Navy sought to strengthen South Vietnamese naval capabilities by supplying both equipment and advisors, while also conducting surveillance and reconnaissance missions. Naval personnel also participated in counterinsurgency programs; President Kennedy created the Navy SEALS (Sea, Air, and Land Forces) in 1962 to increase the United States' guerrilla capabilities in coastal and river areas, while other naval units built infrastructure such as houses, roads, and hospitals to support the South Vietnamese population. Throughout the war, naval personnel serving throughout the Pacific facilitated wartime supply routes, while naval destroyers and submarines secured the Vietnamese coast. Within Vietnam, naval personnel were active both in the air and on water, as naval aviators and helicopter units participated in bombing campaigns and combat, naval flyers took aerial photographs, naval swift boats patrolled rivers, and naval river convoys resupplied Army and Marine units fighting on the ground. The experiences described in this chapter capture the varied and wide-ranging functions fulfilled by the Navy in the early years of conflict and beyond.

Bill Moore, Greenfield (Navy, Seventh Fleet)
Wayne Jensen, Milwaukee (Navy, Coastal Division 12)
Bruce Jensen, Milwaukee (Navy, River Assault Division 111)
Dan Schaller, La Crosse (Navy, Fleet Air Reconnaisance Squadron 1)

Bill Moore on the USS *Perch* deck, summer 1965. *Bill Moore*

BILL MOORE I was getting out of high school and my dad had some bad health problems. My plans to go to college went down the tubes; I was all set to go to Marquette but we couldn't afford it. A buddy of mine came over and said, "Wow, we can get all this good schooling by going in the Navy." We got looking at it and I still have the flyer showing the outline of the *Nautilus*; it was the cutting-edge submarine back then. We got a hold of the recruiter and August 8, 1961, off we went for our Navy careers.

WAYNE JENSEN My dad had been wounded in World War II. That had always had a great significance to me. Growing up I always had an affinity towards the military. And in high school it was evident to me that I was not college material. What was I going to do with my life? I always felt that I wanted to make a career in the military. I didn't know what branch I originally wanted to go into. The deciding factor was I loved swimming. I opted for the Navy.

That would have been January of '63. I remember it well because my mom and dad got into a big argument. My mom didn't want me going in the service. The Bay of Pigs was a big issue at that particular time. Everyone thought we were going to war. She didn't want my dad to sign for me. The deciding factor was my dad telling her, "Look, he is going to go when he is eighteen and he is going to be bitter at you for the year that you wasted of his life." She finally consented and my dad took me down to the recruiting office. I took the test and they said, "You can join."

BRUCE JENSEN Wayne was born almost two years before me. I looked up to him. He was the big brother. When we were growing up, he would always get out of trouble and I'd be the one to get into it. He just got home quicker than I did and made like he was not involved in anything that I was doing when he was the instigator. He went into the Navy. I respected him a lot and I thought, "Gee, what else am I going to do with my life?" My uncle Roy was my godfather and he was in the Navy in World War II. Wayne went into the Navy and I thought, "I might as well join the Reserves and go into the Navy myself." Right after I turned seventeen, I got my mom and dad's permission and I joined the naval reserve.

DAN SCHALLER I'm from La Crosse, Wisconsin. When I joined the service I'd been in college and I don't think I knew about Vietnam at the time. That was in February of '62. I went to boot camp and then I went down to electronics training in Memphis, Tennessee, for nine months and on to San Diego for three more months of electronics. While I was there I had to go through a week of survival training. I wasn't sure at the time why, but I think I found out later. A lot of it was for escaping invasion. They'd "capture you" and throw you in a prisoner of war camp and treated you just [as though] you were a prisoner of war. They made you believe it after a while.

BILL MOORE I did my boot camp at Great Lakes. After I got out of there in roughly November of '61, I went back to Great Lakes for twenty-eight weeks of electronics school. I got done with that and went off to New London [Naval Submarine Base] and learned how to be a submariner. You have to learn the basics of every system on the boat. When you graduate, you go to your first submarine and you get to be qualified and that's where you [earn] your Dolphins [submariner's badge].

Going through sub school, I saw some guys freak out when we went through the diving tower. Their ears would not take the pressure change and they washed out right away. They pressurize you at the fifty-foot level. It's a 119-foot tower. They open up the side door into the main tower, which is like a chimney full of water. You do a "blow and go" and ascend to the surface. You just blow the air out, you keep saying "Ho, ho, ho," and up you go. If you didn't do that, the air would expand and your lungs would explode because of the pressure.

It was a tight-knit bunch of guys. When you look back on it, all the training you had, everybody has to be able to do everybody else's job. Obviously, each person is very professional at his own job, but you also learn to do other peoples' jobs. You learn all about the systems. You have a working knowledge of everything that is going on around you. It's probably the safest place to be.

WAYNE JENSEN My first day on active duty was the day President Kennedy got assassinated. I was in a school in Treasure Island, San Francisco. We were sitting in class all morning waiting for orientation and about noon a [chief petty] officer came in, tears in his eyes. It was very ironic for us because chiefs are everything in the Navy and grown men don't cry routinely. He stood in front of us and said, "Gentlemen, your commander-in-chief has been assassinated." The first thing that crossed my mind was, "Mom, you were right, we are going to war." What did I know? Needless to say, at that particular time we were involved in Vietnam but not anything that a seven-teen-year-old kid would be [cognizant] of.

DAN SCHALLER [My training was in] electronic countermeasures. It was basically in the receivers that were picking up all the radar equipment. When I first got overseas, the squad room was based there to pick up radars and track radars in Russia and China and Korea. In May of '64, we found out we

Dan Schaller, first from left, at work with fellow crew members in the electronics repair room of their air craft carrier. *Dan Schaller*

were going to Vietnam. We tracked bombing missions, surface-to-air missiles, and ground fire. When we'd go on a bombing mission they'd have a track laid out for us and we'd go with the bombers and fighters [jets]. As soon as a surface-to-air missile came up in one area, I'd know where we were. I'd say, "Area Z, condition yellow," which means it was tracking. I knew when it was fired and I'd let them know. After a couple of years, I kept waiting for one to come right up our butts. You imagine those things being shot all the time. You think you've missed one somewhere along the line.

WAYNE JENSEN In early August 1964, we picked up a group of marines and we wound up off the coast of Vietnam. There were about thirty ships in convoy and for eighty-four days we were steaming back and forth in front of the mouth [of the river] to Da Nang. I was a radio man at that time. I was on watch at the time *Turner* and *Maddox* were attacked by a North Vietnamese gunboat. We heard the chatter on the radio, saying they were being attacked, but I didn't attribute any significance to it. We continued back and forth in front of the mouth of the Da Nang River.

There was the historical significance of it so far as it [was] the catalyst for our active involvement in Vietnam and also with the conspiracy theories as to whether they were actually attacked. I heard radio chatter that the North Vietnamese gunboats were attacking them and they were taking them under fire. I remember it was at night, and of course I was on watch in what they called CIC, Combat Information Center. We had about seven different radio frequencies that we would be monitoring at any time. I do recall that it was pandemonium. Where they were in the South China Sea was so far north of where we were that an immediate response from us wouldn't have been [possible].

BILL MOORE In August '64 [in Subic Bay, Philippines], everything kind of changed. I mean, we were doing our operations like all submarines. We really didn't know what was going on in the world that much because you are kind of in your own little world; being in your sub, being concerned with keeping your gear running, and so forth. One morning [shore patrol and armed forces police] were coming down the middle of the streets [of Olongapo], saying, "Everybody back to the base, war's broken out." We didn't know what they were talking about. War? They said, "Yeah, yeah. The Vietcong fired on the *Maddox*." And we said, "Who are the Vietcong and what's the *Maddox*?" You know, we didn't even know that the North Vietnamese

Right: The USS *Perch.*
Bill Moore

Below: Crew members
of the USS *Perch* prac-
tice maneuvers off
the coast of Korea in
preparation for Viet-
nam. *Bill Moore*

had fired at one of our ships. That was the beginning of it. Well, we went right over the fuel piers and once again, bullets, beans, and black oil. We took on food, fuel, and ammunition and headed over.

We started operating with Special Forces and started doing beach recon work where we'd actually submerge to periscope depth where we would do time bearing photography and take pictures of the shoreline. We'd tape them together, like a panoramic picture. Then they'd send them off to intelligence for future recon. You'd get to know the topography of the beaches all around North Vietnam. Then as we got operating more and more with the Special Forces, we actually started getting into the really interesting stuff as the war progressed. The [USS] *Perch* had a history. She did these operations in World War II. She did the same operations in Korea. And she did the same operations in Vietnam. She has the combat patrol pin for World War II, for Korea, and we were nominated for the combat patrol pin but because of the secrecy of the operations we were doing, the covert stuff we were doing, it never got awarded. She got four battle stars for World War II and was one of only two submarines that were in the Korea war.

Bruce, left, and Wayne Jensen on liberty in June 1966. *Wayne Jensen*

WAYNE JENSEN [After war was declared] I received orders transferring me to the USS *Stone County*, which was an LST [Landing Ship, Tank] out of San Diego. I came home, on leave, reported on board the ship. I don't recall if it was Christmas Day or the day after Christmas, the ship was in dry dock in Long Beach, California. One morning I had a shoe thrown at my head. I woke up, ranting and raving, "What the heck was going on!" Lo and behold my brother had put in for brother duty unbeknownst to me.

BRUCE JENSEN [After boot camp] they sent me to Philadelphia Naval Station to await orders. I had requested that I get brother duty with Wayne onboard the *Stone County*. I thought it would be neat if I could get stationed with him. Lo and behold, [the order] was approved. I got my orders to report to the *Stone County*. Wayne didn't know anything about this. I walked into the barracks just as reveille was going off and I asked the first guy who got up, "Can you tell me where I can find Jensen?" and he says, "Hand me my shoes." I gave him his shoes, and he turned around and he ripped one of them and hit Wayne in the head. That was Wayne's first idea that I was going to be stationed with him.

We both ended up in the rivers. I was up the small rivers and he was mainly on the coast on major rivers with the swift boats. We went up some rivers that were barely wider than the boats. We had to pull up onto the beach and back down just to turn around. We couldn't even turn around in the river because the boats were longer than the river was wide. You had beautiful green, lush vegetation most of the time, so it wasn't all that bad.

BILL MOORE The USS *Perch* became my real home and my family of submariners. You do get very, very close. It is a trusting group. You're screened for all the psychological problems you might have.

The only legal [acceptable] thing to steal on a submarine is a white hat. You're in a filthy environment. It's dirty and greasy and everything and you get your uniform on to go out on a liberty and you need a clean white hat to get off the sub. You usually cross a sub tender when you are out in San Diego. I've had…my white hat on top of my bunk with my wallet, my change, ID, all my junk in it and I'd have to hit the head to go. I'd come out and someone had dumped it all out. There wasn't a penny missing but my white hat was gone. You'd have to go steal one or hopefully you'd have another one. But it was a trusting group.

DAN SCHALLER There were so many people on the carrier, like five thousand people. It is so hard to imagine that so many men can be on board. At that time there weren't any women, but so many men aboard one aircraft carrier. The first time I went aboard one I went touring around, trying to find my way around. It was so huge. You get lost. I was wandering around with my flight suit on and I wandered into the admiral's territory. You weren't allowed in there. I was walking down and said, "Boy, these stairs get nice all with braided rails on them." All of a sudden here comes the Marines and the admiral of the Seventh Fleet behind them. He stopped and talked to me and said, "Are you one of the young fliers?" I said, "Yes, sir. I am with fleet air squad." He said, "You are doing a darn good job," and he walked off. I found out later from my pilot, he said, "Holy shit. You really get hell for being in places like that."

WAYNE JENSEN My brother was striking for gunner's mate and he was assigned a .30-caliber machine gun on the main deck. I was on the radar gang and I got special permission from the CO [commanding officer] to man the .30-caliber on starboard side of the ship so that Bruce and I would be across from each other as we were pulling in, anticipating that we were going to be under attack or shooting. So I'm loaded; I'm John Wayne. Got my cigar in my mouth, my helmet on. Manning a .30-caliber, you know;

Dan Schaller preparing for a bombing run, May 1965.
Daniel Schaller

how significant that my brother was on the other side of the ship from me. As we pull into this landing ramp there were about a hundred Vietnamese with signs, "Welcome U.S. Marines." So much for dramatics.

DAN SCHALLER It was around May 1964 when we started flying and landing and doing surveillance. I don't know if it had ever been done before there. That was the first time that one of the pilots was missing. His plane got shot down. We got back and they told us about it and wanted us to go back out and search for him. We went back out, doing low-level scanning on the ground looking for him. In later years so many were shot down, but this was when it was starting with those pilots. That guy, I'd sat right next to him in the ready room and then he was missing.

Nine years later when I'm sitting at home with my daughter watching the POWs come off on the television, I hear this guy's name and I just sat there and started crying. I just couldn't imagine. All the time I was over there and then I've been home all those years, and he had been locked up for nine years. I just couldn't imagine how anyone can go through that.

WAYNE JENSEN A lot of our duties were primarily stopping and inspecting boats; anything from a basket boat, which was one Vietnamese fisherman with a paddle, going out into the South China Sea to do his daily fishing, to a sampan that could hold fifteen or twenty people....One of our jobs would be to get on board a little basket boat and put your hand down to the bottom and fish around to see if they had grenades or mortar rounds that they were trying to smuggle in. Some of their catches were sea snakes and if you reached in and startled a sea snake you were going to get bitten. You had to gently put your hand down to the bottom and then when you moved it around it wouldn't startle them. You could feel fish sliding past your hand. You got used to it and knew that if you didn't grab or startle it you were safe.

The part of it that really disturbed me was we had individuals that might

Wayne Jensen conducts a routine check of Vietnamese fishing boats. *Wayne Jensen*

be seventy years old out there fishing who had been doing it for sixty-five years. Along came Uncle Sam and said he could no longer fish in that particular area, where he'd fished his whole life. It was very difficult for me to accept the fact that I could turn around and tell somebody that you can no longer fish in that area. We used to spray paint a portion of their boat a certain color. The next time they were caught in that area it would be spray painted a different color. The third time, they would be thrown in the water and we would blow their basket boat up with a grenade. A fisherman's income in Vietnam at that time was like eleven dollars. Their fishing nets cost three hundred dollars. I don't know what their basket boats cost, but to throw this person into the South China Sea and say, "OK, swim back three miles," and then blow their boat up...To this day I have a hard time dealing with that. It just never seemed right. Even though I understood the theory behind it, we never did see a fisherman with a hand grenade or mortar in his basket boat.

Wayne Jensen and fellow swift boat crew members patrol the waters outside of Da Nang. *Wayne Jensen*

BRUCE JENSEN We all shared the duties driving the boat, answering the radio. Except for working on the engines themselves, we all did everything. I changed the filters down on the engines. I drove the boat. It was fun. What we did in the delta was keep the supply lanes for Charlie pretty much closed off. I was part of a big unit, but we cut off Charlie's supply line for food and weapons. We kept it pretty minimal. They didn't get a whole hell of a lot through on us.

My boat was equipped with a helicopter pad. We were the medical aid boat for the division. I think there was a couple of doctors and then three or four male nurses. When we got into firefights, they would bring them back to our boat and they would do like a triage, like MASH. We would get to a relatively safe area and bring in the helicopters. When the helicopters would land on the flight deck we would bring the wounded up and put them on the helicopter and the helicopters would take them to the base hospitals. If they were really bad, to one of the hospital ships. Whatever was closest.

BILL MOORE Usually, we didn't know much except they were going in to do whatever. They would just say we're going in to do recon. A lot of times we didn't know what we were going to run into. I've heard some of the guys tell me tales of the UDT [Underwater Demolition Team] guys and the SEAL guys. These guys would jump out of a plane at night, parachute down to the water, and get their chute all together and make sure it sinks or whatever. They'd dive down and lock into the submarine, and go off to war. It's a pretty neat way to go to war as opposed to airborne. The officers knew pretty much about what the missions were, obviously, but our job was to make sure everything was set up. Whether it was dry deck, wet deck, tank launch, or if we were going to sit on the bottom and wait for them. This is what we did a lot of the time too — sit on the bottom with our scope out of the water, watching for them.

Our Special Forces actually got two Vietcong prisoners. The hatred between the armed forces and the two Cong they had caught, you could cut it with a knife. They had them bound and gagged on the deck of the sub with their hands tied to their heels, gagged and blindfolded. They were just two guys, but they were prisoners; they took them down. We also did operations that were more humane.

BRUCE JENSEN We knew something was going to happen sooner or later. Very few missions that we went on did we go in and out without receiving

Bruce Jensen mans a 20-millimeter cannon while patroling the My Tho River. *Bruce Jensen*

fire. One time we were on our way up the river from Dong Tam. It was called Route 66. It was long, straight, and narrow. We would fire our small arms and whatever on occasion just to keep Charlie's head down. We were coming to a friendly village. It was maybe a mile inland. Any time you were nearing a friendly village you stopped firing because the rounds would carry in and you didn't want to hurt innocent civilians. The boat captain gave me the order to go up and tell the engineers down in the well deck to cease fire. I yelled down in the well deck "cease fire" and they stopped shooting. Then something caught out of the corner of my eye. I look up and there was a mortar shell going up. I was just mesmerized by it. Then it started coming down. It dawned on me exactly what was going on. I thought, "Oh hell!" I dove four or five feet to my gun mount. I went right through the opening of the gun mount straight down. Slithered down, hit the bottom, came up, and I was firing my gun. The mortar hit, exploded in the vegetation right off the port side. I could feel the heat of that mortar. That was a close one. When I realized that we were receiving fire, I turned around and screamed, "Open fire!" How I dove as far as I did and made it is a wonder. You don't have time to think. You react. The adrenaline starts going and you just do what you were trained to do, what you are there to do.

[In another incident,] we had several rockets fired at us, but only one hit our boat. [It happened when] we were heading [up] the inner section of two rivers. We were heading west and the lead boats got partway up the river. It was blocked so they had to turn around and head back out to the main intersection of the two rivers. While we were turning around, all hell broke loose. Charlie started shooting at us with rockets, small arms, machine guns, and whatever, and I saw the rocket coming straight for where I was standing. I thought, "Oh hell, this is it." At the last second, the rocket dipped down and went through a deck farther down than I was, and exploded. It went through the lockers and exploded. Fortunately, there were no injuries. Matter of fact, during the damage report, the engineer called up that it went through the middle locker. We had booze in the lockers on both sides of it and not a bottle was broken. We didn't lose a drop.

WAYNE JENSEN The first time we took fire we didn't even know we were being fired at. It was a Marine recon patrol on the beach that had to call us on radio and say, "Hey, you're under fire. We can see the tracers coming at you." You can't see tracers coming at you. Then of course we saw the splashing and we started firing back. Those were my only three KIAs over in Vietnam; I don't know if they were men, women, [or] child. I never actually saw them. They were behind a sand dune and I was firing into that sand dune. It was the Marines recons that went up and advised us that they were killed by a .50-caliber. The other gun crew was operating a mortar. That was the only time I actually knew that I had taken somebody else's life. When you're under fire it's so intense and so rapid. It happens spontaneously. You don't have time to think, "I am afraid."

Bruce and I spent two or three trips going back and forth into Vietnam up in Da Nang. When we would get bored, we would go down and talk the Marines into letting us drive their forklifts to unload cargo because there was nothing to do. In October 1966, we pulled into Okinawa and my term of enlistment was due to come up. So Bruce carried my sea bag off. Then I was at the Air Force base waiting to fly back to the U.S. and I watched the ship pull out with my brother, going to Vietnam. That hurt because I wasn't there with my brother going into harm's way.

BRUCE JENSEN Wayne's end of enlistment came up, so I had to carry his sea bag off in Buckner Bay. It was tradition; he stood there and watched the ship get under way and we went back to Vietnam for a while. I was missing him

Bruce Jensen, front center, with his swift boat crew. *Bruce Jensen*

already, but I didn't have time to think about it because I had my chores and my duty to do.

When we went over, it was a one-year tour of duty. The ones that were ending their tour were grateful when they saw us. I met my buddy Herman Danford — Dan Danford — he doesn't like to be called Herman. He was the only crew member that was on the boat that I am in contact with after all this time. He was on board before I got on board. I was part of class R-1, the first replacement class for the Riverine Force. He said, "I don't want nothing to do with you. Every time you make friends, they get shot and killed. They don't last long. Friendships don't last long," He didn't want anything to do with me, but he took me under his wing and showed me the ropes. We became very good buddies.

BILL MOORE   The word we had gotten up around Qui Nhon was, you know, that the North Vietnamese were coming down from the North, just slaughtering and doing whatever they had to do against their enemy, which was the side we were on. There was an APD [attack personnel destroyer] out, a small ship that had gotten its rudders punched into its screws, so we had to take over her operations. We were actually rigged on the surface. We went up about fourteen miles north of Qui Nhon and evacuated a village up there. We brought on men, women, and children from that area because had they been left there, they would not be alive because they would have been slaughtered. I'm not comparing it all to what the guys in the bush were doing. God, I'm glad I don't have to even remember any of that stuff. It just made me feel good that we were doing some constructive stuff rather than just damaging, blowing up, and killing.

We were also saving and salvaging. You see a guy, looking similar to a Huck Finn with a stick over his back with a knotted bag on it with his life's possessions. Everything he owns. There's his wife and two or three kids getting on our submarines. That's all he has in this entire world. You think back of home with your tape-recorders and your stereos and your car, and your clothing, and all the stuff that you have, that we like to have in America. And you figure this is what this guy has. It's all he has. It just brought it home that a lot of the old-timers call World War II "the big war." You say, "Well, this might not be the big one, but this is real. There are people getting killed. And these are refugees." We were helping them and they were losing everything they owned; possibly relatives are already slaughtered. There are people getting killed on both sides. It just brought it home that this is just as real. There is real red blood flowing just like there were in the other conflicts you know. It's a shame that man has to always settle our problems that way. But that seems the way history seems to go.

BRUCE JENSEN You just prepared for everything. When one boat would open up [fire], everybody would. Charlie was lined up back and forth and up and down the river. It wasn't in just one [place]. Most of the time the most we could hope for would be to keep their heads down. We would put out one hell of a barrage of gunfire. We would get through them, pull up onto the beach, and let the Army [men] off. The Army would sweep back the way Charlie was and hopefully we'd catch them in a pincer movement.

DAN SCHALLER I asked to sit up front for just one landing. So I went up and took the navigator's seat. You come in looking at the carrier and it looks like a postage stamp. You're coming into it and wondering, "How in the world could a guy be trained to land on that thing?" The nerves it would take to land on that the first time when you are practicing! There were four cables down there and you caught one of them with the hook. As soon as you

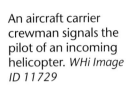

An aircraft carrier crewman signals the pilot of an incoming helicopter. *WHi Image ID 11729*

touched down you gave it full speed because if the cables snapped, you wanted to have the power to get back off again. If it pulled you out like it did sometimes, maybe it would pull the cable halfway out, and the cable would snap and then you were going over. Usually they didn't find people when they went over.... You always thought, "My goodness, it might be your time." You always wonder how you get by.

We took off from carrier and I was always in the back. It had to be totally dark. Look at me now, now that I am totally blind. I used to say that I could hear those sounds over my headsets — I could hear the sounds of the different equipment, ground fire, surface-to-air missiles and different radars. I could tell what they were by the sound of the frequency. I was always in the dark looking at the scope. I'd put the point on it and pick up the direction that it was at and give them the direction by the sound and I could tell when it was fired.

BILL MOORE It is a special force: the brotherhood of the fin. You've all gone through the training so you all basically know the submarines inside and out. I'm not saying that destroyers or carriers or flattops or battleships or cruisers [don't have a bond]. But with a carrier, you have five thousand guys on a carrier. You talk to two guys on the same carrier and they have no idea

U.S. navymen look at maps on the deck of the USS *Perch*, with ARVN soldiers gathered on the lower deck. *Bill Moore*

who the other is because one is serving forward and the other serving aft. You don't know everyone in a city of five thousand. Yet they might be just as prideful in their jobs. In a submarine, you all know each other. You go out drinking together, you party together, and you throw up over the side together. You do everything together. You are out to sea, faced with an enemy. You are all depending on each other. When you are sleeping, you don't worry about it because your buddy is on watch and he will keep you safe until it is time for you to watch his butt when he is sleeping. It is just pride. [We] call them "brother of the fin," short for dolphin.

Several of the guys that we did operations with got killed over there. I remember one by the name of Sullivan. And a close buddy of mine named Bob Neil whose name I saw on the Wall in Washington, D.C. You're with them, out drinking with them on the beach, having fun. You are out there going to war with them and then they aren't around anymore. You know it's not just stories: it's real. They were an honorable bunch of guys, all the Special Forces we operated with. They just did a bang-up job.

DAN SCHALLER I was supposed to get out in February of '66. That would have been four years. In late '65, they started talking about extensions and they were running out of people because they were building up more and more in Vietnam at the time. I got extended for four months because I was in a critical rate. I didn't even vote for Johnson, so I didn't think it was fair that he got to extend me. I was pretty upset about it. I got back to Japan and I knew that was my last time and I was going to go home, and then they told me, "You've been extended and because of that you are going back to Vietnam again." That really upset me because I really thought, "This time I'm going to die. This is out of the norm and if I go back this time I'm going to go down." I thought about that an awful lot. I was more scared than I had ever been before because I was sure that I was going to die. I'd never been that way before until that extension.

BRUCE JENSEN   It was pretty near the end. I wanted to go out on operations less and less. I didn't want to push my luck in that. As much as I could, I got to go into the Dong Tam and stay on the base. I tried to stay off of the boats as much as I could. I was a short-timer and I didn't want to push my luck any more than I had. One of the officers came up to me and said, "You've got a year left on your enlistment. If you re-up for six more months in Vietnam, you can get a six-month early out. You'll only have six months to go on your term." I looked at him and I said, "Lieutenant, I'm one of 10

Wayne Jensen, left, and shipmate Henry Clark enjoy a drink at the British Seaman's Bar in Hong Kong before deploying to Vietnam. *Wayne Jensen*

percent of our class of 126 people that have made it through this far without a scratch. I'm not pushing my luck. When my time is up, I'm out of here." A good buddy of mine decided to go for the six-month early out. He was in the hospital three times within the next three months with wounds. He pushed his luck. I didn't.

When my year was up, that was time. I had seen enough blood and gore to last me a lifetime. At the time, it was all adrenaline. You did what you had to do. You didn't think of it. My means of coping with the bad when we got done on an operation or we got rid of the wounded, and we had time to sit and reflect, I would open a case of C-rats and I would start eating. World War II C rations were not the greatest four or twenty years later. One particular night I ate seven boxes of C rations, just one after the other after the other. That was my way of coping with the stress, besides having our booze locker.

DAN SCHALLER I think deep down you were probably scared. It was one way to deal, going out and drinking a lot when you had a couple of days off. It was like you were treating yourself to your last day of fun. Go out, find some girls and some beer, and then you'd be back, back aboard a carrier and flying again. I think one of the toughest times was when I was out three weeks and we changed carriers. I'd been [out] three weeks straight and was pretty ragged. There was only one time a day that you could use water or take a shower, so a lot of days you went without being able to shave or shower. Sometimes when they'd turn on the water, you'd be out flying and you'd come back and it was tough luck. You'd missed out on having the water on.

I was fearful [in Vietnam], but it is like sitting here now blind. I know if I sit here and think about nothing but the blindness I'm going to lose it. If all I thought about in Vietnam was getting shot down or getting hurt, I wouldn't have been able to do it. We had our minds on something else. Obviously, when we were watching the scopes, we were looking for surface-to-air missiles, but on the way out, we were always kidding, laughing, joking about something. I think that is the way most people in the service get through it: by talking, by making jokes all the time, doing stupid things to get your mind off what is real. What is real is that you had a chance to die when you went out. We all knew that. If you thought about it all the time like I said, you couldn't go up. And I know that happened to some people because they'd fail out. I don't know what happened to them, maybe they got sent back to the States. It takes a tough mental constitution, I guess.

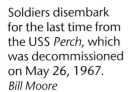

Soldiers disembark for the last time from the USS *Perch*, which was decommissioned on May 26, 1967.
Bill Moore

We were very young. God, I was only twenty-one. After you have been flying there for a year, you feel like an old man. I guess I never thought about it that way, but you did get old in a hurry.

BILL MOORE To give you an idea of how out of touch we were, the captain gave us a speech on psychedelic drugs, only he didn't know how to pronounce the word *psychedelic*. We didn't know what he was talking about. He gave us this speech on these drugs before we pulled into Hawaii, telling us that they had some sailors that were on psychedelic drugs and they were both locked up in a jail cell. One of them thought he was an orange and he was going to squirt juice at you if you got near him. The other one was screaming out of his mind because his arms were melting off his body.

Well, they were all psyched out on these. And he said, "It's called lysergic diethylamide or LSD." And we thought, "LSD, that's 'landing ship dock.'" We'd never heard of any of this stuff. Outside of hearing about marijuana we knew nothing about all the hard drugs. It was an automatic bad conduct discharge if you got caught with drugs on your person, so we skipped out of that part of it altogether. I was just working on quitting smoking. When I got home, I thought, "What is going on with this country?" — not honoring the troops coming back and so forth.

DAN SCHALLER We always got the *Stars and Stripes*. We did know about the protest going on back in the States, back in those days. That was early in the war. They were protesting then. Then of course, we thought we were there for an awful good reason. We knew about the guys that escaped the draft by going to Canada. It was upsetting to people that were over there. We were pretty upset by [the protestors] in those days. We were upset about us being over there. We all knew that we were over there putting our lives on the line every day. They were protesting us being over there. We didn't understand.

BILL MOORE I used to get in arguments with people all the time. One gal said to me, "I don't like it. It's a war, it's wrong. We should not settle things with war." I said, "I agree with you. I wish to God we could just sit down and talk things out. But if you look back in history, everything in history has been settled by a war. I don't like it. It's not the way we should be." That's how we settle our differences. I wish it could be different but it isn't. You have your neighbor's kids and your own sons and daughters over there fighting; let's back them.

DAN SCHALLER When I lost my sight, the VA sent me down to a blind center in Chicago. I met guys from WWII, Korea, and Vietnam. One guy that I met down there from southern Illinois, he was blind. He was getting disability because he had been blinded by Agent Orange. He said, "You should get it too, Dan, because you were there the same time I was." I said, "But I wasn't on the ground very often. I was probably the asshole that was dropping it on you, for all I know." I didn't know when that was happening, but I did know when we were going out bombing. A lot of times I knew what we were going to be hitting.

Lord knows I was around that stuff enough, I guess, but I have no idea why this hit me. When I first got out of the service I had a problem with my eyes the first summer I was home. They gave it a name but they really didn't know what it was. I never thought anything about it. It just happened. Years later, all of a sudden I had problems with my internal organs. They didn't know what that was. I was in the hospital for a week trying to figure out what caused it. It was affecting my lungs and kidneys and they finally got that under control. One day, I was golfing and I knew my eyes were getting blurry again. I thought I had to get different glasses. I went in on Monday morning to the doctor and they put me in the hospital, but by the following

Saturday I was totally blind. If they knew [what it was] they weren't saying. They said it was some kind of virus.

BRUCE JENSEN One of my best buddies at work finally talked me into going to the VA and seeing a counselor. He took me one night and sat with me, and I wound up seeing a counselor several times a week for a couple of months. We figured out the times when the nightmares would come back and hit me the worst was at the lowest points in my life. The lowest points in my life are when I'm drinking more and more susceptible. I still love my beer, but I don't drink anymore. I love the taste of it, but you learn what the triggers are. It helps to discuss my time over in Vietnam and being in contact with Dan [Danford] every year down in Florida. One of the nights that I'm down there is our time to sit and talk by ourselves with nobody around. It helps both of us through our post-traumatic stress.

WAYNE JENSEN It was emotionally traumatizing to me. On the one hand, I was a flag waver out of high school. I couldn't wait to get in and serve my country just like my dad and forebears did. Then, at the other end of it, I had a feeling like I had been given a bad bill of goods, like, "what a sucker I was." That lasted for quite a few years. It wasn't until the Vietnam Wall in Washington, D.C., was constructed and the movie *Platoon* came out. I went and saw that movie by myself and I was not prepared for what impact it was going to have on me.

I still have trouble with Uncle Sam and the trust factor with our government. I was awfully idealistic and naïve, whereas today, I'm probably cynical and suspicious. It's still the best country in the world and it still carries the bird of democracy and freedom. I'm still that flag waver that's willing to go and bear that particular burden in a heartbeat . . . saying, "I have to do my part. I owe it to my country." Knowing what I know today, abhorring an awful lot of what I see and hear today, I would still go back and do it because I owe it to our country.

Send in the Marines

"I didn't really fully understand why we were over there or what the hell we were doing, but I did what I was told. If they sent me to Vietnam to be a sniper, that's what I would have been. If they sent me to be a grunt, that's what I would have done."— Al Sobkowiak

In the aftermath of the Gulf of Tonkin Incident, U.S. involvement in Vietnam escalated dramatically, both in the air and on the ground. U.S. policy-makers believed that if the United States did not stand strong in Vietnam, the United States would lose global credibility; as Marilyn Young states, they feared that "withdrawal from Vietnam [would] expose American impotence."[1] Yet in the early weeks of 1965, U.S. policy makers also feared that they were losing their ability to control events in Vietnam. Though the United States tacitly agreed to the assassination of Diem, his fall was followed by ten consecutive governments, none of which succeeded in establishing political legitimacy apart from U.S. support. Johnson's escalation of U.S. involvement thus sought not only to maintain U.S. credibility but also to ensure that South Vietnam did not completely collapse or negotiate a settlement with the National Liberation Front (NLF) and the North Vietnamese government.

On February 28, 1965, after the NLF attacked U.S. military outposts at Pleiku and Qui Nhon, the United States and South Vietnamese governments announced the start of Operation Rolling Thunder, a sustained campaign of air attacks on North Vietnam. Air bombing would become a major feature of the war throughout the next few years, as the United States waged sustained air campaigns over North and South Vietnam. The introduction of U.S. ground troops followed soon after, and on March 8, two Marine battalions (3,500 troops) landed at Da Nang to protect U.S. military installations. They were followed by two more Marine battalions in April and U.S. Army personnel in May. Confronted with the NLF's strong position in South Vietnam, the Marines' role quickly changed from simply guarding U.S. bases to include ground combat, activating mobile patrols to locate and eliminate insurgents.

This expanded U.S. presence in Vietnam, however, did not mean that the U.S. leadership and the South Vietnamese held the same views vis-à-vis the war, the NLF, and North Vietnam. Cautioning the United States against taking on a direct combat role in Vietnam, U.S. Ambassador and former General Maxwell Taylor had noted "there would be the ever present question of how to distinguish between a VC and a friendly Vietnamese farmer."[2] Indeed, in the process of attempting to secure South Vietnam from insurgent forces, U.S. troops often destroyed homes, villages, and rice paddies, killing members of the NLF and South Vietnamese civilians alike, uprooting the very lives of those they were ostensibly there to protect. The experiences of these Marines highlight the complications of fighting in Vietnam; jungle terrain, difficult weather, and unclear objectives only heightened the difficulties resulting from a complex relationship with the often-suspicious local population. As the United States sought to achieve a politically stable, non-Communist, pro-Western Vietnam, Vietnam became a war for the "hearts and minds" of the southern population. Yet many Vietnamese civilians did not see the war as a fight against the Communist North — especially since the NLF had originally developed in response to the repressive Diem regime — but instead viewed the war as legitimate resistance to domestic and foreign repression.

The presence of U.S. troops thus often reinforced, rather than undermined, the NLF's position in the South. CIA surveys of war support among the South Vietnamese population, for example, showed that only 1 in 25 South Vietnamese strongly supported air strikes on North Vietnam.[3] The U.S. bombings depressed southern morale while elevating that of the enemy; in the words of one South Vietnamese member of the NLF, the attacks "pushed us to fight harder so the South would soon be entirely liberated and the North would be spared further destruction."[4] In addition to the destructive nature of combat, U.S. pacification programs further undermined civilian support for U.S. actions in the South. The strategic hamlet program, for example, moved entire villages away from family land into barbed-wire enclosed "hamlets" that could theoretically be easily protected; however, it also fostered resistance among the villagers and failed to destroy the deep connections that many communities had with the NLF. As one hamlet village chief stated, every family "has someone in the insurgent ranks. If one does not, then perhaps his wife, or a husband, or a neighbor has a relative fighting for the National Liberation Front."[5] By early 1965, the U.S. presence in Vietnam operated on three fronts: direct combat and pacification programs in the South, and extensive bombing campaigns in the North. Yet neither the United States nor the South Vietnamese government was able to gain allegiance, much less support from the general population of South Vietnam, a failing that would plague the U.S. war effort for years to come and haunt the memories of the first Marines who served.

Roy Rogers, Neenah (Marines, Fourth Marine Division)
Al Sobkowiak, Onalaska (Marines, First Marine Division)
John Dederich, De Pere (Marines, Third Marine Division)

Before his tour in Vietnam, Al Sobkowiak was a drill instructor in San Diego, training recruits. *Al Sobkowiak*

ROY ROGERS I went in with a fellow named Doug Harper. We joined on May 3, 1963. We were taken to San Diego Marine Corps recruit depot. I was a big fellow at that time, so we got split up right away. I had to go to the fat man's platoon. I lost a hundred and some pounds in four months. When I went into the Marine Corps I guess I weighed 250 pounds. We had Mr. Universe from 1952 as our drill instructor and you had to do physical exercises about twenty hours a day in order to get your weight gone. When I went into the Marine Corps, I couldn't do a pull-up or push-up or a squat-thrust or anything. By the time I got my weight loss I could do all that stuff and many, many of them. I was really good then and capable of being a Marine.

AL SOBKOWIAK In 1951, my brother and I worked on a farm. We cut logs every winter for five dollars a day. We would start at eight o'clock in the morning and cut until six o'clock at night. We did that for about four years. In 1949 and '50, it was cold. I told my brother, "We're not going to do this again." We put our heads together and we [said], "Let's join the service." I stayed in the Marines until 1972 and then I retired. I had put in my mind that I was going to do my twenty years. And I did a little over twenty years.

JOHN DEDERICH I made the decision probably my junior year in high school. It was either go to college, get a real job, or the military. When I looked at the military, the Marines were the only choice for me. Once a Marine always a Marine. I joined the reserve unit during my senior year in high school.

Roy Rogers trained at Hawaii's Kaneohe Marine Corps Air Station, where he was an extra in Otto Preminger's World War II film, *In Harm's Way.*
Roy Rogers

ROY ROGERS We were actually the first troops that went to Vietnam as combat [troops]. [In training] Vietnam never came up. We never talked about it. All of our classes that we went to, we never discussed Vietnam because it just wasn't part of the itinerary back then.

March 10, 1965, we were woken up very early in the morning and they said, "Pack all your stuff. You've got about two hours to box up your goods and send them home." They put us in the trucks and never told us where we were going. They took us to Pearl Harbor and put us on a troop carrier and fifteen days later we were in Okinawa. We spent a little over three and a half weeks in Okinawa, and then we went to Vietnam. We never knew we were going to Vietnam even then I don't think. It must have been the best-kept secret.

Once we got to the beach, there were all kinds of women and kids there. They had bottles of Coca-Cola and flowers for us. Everyone in the landing craft got a bottle of soda and a flower if I remember right. We had to drink the bottle of soda while we were on the beach because they wanted the bottles back.

JOHN DEDERICH [At the time] there really was not a lot of stuff going on in Vietnam. The word was, "You're going to go over there but there's an awful lot of training, an awful lot of boredom. You no longer can go on liberty; you can't do anything, you're just in that situation." When we got there we went to Da Nang airstrip. For three or four months all we did was expand the perimeter. We would take a little sniper fire here and there, but it really wasn't a full-fledged combat situation when we first got there. Mostly, we were moving the perimeter out and filling sandbags.

As we started going into sweeping operations and movements, somewhere in the middle of it, I lost track of what day it was or what month it was and really didn't care. Sometimes you ran into hostile actions and sometimes there were none. It really picked up somewhere after about six months over in Vietnam.

We started to take casualties. The reality set in. We were with the same unit, the same people for a year and a half. These were the closest people you know in the world, and all of a sudden they started to take injuries and die, and that was really hard. You would resign yourself that you could be next. You don't want to do anything that would put somebody else in harm's way because of something you did wrong. You became extremely conscientious of how you went out on ambushes and night patrols.

We took some injuries and you start medevacing people and everything. And that becomes extremely hard, extremely difficult. And over the course of, you know, three or four months, I think of the original unit or at least our platoon was down to twenty-three, and then there was...I think when I was wounded, three of us had neither been killed or wounded out of forty-five. You were never sure where the rest of the company was.

Al Sobkowiak outside his tent, March 1966. *Al Sobkowiak*

AL SOBKOWIAK I didn't really fully understand why we were over there or what the hell we were doing, but I did what I was told. If they sent me to Vietnam to be a sniper, that's what I would have been. If they sent me to be a grunt, that's what I would have done. That's what I was. My tour over there was in the infantry: patrols, patrols, patrols, and ambushes and night-time fighting. [I was with] the Special Landing Force. That was in 1966. We would come off the ship and locate the enemy and destroy them. Normally the operation would last about ten to fifteen days. We were just eating C rations. Your feet would get all wet and the skin would start coming off your feet. You would start getting jungle rot around your body. [Then] they would bring you back aboard ship.

[This] was out around the Da Nang area. We didn't go up to the DMZ [demilitarized zone] at that time. It was mostly in the southern part of Vietnam. I don't even know the names of the towns. I can't remember the names of the operations. I was a staff sergeant at that time, and I was a platoon commander. I was a staff sergeant doing a lieutenant's job.

We would land in a certain zone. Everybody would have their mission cut out for them. We would have the maps and know exactly what we were going to do. We would land and set up our battalion perimeter. We would start sending out patrols and set up night ambushes. Then we would all get back to the ship again. We took quite a few casualties, because some of the areas we landed in were pretty hot zones. That was our job: go out there and wipe them [the Vietcong] out, capture them and see what information we could get. We captured quite a few. Once we captured them, I never knew what would happen to them. They would go back with the intelligence department and they would be debriefed to find out what kind of information [we] could get. You could do that day in and day out and nothing would ever change. You could never say we were losing because you never knew. You just did what you were told.

ROY ROGERS I got to Vietnam early in May of '65 and we didn't get new clothes until September of '65. We completely wore out our clothes, our underwear, and our boots. I remember the day we got new boots everybody was just thrilled. [We'd been getting] jungle rot when we walked through the rice paddies, so it was really bad.

Anticipating the Vietcong coming was an eye-opener. We all got in the trucks one day and went to Quang Ngai, fifteen miles or so south of Chu Lai. We were in a skirmish through rice paddies. That was the only firefight that I can really remember. This Vietcong opened up on us, and we dropped down on the rice paddies and opened up on him. We wounded this fella and my lieutenant sat him up on the side of a building and asked me to guard him. We sat there and guarded him while he bled to death. Then I knew where I was.

AL SOBKOWIAK We'd capture what we could and kill what we couldn't capture. We'd go from village to village. We had interpreters with us. You would have the interpreters ask, "Any VC around here?" [They'd say,] "No, no VC."

Al Sobkowiak and his troops fill their canteens at a village well during day patrol.
Al Sobkowiak

You would walk out there about a hundred yards and would get all kinds of fire from the rear where the VC were buried in little holes. They would come up shooting. We would have to go back and wipe them out, digging them out, and get them out of the trenches. That was an everyday occurrence. It went on, and on, and on. It wasn't any fun. We were so tired. Living on C rations, with no sleep, in the rain, in the sun. We were constantly moving, getting different objectives. "Go up to this hill" or "Take that hill." You'd set your perimeter up and dig some foxholes. [Then you'd be] moving out again. Back down and back and forth. It was just constant movement. I don't know who was making decisions. I suspect that they were com[ing] from regiment and from the divisions. We just called ourselves goats because we were going from hill to hill: "The goats are ready to go again." Sometimes it would be steep hills. Other times we were in rice paddies. You would have to adjust out in the rain. The heat was just unbearable sometimes: 100 degrees, 110, 115, 120 degrees, and just sweat, sweat, sweat.

The first time I was over there, we had the biggest problem getting water. We would drink the water that the locals had. We would go to the wells and steal their water or we would drink out of the rice paddy. Wherever we would find big puddles of water, we would take our canteens and fill them up. We would put our halizone tablets in the canteen to kill any disease and germs. Little did we know that in some of the areas they had defoliated them with Agent Orange. I would say, "This is a nice area. We've got no brush to contend with." It was all defoliated. I didn't know at the time that we were in a contaminated area. We would fill our canteens and drink that water. We didn't know. They had a very hard time getting [us] water and supplies because the area would be fogged in sometimes for two days. Three days was the most we ever went without food or water. We would go into these villages and pick the fruit that was on their trees. We would never eat any of their meats because they were so infested with lice and fleas. I have seen what happened to people that ate that meat. They would take about six feet of guts out of their stomachs because worms would eat through their guts. It was very sad to see that. We didn't have anything that we could cook with. Just a little bitty something to heat the C rations, you know. Water was the big thing the first time. The second time it wasn't so bad. We had more supplies.

JOHN DEDERICH You resign yourself. After about six or seven months I never thought I was going to come out of that country alive. You pretty well knew that. [You said,] "Let's do the job." We were starting to get new people into the unit, and you wanted to be that leader that those Korean veterans were to us. You wanted to do everything to make sure that they weren't doing something stupid like stepping on a land mine or making noise during a night ambush.

Most of our operations were smaller operations. We would be guarding a bridge maybe for a week at a time, and then four or five or as many as ten people would go out at night, either on a patrol or an ambush. You would just sit and wait because a lot of these people were farmers by day and military by night. You were never sure, so you had to be really careful. When night went down and they were moving around in their black uniforms, you would be extremely scared. I can remember one time going out with a full moon and I'm rounding the edge of a village and I think a water buffalo kicked or made some noise or something. I hit the ground and I turned around and fired. You're silhouetted out there and extremely vulnerable. You're trained to be cautious, but you still have an awful lot of fear. You're looking for all different kinds of booby traps and at the same time making sure that you're not hearing anything else that's out of the ordinary. You really are trying to get from point A to point B without anything happening.

ROY ROGERS My father sent me over a 16-millimeter movie camera, and I hung that around my neck with a shoestring and carried it around. My sergeant said I could take photos and pictures, whenever I wanted to, unless we [went] into battle. Quite a few times during the patrols I'd push the button

Left: Roy Rogers enjoys a moment of down time. *Roy Rogers*

Above: After finding an extra twenty dollars, Roy Rogers placed an order to the Scrafft's Candy Company in Boston. They sent him a 50-pound box of candy, shown here with his gear. *Roy Rogers*

down, hold it, or have somebody else hold it so that I'd get into some of them. I got some very interesting photos [and] movies out of Vietnam. One of the things I filmed was kind of like a play-acting firefight on top of one of the hills at the foxhole. I asked two of my fellow inhabitants of one of the foxholes if they'd take and play-act like they're being shot at. We had quite a time on that one. They made believe they were shot and falling back. This was pretty early in when we were over there. It was easy to play-act, but once you knew what it was like to see people shot and hurt, then it got kind of difficult. I see the films and the tapes and it bothers me because we were making fun of something that was actually enough to kill or hurt somebody.

AL SOBKOWIAK We were on the way out on a good day or two patrol and we got about halfway and we'd had no contact with the enemy. We got to a river but it was only a couple feet deep. I knew from all of the training that I'd had that rivers are ideal places to set up an ambush because you're in the open. My point man said over his little radio, "Lieutenant, we're up to the river now." I said, "Well, you just wait there, I'll be right there." I was a hundred feet behind him. We went up to the river and I said, "Well, look, what we're going to do before we cross the river, we're going to just set up here and observe what's going on before we start crossing that little stream." We were all down on our bellies just watching across the river, looking up and down the little stream to make sure nothing was happening. I had been in the Marine Corps fifteen years by that time and I was pretty streetwise to what's happening. I said, "There's no activity across that river." Nothing. Where there should have been birds around, there were no birds flying. Where you should have seen monkeys jumping through the trees, there were no monkeys around. It was too quiet. We sat and watched for twenty minutes. My point man was over here, my radioman was there, and I was in the middle and I said, "We're going to have to cross the stream." I stood up and I said, "OK, we're going to move out." My platoon sergeant was way in the rear with the radio, and I said, "Put them in groups of two. We'll get to the other side and regroup and then go on with our patrol." I stood up and just as I [did], seven or eight Vietcong on the opposite side of the river jumped out of these little holes and opened fire. They were so close when they fired I recall my mouth going [makes sound]. It opened up and it was just stifling because I couldn't breathe and I couldn't even see because my eyelids hit the back of my head. That's how much concussion there was. They just opened up and fired like crazy and my guys got online and they started firing like crazy. We had a good little battle there going, and then it went silent. They were gone. They just opened fire and then they'd take off back into the bushes. I got hit in the legs.

I told my radioman as soon as we got hit. He picked up his radio and a bullet went right through and knocked his two fingers off. He said, "I can't talk." I said, "Well, use your other hand!" The corpsman said to me, "Holy shit, you're going to bleed to death if we don't get this blood stopped." They put a tourniquet on me and a tourniquet on my radioman. My point man was on his knees. He'd gotten shot right through the chest, three or four times. He was lying there and all kinds of foam was coming up from his chest because he was breathing through the holes. I said to the corpsman,

Ground troops carry a wounded soldier towards a medevac helicopter. *U.S. Aviation Museum Archives*

"Don't worry about me, just take care of him." He ripped his clothes off and put pieces of tape across the holes so he could breathe through his nose. I called some artillery in to get those Vietcong who were running. I said, "Drop some artillery on them."

I called in medevac and they said, "You're going to either want the medevac or the artillery; we can't give you both." I said, "Cancel the artillery and let the Vietcong run, and get the medevac." It took maybe a half hour before we could get a medevac in, and they kept the guy breathing. When the medevac came in, they loaded my point man, my radioman, and me all on the medevac at the same time. I gave my radio to the platoon sergeant and he took care of everything.

ROY ROGERS I had a good friend over in Vietnam, Jim Highland, who was a cryptographer over there. He said, "Don't volunteer for anything. The short-timers are getting hurt." I let it slip through my mind and I volunteered to go out on a patrol. I was singing "Handyman" and weaving back and forth and all of a sudden there was a big explosion. I looked down and there was blood shooting out of my hand just like a bubbler. Someone was yelling, "Corpsman!" The first thing I thought of was my training in guerrilla warfare. I told the gang, "Don't jump in the ditches because they might have [pungi] sticks." There was quite a crater in the ground where I was standing.

The corpsman was quite a ways back. He ran up, put a tourniquet on me. I never lost consciousness. They brought a helicopter in. The helicopters at that time were pretty small. They put me on a stretcher. They told me to close my eyes and hold my breath [because of the dust that the helicopter blew up]. They took off and I was on the outside of the helicopter, flying from there to the field hospital, facing straight down. It was almost scarier than getting hurt. Of course I was in a little bit of a shock from when I got hurt but never passed out or anything.

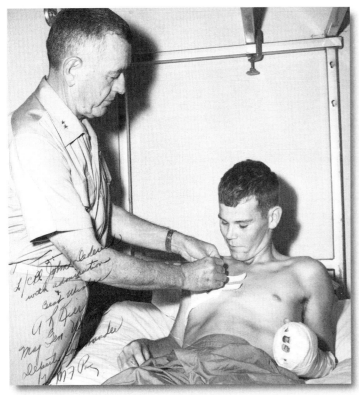

Major General Kier, pictured left, attaches John Dederich's Purple Heart to bandages on his chest. *John Dederich*

JOHN DEDERICH When you're fired on the first thing you do usually is hit the deck, and then you try and find out where the enemy fire is coming from and return it as quickly as possible. Then the next thing that kicks in, but it only kicks in with training, is to attack that enemy, because you're in the middle. So if it's coming from your right side, you want to turn around and fire from the right and attack to the right.

Your entire life depends on the guy next to you. It's a great equalizer of human beings, because you don't care who they are, what they are, your life depends on them and vice versa. We were moving at night. You would sleep for two hours, be awake for two hours. Those two hours that you were sleeping, that [other] person had your life in his hands.

[After a firefight] there was a great deal of anger because people were wounded. People who I loved, who I had been with for a year and a half, they were either wounded or killed. I had a great deal of anger. Eventually it would subside and then you would just realize that that's what you're there for.

ROY ROGERS I remember Vietnam being very hot and very wet with monsoons all the time. The children were friendly, singing all the time. Toward the end of the time that I was over there, a lot of the kids would walk around with hand grenades. They'd walk up to the Marines and commit suicide and kill or disable the Marines with them.

AL SOBKOWIAK This still bothers me. One night, we were set in at night and there was a village out there about two hundred yards, across the rice paddy. The villagers knew that at night they went into their houses, their hooches, and they didn't come out because if they came out, they might be shot. They'd stay in their hooches till the sun comes up. I was a company commander at that time [and] the security around our area said, "Hey, there's activity out in the rice paddy." I said, "How far out?" "Oh, it's over by the village." He said, "Maybe they're going to mortar us." I said, "Well, I'll be right out." I went out there and I lay there with my binoculars, looking. I saw people running around like rats out there. I said, "There's something going on over there." We watched and watched. It got to be around 11:30 p.m., and there was still activity. I said, "I don't know what the hell's going on out there." I called for mortar fire to drop in the rice paddy, not back by where they're living, but in the rice paddy. I called for some mortar fire. I said, "Drop about three or four rounds of mortar fire out there and if there's somebody setting up to mortar us, they'll get the hell out of there; they'll know that we're on to them."

They fired a couple mortar rounds. One of the rounds for some unknown reason was overshot and landed in the compound where the people live[d]. Five minutes later, one of these hooches [was] burning with all these banana leaves going up. They started burning torches and coming toward our compound because we had a dispensary set up out there. Whenever they'd be sick or something, they'd come there and we'd treat them. They were walking with these bamboo-lit torches and wailing and crying. When this mortar landed in there, it hurt some people. There were fifteen of them that were coming with shrapnel, and we got the doctor and the corpsman out there. I went out there to meet them and they said, "Oh, look at what happened." One of the ladies had half of her face blown off when that mortar round overshot. This lady [inaudible]...I can't say it. She put her baby [inaudible]...I couldn't handle it. The next day she [inaudible]...the baby ...[inaudible]. I said, "What the hell am I going to do with this baby?" I gave her an ammo box. She took the baby and buried him. It was the worst thing that ever happened to me. My guys got shot, but that was the worst thing. I still think of that sometimes.

JOHN DEDERICH Most of the people in my original platoon were either wounded or killed or gone somewhere. They reassigned everybody to different units. I was reassigned to the group that was guarding the radio relay on Operation Double Eagle. At the end of the operation, we were coming down out of the mountains to rejoin the unit. I rounded a building and stepped on a land mine and went fifty or sixty feet into the air. My right leg went

On February 24, 1966, John Dederich's mother received this telegram informing her that her son had been wounded in action. *John Dederich*

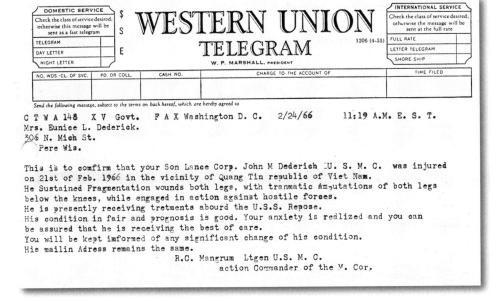

one way and my left leg went the other way and I got a little bit charred. The first thing I thought when I came back down was, "Where's my rifle?" I remember crawling for my rifle. I moved a little bit and then another person came and stopped me. We were probably a little bit into a land mine area and I had at least brought the unit partially into it. Because we didn't have the radio relay, we couldn't call in a medevac for me. The corpsman stayed with me, and it was about three and a half hours that I laid in the field. I stayed conscious that whole time until that helicopter picked me up and was on the way to the hospital ship.

I didn't think I was going to live because I looked down and I could see the mess I was. Almost everything was black and my left hand was shot and my right hand was pretty damaged. I didn't know it at the time but I had a collapsed lung and head wounds. I didn't think I was going to make it. I was happy because they had morphine. They were trying to end some of the pain. They put tourniquets on my legs. Once the helicopter came, I said, "OK, their job is done," and then I blacked out. I didn't come to until we were just landing on the hospital ship.

ROY ROGERS Vietnam helped me grow up. The Marine Corps helped me become a man and realize that I could actually do something with my life helping others. When I was wounded I figured God had a reason for me to live because he didn't kill me. The Bouncing Betty that I stepped on is meant to make a T-bone out of you [but] it [only] caught me in the left hand. The hard part about that is that I was left-handed at the time, so I had to relearn everything right-handed. I was alive [though], so once I left the Marine Corps I spent forty-five years volunteering my life away.

Tired Marines rest after patrol, October 1965.
Roy Rogers

AL SOBKOWIAK You'd always hook the new guys up with an old guy that's smart. You'd say, "He'll take care of you, that old sergeant will take care of you." I remember I did that with a lot of lieutenants that I got. Most of them were scared shitless. After a couple months, they'd get their feet on the

At the April 2009 grand opening of the Onalaska Library and Museum, the Sobkowiak brothers were honored for their service in the Marines. Pictured left to right are Donald, Charles, Ronald, Bernard, Al, Dennis, and Robert. Al, Dennis, and Donald served in Vietnam at the same time.
Al Sobkowiak

ground, the same with the new troops. They get their feet on the ground, and pretty soon they'd die for you. Some do.

JOHN DEDERICH I run into a lot of people and some have a guilt complex because they weren't wounded. I say, "Are you crazy? Is there something wrong with you? Why would you think that?" They say, "Because all my friends were hurt and wounded and I wasn't, and why not me?" And I said, "Well, why you? Go out and do something about it then." If somebody said to you, "I'm going to spare you, go do something," well, do something. There are a million things you can do to make this a better world. Go do some.

4 Elusive Enemy

"The only way things were measured was with a body count. If you didn't have bodies to count when you were done, you'd failed. Your mission was a failure."
— *Daniel Hinkle*

Though the U.S. ground combat presence in Vietnam began with just 3,500 Marines in March 1965, it expanded quickly; once U.S. policy makers committed to a ground war in Vietnam, it became clear that Army forces would be necessary. With its previous policy of training and support for the South, the United States had resisted full U.S. participation in the war. By the middle of 1965, however, U.S. policy makers came to believe that they had no other options; the Army of the Republic of Vietnam (ARVN) seemed woefully inadequate as desertions increased; North Vietnamese soldiers, materials, and supplies poured into the South; and U.S. intelligence predicted that North Vietnam would soon be able to take control of six of the northernmost southern provinces.[1] Pulling out, President Johnson's advisors argued, was an untenable option, far worse than committing more troops. After a lengthy discussion of Vietnam policy, Johnson committed fully to ground combat, announcing in July 1965 that he was sending more troops to Vietnam — bringing the number of troops from 75,000 to 125,000 — and doubling the draft call.[2] Johnson did not publicly discuss this as a major change in U.S. strategic policy, yet the United States was fundamentally expanding its responsibilities in Vietnam. In the words of Defense Secretary Robert McNamara, the United States would now carry the "brunt" of the fighting and be responsible for a "satisfactory military outcome."[3] With this new commitment to Vietnam, the number of U.S. forces rose dramatically, reaching 385,000 by the end of 1966 and rising to 535,000 by the early months of 1968.[4]

Despite the increase in numbers of troops, the United States struggled to develop a successful strategy for waging war in South Vietnam. Rather than large-scale, unit-level confrontations with the National Liberation

Front (NLF) or the North Vietnamese Army (NVA), U.S. troops often fought a grinding war of attrition in which they followed a practice known as "search and destroy." U.S. forces would identify the location of the enemy and then call in airpower to destroy it. Relying on superior U.S. technology, especially helicopters, U.S. troops would fly out from South Vietnamese bases to search hamlets and villages, patrol jungles and rice paddies, and engage in combat, using body counts, rather than territory secured, as their metric of success. U.S. troops constantly contended with snipers and land mines, fighting an enemy well-versed in Vietnam's often difficult terrain. U.S. military leaders sought to reach the elusive crossover point where they killed Vietnamese faster than they could be replaced, thus breaking the enemy's will to fight. This battle logic led to a "shoot first, ask questions later" mentality, and U.S. troops regularly patrolled through populated areas where, unable to differentiate between combatants and civilians, they often left destruction in their wake.

U.S. search-and-destroy tactics created great frustration for American troops. Simply put, there was no one to secure the areas that U.S. forces cleared: both U.S. troops and ARVN lacked the means to hold large tracts of conquered territory. As Daniel Hinkle states, "We would take the same ground over and over and over.... We fight in the same rice paddy four or five times. Our victory amounts to a body count. Then we go drink beer. We clean our weapons, we write letters home, and then next week we go to the same spot and do it all over again for a week or so." Ultimately, the United States developed a strategy based almost solely on its destructive capacities. This strategy, however, further undermined any chance of support from the South Vietnamese people, and the political victory that the U.S. ultimately sought — a politically and militarily secure South Vietnam, capable of standing strong against the North — remained elusive.

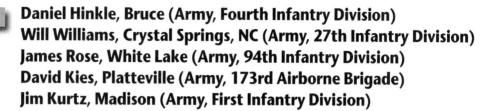

Daniel Hinkle, Bruce (Army, Fourth Infantry Division)
Will Williams, Crystal Springs, NC (Army, 27th Infantry Division)
James Rose, White Lake (Army, 94th Infantry Division)
David Kies, Platteville (Army, 173rd Airborne Brigade)
Jim Kurtz, Madison (Army, First Infantry Division)

DANIEL HINKLE I never hesitated about my responsibility. I was raised in a family with values and one of the values was knowing how we got where we are and holding that dear. We have a responsibility to uphold, so I didn't have a problem with going into the military. I didn't wait to be drafted; I enlisted. I had enlisted originally to be a chaplain's assistant. And I got a guaranteed three-year tour in Germany. I had to give that up when I went to Infantry Officer Candidates School. I often wonder how it would have been the other way. It was pretty much a snap decision. I was enthralled with the idea of being an officer, so I went to Fort Benning for 1965 and '66.

I guess I don't regret any of that experience. I certainly would like to know how the other road would've been because one of the things I lost was God. I've tried to pick it back up, but it doesn't work anymore. [Mankind]

An Army recruiting office in Madison, Wisconsin. *WHi Image ID 54585*

can't go too long without killing somebody, or without being superior in some way or another to someone else. The last hundred years it's been about money. You know, before that it was about land.

WILL WILLIAMS I joined the military immediately after graduating from high school in 1962. I was with the 54th Infantry in Germany with the missile unit. I departed for Vietnam on January 3, 1966. I was a Wolfhound, Second Battalion, 27th Infantry. We were the dogs of the unit. [The name] came from one of the battles they had during World War II.

When I joined the military I looked at it as a way to get out of Mississippi. I remember my mother and grandmother used to tell me I wouldn't live to be twenty-one if I didn't change my attitude. I was always compared to Emmett Till. I was told, "The same thing will happen to you that happened to Emmett." When Emmett was killed, I was twelve years old. [When] people told me that I'd end up like that, I needed to get out of Mississippi in the worst way. And the military was that chance and it also helped economically. I could send a few dollars back to my mother.

James Rose poses with a front-end loader, used to fill trucks with blast rock from a quarry in Gia Ray. *James Rose*

JAMES ROSE I quit high school when I was sixteen. I decided to go into the military and be a heavy equipment operator. I went to the recruiting station and I got the paperwork and took it home. I showed my mother and I had to have my dad's signature on there. It was early in the morning, my dad was in bed, and my mother took the paper in. She came out and she said he wouldn't sign, [so] my mother signed for me. I did my basic training and then I did all my heavy equipment school at Fort Leonard Wood. I was shipped to Germany for three years. In 1966, I got married. At the end of '66 I got orders to go to Fort Campbell, Kentucky, and test a 40-ton shovel that was going to be used in Vietnam in a rock quarry. They assigned me to the 94th Quarry Detachment, and there were twenty-seven of us in the detachment.

In November 1966, members of the 173rd Airborne Division practiced jumps in preparation for their April 24, 1967, combat jump into enemy territory. *Dave Kies*

DAVID KIES Before the military, I was in college. Actually I got kicked out of college because my pants were too tight and my hair was too long. I was too much for the school, so I left. I got a job with American Airlines at Chicago O'Hare. I was there about a year and I got my draft notice. About four months later I went in. Of course I knew where I was going about that time because everyone was going to Vietnam or being trained for it at least.

I went to Fort Knox, Kentucky, and then to Fort Polk, Louisiana, and that was hell. It was worse than Vietnam. There were spiders, snakes; it was cold at night and hot in the day. Then I went to jump school in Fort Benning and that was a pretty nice place. Jump school was my choice. [It paid] fifty-five dollars a month. I was scared to death of heights but for fifty-five dollars a month! In today's dollars, that'd be quite a bit.

JIM KURTZ Growing up in the 1950s in Madison, Wisconsin, is a very different experience than it is today. The Cold War was very much of a reality. There was a fear that the Russians were going to come across the polar ice cap and bomb the United States. At Truax Field, there were two air defense squadrons operating, one with night fighters and one with regular fighters. On top of the YWCA building on the corner of Pinckney and Mifflin Street they had a ground observer corps that was [manned] with people looking for Russian aircraft coming in. It was a reality that if you were a male you were going to serve. I graduated from high school in 1958 and the choices that you had were to go into the military. If you went to college it didn't exempt you from the draft. If you went to Madison [the University of Wisconsin], you had to attend ROTC for two years mandatory. The Madison campus on Fridays was a sea of military uniforms.

They had very good instructors in the ROTC at that time. They had young men that had served in the Korean War who needed college educations that would come in and teach. I had an opportunity to meet a cadre guy by the name of Harry P. Mueller. He was a captain at the time, from Waukesha, Wisconsin, and he'd won the Distinguished Service Cross in Korea. He was a very charismatic person and he was the one who suggested, very strongly, that I should stay and move on to the advanced course and that I should be in the infantry. I had some discussions with him about that, saying that I was going to law school and I thought it would be more appropriate to be involved in the JAG Corps or intelligence or something like that.

He told me basically, "If you are going to be a warrior, you've got to be in the infantry. You're too intelligent to be doing any of these other things." [Laughter.]

Many of my [ROTC] classmates went right in the military, but I decided that I wanted to get rid of school and get it behind me, so I went to law school. I attended the university's law school from 1962 to 1965. I really didn't think a lot about the military. Law school was a very rigorous intellectual experience. I was aware of the Vietnam situation to the degree that I've always been interested in military history and I knew about Dien Bien Phu, which happened in 1954. John F. Kennedy [said] in his inaugural speech, "Ask not what your country can do for you, but what you can do for your country." [That] had a big impact on a lot of people in my generation or pre–baby boomers. Kennedy was of a new generation, a World War II hero, and so it had an impact. The day I graduated from law school I received a letter with orders to go to Fort Benning, Georgia, in September 1965. I got my orders to go to Vietnam in mid-April [1966].

DANIEL HINKLE I was assigned to Fourth Infantry Division. The next day I was on a chopper and we flew out to the base camp. I was assigned to a battalion and then assigned to a company and given a platoon. I was in country forty-eight hours and I was an infantry platoon leader with a combat mission. At that point I was second lieutenant. Life expectancy was seven seconds. I guess you knew but you didn't realize it. The training kicks in. You start taking fire. It's only after it's over that you have time to consider what was going on and [think], "Jesus, I could've been killed." Thirty days after I arrived I was crawling through tunnels in Cu Chi with a .45 and I didn't care. People got killed. People got blown up.

WILL WILLIAMS We went by ship. I can't remember the name of the ship that we boarded, but I remember the families that were standing on the dock when we loaded and pushed off and the sorrow, I think, in everyone's heart that we were leaving, both the military personnel and the dependents that we were leaving behind. My wife talks about it now, how it hurt her to see the ship pull away from the docks.

I think about eighteen days later we docked at Vung Tau. We had a staging area in Bien Hoa to get orientated to the country. We were in Bien Hoa a couple of weeks and from there we convoyed to Cu Chi, which would be my duty station the remainder of my tour in Vietnam. That's where the rubber hit the road. We hadn't had any battles prior to that. We were inside another unit's perimeter at Bien Hoa. In Cu Chi we were out to do the fighting and that's what we did. We built our base camp right above the tunnels. I don't know why the military didn't know [the tunnels] were there. They had intelligence people and those tunnels were old, so I hear. We started taking casualties as soon as we got into Cu Chi from the VC coming out of the tunnels inside our perimeter, sniping on people. It took a while before we realized that the tunnels were there. It was pretty hectic.

By then I was an old-timer compared to the rest of the people in the unit. Coming out of Mississippi I was prepared for survival. During the time I grew up there, in Jim Crow, you had to know how to survive. My preparation started as a kid, really. I think I was more prepared than the ones who had never learned the tougher things in life.

JAMES ROSE We flew from Fort Campbell to Oakland and boarded the ship. Twenty-two days we were on water, and for twenty-two days I was sick. When we landed, we landed at Vung Tau late at night. We were all above ship and you could see the helicopters and the gunships flying over and all the tracer rounds shooting into the jungle. You could see the big nine[-inch] howitzers shooting and you heard the sound, and then you saw the big flash and the flare of the fire. This went on all night long. At that time, I was going to be twenty-one years old. We all sat up above and watched this and wondered what we got ourselves into. The rest of the guys in the 94th Quarry Detachment were all between the age of eighteen and nineteen years old, so they had no military experience whatsoever besides their training.

Huey helicopters transporting troops to the field. *Dave Kies*

DAVID KIES We were the first wave of replacements. We were thrown in and the first day in the field, I'll never forget it, they kept dragging American bodies out of the jungle. I thought, "This is not going to be good." [Laughs.] A helicopter was shot down like a hundred yards away in a rice paddy and I thought, "I don't know if I'm going to make this or not."

I thought every day was my last. I really did. My unit lost almost 1,400 guys, which is more than any other unit lost over a six-year period. It was pretty tough; you didn't get attached to anyone. It took a toll on everyone there. You can't keep that up. You'd go out on a listening patrol or an observation post,

Troops from the 173rd Reconnaissance set up camp. *Dave Kies*

they'd send two people out... You might be a hundred yards out in front of everyone else and you know, you're on these bennies [amphetamines] and it was perfectly dark. You couldn't do your Zippo. You broke the squelch on the radio every fifteen minutes so we knew you were still alive. You saw things that weren't even there. I'm sure if you went back in the archives, they would deny they ever gave those to us, the speed.

JAMES ROSE At night, you got in your sleeping bag and you just had a little hole to breathe through because as you lay there at night, you could feel the rats run across the top of you. We had a few out of the twenty-seven guys on the 94th Quarry Detachment who got tied up with marijuana and all kinds of stuff. At night you'd come in and one of them would be lying on his cot holding his rosary beads thinking he was going to die from these drugs. These young kids didn't know what they were getting themselves into when they started taking this. We had one young kid who was eighteen years old. He was high and picked up an incendiary canister. He pulled the tab on it and held it in his left hand and it burnt half his hand off. One of the other guys slapped it out of his hand and wrapped his hand. They called for medevac and they hauled him off and we never saw him again. Drugs were all available for these guys, and these guys got on it.

WILL WILLIAMS I think on my first tour in Vietnam, I carried a lot of hate with me to Vietnam, hate from what was happening in Mississippi to my people. It was a way of venting it. Even though I was in Germany for three years, I still saw prejudices and racism. Not from the German people, but from many of my fellow soldiers from the South, who had the separate places where they went and treated us differently. I had that hate in me when I went to Vietnam. It was easy for me to be destructive, because I grew up with that instilled in me.

My grandmother was Seminole and she had told me much of what had happened to her people. When I started getting higher in school and learned about the Constitution and the Declaration of Independence, I couldn't square it. I couldn't understand how this could be true. We were created equal, and I'm seeing people being lynched, beaten for nothing other than being themselves, a different color. Right away I had problems with government, with those documents, and hate for what the people were doing. My grandmother recognized it and she told me that if I didn't learn how to harness the anger and hate that I had, that it would destroy me from within. I didn't know what she meant until I was almost sixty years old. It was easy for me to fight, to kill. It was part of that hate that I had harbored for years, from childhood. It was only after my second tour that I began to turn it around, to think about what I had done and why this wasn't me.

JIM KURTZ We flew into Tan Son Nhat, which is the main airport in Saigon. We came in at a very steep level because the VC controlled the land on the approach. Walking off the plane was just like walking into a blast furnace. This was at three o'clock in the morning. It was probably about ninety degrees or so, and there was tremendous noise from aircraft taking off on missions. The smell would just knock your socks off. I've interviewed quite

Jim Kurtz during his last days as platoon leader in September 1966. His socks dry on a makeshift clothesline in the background. *Jim Kurtz*

10 Jan 67

Dear Folks,
The impossible has happened. Division came down & asked for me by name. Right now I'm sitting in as the G-1 officer as an Asst G-1. I must admit that it didn't come any too so. I was involved in a few "minor engagements" one of which cost us six. The job is challenging & not much more dangerous than during a Labor Day weekend except for an occasional patrol. The only thing is that already I'm feeling guilty about not being where the action is, particular when some of my friends are really putting out.

I had a very interesting talk with the Lutheran Chaplain today. His name is Lt Colonel _____. I think that he is American Lutheran.

Food wise there isn't really a lot that I need. I always like nuts & cheese. They sure were appreciated over Christmas. The fruit cake was outstanding but once it was opened we had to eat it right away. One thing I would like is salami. One of the officers got some pre-packages in a vacuum scardboard cylinder & it was great.

It looks like I'll have to put my R&R off for awhile. With the change I won't have to go until April. Are there any things that you would like me to get. I'll probably get a tape recorder & slide projector. So I have a good watch at home? I might pick up one. That one you sent me is running real well.

I have to get to work now. I'll let you know what my job is when I have a better idea myself. I should be mailing some pictures one of these days.

Say hello to everyone for me.

Jim

P.S. new address:

HHC, 1st Inf. Division
APO 96 345

Jim Kurtz wrote this letter home on January 10, 1967.
Courtesy of the Wisconsin Veterans Museum

a few Vietnam veterans and that's one of the impressions most of them had: the smell and the heat at any time of the day.

It ended up my company commander was on R&R in Hawaii with his wife. The first sergeant comes and gets me and takes me down to the platoon tent. In the military the word travels real fast about people and they knew that I was a first lieutenant and I was a lawyer. There were twenty-three people in this platoon, and I'll never forget walking into this tent. Some of the guys had been in Vietnam for nine or ten months. They looked at me like, "What in the hell is wrong with this guy that he's a lawyer and he's down here at the bottom of the line. What the hell did he do wrong?" I recounted this to Colonel Mueller and said, "The only excuse I could give other than saying it was my duty, which nobody [was] buying, was that basically they needed infantry lieutenants at that point in time. I was given an opportunity to go in JAG, but I didn't want to be in the Army for eight years.

I wanted to do whatever I had to do and get out. And besides, this guy told me that infantry was the place to be, so here I am."

A platoon's supposed to have forty-four people in it and this platoon was down to twenty-three. During my time as a platoon leader I don't think I ever had more than thirty people. [We didn't have] enough replacements. They were trying to have people with different times in country so everybody didn't leave at the same time.

DANIEL HINKLE You wrote letters back home almost in the abstract. My mom gave me a stack of letters that I had written to her. I don't even know who that person was. I never really mentioned anything about what was going on. You'd thought I went to summer camp. But that's good. I don't regret doing that.

We would take the same ground over and over and over. I didn't know until twenty years later that it was a war of attrition. It's acceptable to us if we only lose one guy to your six. We fight in the same rice paddy four or five times. Our victory amounts to a body count. Then we go drink beer. We clean our weapons, we write letters home, and then next week we go to the same spot and do it all over again for a week or so.

WILL WILLIAMS Cu Chi, which is about thirty clicks from Saigon, was in the heart of the rubber plantations. We saw the Firestone, Michelin, Goodyear plantations around the area. The rubber trees were right where we were fighting and [what we were] fighting for, I think. That's part of why I was there: protecting the corporate interest.

JIM KURTZ Rubber plantations were extremely [difficult] to operate in. The ones that were still operating were brushed out pretty good between the trees. They don't look like apple orchards, but the trees are spaced like that. There were always big ant hills in these rubber plantations. The ant hills could be twelve feet high and they provide pretty good cover for somebody. They would have snipers sit behind them and shoot at you from a long ways away because there were these alleys. Rubber was also difficult because if you were away from your base, radio communication was very difficult. I don't know if there was latex in the leaves of the trees [but] if you wanted to make communication you had to have somebody climb a tree with an antenna.

DANIEL HINKLE One of the things I've never been able to come to grips with is in the area of the Iron Triangle. I was in a mechanized battalion, so we had tanks and armored personnel carriers and self-propelled artillery. When we moved, the thunder of us moving — you could hear it for miles and there were things that fell by the wayside like trees. We had a Frenchman attached to the battalion that would follow along behind us and count the number of rubber trees that would be destroyed as we went through a rubber planta-tion, so that the United States could reimburse these people for the trees we destroyed. Is that not insane? That flies right in the face of what I was told I was going over there for, to stop the aggression of Communism. What a line of horseshit. I think the Vietnam vets, more than any other vets, have to deal with the atrocities they witnessed, the atrocities they were involved in. They also have to deal with the guilt. They have to deal with the betrayal. I've never talked much about that except to my wife. The sense of betrayal, sometimes it's overwhelming.

DAVID KIES It was Sunday morning on January 22 at approximately 7:20 in the morning. I was in recon so we'd walk around all day. At night, just as the sun was going down, we'd go back and pick out our spot, usually at the cross trails. We'd set up three-man teams and just ambush. We'd stay up all night after being up all day. They were feeding us Benzedrine to stay awake. It was 7:20 in the morning along a river pretty close to Cambodia, [and] the Vietnamese [were] unload[ing] our ships. I think it was Parrot's Beak or Iron Triangle, which are right next to one another. The naval ships would come in loaded with supplies and we'd hire the Vietnamese to unload them. That wasn't smart because they'd back their little trucks up there and take off the equipment: uniforms, explosives, whatever. I still don't know what hap-pened exactly. They would turn things around at night.

[The explosion] flipped me up in the air, like you see on TV when some-body gets shot. I tried to get up, and I couldn't get up and I looked down. [One] leg was gone and [the other] was hanging on but it was just dangling there. I knew right away what was going on. The medic came over. He really did save my life. It took seventeen units of blood, and that's pretty much what you have in you. So I guess I got a change out of it. I've never been absolutely certain, but I think the guy's name was Pedro Verera who helped me. He shoved a cigarette in my mouth and gave me a shot of morphine. I said, "Give me another one," and he said, "I can't. It's against regulations," but he did. [Laughs.] That's probably why I didn't pass out. I was pretty

Helicopters and tanks provide support to combat troops in the Tay Ninh area. *Dennis Bries*

Members of the 173rd Reconnaissance crossing a stream. *Dave Kies*

doped up. They called for a medevac, but there was none around. There was a helicopter in the area so they called [it] in. The pilot said, "I can't come down. This is the Colonel's helicopter." If you knew my colonel, he was the best guy in the world: Colonel Zeigels. We were all scared to death of him at the time, but he turned out to be a great friend. He said, "Get this blankety-blank helicopter down there right now." They came down and picked us up and we were back in a MASH hospital in twenty minutes. I never lost consciousness. I remember the whole thing. I was in shock I'm sure, but I had good care.

I remember they made a litter out of a poncho and a couple sticks and they took me to the helicopter. One of the guys I met at my first reunion said, "I've been holding this back for thirty-three years but I threw your legs on the helicopter." He was very relieved to tell me that. The pilot of the helicopter has called me since. I talked to him just a couple years ago. Colonel Zeigels just passed away a couple years ago but what a great guy. He actually had a son killed in Vietnam as well.

DANIEL HINKLE There's a transition you go through mentally when you're with a combat unit. Your values quickly change. The things you hold dear quickly change. I had a watch that my mom helped me pick out before I left. That became one of the most important things in my life — protecting that watch. Only after reading the book *The Things They Carried* did I realize the significance of that watch. That was something I could touch. [It] was part of the world I came from and no matter what, I had to keep that. You learn to value the most basic things. I don't remember thinking about it much until I got home. You think about your friends dying. You don't care about you dying until your friend dies. You can't carry that and survive.

During a firefight that lasted a couple hours, there was a chopper that called in and requested permission to land. Of course [he was told] to get the hell out. It was a slick, so it had no defenses, no armaments on it. On the belly of the helicopter was a cable attached to a palette. On the palette were gallons and gallons of ice cream. Some well-meaning person back in Saigon or Cam Ranh Bay or somewhere, somebody who had absolutely no freaking clue what we were doing and no concept of what we were involved in, thought that they would do something good for us. [These guys] are fighting for [their] lives and somebody sends [them] a pallet full of ice cream. [They] could have used some ammunition, some water.

WILL WILLIAMS I remember when we were building the base camp in Cu Chi, before we got a watering point, we used to stand out and take showers in the rain. It rained almost every day for quite a period of time. So it was rainy for a while, and then after the monsoon, it seemed like it was in the hundreds every day. I don't know what the temp was, but it was almost unbearable. I think Vietnam was the hottest place I've been in my life, both from the heat and from the war itself, from what was happening.

People within the perimeter were getting wounded or killed and the perimeter hadn't been breached. No one had gotten in. We couldn't understand it. After we discover[ed] tunnels, we went on special missions to locate them and try to blow them. You could do damage, but I don't think you could destroy them. Even the bombs didn't destroy them. So we took a lot of casualties from the people in the tunnels. You could see the so-called

Will Williams's friend Johnny H. Johnson explores an enemy tunnel in Cu Chi, spring 1966. *Will Williams*

enemy in the rice paddies one moment and the next moment they were gone. They had hit the tunnel entries. At that time they [the U.S. military] didn't have the dogs that'd do the sniffing or search the tunnels. We had what we called tunnel rats. They used the smallest people in the outfit, the ones who would go into the tunnels and search. I think some enjoyed it. The young man in my outfit, Johnny H. Johnson, was our tunnel rat. He loved the adventure of it. He was wounded and I went in to get him even though I am bigger in stature. It was something. I liked going in them myself, just to see how they were built, how they were constructed with the different levels, the different rooms. It was amazing. It aroused my curiosity. It wasn't like going into a cave where you're on one level. It was winding. They knew we had grenades. They were built in a way where when you'd first go in, you would go around the corner or down and up again. It kind of protected them from explosives and from bombs. They had kitchens there where they cooked and hospitals. You name it, it was there. They lived as they fought, right beneath us. That was our staging area. I never heard them talking or anything at night. We never even detected the smoke when they would be cooking.

DANIEL HINKLE The tunnels were a result of the conflicts that started during the Second World War. These tunnels were first started in the area around Cu Chi to hide people and weapons from the Japanese. Later, they were expanded. There were entire little communities down underground: ammunition storage, food storage, hospitals, and hundreds of firing perches. The first casualties we took moving into a new area would be from VC firing up

A "tunnel rat" discovers a well-concealed NLF tunnel. *Dennis Bries*

through portals as we walked along the path. They'd be six feet over in the vegetation and there'd be a breathing hole or something that they could see out. That would be our cue to start searching for tunnels. They were linked by a series of smaller tunnels and the entrances were booby-trapped. The entryway would simply collapse and there'd be no way to get to the rest of the tunnels.

WILL WILLIAMS Most of the fighting that I was involved in was at nighttime. We would search a village and if we were staying out for a while, we would set up a temporary perimeter to continue the mission. We'd get hit at night, rather than during the day when we were out actually searching and destroying. At times we did get hit pretty hard. I know right outside of base camp, at Hobo Woods, was one of the places where we always had contact anytime we were there, whether it was day or night. It was always an area that was crazy. I couldn't understand why we kept going in there. We never kept security; we would go [one] week, lose a lot of people, and a week or two later we would go right back and the same thing happened. I didn't see where we were making any progress at all in that area. It was that way even when I left.

JAMES ROSE On May 27, 1967, my company commander wanted to learn how to run an APC, [an] armored personnel carrier. He took position in [an] APC and they had one .50-caliber machine-gun operator in each APC. They crossed the river right next to Gia Rai village, and the Vietcong waited and they opened up on them. They had mortars, RPGs [rocket-propelled grenades], AK-47s, machine guns, and the ammo belts were wrapped around their neck. They had five hundred rounds attached to each one of them. The Vietcong, they wore black pajamas and straw hats, and the [North] Vietnamese had regular uniforms. You could tell them apart. The convoy got hit. It was only a quarter of a mile down the road from our base camp. They hollered, "Ambush! Ambush!" D Company left their posts and we followed the APCs down across the river. We spread out and started shooting at the Vietcong in the black pajamas. They would be running in and out, carrying litters, picking up wounded, and trying to get away. You would shoot them down as they carried their bodies out. It lasted for about an hour and a half. The bodies [were] everywhere. A lot of civilians and a lot of our people. We lost three guys. Sixteen from K Troop were killed.

The Vietcong that lay dead out there, we took a bulldozer and we went down into the rubber tree plantation and dug a big hole. We picked up all the bodies and laid them down in the hole and then they sprinkled lime over the top of them. The civilians came up and gave [their own] a burial. Little kids, babies, anything that moved, the Vietcong shot. Right after that, my brother got drafted and got orders to go to Nam. They wouldn't send two brothers over there at the same time. So I extended and I took his tour. They sent him to Korea and I stayed.

JIM KURTZ I was in the infantry platoon for just about three months. Then I got promoted to captain, so they put me on the battalion staff. We were spread out all over the place, so I flew around a lot. Actually, that was more dangerous [because] I was alone most of the time. A couple times they'd drop you off at one these airfields and your unit was supposed to show up. You're sitting there alone and there's somebody shooting at you. It weighed heavily on me because the week before I left for Vietnam, I went down to Milwaukee to see my uncle who was in the Bataan Death March. He said, "The one thing you do, Jim, is you don't get captured. You just don't get captured." That went through my mind. I was much more concerned about getting captured than getting killed. If you get killed, there's no problem. If you get captured there are a lot of problems.

I was in the infantry battalion for seven and a half months. That was kind of unusual because officers were only in a combat unit for six moths, whereas the grunts had to stay for a year. That really wasn't fair to the grunts. Some of them were able to get different jobs. They would move you out whether you were good, bad, or indifferent in that six-month time range. The reason I wasn't moved was we were on a big operation. Operations Attleboro and Cedar Falls were happening, and they didn't want to make any changes in that. This was when a friend of mine, Fred Victoria, got killed. He was platoon leader in Charlie Company and when I came into the company, he had just moved to the recon platoon. They would take a line platoon leader that was really good and have him head up the battalion recon platoon. The battalion surgeon and I were noticing that Fred was making mistakes that he wouldn't make ordinarily. One day we were out in a battalion position and a general came in to give his usual helpful stuff. As

North Vietnamese soldiers with their machine guns at the ready. *WHi Image ID 55009*

Nicknamed the flying banana for its distinct shape, the Piasecki HRP helicopter transported troops and supplies to the field. *WHi Image ID 11741*

his helicopter was leaving, the VC shot at it. Our battalion commander was scared of his own shadow and the General calls up and yells at him: "What are you doing letting somebody shoot at my helicopter?" He was going to send out the recon platoon to find out where this problem was. Both the battalion surgeon and I went to the battalion commander and said we don't think he ought to go. In fact I said, "I'll go." He said, "No, no. You're not going. He's going to go."

We were in a battalion position and he [Fred] went out and we started hearing the shooting. They had an ambush set up out there. They sent out another platoon. I found out when they brought the body bags back and Fred wasn't walking with them. That just hit hard. I had to walk away because I was so mad at that battalion commander. I never really forgave the guy. He [Fred] had eight days to go in the Army. It hit me really, really hard. I've never felt good about that. Could I have done something to stop this? I tried. I was supposed to be able to persuade people. It affects me to this day. Many years later, my father died on the same day, November 18. That's not my favorite day of the year.

DANIEL HINKLE The only way things were measured was with a body count. If you didn't have bodies to count when you were done, you'd failed. Your mission was a failure. You've heard stories about our troops cutting off the

During patrol, troops took every opportunity to rest, even for just a few minutes.
Doug Bradley

ears of the Vietcong. True story. It started with colonels and generals that didn't believe the body counts being turned in to them. They wanted some proof, so by God, they got it. That's insane. But that was normal. That's what we were expected to do.

WILL WILLIAMS It was amazing that DeMarchi was the only one during my time, from the squad, who was killed. That [happened] on a patrol where we got hit pretty hard. We couldn't come back into the perimeter because the company was getting overrun. So we had to spend the night out and that's when he took it. We just disengaged and sat in a bomb crater until the next day when Fifth Med came and brought us out.

I don't know how you can make one understand it, what it means to lose someone. If it's not you getting hit but someone you've known. To see them die. There's no way you can explain where they are. I think you are in shock initially, but you are able to function. You'd still be in that survival mode, so you do what you have to do to save your life and the lives of the rest of the squad. I think it hits you more when you are out of that situation, like when you come back to the base and you have the time to reflect. Then it hits you hard. Grieving starts at that time. But in the event, there's no grieving. You don't have time for it. Your survival doesn't allow you to do it. You move by instincts when one gets hit like that, especially if they die. I don't think anybody can explain what it really, really feels like. At the time I felt like it's no feeling, like you're just hollow for a moment. That's the way it was the complete night when DeMarchi was hit. We sat in the hole with him and we couldn't fight because we had a team, [a] small patrol out. We had hundreds of people that were coming through, going to the perimeter. We were just trying to stay down and make it until day, when the fighting would stop. That's what happened; we did make it. It was really painful to be in close proximity to a friend of yours who is with you no more. And you're seeing him there when in reality he's not. It has an effect on you that you never forget it. I still think about it often. I still think about DeMarchi. We were close too. We had a little singing group. We used to call him Frankie Valli. DeMarchi could carry the high notes. When we had a chance in base camp, we used to sit around and do doo-wops, harmonize. He was a close friend.

JIM KURTZ The emphasis was if you ever got into a firefight, they'd want to know body count and they'd want to know it right now. If you didn't [know], they'd get really irritated. [We'd get chewed out] for not moving fast enough and not killing enough. At the end of my tour, I was in a G-1 section and one of my jobs was to deal with body count. At night each battalion would have to call in what happened during that day. My job [involved] a big chart on the wall with each battalion [listing] how many people we'd killed and wounded. This general walks in and he says, "Captain, I don't like these numbers." And I said, "Sir, I agree with you." We'd had a bad day that day. The First Division had a bad day, took some bad casualties. He said, "I don't think you understand, I don't like these numbers." What he was suggesting was that the body count wasn't high enough. [He said,] "I want you to talk to these people, get more bodies." I said, "Sir, here's a grease pencil and a rag. You do what you want to do." He blew up. He said, "Captain, you're insubordinate. Your career is over." I said, "Well, I'm glad you agree with me at least on that because I'm going to be back in Madison in two weeks. I'm really not going to do anything like that because it's wrong." He stormed out of the room. He was really, really very unhappy with me.

DANIEL HINKLE I was in country for nine months. I got blown up in June or July. I spent four and a half months in a hospital in Japan. I stepped on a land mine — one left there during the Second World War. The VC had planted it there, I think — at least that's what I was told — but it was one we left or the British or the French left during the Second World War. The Vietcong were very ingenious people.

I didn't know what I was doing. I was playing it by ear. Training kicked in and if it didn't, I was winging it. After a while you learn what not to do, but you're always learning what to do. Learning what not to do sticks with you. I got wounded right about Christmas or New Year's '66. As a result, I

Bob Hope's USO show at Cu Chi, December 1969. *Dennis Bries*

was reassigned because I wasn't able to continue as a platoon leader. I went from the tunnels and carrying a .45, hopped on a chopper, landed at Tan Son Nhat at around six o'clock in the evening.

It must have been a Sunday because there wasn't anybody there. I went from tunnels in a jungle to having a hot meal in the officer's club at Tan Son Nhat Air Base. Bob Hope happened to be there, doing a USO show.

WILL WILLIAMS I got hit in August of '66. I took grenade frags to the head. I had other people in my squad who were wounded. Linwood Puryear, Ernest Dawson. I still wonder what happened to some. Dawson was medevaced to Japan and I never heard from him. Never knew what happened. It still bothers me. I'd like to contact some of these people if they are still alive. Linwood Puryear was wounded and I contacted his parents last fall. He had just passed away, but I had been trying for years to get in touch with anyone from the Second Battalion, 27th Infantry during '65 and '66. Puryear was the only one, but his injury wasn't serious. Wilson, another guy, lost his arm. Life goes on. We handle it the best way we can.

I think a bond is built between vets that can never be broken, regardless of their philosophies. They'll always be vets and I think they'll always respect each other to that extent. But I think where the problem comes in is that many don't know the history, they don't know why we have gone into war after war, and it's hard for them to accept it. They look at patriotism as being, "Support my country, my commander-in-chief, right or wrong." I don't believe that way. I believe that if someone is taking you down a wrong path, the thing for you to do is to speak about it. That's patriotic. Patriotism has been something that has been used, so has religion, to divide people. I've been called unpatriotic, but it doesn't bother me. It took me a long time to find myself, to know who I really am and what I stand for, and that's something that no one can take.

JAMES ROSE A month before I left the States, my son was born. After the massacre with K Troop, I had the shakes so bad, I couldn't write home for over a month. My wife contacted the Red Cross. The Red Cross finally found me. My company commander came to me and asked when I had last written home. I told him I couldn't remember. He said, "It's been over a month." When he asked me why, I held out my hands. I was shaking so bad I couldn't hold a pencil. He said, "I'll get the company clerk and you'll sit down and get something out to your wife." We sat down and we got a letter out.

I don't know if it was from the Agent Orange. I was tested and with my nerves and shakiness they said [I was] a candidate for it. I don't speak about it at home. I don't speak about it around my kids. I got three sons and two of them were born in the military and one was born here in Wisconsin. I don't talk about it at home. This is the first time I've ever discussed my role in Vietnam.

DAVID KIES I went to Walter Reed [Army Medical Center]. It was a great place. There was an amputee ward. Some guys by that time were hooked on morphine, so there was a lot of screaming. If you didn't know you'd swear you were in a crazy house. It was just like a mental ward. They'd come around for medicine. They'd give each guy a six-pack every night; instead of getting a shot you'd get a six-pack of beer if you wanted it. We used to go to New York City every once in a while. I had a doctor one night who came to me and said, "I know what they're going to do to you." They were going to give me a knee disarticulation. They were going to take my knee apart and everything else would be gone below. He said, "Don't let them do it." He said, "I know where you're going. You're going to Madison when you get out of here. There are some really good doctors in Madison." I wouldn't let them do the surgery. I wasn't there very much longer. I went to be discharged from Walter Reed so I'd be out of the Army. This was in June. I'd been there since January. I had my wheelchair and my uniform on. I had a pair of jump boots on the platform even though I didn't have any legs or feet. [Laughs.] I rolled into the General's office to get discharged and he said, "Your hair is too long. Go get a haircut." I had to go down to the barbershop and get a haircut, come back, sign my name, and I was out.

JIM KURTZ A couple days before I was going to leave from the Bien Hoa Air Force Base, they had a little party. It was real nice. They took me in a jeep down there, and we sat around for a day or two waiting for the airplane. When it was our turn to go, when the pilot said, "We are now leaving Vietnam airspace," there was just a huge cheer on the plane. It was just, "We're out of here. We made our year." They sent me to Fort Dix. Fort Dix was a basic training center. I was a captain; I was quite a bit thinner than I am now and very tan. I had a few ribbons. I was going to go off the base to see this guy that I served with over in Vietnam. He and his wife were in that area. I got stopped by the MPs [military police] at the gate because I didn't have an ID card and they were accusing me of being a basic trainee who wanted to sneak off the base. I did have a copy of my orders, but I didn't have an ID card. I said, "What is this?" They said, "Well, some of these trainees, they try to look like generals. They go to the PX and buy stars and try to leave." I said, "Well, do I look like a basic trainee?"

When I got back to Madison, I was very happy to be home, but it was interesting. My family was happy to see me, but there was apathy at that point. It was, "You've had a job somewhere and you came back." I had just been through the most intense experience of my life and there was no way to really decompress from that. You're expected to be normal. You've had this experience and you're supposed to be just exactly the way you were three years before it ever happened. They are doing a better job now in the military when they're letting people out. They never told us that this was an issue. I never even thought about mental issues and stuff like that.

After practicing law for a while up in Chilton, Wisconsin, I came back and started working for the legislature and then the Department of Natural Resources. Working for the DNR, my first job was advising the conservation warden staff. The riots had started and the State Patrol and conservation wardens were brought into Madison as a group to protect the capitol and the state buildings on either end of State Street. Our guys were very good policemen, but had not been trained in this. I went down on the police lines several times to help out, not to deal with it, but to give advice to the offi-

Protestors assemble at the Truax Air Force Base in Madison, October 1965. *WHi Image ID 54588*

cers in charge. The things the protestors were saying about the soldiers were horrible. I can't even repeat it. Saying they were mass murderers. Then it occurred to me that they were talking about me. They didn't know that I was a veteran, but they were talking about me. The only way I could deal with that is to forget that I was a veteran, just to blank the experience out totally. That's about 180 degrees the wrong way to [deal with] something like [this]. My wife asked me about some parade somewhere and [said how] I ought to go to that and I said, "I'm not a veteran. I'm not going to go to any parades."

DANIEL HINKLE I will never get where I was before, and I've accepted that. I will never be who I was before. Not even close. I don't know why we have such trouble differentiating the war from the warrior. You can hate the war but why hate the warrior? He's doing what's asked of him or her. They believe the hype; they believe in what they're doing. I hate the war, but I don't hate the warriors. I think we're great at war. We'll kick the hell out of anybody, but we suck at peace. We're not good at it. Our soldiers are the ones that suffer because of that.

JAMES ROSE In June '74 I retired. I wanted a career as a military person and spent twenty years in there. It just didn't happen. When I came back from Vietnam, I was a whole new person.

WILL WILLIAMS I tried to block what was fun, like when we used to sing. We used to sit around and do doo-wops. That was good early on, but after DeMarchi was killed, the group stopped. We did a song that I sent home that the wife thought was a professional group singing. It was called "For You Girl": "I'd cross the desert sands on my knees and hands for you." She thought it was a pro group that did it. We were sitting around in the base camp and did it one night. I blocked that out because he was no longer a part of it. I didn't want to remember it.

DAVID KIES I still get chills. I thank God there aren't too many Hueys around anymore. Med flight has more of a jet helicopter. Those Hueys just have that "bum bum bum bum bum bum" — you can hear them from miles away. Sometimes the skies would be black with helicopters, like a bunch of black birds up there. You talk about emotions getting me. Once in a while, if I'm driving down the road and go by a Chinese restaurant and smell the spices they use, it sends me right off. It's just like, "Oh, God." It's the smells more than anything else that brings the senses around. It's just like hearing that Huey. Those are probably the two biggest things. They just bring things back.

If there had been veterans against the war [groups] at that time I would have been there. I'd still wear my khakis a lot or my field jacket and my cargo pants. That was my dress for years. I did run into trouble one time in Milwaukee. It was the only time I was ever spit on. You always hear we were spit on. That time I was dressed in my Army clothes and a guy came up and spit on me. Other than that, I got treated very well.

WILL WILLIAMS I went through a program for PTSD [Post-Traumatic Stress Disorder]. I didn't realize I had it for many years. That's what I was saying earlier. My wife used to tell me I had changed and my daughter had told me. I didn't understand what they meant, so I actually went through a program for PTSD. It's something I learned that I couldn't change. Those thoughts will come and they'll go and it's just the way I deal with them now that makes them different. That's why I laugh when I hear people now who say they have this new way of treating PTSD. One lady even said they were curing PTSD. I think it's a joke. Because I think to cure it you'd [have to] be able to take away those memories, those nightmares, the flashbacks. I don't think one will ever be able to do that unless there's some way you can alter the brain. I think you can get to a level where you can deal with whatever happens that carries you back to that time and the ghosts of war visits you. I think you learn how to cope with it.

During Desert Storm I tried to watch TV and it really set me off. My counselor and doctor at the VA told me, "Don't watch the news; don't read the papers." I couldn't deal with it. Even the Wall, the names on the Wall, I know so many people on there. The first time I saw it was last year when it was out at the VFW in Madison. Even though I had been to D.C. six or seven times, I never had the courage to go up and read the panels. When it came here, I thought I could do it by myself, go early in the morning. I went about three o'clock in the morning and read a few names and then went home. A couple of hours later, I went back. I went about five or six times and my wife went with me a couple of times. She knew many of the people that were on that wall too, that I knew. Just dealing with it, dealing with the memory of it, trying to forget it. I think trying to drop that stigma that many people have, about how we were nuts and all of that, played a big part in it. I think that's why a lot of vets don't go for help for PTSD, because they're afraid of being labeled a psycho when they're just dealing with something that happened beyond their control. You got to live with it, accept it and go on.

JIM KURTZ In a lot of ways it was a lot harder being home. When you were there you were with people, even [if all you] knew [were] their nicknames, it was a brotherhood of "We're in this together, we've got to help each other" and all of that. There just wasn't that type of thing coming back here. There was not the cohesion. World War II veterans participated in the veteran movement — not all of them, but it was readily available and it was a welcoming thing. We didn't have that opportunity.

5 All Hell Broke Loose

"Then when it's over, everything hits you. The adrenaline starts to wear off and the reality sets in of what actually went down, the pain that you saw on your fellow Marine's face or the vision of a Vietnamese head exploding because you shot him in the eye. No time during the firefight but afterwards, much reflection. Much reflection."— Daniel Pierce

Throughout 1966 and 1967, the number of U.S. troops in Vietnam continued to escalate as fighting intensified. As the U.S. presence expanded, so did the infiltration of men and material from North Vietnam; though the United States bombed the North heavily throughout 1966 and 1967, the number of people and amount of supplies entering South Vietnam actually increased, much of it through the painstakingly maintained Ho Chi Minh Trail, which ran along the border between Vietnam, Laos, and Cambodia and along the demilitarized zone (DMZ) separating the North from the South. Along with National Liberation Front (NLF) fighters, the number of North Vietnamese Army troops (NVA) in South Vietnam also increased, and for U.S. troops, contact with the uniformed NVA became increasingly likely. In response to a growing enemy, the United States and the South Vietnamese Army (ARVN) continued to use search-and-destroy tactics. Seeking to ensure that enemy forces would not have anything to reoccupy once U.S. troops had patrolled an area, *destroy* came to mean the destruction not only of enemy combatants and civilians but also of villages, homes, jungles, rice paddies — all of the infrastructure and plant life present in a given area. As Marilyn Young notes, "The American war against the NLF and its northern ally transformed every aspect of Vietnamese society and became a war against Vietnam."[1]

For the purposes of waging the war, Vietnam was divided into four tactical zones; the Marines in this chapter fought in I Corps, which consisted of the five northernmost provinces of South Vietnam. The terrain in I Corps varied, from isolated mountains and jungles in the east to rice paddies,

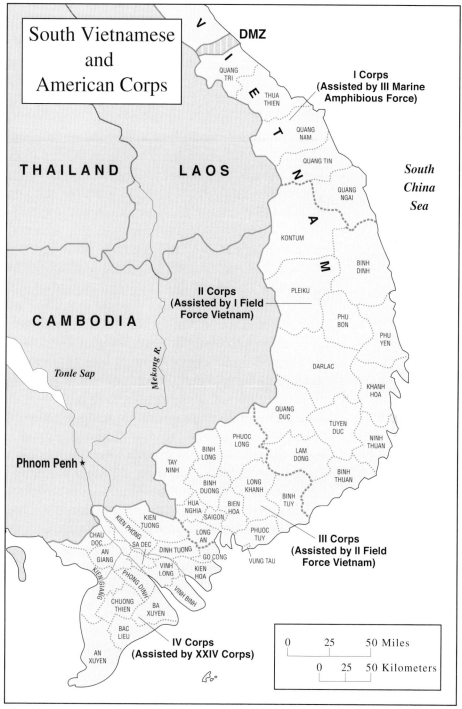

South Vietnamese and American Corps

DMZ

I Corps
(Assisted by III Marine
Amphibious Force)

II Corps
(Assisted by I Field
Force Vietnam)

III Corps
(Assisted by II Field
Force Vietnam)

IV Corps
(Assisted by XXIV Corps)

South
China
Sea

THAILAND

LAOS

CAMBODIA

Tonle Sap

Mekong R.

Phnom Penh ★

V I E T N A M

QUANG
TRI

THUA
THIEN

QUANG
NAM

QUANG TIN

QUANG
NGAI

KONTUM

BINH
DINH

PLEIKU

PHU
BON

PHU
YEN

DARLAC

KHANH
HOA

QUANG
DUC

TUYEN
DUC

NINH
THUAN

PHUOC
LONG

LAM
DONG

BINH
THUAN

BINH
LONG

TAY
NINH

BINH
DUONG

LONG
KHANH

BINH
TUY

HUA
NGHIA

BIEN
HOA

SAIGON

KIEN
TUONG

LONG
AN

PHUOC
TUY

CHAU
DOC

SA DEC

DINH TUONG

GO CONG

VUNG TAU

KIEN PHONG

AN
GIANG

VINH
LONG

KIEN
HOA

KIEN GIANG

PHONG DINH

VINH BINH

CHUONG
THIEN

BA
XUYEN

BAC
LIEU

AN
XUYEN

| 0 | 25 | 50 Miles |

| 0 | 25 | 50 Kilometers |

Patti Isaacs, Parrot Graphics

villages, and coastal plains in the west. I Corps included the Marine bases at Khe Sanh and Dong Ha along with the large cities of Hue and Da Nang, also the site of a major U.S. air base throughout the war and the arrival site for many U.S. troops. Marines began extensive pacification and battle operations in I Corps in 1966; because I Corps bordered the North, it was also the responsibility of the Marines stationed there to clamp down on the infiltration of the NVA through the DMZ. Indeed, in the early months of 1966, Military Assistance Command in Saigon (MACV) estimated NVA infiltration into the two northernmost provinces of I Corps at 7,000 troops per month; when "possible" infiltration was included, the numbers reached 12,500.[2] In Operation Hastings (July 1966), for example, approximately 8,000 Marines and 3,000 ARVN troops fought a bloody battle in difficult jungle and mountainous terrain, hoping to prevent the NVA from taking control of northernmost Quang Tri province and from massing south of the DMZ. I Corps was the site of fierce fighting throughout 1967 and 1968, and combat bases such as Con Thien, a strategically vital group of hills near the North Vietnamese border, sustained heavy attacks as the Marines continued to engage with NVA troops to maintain U.S. military positions and prevent the NVA from gaining a foothold in South Vietnam.

Despite U.S. efforts, however, it was still the enemy that largely determined the site of fighting; according to one National Security Council report, in 1966 and 1967, approximately 75 percent of battles were "the enemy's choice of time, place and duration."[3] Moreover, along with continuing to prop up an unpopular political regime, the United States was facing increasingly insurmountable odds. While the United States had to "win" the war, the Vietnamese — both the NLF and the North — had to outlast the United States; not a simple task, to be sure, but the NLF often had popular support on its side. Indeed, in the U.S. mind, Vietnam was becoming a war of wills, one that the United States, particularly President Johnson, was determined not to lose.

Daniel Pierce, Stone Lake (Marines, First and Third Marine Division)
Don Weber, La Crosse (Marines, Fourth Marine Division)
Larry Miller, Rice Lake (Marines, Third Marine Division)

Daniel Pierce served three and a half years with the Marines after enlisting on August 15, 1965. *Daniel Pierce*

DANIEL PIERCE I grew up in small-town southeastern Minnesota. I got in a little trouble when I was a youth and my probation officer was a Navy Reserve officer. He thought it would make a man out of me if I joined the Navy Reserves, so I was in the naval reserve but every time I went to a meeting, I was always peeling potatoes because I had lint on my uniform or, shoot, something. They were going to send me to active duty, so I thought I'd fool them and instead of getting a tan in the Gulf of Tonkin on a two-year Navy stint, I joined the Marine Corps for four years. I knew that there was a conflict going on, but my road was to take the Marine Corps to get out of small-town [Minnesota]. I wasn't very good in academics, and there was only one other avenue to leave the village and that was the Marine Corps.

In 1965, I joined the Marine Corps and went to boot camp in San Diego. Virtually 100 percent of the people in boot camp went to Vietnam. I was a very bad Marine. Unmotivated. I spent time in the motivation platoon, watching John Wayne movies all day long. I tried to smuggle in food to the guys in the fat farm because they were crying at night and stuff. My boot camp experience was not pleasant. I guess my only salvation was that I could PT the hell out of anybody. I could out-push-up, out-pull-up, out-sit-up everyone. That's what saved me basically. I finally got out of boot camp and ended up in Vietnam as an infantryman.

DON WEBER [I grew up] about twenty-eight miles east of La Crosse on a dairy farm. I went to grade school at a little one-room school. We had all eight grades in one room until I was in fifth grade. I had a hard time in school. I was always the one that got the lowest score on a spelling or math test. I would sit in the back of my row. I grew up and went to high school thinking that I was just a loser. I'd been told that "You're not a good student, you're not going to make it." I would get in fights. I worked when I was fourteen. My uncle was a farmer, had a very serious accident. I was sent to his farm.

Don Weber, center, poses with his family before departing for Vietnam. *Don Weber*

So I was running his farm and going to school and getting up very early. I'd get all the chores done at the dairy farm, go to school, come back, and do chores.

I graduated from high school in 1966. Vietnam was getting very serious at the time. I had no idea what I was going to do with my life. I couldn't go on to school. I didn't have any grades where I would get accepted with a scholarship of any kind and my mom and dad could not afford to put me in any school. I always had this sense that I wanted to serve our country, because my father [did] and he was a prisoner of war. He went through all of that. I really felt it was my duty to do this. At the time I thought Vietnam really was a war that we needed to participate in. There was more and more protest. You could start to see more and more rejection by America and younger people. I still thought, "We need to do this, we need to help stop the spread of Communism."

I had no idea what I was going to do, [but] I decided I'm not going to wait until the draft comes up. I went to see a couple different recruiters; the Navy, the Air Force, and I went to the Marine Corps. The Marine Corps said, "We'll get you in as soon as you want to go." I just wanted to get in, so I enlisted.

LARRY MILLER My older brother was in the Marine Corps right after Korea. I had five uncles in World War II. One did Normandy, one in the Marines, one in the Navy, and one was captured in the Battle of the Bulge. So my whole family has been military oriented. I graduated from Rice Lake and I just figured it was the thing to do, so I joined in October 1965. Do my patriotic chore. It was my turn.

DANIEL PIERCE My first time over was on a ship and we picked up the 25th Infantry in Hawaii. It was quite interesting landing in Da Nang a month later. Landing on landing craft with a sea bag, no guns, I thought, "What are we, nuts?"

We were all separate. There were about six hundred of us from [the] staging battalion out of Camp Pendleton. I was assigned to First Battalion, First Marines, Alpha Company. Battalion area was located south of Da Nang around the historical old city called Hoi An. Very, very beautiful city. It was one of the few that didn't sustain too much damage during the war. For some reason no one wanted to destroy it. It's an old, beautiful provincial city, very upscale. Most of the Vietnamese women you'd see all had the traditional Vietnamese dress on. Of course we didn't spend any time there. We were out in various places: Mud Flats, the Sand Dunes, and the Island.

DON WEBER I landed in country on April 6 at Da Nang. It was dark and you could hear artillery rounds going off. There were these sand-bag bunkers right off of a man-made runway. I was put in one of those bunkers and that's where I stayed for the night. The next morning they came and said, "You're going to be reporting to the First Battalion, Fourth Marines, Charlie Company. They are up on an outpost called Con Thien." I wasn't quite sure where that was, but it was on the very northern tip of South Vietnam. The outpost was there to provide security for CBs [construction battalions] as we were developing the demilitarized zone. They were bringing supplies down Route 1. It's the narrowest point between North and South Vietnam. They were developing this demilitarized zone and clearing all of the trees and elephant grass. They had dozers and heavy equipment, and we were to provide security and set up ambushes. We were constantly taking on small-arms fire and mortar rounds.

LARRY MILLER I shipped out and went to Vietnam. We flew in to Da Nang and joined up with the Ninth Marines. Hill 55 south of Da Nang. I was attached out of a battery where all they did was force. I spent all my time with the grunt units. They shipped us up to Marble Mountain, which was a mountain just outside of Da Nang. We had an observation post up there. The five of us would sit on top of the mountain and just watch the whole area for any activity. In May, they had a big uprising in Da Nang with the Buddhists. It was a big civil issue. They pulled us off Marble Mountain and we went into Da Nang to protect some civilians that were working there. I really didn't understand the Buddhists burning themselves. The South Vietnamese were opposed to that. We started taking civilians on May 18. Two sky raiders bombed some of the wrong guys. We had a lieutenant get killed and a bunch got wounded. We tried to shoot down the sky raiders, which we weren't supposed to do but they were killing us. Two or three hours later I got wounded. I never knew if it was a rocket round or a mortar round, but it wounded about twelve of us. I was in the hospital from May 21 and didn't return to Vietnam until the first part of July.

I went to the Fourth Marines. I got back to Vietnam on a Friday or Saturday evening. I joined my unit out in the field, and Sunday afternoon I got hit again for the second time. I was back only three days. A guy stepped on a land mine and it killed him, killed the next guy, and I was the third guy. I got the leftover shrapnel. Sergeant Jones got down and picked it all out. He said, "You're OK, don't worry about it." He cleaned me up and I had a bunch come out of me for the next three, four months. It just kind of oozed out of the right side of my face and my shoulder. I didn't put in for a Purple Heart because it got screwy the first time [I was wounded]. The recruiter sends a telegram [to your family] telling them: "Your son has been wounded in Vietnam. Stop." Nobody knew how bad I was or anything and that didn't sit well with my mom. When I got hit the second time I said, "Do not put me in for a Purple Heart." It wasn't that bad. I could have been medevaced, but I stayed out in the field.

DANIEL PIERCE The first operation I went on was Operation Virginia. It was kind of a joke and it formed my opinion about Vietnam right from the beginning. A general in the Army bet a general in the Marine Corps that the battalion of Marines couldn't march up Highway 1 to the DMZ. So, of course, we had to march up Highway 1. We got up there with virtually no contact with the enemy. [There were] a few here and there but nothing even approaching any kind of major confrontation. It took us about thirty days, and we were all ragged. They flew in a water buffalo, a big tank of water with a high-pressure hose on it, and made everybody get in front of it. They brought in all new utilities and made you put those on, and then the generals flew in and they had a big photo op. It made me understand that this was not really a place that I wanted to be.

In the rear, the officers would live in air-conditioned trailers, eating steaks and shrimp and we had to steal C rations. It just didn't make much sense. I wanted to be there to make a difference but soon as I got there everything was contradictory. There was no making a difference; there was no domino effect. It was just keeping your ass alive and hoping that everyone else stayed alive also on both sides.

Daniel Pierce, pictured left, poses with fellow Marines George Martzo and Glenn Norris while on R&R in September of 1966.
Daniel Pierce

DON WEBER And gosh, here you are. You train, but this is for real. I still felt I'm immortal — then you start to see a few casualties taken. On May 4, we got overrun. I have no idea to this day why I survived and almost my whole platoon was wiped out that night. We had been issued the M-16 and we had trained with the M-14. On the way over we landed in Okinawa to get our gear and they gave us the M-16s. It was the first time we worked with the M-16. It was made for jungle warfare. The M-14s were heavier weapons, with longer barrels. You could bury them in mud, come back, and a month later dig them up and as long as the chamber and everything was clear, it would fire. Not the M-16s. It was the first version of them. I think today they're on the fourth version. We had a lot of problems [with] jamming.

Well, that night, we started taking incoming, mostly mortar rounds, really early. It was still light out. It just kept pounding our perimeter. We had land mines, we had concertina wire, and then we had our first defense, where we had our Marines in foxholes. The main perimeter was further back. They kept dropping mortar rounds and trying to break up our perimeter. That went on for hours and we knew we were in for a long night. Then they started with the ground forces. They just kept coming and coming.

The M-16s just couldn't tolerate any dust or dirt. Once they got inside our perimeter, our fellas didn't have anything to fight back with other than hand-to-hand. They would come at you and they were all drugged up. You could take somebody's arm off and they would still come at you. It was very scary to see that and experience that. I'd only been there for a month. My squad leader, he'd been there for almost ten months. I made up my mind when I got over there to do whatever he told me, because he had survived. We called him Sergeant Rock and he had gone home just before that on emergency leave, because his brother had drowned. He was married and when he was home, his wife got pregnant, so he had gotten word after he had came back and he was really excited about that. He only had a few weeks left and he was going to fly home. But he came out to get me out of my foxhole because [the NVA] were going to overrun the area. As we were running back inside the perimeter, a mortar round came in and killed him. He never got to see his child. He saved my life and you have to live with that. I survived the night and most of the rest didn't. I have no idea why. Those things change you forever.

LARRY MILLER I stayed with Fourth Marines. We were fighting VC mostly. When I came [back] in July, we started Operation Hastings. That was a big multibattalion operation. That's when we ran into the NVA for the first time. Operation Hastings went on to Operation Prairie, [then] Prairie 1, [then] Prairie 2. It basically lasted the whole summer and into the fall. That was the first time we ran into the NVA. They were good. The VC didn't even bother us; they had poor weapons. They were really bad marksmen. On the Hastings we ran right into the NVA. They were using flanking tactics on us and everything. They knew their business. That's when it turned into a different war, with the transition from the VC to the NVA.

We went north after that. I started on Da Nang I Corps, then went to Phu Bai, Dong Ha. We spent that winter in Dong Ha, 1966 into '67. Things really heated up in early '67. Then I changed; went on a helicopter ship, an LPH, a landing platform helicopter. That was with First Patang and Third Marines. We all went on a float. We cruised up and down the coast. [If there were] any hot spots, we'd go in. We'd shoot and take care of business, then come back for two or three days and wait for another one to happen. I was always assigned the first wave. We basically went in with five helicopters. There were five grunts to a helicopter and that would be a first wave. We'd start setting up a 360 [degree] perimeter. The North Vietnamese, they basically wanted to come down across the DMZ. They did not want to do the Ho Chi

Marines relax at Phu Bai between search-and-destroy operations. *Larry Miller*

Minh Trail. The Marine Corps wasn't going to let them. We were going to stop them at the DMZ. In the summer of 1967, the spring and summer of that year, that was when the action was. That's when it happened. Four to five thousand at a time would come across the river. We were up there trying to stop them. It was just operation after operation after operation. I think the longest we were out was forty-two days. The clothes just rotted right off you. We'd go back to the ship for maybe two or three days, and then go right back in again. We basically stayed in the bush for the whole time.

Larry Miller and his spot team return from an operation in which all members survived. Miller is pictured front, second from the right, with a rifle. *Larry Miller*

There were only two other people to live out the first wave from May 18. I pulled sixteen major operations, sixteen assaults. Major ones. We [were] first there in '66 [and] we did, Marine Corps calls them "county affairs," and that was, that helped the South Vietnamese people. We'd go in the village with medicine, but the deal was there were people we didn't know about. First we surrounded the village. And we sent people in, and whoever ran out we just killed, we just killed whoever ran out. 'Cause we assumed they were the bad guys. Then they went in and gave everyone medicine, patched them up, and stuff like that. We did effort. That was early '66 we did that. Called 'em county affairs. Then in '67 it just changed, just changed. All the operations out there.

DANIEL PIERCE It was all search-and-destroy missions. It was battalion-sized operations where you would get online and sweep through an area. They would go from one to the next. I can't even tell you what operations I was on. The only one I remember is Virginia. But it was continuous and then the only break from that was you would be off in company areas running squad patrols. The war was so much different in '66 than when I went back in '68. When I went over in '66 there were not only guys that had time in Vietnam but time in life. There were fire team leaders that were E5s, sergeants, guys who could teach you something. I was just a kid off the farm, and I gleaned every bit of knowledge that I could off of these guys. It was a whole different war in '66. Mostly it was small skirmishes, ambushes, operations, sniper fire, and a lot of anti-personnel mines.

Most of the time we were trucked to a certain point and then we humped [marched] in. Other times when there was some activity going on somewhere we would be choppered in. In both instances it was mostly one foot after the other. I went back to Vietnam in 2005 and I got off the plane and I almost died. I couldn't even breathe. I thought to myself, "How the hell did you do all that humping in that sand and that heat?" That's what we did. We humped and dug holes. Most of it was pretty boring stuff.

There were times when we were choppered into jungle situations. I remember being in the jungle where it was so dark you couldn't see the guy in front of you. Most of the time in my first tour it was all along the China Sea from Da Nang down to Hoi An. We did do a lot of things up north also. Quang Tri, Phu Bai, Dong Ha.

DON WEBER I was over there 393 days and I remember most of them. Shortly after that, on June 26, I was taking all my squad out on an ambush when the Vietcong ambushed us. I got shot in my right leg, and seven others were killed. Our radioman escaped without getting shot. I crawled off. At first I didn't even know I was shot. It happened so fast. You just go into this survival mode where instinct takes over. It was like somebody pulled a rug out from under me. I just went down. This happens within seconds; it happens so fast. I tried to get up [and] run and I couldn't. I could feel the blood. I just dragged myself twenty-five or thirty yards. It was over with like that. If the other seven Marines weren't dead, they came down and shot them all in the head. It was over with.

The rest of my platoon understood that we had been hit. It was almost dark when we [went] out. I couldn't get evacuated that night. It was too thick and they didn't know really what was in the area to try and bring a chopper in. The next morning, they brought a chopper in. There was a little river. He couldn't land, so he hovered over the river and lowered a basket. They strapped me in. Right about that time they started taking some small-arms fire and the chopper took off. I was just thinking, "It's either going to get shot down or I'm going to get a round in the back," but it didn't happen. From that point on I realized I wasn't immortal. It kind of changed the rest of my tour over there. I just decided, "Maybe it's meant for me to die over here and if it is, that's the way it's to be." I lived one day at a time.

LARRY MILLER I stayed there sixteen months. A tour is thirteen months. I extended it three months. That's all the time they let me extend because that was what I had left in the Marine Corps. It becomes part of your life. You forget what round-eyed girls look like. You forget what people back home look like. I just wanted to stay. I knew what I was doing there. I got good at what I was doing there. I knew what I was doing from Sergeant Jones. He taught me well. I had a good officer in John W. McCormick. He got killed in May. I was the only FO [forward observer] left basically. I think there was one other guy that was an FO. That place became my second home. That was it. I didn't care about coming back to the States.

I didn't even take R&R over there in sixteen months. It was supposed to be every six months you get R&R. You're young, you start doing this stuff and you know, I didn't want to die, but I already figured it was just a matter of what day and that it didn't make a difference. Combat is a different world. It's really hard to explain. You're with good people. You'd die for these people. In the Marine Corps, if you've got a guy laying out there wounded or dead, we were going to come and get [him]. If it cost ten casualties to come get one, we were going to do it. That's a good feeling if

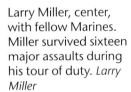

Larry Miller, center, with fellow Marines. Miller survived sixteen major assaults during his tour of duty. *Larry Miller*

you are laying out there because you knew they were coming. They'd sacrifice people to get to you. That's just what we did. I think me being there, as the point of the spear, [is] the only way I would have had it. Anything other than that would be lagging. If you are going to be a bear, be a grizzly.

DANIEL PIERCE Twelve days [before the end of tour], I got wounded. Three of us were wounded the same day. We were out in the field on a squad patrol. It was a 60-mortar round booby trap that was buried in a paddy dike. I was the third in line. The point man set it off, tripwire, and the only thing that saved me was I was just stepping up on the dike and the dike took most of the blast. The other two guys in front, they both were wounded also from the blast that went forward. I had shrapnel in my face, hands, legs, torso, lost a part of my left kidney, some bowel damage, groin. I spent about three months in the hospital. I recovered very nicely. I had a punctured lung but felt no other effects of the wound later.

I was awake the whole time. The only thing I couldn't do was breathe because it had punctured my lung. I was hit all over, but when blood started oozing out of my crotch it was a whole different thing. That was the only thing that was on my mind. I didn't want to have that area of my body damaged in any way, but everything turned out fine.

We returned to Great Lakes Naval Hospital. From there, again, I was not a good garrison Marine. I couldn't put up with all the stuff that was required of you to do [like] spit shine. They put me in Marine barracks because I had a few medals and I was cuter then. Marine barracks was a terrible place to be for me because it was dress blues and escorting bodies. There was guilt and the thought of leaving something behind, whether it was a part of me or some of the fellows who weren't there anymore. It didn't matter who it was. I guess we all just wanted to help each other. I wanted to go back to that situation where I felt I could actually make a difference instead of being some pawn for the Marine Corps. They also had me speak to Kiwanis Clubs and Lions Clubs and Rotary Clubs for the war effort. The hypocrisy pushed me back to Vietnam. Only it was a whole different war when I went back in January '68.

I showed up at staging battalion in Camp Pendleton. I thought I was a pretty salty dog. Turned out I was. There were about six hundred of us lined up on the street and there was a captain in charge of the battalion. There were a few NCOs [noncommissioned officers]. There was me and one other E3. The rest of the guys were right out of boot camp. I had on this cover that was all frayed on the brim and these old Marine Corps boots that were the rough side out where you just polished the toe. We're all standing there and I was talking and the captain got in my face and asked me, "Do you have another utility cover in your sea bag?" I said, "Yes." He picked up my sea bag and dumped it out in front of everybody standing there. Of course my uniform dress greens fell out on the street with three rows of ribbons on it. He about shit his pants then because he didn't know what to do. He was going to use me as a whipping boy and it turns out I was the only one in the whole bunch that had any experience in Vietnam. That kind of ended that tirade. He and I knocked heads right and left. I'd just tell him to send me to Vietnam or don't. Either way, I figured I couldn't lose. Or I couldn't win, I guess, was closer to the truth.

I arrived in Okinawa and couldn't get into Vietnam because they were shelling the Da Nang airport. We were on twenty-four-hour stand-by. And in the interim I had been retrained fixing rifles. I kind of had a plan that I was going to be sitting in the rear getting fat and fixing guns. We finally got to Da Nang and the first thing that struck me was the whole airport was bombed out. It was just a chaotic mess. I heard over the loudspeaker that all NCOs and anybody with prior Vietnam experience were to report to the staff duty officer. I knew right away this wasn't good. I hid out for a few days waiting to get some orders for some cushy job in the rear. After about three days' hiding, they found me and told me I was going to another line company. I go, "No, no, I fix guns now." They said, "No, you don't. You might know how to fix guns, but you're going to a line company." I went to Bravo 1/3 [First Battalion, Third Marines] and they were in a place called C4. It was north of Dong Ha up in the mountains where we had these beehive bunkers. They were huge. I had never seen any bunkers like this. We had the latest night vision scopes and listening devices and we were basically supposed to be Intel for any kind of North Vietnamese movement.

DON WEBER My mother got a hold of Senator Proxmire and said, "Look, my son has been wounded. Why isn't he coming home?" He had made some contacts. She never wrote and told me this. By the time I got to my unit, word had gotten back that I wanted to be sent home. And that wasn't good. I didn't want to leave. I wanted to stay. I didn't know what happened. I felt I really had something to prove. I volunteered for every mission. I walked point all the time. There's a reason why I survived this and there's a purpose in life for things happening.

A patrol is kind of like playing football. You get together and you put your game plan together. The night before, I was always pulled in and told what the purpose of the mission was, where we were headed, and when we were leaving because I was always out in front. One particular patrol we were going to work our way up to what was called Hill 51. We started about an hour before the daybreak. I was told there were no friendlies in the area. Any movement was the enemy. I'm going down this trail and I see a silhouette of a body that'd spotted me coming. I got down on my knee, and I had my M-16 at that point, and I put it on automatic and rattled off all twenty rounds into the direction I last saw him. I rolled off to the side and I reloaded, and pretty soon the CO came running up and told me, "Cease fire, cease fire!" Well, there was a Marine outpost, an ambush they had set up there. It wasn't communicated in our briefing before. I was doing my job. I saw movement, I was told no friendlies, and it happened to be a Marine. He lost his left arm. I think about that all the time. They never would tell me who he was. He's somewhere in this country I'm sure. How that had an impact on him for the rest of his life...

LARRY MILLER The North Vietnamese started a lot of body mutilation when they had a chance. They started it and we perfected it. It was payback time.

David "Moose" Moyer, left, and Larry Miller pose in front of a naval gunfire bunker in Dong Ha. *Larry Miller*

That's just part of it. They did it to us, [so] we did it to them. It gets down to the basic animal instincts of surviv[al]. Fight or flee. We weren't fleeing. If you're going to do that to us, we're going to do it back to you in spades. We did a lot of body mutilation; any chance we had.

We'd be out in the bush, and we'd go into a Marine camp. It struck me strange one day. We went in there and all the Marines looked at us [but] they wouldn't even make eye contact. I thought, "What the hell is wrong with these guys?" Some of [us] were wearing jawbones for necklaces. A lot of us wore black hair. We'd cut it [the hair] off the Vietnamese women. We had black hair hanging off the back of our helmets. We were decorated. Moose, my radio operator, he had a shin bone for a stick for a short time. We just picked up body parts. The gold teeth, of course, we always got those.

How strange it got. I remember [Moose and I] carrying a dead body back to this CP [command post] area, a piece of bamboo [around] his feet. It was like eight o'clock [in the morning]. We set him down and I said, "Moose, he's got a gold tooth." Moose said, "OK, we'll get it." We were going to have breakfast. I had ham and chopped eggs. We used this dead NVA for a table. We're eating breakfast off the dead guy. He said, "Larry, that captain is watching us over there. I can't get this gold tooth now." It dawned on me this captain was pretty new. I said, "Moose, he can't see this gold tooth." So we finished our breakfast, got the gold tooth, and everybody was happy. It was just a mind-set that you get into. There is no other world than that world right there. That world will change from me and him in a hole and fifty feet away two other guys in a hole. [Those] are two completely different worlds. It's hard to explain. [You] don't care what else goes, it's your world. I think you can stay there too long. It gets in your blood.

Combat brings out the best or worst in people. Some of them were just bad going in. We were going through a village one day. There was nothing going on, no shooting or nothing. I heard a bunch of screaming coming out of a hooch. I poke my head in there and hear one of our guys. He was an

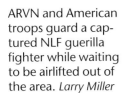

ARVN and American troops guard a captured NLF guerilla fighter while waiting to be airlifted out of the area. *Larry Miller*

M-79 man, a little grenade launcher guy, and he had Mamasan and Papasan over in the corner of the hooch and he was raping her twelve- or thirteen-year-old daughter. I just told him to get off her or "I'll kill you right there." Everyone has this assumption that all the Marines and all these guys in Vietnam were good people. A lot of them weren't. Some people were just bad going there, and [that] gave them a license to be worse. I can truthfully say the people I was with, with the exception of a few, didn't kill civilians if we had a choice not to. I think that has a lot to do with your moral upbringing, who you are as a person, because you have a license to kill right there. And the people I was with never did it and I never did it. I could have many times. In all three battalions, the Ninth Marines, Fourth Marines, and the Third Marines, I never witnessed that.

DANIEL PIERCE One thing that separates me from a lot of vets is that I do care about lives on both sides of the fence. I think a life is a life and I respect the hell out of them [the Vietnamese] for what they put up with and how they could go on with daily lives with all the war around them. All they wanted was a little peace.

[In] the first tour we fought mostly VC. [I]n '68 it was all NVA. These NVA were 100 percent better equipped and better led and better trained than we were. We didn't know anything. We didn't have any leadership. We were TDY [temporary duty assignment] to 2/4 [Second Battalion, Fourth Marines] on an operation to save Dong Ha. NVA was in the area and the intel we had was that they were going to overrun Dong Ha. 24 was led by then Colonel Weiss; he's a general now but colonel then. He took 24 on a pinching maneuver to get the 321st [Division] between them and us. Well, they got in between us and he got them behind us and he got them everywhere because they virtually wiped us out. We were only a company.

We crossed the Bo Dieu River on April 30, 1968. Forty years ago. It's amazing to me that all this happened that long ago. Three platoons got on these amtracs across the Bo Dieu River, which was a tributary to the Qua Viet. We were supposed to land at a spot called An Loc. On the map An Loc was way south of where we landed. We landed right in a hornet's nest. They were shooting us off the amtracs before we even got to the other side. There were so many inexperienced guys that this was really the first sustained action they had seen and they reacted accordingly. In their defense, the company commander, the company gunn[er]y sergeant, the company executive officer, and the third platoon commander were all killed before we even got to the other side. We had one officer left, and basically confusion ruled the day. There was a fortified vil [village] right where we crossed the river, and the NVA had dug in there and they picked us off crossing the river.

We didn't have a clue what was going on when we came across that river. There was no intel. Later [we found] out that there was a Mike [communications] boat that was fired on from that vil the night before. So someone had to know that there was activity across the river, but we were not informed about it whatsoever. We finally made it across the river and got on line to go into the vil and sustained more heavy casualties. We had to back out of the vil and set up. It was a pretty harrowing night. Lots of scared young kids.

LARRY MILLER The hardest part of Vietnam was coming home. Over there I knew what I was doing. I knew what was expected of me. You really lose track of time. Days. I left there on a medevac helicopter with wounded guys. Flew back to the ship, grabbed my gear. I flew to Da Nang [and then] to Okinawa. I grabbed a flight, and in a matter of three days, I'm sitting home with my mom and dad. Three days. I was happy to be home. I was only twenty years old. I got out of the Marine Corps, I was twenty years old, and I couldn't even get a mixed drink in Rice Lake because at the time it was nineteen for beer, twenty-one for hard liquor. I bought a pistol when I got out because I thought I had to carry a gun. I had to get my dad to go down and sign for it at the Gambles hardware store because I wasn't twenty-one. Pretty ironic. I don't know if staying back and decompressing for thirty days would have made a difference or not. That was a bad mistake on the Marine Corps' part. They should have never turned me loose on civilian population after three days. It takes the rest of your life to come to terms with this, let alone, "Here you go, you're gone." It's a bite.

DANIEL PIERCE I felt pretty out of place. I had lost my closest friend and it was kind of strange how it happened because when I arrived at Bravo 13, I was an E3. They needed a squad leader and the guy I was closest with was an E4. They wanted to make him the squad leader, but he turned it down. He said I should be leading the squad. They promoted me to corporal and they gave me the squad. When we crossed the river and all of the leadership was killed, I went to the platoon sergeant and he [my friend] eventually took the squad anyway. He was killed on that assault on the vil. I went wacko, thinking that it should have been me who was killed there. I started taking a lot of chances. The next day we went into the vil again. The Vietnamese had crept out during the night and reformed across this canal. Again, we got on these amtracs and start[ed] crossing this wide-open graveyard. It turned out to be aptly named because they were picking us off the amtracs and we disembarked again. We got pinned down in this graveyard. I was taking some chances I shouldn't have been doing. Doing stuff I shouldn't have been doing.

I got shot on May 1, 1968. I was running around exposing myself. The only cover we had were grave mounds that at best were anthills. I was trying to get to the tree line, which I had no business doing. The only problem with that was that I had my radioman with me and I had no business taking chances with his life also. We both were hit, and I got hold of him about five years ago. I didn't know if he'd even made it. I apologized to him. He didn't think there was anything wrong with it. There were seven left in my platoon. I'm not sure how many [were] left in the company. We took massive casualties. They weren't all KIA but a lot of WIA who were left out there. I talked to a few folks afterwards and they said they tried to get to me but they couldn't. They were basically left to their own devices to survive. There was so much heavy fighting still going on they wouldn't bring any medevacs unless absolutely necessary.

[I'd gotten hit] through my diaphragm, so I couldn't breathe again. Well, at least I had experience at it, so I knew how to do it this time. I didn't freak out so much. They put me in the back of this amtrac because they were doing their triage deal figuring I wasn't going to make it. Every once in a while, a corpsman would come back and check on me. Finally I grabbed him by the shirt and I said, "Get me the fuck out of here because I ain't dying." They called the chopper in and I was awake the whole time. I remember getting on the chopper and I was hurt pretty bad. They didn't expect me to live. There were excellent doctors at Dong Ha Field Hospital. They saved my life.

When you're in a firefight and someone is injured or killed, you don't

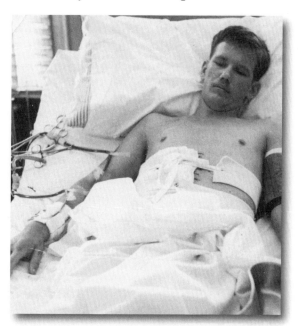

Daniel Pierce receives dialysis after suffering an abdominal gunshot wound. *Daniel Pierce*

have the time or the capacity to grieve or to cradle them or give them comfort. You have to keep alert and keep on going. Then when it's over everything hits you. The adrenaline starts to wear off and the reality sets in of what actually went down, the pain that you saw on your fellow Marine's face or the vision of a Vietnamese head exploding because you shot him in the eye. No time during the firefight but afterwards, much reflection. Much reflection.

DON WEBER I often think about the times that I had to take somebody's life. You try to justify it and say, "Well, if I hadn't taken theirs, they would have taken mine," which is true. That's not justification. I have a hard time living with that and I'll never forget. There's a lot of times when there's a confrontation going on and firefights, and it's back and forth and you don't know really; it's just you're shooting in the direction of where gunfire's coming from and mortar rounds. You're dropping in artillery and you're throwing grenades and you don't really know if you took someone out or... When you personally walk up on somebody who's on an outpost, who's supposed to be on watch, and he doesn't see you and you take that person out...

when it's all over you walk up and you look. You start thinking; "They're no different than I am." He's probably the same age. He had a mother and a father, probably brothers and sisters. If we could have met in a whole different situation in a corner bar, we probably could have had beer together and worked things out. You'd like to think that. I see his face as clear as looking at yours. I'll never forget it. At the same time, if he had spotted me first, it would have probably been the end of my life.

LARRY MILLER [I remember] everything like it happened this morning. Funny. I'm sixty-one. That shit will never go away. You learn to deal with it. You stay away from the situations that will remind you of it, but you're constantly reminded of it anyway. When I first came back I never thought of Vietnam. When I left there I didn't even look out the window, never even thought of it. [With] the years it starts creeping back in. Age has got something to do with it. You start getting mellow. Before it was no big deal. Back here it is a big deal. "You did what to them dead bodies?" "We cut them up, ears, hair, whatever." It's not a big deal. It's the world you're in. But I really

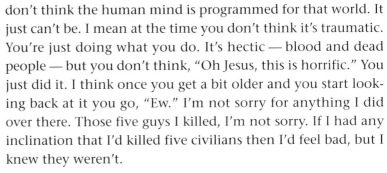

don't think the human mind is programmed for that world. It just can't be. I mean at the time you don't think it's traumatic. You're just doing what you do. It's hectic — blood and dead people — but you don't think, "Oh Jesus, this is horrific." You just did it. I think once you get a bit older and you start looking back at it you go, "Ew." I'm not sorry for anything I did over there. Those five guys I killed, I'm not sorry. If I had any inclination that I'd killed five civilians then I'd feel bad, but I knew they weren't.

DON WEBER On Christmas Eve [after I got back], I went up to see my mom, and she was reading a letter. She had a shoebox there. I said, "What are you doing, Mom?" She said, "I'm reading one of your dad's letters." I said, "Really? You have his letters saved?" "Every one." she said. "How many letters did he send?" She said, "One hundred and sixty-seven."

She was telling me that on December 20, 1943, the War Department notified her that he was MIA. Ninety-nine point nine percent of MIAs never return, casualties. I was thinking what that holiday season must have been like for her and my grandparents. It wasn't until April 4 that they got word that he was a POW, in a Nazi prison camp.

Don Weber in full Marine regalia.
Don Weber

He went through hell. I understand what was going through his mind all those times I would see him sitting there. Yet he came back and he pulled himself up and struggled all his life working. He coped with that. Today, I understand almost a quarter of our homeless are veterans. It could have been me. Most of those men and women were pretty healthy, physically and mentally, before they went through this. And when they came back, and particularly the time we came back, it was really sad. I remember when I landed, coming home. I had to take my uniform off in the airport, because people would spit at you. I really was concerned. It was a sad, sad thing. It was like you were ashamed to tell anybody you were serving your country, you were in Vietnam. All these veterans today who are homeless, who never were able to transition back into society, to become productive citizens: no one was there to help them. We never reached out and said, "Hey, let's talk about this." That's just sad. It's very wrong. Whether they were drafted or whether they enlisted, they served this country. Whether you believe in a war, support it or not, you still take care of those people.

High school class-mates Mark Chartier, left, and Larry Miller met in Kobi Ton Ton on June 19, 1967.
Larry Miller

LARRY MILLER [I visited the Wall] twice. The first time it was just unbelievable. It's an amazing place. People whisper. A bunch of young little kids were running around, and as soon as they hit that sidewalk with their parents, they just whispered. It's a nice memorial. It's moving. The first time you really get the butterflies going. It's hard to explain. I know a lot of people on that wall. You look up and you say, "How you doing?" I told a friend one time, "I'm going up to D.C. on vacation to see some friends." "Oh yeah, have a nice trip!" he said. I come back, he goes, "Did you see your friends?" I said, "Yep." He asks, "How they doing?" I said, "They're still dead." That's how I put it. I go up to say hi to my friends.

DANIEL PIERCE I don't understand this hero stuff that America has to have, because the only heroes are the ones that are on that wall. The rest of us were just doing our job, that's all. I've looked at many avenues to stop the hurt and the guilt and the pain. I went to the Wall about eight years in a row. Kept looking for something. Never on Memorial Day. Never with crowds around or anything. It was an eerie yet special place, and those guys talk to you. The last trip I made there was in 1995. I left all my medals there because I thought that's where they belonged. Those medals were like an albatross on you. The military used them to promote their sick war effort. I knew different. It wasn't that glorious. I wasn't heroic. It's just a bunch of old men in Washington sending kids off to fight. I'd wanted to do it for a long time. I didn't want to be disrespectful. [The medals] were meaningless to me, yet the respect or pseudorespect that you get because of that stuff is amazing. I might have conjured [this] up by myself. I don't know. I don't really care. That night [at the Wall] I was sitting there. It was dark and everybody was gone and the fellas said, "It's OK, you can go home now." So I went home.

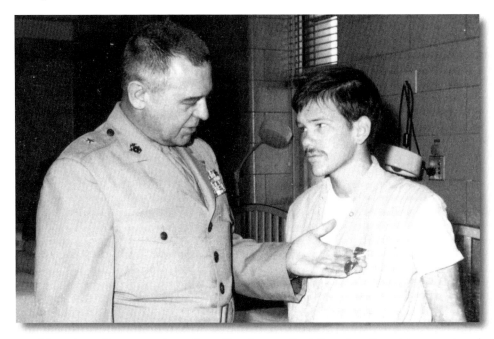

Daniel Pierce was presented with the Purple Heart at the Bethesda Naval Hospital in summer of 1968. *Daniel Pierce*

There's really no explanation. You know that figuring it out is a waste of time. I think a lot of vets try to justify, try to rationalize why, and they can't unless they have something to blame for all the death and dying. It was just another war started by old men and fought by young boys that benefited a few and destroyed many. All you can do about it is try to survive in this world.

I went back to Vietnam in 2005 and tried to atone to those people for some of the things that [my] government created. I visited many pagodas, lit a lot of incense, and said a few prayers. I talked to some folks. They don't hate us. When I went back to Vietnam I flew into Saigon. I was trying to atone for my sins. I had done everything else, so I tried to go back to Vietnam. I flew

In 1995 Daniel Pierce left his medals at the foot of the Vietnam Veterans Memorial Wall in Washington, D.C. *Daniel Pierce*

out of Bangkok on Vietnam Airlines. I was sitting next to this middle-aged gentleman. He was from Vietnam and worked in Bangkok and came home every four months to see his family. I thought he was too young to know the Vietnam War. [It turns out] he was a captain in the NVA. We talked about places we had been. It was amazing how close we came to each other. He was in Hue City when I was in Dong Ha. We respected each other; neither one of us wanted to hurt the other. If things had been different we could have possibly even been friends. He gave me a little pin and I've kept it.

DON WEBER What really hurts is it all seems like it was for nothing. It's terrible how it all ended. I don't like to think about it. If it was World War II and some of those things happened — wars are ugly, things happen, and I understand that — but we were so respected. I mean the world carried us, this country, in the palms of its hands. That was part of the battle. Lives were lost, limbs were lost, but the sacrifice, was it worth it? Here, you can't say that. My dad and I never [talked]. I couldn't ever talk about what I went through. I never talked to anybody about that. I'm going to go to my grave not talking about some things.

DANIEL PIERCE I'm still looking for peace. I think a part of you is forever lost. There's got to be a landing zone somewhere that we can go on from. You'd think we'd be there by now, but still [there are] a lot of guys that haven't found their way home.

6 Khe Sanh

"The papers in training were all about these little farmers with old rifles [who] take potshots at you and then sneak back to their hut. I'm sitting there with a reinforced regiment of Marines. We're talking six thousand Marines, fully armed with tanks. It was a wake-up call for me."— Lance Larson

The combat base at Khe Sanh, only fourteen miles south of the demilitarized zone (DMZ) and seven miles from the border with Laos, served as a lynchpin in the defense of I Corps, the northernmost provinces of South Vietnam. The base dated from 1962, when a team of Special Forces created it to monitor Vietnamese activity along the Ho Chi Minh Trail, a key supply line for the North Vietnamese. In 1964, U.S. Special Forces expanded the base and built a small airstrip; Marines arrived at Khe Sanh the same year and used the base to monitor North Vietnamese and National Liberation Front (NLF) communications. By 1967, Khe Sanh had become the "western anchor in a chain of strong points stretching from the border with Laos to the city of Hue in the east that were designed to thwart any [NVA] invasion across the DMZ."[1] Strategically situated amid jungle-covered hills, Khe Sanh required the defense of the surrounding high ground, which included Hill 881 North, Hill 881 South, and Hill 861. Indeed, in 1967, Marines fought the NVA in the "Hill Fights," a series of difficult engagements for control over these three vital high points, which led to further fortification of the base itself.[2]

By late 1967, with NVA troops massing in the area surrounding Khe Sanh, it became clear to U.S. intelligence that the base — manned by only a single Marine regiment — would be the site of a major battle. However, U.S. intelligence did not know that for the NVA, Khe Sanh was simply a diversion for a large-scale surprise attack that would come to be known as the Tet Offensive. Indeed, North Vietnamese general Vo Nguyen Giap later asserted that "Khe Sanh was not that important to us. Or it was only to the extent that it was to the Americans."[3] Ironically, the United States came to see Khe Sanh as the main target of the NVA offensive.

Prior to the main assault, on January 17, 1968, NVA troops ambushed a Marine patrol on Hill 881 North; a second attack on another patrol two days later revealed that the NVA had actually retaken control of the key strategic hill. On January 21, shortly after midnight, the NVA attacked Hill 861 and then proceeded to lay siege to the base itself with a barrage of mortars, rockets, and artillery.[4] This initial shelling was the beginning of a major battle that would last a total of seventy-seven days.

Among U.S. policy makers, fears were widespread that the outcome at Khe Sanh would replicate the 1954 French defeat at Dien Bien Phu, putting America in an unfavorable position; indeed, President Johnson had a replica of the base built at the White House in order to follow the battle, reportedly commenting, "I don't want any damn Dinbinphoo."[5] With the major land supply route to the base — Route 9 — cut off by the fighting, the Marines, outnumbered 3 to 1 by NVA forces, fought fiercely to defend the base and the surrounding hills but were dependent on air reinforcement for both supplies and battle support.[6] Throughout the siege, which lasted from January 21 to March 31, U.S. airpower played a vital role in destroying the NVA and NLF troops surrounding the base, and the U.S. Air Force and Marines flew a total of 24,000 tactical air strikes, dropping around 40,000 tons of explosives.[7] B-52 Stratofortresses, flying from bases in Guam, Thailand, and Okinawa, also flew an estimated 2,700 missions, dropping over 50,000 tons of explosives on the surrounding NVA forces.[8] U.S. air strikes targeted NVA troops, bunkers, and supply areas; they also used large amounts of defoliants (including Agent Orange) so that the "green jungle surrounding Khe Sanh soon became a desert."[9] On April 8, 1968, at the conclusion of Operation Pegasus (the relief of Khe Sanh), U.S. forces reached Khe Sanh via Route 9, ending the siege. U.S. Marines were airlifted out of the area ten days later. U.S. and South Vietnamese forces suffered heavy losses both defending and relieving the base. Due to the difficulty of assessing enemy casualties, U.S. estimates vary widely from 3,000 to 15,000 NVA casualties, from both ground artillery and air strikes.[10] One of the war's most difficult and exhausting battles, Khe Sanh proved to be a costly diversion in the weeks surrounding the Tet Offensive.

Ray Stubbe, Milwaukee (Marines, Chaplain Corps)
Lance Larson, Appleton (Marines, Third Marines Division)

RAY STUBBE I went to Washington High School in Milwaukee. The summer before my senior year I decided that I wanted to go into the military. It shocked people because everyone thought I was going on to do more schooling. I was very interested in science. I had received perfect scores on my chemistry and physics final exams. At the same time, my local pastor wanted me to consider the ministry. I decided to join the military.

LANCE LARSON I went into the military in February of '67. I knew there was a Vietnam. It's one of my earliest memories in a sense. My dad was a World War II vet, and it just seemed strange that there was a war going on. By the time I got out of high school, the big question for all of us was, "Are you going to join? When?" Some went off to college and some got jobs and waited to get drafted. Others just enlisted. I went off to college for a semester, but there were so many guys going, I just wanted to get in.

RAY STUBBE I joined the Navy Reserve on the 28th of September, '55. I made second-class petty officer and then was separated [fulfilled my terms of enlistment] and went to college. I graduated from St. Olaf and then went to Northwestern Lutheran Theological Seminary. I graduated and was ordained a Lutheran minister. I went into mission development in Oak Creek, a suburb of Milwaukee, and started a church that is still there, All Saints Lutheran Church. I was still drilling in the Navy Reserve. I applied to the University of Chicago graduate school, which, at the time, was considered one of the five top theological schools in the nation. To be accepted was very gratifying. I went down there for one year in a PhD program in ethics and society. I learned a lot that was helpful later on in trying to reconcile things in war.

The Navy at the time was asking for chaplains because of the buildup in Vietnam during 1966. That summer, I went on a two-month active-duty assignment. That was a positive way to leave graduate school. I went to Washington to be interviewed and they asked if I'd waive my thirty-day waiting period and I said, "Sure." The first week of June, I went to Camp Pendleton to take a course for chaplains going over to

Ray Stubbe's ordination photo, May 1965.
Ray Stubbe

Vietnam. I was the only chaplain at the time. I had a sergeant major who was retiring take me around to different places to see how an M-79 is fired and how artillery is fired and how a LAW [light antitank weapon] is fired. As an enlisted person myself, I had a real sensitivity for the separation anxiety, the aloneness, the helplessness that the troops felt.

LANCE LARSON I got into Vietnam at the end of November 1967. In January all of a sudden everybody was buzzing and screaming, "Get your gear together! We're going to Khe Sanh." Nobody knew where it was. I remember all this activity. There were nine hundred men running around, screaming, yelling, filling canteens, and getting ammunition. We all flew to Khe Sanh. And nobody really knew where the hell we were going. We landed in Khe Sanh from Camp Evans. We had a tent with cots. It was a lot worse than in the States so I thought, "This is war." Now I think of Camp Evans as luxury because it was never like that the rest of my tour.

RAY STUBBE I was sent to Khe Sanh as a replacement because the chaplain who was there had rotated and they didn't have a chaplain. They had a Catholic chaplain, but they didn't have a Protestant chaplain. At that time, chaplains were assigned to battalions. A battalion is about twelve hundred men. They assigned me to Third Shore Party, and I went to Khe Sanh that way. Shortly after I was there, the Third Battalion 26th Marines left and I "was the only chaplain there. I immediately decided that the only way to communicate what I felt needed to be communicated, namely that people aren't alone, that God is with them, that they're of inestimable value, and not just grungy, dirty Marines, was not by word, but by being with them. I went out to Hill 881 South. There was a Captain John Raymond, who was the company commander at the time. I decided to give a talk on the prodigal son, Luke 15. One son goes off in a far-off country and it seemed to apply to these men living a very uncomfortable and despicable kind of existence, realizing that home [is] far off. The company commander, John Raymond, saw me afterwards, and he said, "You know, you shouldn't really talk about how life is with these men, unless you know how life is." He says, "We have a patrol that's going off within half an hour. If you want to, you can accompany them." I said, "OK," being the foolish person that I was at the time.

This sign greeted troops as they entered Khe Sanh Combat Base. *Ray Stubbe*

Sandbags protect a valuable 60-millimeter mortar position on Hill 881 South, Khe Sanh, in August 1967.
Ray Stubbe

We went off on this patrol. It was eight hours of constant movement up and down. I could never understand how Marines were able to attack like that. It was almost like a cliff. It wasn't walking down the slope. It was falling down the slope. We were going up and down streams with large boulders. We were going through bamboo thickets in which we would get lost. Grass that was razor sharp that would cause cuts, and leeches: little two-inch wormlike things that were attached to a leaf on one end and wiggling and hoping to attach to your skin with the other. They said you should never pull them off because the head would remain under the skin and cause an infection. Marines would usually roll up their jungle shirts exposing their forearms and get leeches. They would eventually cause festering sores that no matter what antibiotic they put on it, would remain there for a long time.

It became sheer exhaustion after one hour because at the time, I had just come from the academic world and being a pastor and here I was in Vietnam, grossly out of shape. I never participated in high school athletics. I wasn't an athlete. I was a bookish-type person, an academic, and a nerd. Here I am climbing these hills with these young Marines. Finally we were climbing up the southern slope of 881 South, which is a rather gradual slope, but I had gone through my water. I savored each drop, each little half

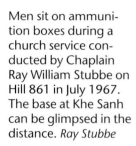

Men sit on ammunition boxes during a church service conducted by Chaplain Ray William Stubbe on Hill 861 in July 1967. The base at Khe Sanh can be glimpsed in the distance. *Ray Stubbe*

mouthful. I'd rationed it out. A corpsman fortunately gave me some of his water after we returned. They filled me with juices that they had. They gave me their pine-apple juice and apple juice and orange juice, and I got re-hydrated, but I learned. I learned that these Marines did this every day.

I learned the way to get the most people for a worship service was to go in during resupply, and stay there overnight. I could hold my worship service for all the Marines, stay overnight in one of their bunkers, and talk with them. I'd go on a patrol in the morning, come back in the afternoon, go to the next hill and the next resupply. That's what I did for July, August, September, October, and November. They liked what I was doing. The division chaplain got a hold of Washington, and I got transferred as a Third Marine Division chaplain.

LANCE LARSON [When we arrived,] Khe Sanh was relatively quiet. There had been a recon patrol that was ambushed in December or early January. It was not anything out of the ordinary, because things like that happen, you know. The 26th Marines, the whole regiment, all three battalions, were at Khe Sanh. All of a sudden out of nowhere they got hit with a heavy artillery barrage and rockets. It just saturated the whole airstrip and the whole base and knocked out a lot of trucks and helicopters on the ground and did a lot of damage. There were a lot of casualties. They had a couple companies from the regiment up on Hill 861. I don't remember if it was North or South. All of this was coming from Co Roc Mountain in Laos, which was just west of our position. They [the higher-ups] thought we were going to get hit the way Dien Bien Phu was. They took my battalion to reinforce the 26th Marines. The NVA were coming into the valley west and south of there. They were mortaring the base. They figured they could launch a ground attack from that position. They could sneak up from that rock quarry and just swarm that one corner of the base. They wanted the battalion out there. We used to say we were just mortar bait. From where we were, we could see that whole valley. They couldn't use mortars because they would be too far out to hit the base. They could hit us farther back. That was the purpose of why we got there right away.

Khe Sanh Combat Base, photographed from the air by the 460th Tactical Reconnaissance Wing a week into the siege on January 28, 1968. *Ray Stubbe*

The day we arrived was the day after all of this had happened and I remember everything was shot up. They didn't have time to clean up anything. There were trucks with the windows all smashed and the tires were flat and helicopters wrecked. This corporal comes up and he says, "Can you help me with this detail?" He said, "A plane's going to land. We've got to put these on." They were dead Marines on stretchers with ponchos over them. They weren't even in body bags. He said he'd run out of body bags.

He didn't have that many. He was the corporal in charge of grave registration for the regiment. I'll always remember my buddy Saxon and me loading these guys on and one of the ponchos blew off. It was the first time I saw a dead Marine close up. That was my first day there.

RAY STUBBE The siege began on Sunday, January 21, at about 5:00 in the morning. I was going over my sermon notes because I was going to have my three services on the base. All at once there were explosions like you wouldn't believe. The sky was illuminated with red explosions. On one side of us, there was the petroleum-oil-lubricants dump in big fifty-five-gallon drums, and that was on fire with these orangeish, yellowish billows of fire. On the other side of us was the supply depot. It was a very small supply depot, with lots of sandbags, and that was on fire. Further on was the ammo dump, which was cooking off, spewing off all sorts of rounds while we were taking rockets and mortars.

I was in my bunker, which I had built myself, alone. I was in the medical area and I was debating whether I should run to that trench for cover, or stay in my own bunker, which I had built rather substantially. I had put air matting along the walls. I had filled fifty-five-gallon drums with dirt and placed them around the bunker. I'd filled sandbags and put them around the drums and the rest of the bunker. I'd then covered the whole thing with plastic because of the monsoons. It would protect me from mortar shrapnel. I had an L-shaped entrance for blasts, but I was alone, and you don't want to be alone in those times. I knew, however, that you don't run during a mortar attack because mortars explode in a V-shape. If you're standing, you'll probably get shrapnel in your head and chest. If you're crawling, you could probably crawl right next [to one] and you wouldn't get hurt. Rockets splatter laterally. There was ammunition cooking off so I knew I shouldn't run and yet I wanted to run. Eventually, I ran, stooped down into the trench. We had four doctors at the time and the corpsmen were in there. All of a sudden we started getting tear gas, from our own ammo dump. We had powdered tear gas drums there and it was spreading through the whole base. I had my gas mask with me always, and so I put it on. I immediately felt claustrophobic. I just wanted to tear it off, and yet I knew I had to have it on. There were some of our guys who didn't have masks with them and they tried to wet their shirts with water to protect their face from the tear gas.

It lingered for some time. We weren't actually under attack for all that long, but our ammo dump kept spewing and our POL [petroleum, oil, and lubricants] kept burning. Eventually helicopters started to take casualties out. I emerged with my brass cross, a container with wine and some little hymnals, and was going to hold church services. I walked towards the eastern part of the base where the ammo dump was, towards the mess hall, which was where I was going to hold church. The mess hall was completely caved in, as were all the above-ground wooden, plywood bunkers, of recon, and the Seabees. They were all destroyed. I remember helping dig out some people with tears in my eyes from the tear gas.

That was the first day [of the siege]. I remember walking around the base just stunned. I knew I couldn't hold church services. Everyone was busy anyway. They were building, filling sandbags, rescuing people, and assessing damage. I remember passing our own 1/26 Battalion Aids Station and seeing from a distance, a man on a stretcher, whose abdominal wall was missing. You could see his intestines. I remember in my mind, asking why they weren't covering his intestines with a wet cloth. That's what you learn in first aid. I asked a corpsman, and he said, "Well, that man's dying. He's going to die." To my shame, I just stood there. I've learned to forgive and not to be so hard on myself because I was probably in shock. People wonder, "How are you feeling? Why don't you cry? Why don't you get angry? Why don't you do this? Why don't you do that?" The emotions become frozen.

LANCE LARSON The next day we went out to the rock quarry and started digging in. That night we got hit. We got probed and then they hit us. Before it was dark, they launched another heavy artillery attack. It was Russian 152s. You haven't lived unless you've been in an artillery barrage, because artillery is nasty stuff. It's like the loudest train roaring right by your head. Then the ground shakes. With the noise and the concussion, you can start bleeding from the ears. I can't describe the fear. It's terrifying. It was at that moment I said, "This is not the war they talked about when I was in training." The papers in training were all about these little farmers with old rifles [who] take potshots at you and then sneak back to their hut. I'm sitting there with a reinforced regiment of Marines. We're talking six thousand Marines, fully armed with tanks. It was a wake-up call for me.

The American forces bombed more around Khe Sanh when I was there than the entire total tonnage of all the planes that bombed in World War II. These B-52s were incredible. They bombed every day that I was there. We didn't have any good fields of fire. It was all elephant grass right up to our lines. Every day the men would try to cut that away. At night the enemy

Shot down on February 22, 1968, this CH-53 crashed on the Khe Sanh Combat Base, killing Captain James Thomas Riley and First Lieutenant Cary Carson Smith.
Ray Stubbe

came right up to where we were. You couldn't fire artillery at them or mortars; they were too close. As the siege went on, they started digging trench lines every night. You'd wake up in the morning and there'd be this trench line all the way around your position. You could hear them digging at night; it was like too close to bomb. We'd fire M-79s out there, but they'd still dig all night. So then in the morning there were these trenches. We figured they were trying to dig trenches to launch an attack. In the morning, we'd go out and try to fill them [in].

RAY STUBBE According to the Air Force, more bombs were dropped at Khe Sanh during the siege, in terms of tonnage, than were dropped in the entire Pacific during World War II during 1942 and '43. The ground was rocking constantly. There were B-52 strikes constantly. It was just a constant bombardment. There were some days that we would take up to thirteen hundred incoming rounds. This Garden of Eden vegetation was soon a moonscape. It was literally hell. There are many passages in the Book of Isaiah that talk about the earth being shaken and the mountains trembling. All of those words in the Bible suddenly became very real. I had a casualty one time lying on a stretcher ask, "Chaplain, would you say 91st Psalm with me?" I never really thought much about these things existentially. "A thousand may fall at your side, ten thousand at your right hand...you shall not fear for the arrow that flies by day nor the pestilence that walketh, it stalketh at noon day." All of a sudden that psalm took on existential significance to me.

The days all started to merge. I did keep a diary. Every day I'd go to my bunker and write down what happened during the day from my briefings, from my observations. I was able to keep things in chronological sequence so I can talk about it in a somewhat knowledgeable way.

LANCE LARSON You lose track of what day it is. I had no idea what was going on in the world because we were not getting regular newspapers. Somebody would come back from R&R or a new guy would come and he'd say something. Martin Luther King was killed when we were at Khe Sanh and we didn't know. This guy was talking about Robert Kennedy being killed. I said, "What the hell are you talking about? That didn't happen." I thought he was talking about John from '63. I didn't get news.

RAY STUBBE I'm a cool-blooded fellow. Ninety-seven degrees is a normal temperature for me. I had a fever, near 102 degrees. I was very weak. I had lost a lot of weight. I went over in the 108 range and [now it was in] the 120s. We were down to one C ration a day. We were supposed to have at least three. With all the excitement and the stress of running around, our calories were very depleted. We were down to one canteen cup of water a day because our water supply was destroyed several times. I was in a bad way. I continued and I collapsed, but I was still there. The next day I was getting ready to go out on my rounds again and I just fell down. The corpsman manhandled me onto a stretcher, and the next thing I knew, I was down at Quang Tri, and then to Da Nang.

LANCE LARSON It must have been in February, we were down to like one meal a day. A lot of food wasn't getting in and it was starting to wear us out. We were really tired. We didn't have a lot of water, even with the stream. There'd be days where suddenly twelve hundred rounds would come in and the next day you wouldn't have anything. Then you'd get fifty mortar rounds the next, four hundred the next, and then you might get a thousand again. Nothing changed. You really didn't leave the perimeter.

We started getting more food probably in March. We'd have two meals. Everybody was getting pretty weak from eating only a meal a day. We were trying to live on C rations. You start falling apart simply because it's not a very good diet. You can't eat just cans of meat and beans. I had never had a cavity in my life and when I came back from Vietnam my teeth were bleeding. I was a wreck physically. You don't get milk; you don't get vegetables or fruit. Your body is under all that stress and physical work; it wears you down just from lack of good nutrition.

RAY STUBBE They did tests and found blood in the urine. They sent me to the hospital ship, did a cystoscope, and said, "You have kidney problems." I said, "But I've got to get back to Khe Sanh." They said, "No, no. You're out." I argued, "No, I'm the only Protestant chaplain on the base. You don't understand. I've got to get back there." Eventually I got back. It was in a few days, against medical advice. It's all in my health record that I returned. This was on the 29th of January. I know I was back by the 4th of February, because Lang Vei was overrun on the 7th. I met all the casualties that came, that were evacuated. They said, "We'll let you go back, if you get medical attention when you leave Vietnam."

LANCE LARSON By the time we got near the end of March, we wanted to be relieved. They kept saying, "Somebody's going to come and rescue us." We heard the [First] Air Cav was coming. We envisioned they'd come, take our positions, and then we'd leave and go to a safer area. The Air Cav had the most incredible firepower I had ever seen. They had all these Cobra choppers flying around with fire support and self-propelled artillery. They were all gung-ho. They had state-of-the-art weapons. They were ready. They came up and when they got to Khe Sanh, they jumped on their choppers and took off. We were still there.

RAY STUBBE The siege was still going on all through March. I kept going back there. I know I was back on Easter Sunday because I documented that. I went back maybe six other times.

During the siege we were surrounded by at least forty thousand North Vietnamese, which had crept in suddenly. Our base was a little under a mile long, an airstrip. It was about a half mile wide. Usually there was fog in the morning, which we all enjoyed because we could walk around freely. The North's aerial observers couldn't report in targets, but neither could we bring

Delivering ammunition and water to Khe Sanh Combat Base Logistic Support Area, October 27, 1967.
Ray Stubbe

Bru tribesmen make crossbows in Tum Piang village, September 1968.
Ray Stubbe

in supplies. Around noon, the fog would burn off, the planes would come in, and then the mortars would start again.

On the 22nd of March, we started getting a huge amount of ammunition because our ammo dump had been destroyed. Fortunately our S4, Colonel McKeown, the logistics man of the regiment, had established another ammunition supply point on the western part of the base. However, the day we were attacked, Khe Sanh village was also attacked. Hill 861 was attacked and one of our recon teams called Nurse was attacked. We had C-130 after C-130 bringing in pallets and pallets of ammunition. Rather than return empty, they airlifted the twelve hundred Vietnamese who occupied Khe Sanh village. The twelve hundred local mountain tribesmen were not airlifted out because the three-star Vietnamese General Xuan Lam determined that there was no place in Vietnam for mountain tribesmen. Many, many thousands of the local tribesmen perished during those first three months of the Khe Sanh siege battle. I figure approximately 475 Americans died. Two thousand were medically evacuated. Twenty thousand North Vietnamese, by estimation, perished during those first three months of that battle. It was probably the bloodiest battle of the whole Vietnam War.

LANCE LARSON During Pegasus [the relief mission] my battalion snuck out about one o'clock in the morning to take Hill 471. It was about two thousand meters south of our position; almost near Khe Sanh village. We took the hill and they counterattacked that night. We caught them trying to sneak up to the lines. We had artillery with illumination-rounds fire. We had everybody on line. There were like four or five hundred Vietnamese soldiers tiptoeing up. And we opened up.

RAY STUBBE Marines have asked me since, "Where is God in all of this?" I point to the fact that there was humor, which is maintaining life in a situation rife with death. There was sharing and a caring for each other. People in bunkers that would be out of water, and someone else would give them

Chaplain Ray Stubbe conducts a worship service on January 28, 1967, in the midst of the Khe Sanh seige.
Ray Stubbe

their last drops of water or go without food to give their last. I guess because we knew we were going to die we were somewhat freer to live. You don't have to worry about getting wounded or worry about dying because you know you're going to die anyway. Some guy's out there by himself, wounded, and the rounds are going off. You just run out and drag him in. You know full well that you could get killed. I'd tell people, "God is the one who gives courage to live. God gives life, and by having humor, by having courage in the face of death, God is giving us life." I'd say that's God. God is present not in a spectacular show of force but in blessing us with the life and courage and love of each other. Love is always an action, not an emotion. Biblically anyway.

LANCE LARSON They kept telling us to move every day. We moved over and took the hills 552 and 689. We just kept marching every few days and taking another hill. We didn't get off this operation. We started losing more men and we were wondering why the Air Cav didn't do this because this is where all the North Vietnamese soldiers were. We were worn out from the siege and thought we'd be relieved, but we just had to go out and fight in hills. They were also trying to say the casualties were light. One of my best friends, Ron, was killed. My other buddy Saxon was really hurt and medevaced out. The major I was the radioman for was all messed up and he was medevaced. A colonel was hit, his aide was hit...Everybody was hit, except for me. I didn't get hit. I don't know how I got out of that but I did. If you read about Operation Pegasus, the relief of Khe Sanh, Reverend Stubbe wrote a good book and it talks about this in detail about how the casualties don't include airmen, TAD [temporary assigned duty], and ARVNs. There were a lot of men who were killed that they don't include in the casualties. They also stopped Operation Pegasus, but we were still there fighting. They just named it some other operation.

On April 16, my unit took a lot of casualties. They finally took us out of Khe Sanh three or four days later. They talked about abandoning Khe Sanh at that point. The men were really ticked about that. They decided to keep it again and we did for a few months. Eventually it was abandoned. Other Marine units and Army units through the course of the year would go in that area and get in some campaigns. In June or July, some unit got in a big fight on the hill where we were when we left. They were dug in there and got in a pitched battle with some NVA regulars. The place was always crawling with North Vietnamese, because the Laotian border is right there.

The Ho Chi Minh Trail was just the other side of Laos there. So it was a nasty area. I wouldn't want to live there.

RAY STUBBE When I left Vietnam, I went to Parris Island for eighteen months, and there was a little hospital there. I had an open biopsy, and they determined that I had glomerular nephritis disease. The doctor there asked, "Do you want to stay in the Navy?" I said, "Yes." And he said, "You're only going to live twenty years at the most. This disease is an autoimmune disease where the body destroys itself. At any time, it'll start attacking your kidneys, and that's it. Sometime within twenty years." I made the decision to definitely stay in the service. Also I decided not to get married or have a family because I thought it would be very unloving to suddenly die. Obviously I'm still here but I still have blood in the urine, too, so I'm reminded all the time.

Ray Stubbe stayed in the military after his tour in Vietnam. Here he is pictured preparing for a parachute jump with U.S. Special Forces in Okinawa, 1973. *Ray Stubbe*

[When I got back home] my mom controlled herself but she was terrified at the sight of me, that I'd lost so much weight. She was especially terrified when I said I was going back to Vietnam. I didn't really know the full story of that until around 1989 or so. I was asked to give a talk to some sixth graders at a school. My dad said, "Well, I'd like to come along." I said, "OK, come along." I was talking to these sixth graders, and they were asking the most perceptive questions that I have ever heard. I only remember one of them, but they were so intense. One asked, "How was it for those of your family that were still at home while you were in Vietnam?" I said, "Well, I can answer that perhaps, from what I've heard, but my dad is with me this time, so why don't you ask him?" He was standing at the back of the classroom. All these little heads turned to him, and fortunately no one's watching me. He'd done public speaking before, but not a lot. He was comfortable with that, but very uncomfortable now. He said, "My wife and I were watching television one night. They reported a chaplain was killed at Khe Sanh." His voice started to break up at this point. He went on, "It took a week before we knew if Ray was alive or not." He said, "My wife's hair turned white." I was completely unaware of the pain felt at home. I was so wrapped up in my own issues, in my own pain, in my own unraveling pain, which is still unraveling. People in pain are insensitive, and they don't mean to be. They're just focused on their pain. There he was. He was crying. My dad was crying. We went home and didn't say another word. If I knew then what I know now, I would have run to him and hugged him, but I wasn't competent enough or in touch with my feelings enough at that time.

LANCE LARSON Experiencing death is very traumatizing. I'm going to be sixty this year. I've had forty years to [make sense of] this. I've had a lot of post-traumatic stress problems. You have nightmares; you think of these things. The thing that stands out is the men who you knew as good buddies and you lost them. I lost a nineteen-year-old son in a car accident a few years ago. I am hurting from that. When we had the funeral, we grieved. It affected hundreds of people. When these guys, my buddies, would die in combat, you couldn't do that. You had to almost push them aside and say, "We've got a job here to do. There's a battle going on." They'd whisk them away in a helicopter and you couldn't take time to give them a service. You were supposed to suck it up, to finish the job. That's a lot for any human being. When I lost Saxon and Ron...they were my two buddies, they were everything. I spent all my time with them. They were my sense of humor. They were my strength. My wife used to ask, "How did you get through?" We used to kid around, talk about home, crack jokes, brag. We showed pictures of our girlfriends and would say, "Mine's so great." You talked about music. When he's killed or if he's wounded, it's the same thing, he's gone just like that. It's very hard.

7 Tet

"It just seemed like it was getting worse and worse. Areas that we could go through normally all of a sudden, there were all kinds of enemy in them."— *Ted Fetting*

By 1967, the number of U.S. troops in Vietnam had passed 400,000, with no end in sight. In 1965, General William Westmoreland had predicted that the United States would win the war by 1968; indeed, in 1967, with National Liberation Front/North Vietnamese Army (NLF/NVA) body counts rising, he claimed that the United States had reached the crossover point and was killing enemy troops faster than they could be replaced. In late 1967, on a trip to the United States, Westmoreland spoke optimistically about the war at Andrews Air Force Base in Maryland: "I am very, very encouraged. I have never been more encouraged in the four years that I have been in Vietnam. We are making real progress."[1] Westmoreland's public relations campaign was successful in convincing many Americans that the end of the war was drawing near. Despite his public statements, however, Vietnamese resistance remained high and U.S. progress limited. Though some of Lyndon Johnson's advisors had begun to change their position on the war, a group of experienced and respected foreign policy advisors — the "Wise Men" — continued to argue to Johnson that withdrawal was simply not an option.

The Tet Offensive, which started on the Vietnamese Lunar New Year in the last days of January 1968, destroyed any notion that the United States could "win" in Vietnam with its current strategy. In late 1967, U.S. officials had been encouraged by a seeming softening in NLF/NVA resistance in South Vietnam. In reality, the NLF and the NVA were undergoing preparations for a massive offensive, recruiting approximately 17,000 South Vietnamese men and boys to join 67,000 NLF/NVA troops. On January 30, 1968, ten days after the start of a diversionary siege on the U.S. Marine base at Khe Sanh, the NLF/NVA exploded in a massive, coordinated, country-wide attack. NLF/NVA troops fought U.S./ARVN troops for control over five

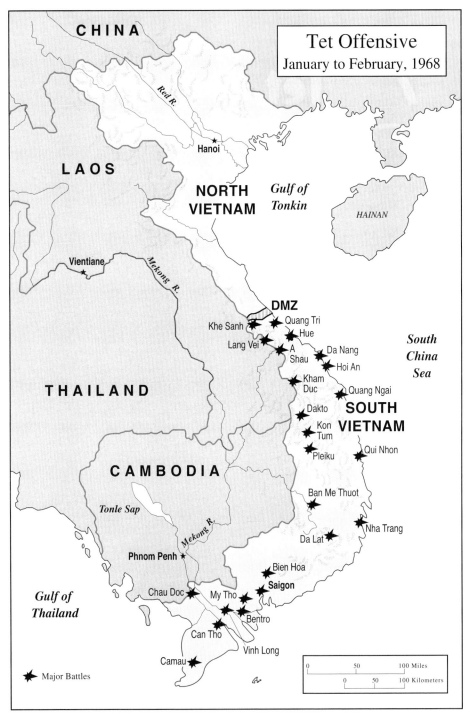

Patti Isaacs, Parrot Graphics

of six major cities, forty-four provincial capitals, and sixty-six district capitals, along with airfields, munitions dumps, and other military facilities. Most shocking, the NLF/NVA forces broached the walls of the U.S. embassy compound in Saigon. The Tet Offensive ended after two weeks of destructive, mostly urban fighting. Militarily, U.S./ARVN troops emerged victorious; NLF/NVA casualties were massive — approximately one-fifth of their total fighting force had been killed.[2] NVA leaders, however, hoped that Tet would spark a South Vietnamese uprising and undermine U.S. will to continue the war. Though the war continued after Tet, the large nature of the offensive eviscerated General Westmoreland's claims about the effectiveness of a continued war of attrition and an imminent victory.

The impact of Tet was felt not just on the battlefields in Vietnam, but also through television sets at home. The most enduring impact of Tet was visual. The fighting produced some of the most lasting images of the war, broadcast into the homes of millions of Americans on the evening news: North Vietnamese troops blasting into the U.S. embassy in Saigon as stunned U.S. forces rushed to react; an NLF fighter shot in the head in the streets of Saigon; the normally composed Walter Cronkite exclaiming on air, "What the hell's going on here? I thought we were winning this war."[3] One American major, commenting on the destruction of the city of Ben Tre, stated, "It became necessary to destroy the town to save it."[4] On February 27, Cronkite stated on air that the United States was "mired in stalemate" in Vietnam; Johnson is said to have concluded that if Cronkite was against the war, there was no regaining popular support for Vietnam.[5] Tet also served as a turning point in Johnson's Vietnam policy, as his advisors, particularly new Defense Secretary Clark Clifford, began to accept that the United States could not simply keep sending soldiers to Vietnam. After Tet, Johnson declined Westmoreland's requests for more troops and decided not to seek reelection as president. Yet even as Johnson rejected further escalation, the question of how to extract the United States from the conflict at a price it was willing to pay remained unsolved.

Ted Fetting, Greenwood (Army, Ninth Infantry Division)
Don Jones, Madison (Army, Military Intelligence Corps)
Joe Campbell, St. Charles, IL (Army, First Logistical Command)
Roger Treece, Cleveland, WI (Navy, Fleet Air Reconnaisance
　　Squadron 1)
Wayne Jensen, Milwaukee (Navy, Coastal Division 12)

Ted Fetting poses outside his bunker with an M-60 machine gun. A Vietnamese child is visible in the lower left. *Ted Fetting*

TED FETTING I was in school the spring of '67 at River Falls, Wisconsin State University at that point. I had been there for three years. I didn't have a degree, but I was relatively close. I ended up volunteering because I was very certain I was going to be drafted anyway. I wanted to get it out of the way. I actually could type better than most women, so I figured, "Well, I'm going to get some admin job anyway, no big deal." The seventh week, they started giving us our assignments and soon as I heard this guy's name from Minnesota, a guy who had a master's in history or sociology, very athletic, very outstanding, my heart just sank. Oh my God. It was all of us wise guys who had some school and who thought we were certainly going to fly right through it. A whole bunch of us went infantry. I was assigned to machine gun and most of the time I carried that.

DON JONES I enlisted in 1957. I decided that I wanted to go into the Counterintelligence Corps and the only way you could get in was to volunteer. I went to Army counterintelligence school, went to Germany, came back, taught at the school, and then wound up going to Vietnam. I got there in September of '67.

JOE CAMPBELL I wanted to get into automotive technology, and I went to school in Chicago. After a couple months of working at UPS and going to school at night and realizing that the war in Vietnam was getting to be hotter and heavier, I heard that you could go in the Army and get really well

Above left: Joe Campbell in December 1967, just one month before Tet. *Joe Campbell*

Right: Roger Treece smiles with family members before departing for Vietnam. *Roger Treece*

trained. I figured, "Well, I'm going to get drafted anyway. I might as well go and pick what I'd like to do." I decided to enlist in the Army.

ROGER TREECE I lived in the southern part of the state, close to East Troy, and I grew up on the farm. My senior year I enlisted on what they called the "Kiddy Cruise Plan." If you enlisted before you were eighteen, you got out just before your twenty-first birthday. I finished high school and in the fall I went on active duty. I went to basic training, then I went to communications technicians school down in Pensacola, Florida, for six months.

I flew from Milwaukee to Chicago to San Francisco. Out of San Francisco I grabbed a plane to Japan and from Japan down to Vietnam. I was gung-ho like most. I was ready to go. I was proud to be going. It was what I wanted to do. I hadn't learned the rules of the road yet. I didn't know what it was really like to have somebody shoot at you.

TED FETTING We would go on these roving patrols, ambush patrols near Tan Tru in the Delta. When we were first there, we were admonished, "Don't walk on the dikes. Don't get near one another so you're an easy target." After a while, you walked on the dikes, especially coming back mornings if we'd been out a couple days. A lot of times you'd do foolish things. You were tired, you were miserable and would break all the commandments. I know people [who] hit a trip wire and set off a grenade or some kind of explosion and lost legs, or it killed them in the process. We would also go on these

Top: A helicopter crewman in helmet and flight suit mans his position. *WHi Image ID 11736*

Above: A row of Hueys prepares for takeoff. *Ted Fetting*

Eagle flights a lot and have choppers taking us into various areas. You never knew from day to day what was going to be the plan for the next.

With the Eagle flights, the helicopters would hover and [try to] land on dikes. People scurried on them. I grew up on a big dairy farm and I was always bothered by heights, but after a while you are just as foolish and stupid as the next. Hell, you got a machine gun and you're sitting and dragging your legs over the edge of [the open door] as this helicopter is moving out. Sometimes there'd be people jumping even though we were going to land because you're such a target. A helicopter is like a bathtub in the air. You're so vulnerable. There's no gliding like you can with a regular plane. People would get off them fairly quick. There were instances where we were jumping from as much as ten feet. You don't know what you're jumping into half the time. You hope it's slop and mud, but that's not always the case. When I think of it now, if my kids ever did that, oh.

DON JONES My group provided air photo and airborne sensor intelligence to the South Vietnamese in support of their operations. The Air Photo Group had Army, Navy, and Marine resources. We could call on the First Marine Air Wing. We had Army aviation. We had our own aviation, Piper Cubs, that we went up in and took low-level hand-held camera shots, which was pretty exciting. We also had support from the Navy who were flying off of aircraft carriers in the South China Sea. They provided some very valuable stuff, mainly because they had the super sophisticated ability to read photography that was motion picture photography.

Acquiring the targets was very difficult. It was hard to find individuals. That was one of our big weaknesses. We got better at it, but senior officers were reluctant to grasp the fact that the North Vietnamese and the Viet Cong were willing to do manual labor, one person at a time. They never asked our troops to do [that]. It resulted in surprises that shouldn't have been surprises. They moved a lot of material by basket boats, which carried about two hundred pounds of whatever: food, ammunition, and material. One person would get behind the boat and push it down the river. You had ten people doing that and that's a ton of materiel moved. That was hard for a lot of Americans, not necessarily just senior officers, but a lot of Americans just couldn't get their minds around that. In a night you could have twenty to thirty tons of ammunition moved into a place with a hundred or so Vietnamese pushing a boat or a basket.

To try to stop them was another thing altogether. I think people have read about it; about bombing craters in the roads and then a photo recon plane coming in two hours later to do the bomb damage assessment to find the road all back in shape because lots and lots of people got out there with shovels and picks and put it back together again. We were so mechanized and so heavily supported by vehicles and things like that that it's really hard to imagine people doing this. We picked up one person just prior to Tet Offensive who had been caught bringing in a section of a rocket near Da Nang airbase. We found out that the way that this happened was that they would pick up sections of rockets on the Ho Chi Minh Trail and each person would put a piece on their back and walk the fifteen or twenty miles to where they were going to launch it.

ROGER TREECE I was assigned to Fleet Air Reconnaissance Squadron 1. [We flew] a four-motor prop. It had four Pratt and Whitman 1250-horsepower radial engines on it. We had a flight time of about twenty hours; we could carry enough fuel for twenty hours. We usually flew about twelve-hour flight ops, but if our replacement couldn't get up because they were shelling or something, we would extend our missions up to eighteen hours. The inside was just completely stuffed with electronics, but we did have our own galley onboard where we could make our own meals. We ate quite well when we were in the air.

We carried a crew of thirty-three. There were quite a few different stations because we had people doing the linguistics, and then the rest were dedicated to radar positions. We could track everything. Our unit was tasked with covering North Vietnam, all the way up and down from the seaside. Our job was to keep the guys off the carriers safe from these enemy positions in North Vietnam. A lot of guys will tell you about their experience in South Vietnam in the jungles and all that kind of stuff and the plantations, but I can talk all about North Vietnam. We used to watch the MIGs come down the Hai Phong River Valley. There's a mountain range on either side of the valley, and they flew right down that valley out of China into Hanoi to land. We would watch them on the radar coming down. Our job was to just keep track of everything that was going on in North Vietnam and try to keep the friendlies out of trouble.

JOE CAMPBELL They sent me to a unit in Cu Chi attached to the 25th Infantry Division. About a month before January '68, they sent me down to Zion, which was the First Infantry Division headquarters. We would assist the units with their artillery and automotive servicing. When you go over there, you have a year. I believe my rotation date was supposed to be February 12, 1968. The Tet Offense broke out on January 30. It was everywhere. All areas were being attacked. The morning of the Tet Offense, my warrant officer was going home and asked me if I would drive him from Dion to Tan Son Nhat airbase in Saigon, which is about twenty miles south of where we were. It was really no big thing. We get in the jeep at about five o'clock in the morning and we drive down Highway 1A, which was a beautiful four-lane highway. We're driving down the road and there's not an oxcart, not a bicycle. There wasn't anything on that road.

DON JONES In September, October, and November, things were looking pretty good. Things got a little tight in December. In the Da Nang area we started seeing a lot of activity to our west between the Ho Chi Minh Trail and Da Nang. There was sporadic rocketing of the air base. The Special Forces were doing patrols pretty far back and giving us indications that more activity was occurring. It was picking up all the way to the boundary with North Vietnam; all the way up to Quang Tri. There was a lot of concern about the area around Hue just because it was closer to the trail. We started to pick up indications of east-west road building from the Ho Chi Minh Trail towards the ocean. We didn't know Tet was coming, but we knew there was something up.

It kept building, building, building during January of '68. It was clear that something was going to happen somewhere along the way. Interestingly enough, it was the American units farther north of both the Marine and the First Air Cav that picked up most of it. Down in Quang Ngai, they were much farther away from the border and so there wasn't very much going on down there at that time. Da Nang was pretty much the southernmost area of where we thought things were going to be getting hot.

WAYNE JENSEN The night before the Tet Offensive commenced, we didn't have patrol, and all of a sudden they went to red alert. Our swift boats and base were about five miles away on the other side of the Da Nang River. All of a sudden we heard over loudspeakers the Vietcong telling these South Vietnamese that if they had any Americans in their hooches they were going to kill them. Mamasan was legitimately petrified and told me I had to leave. Whenever I went into town, I always had a submachine gun — I called it a grease gun — and a .45. I would stop the Vietnamese on their motor scooters and have them give me a ride into town. That's how I got back to the base just in time. Our boat was getting ready to leave.

When I got on board, we had orders to go up to the city of Hue on the Perfume River. Each swift boat would get assigned a particular quadrant, and that's where they would patrol. During the Tet Offensive for three days we were up on the Perfume River. Talk about being around historical events without knowing the significance of them. We were taking Marines from one side of the Perfume River over to the other side, and unbeknownst to us we were dropping them off to go into the citadel. It wasn't until years later that I found out how massive the casualty rate was and the significance of the Tet Offensive. To me, it was just taking a bunch of Marines over to the other side.

Ted Fetting radios from the field.
Ted Fetting

TED FETTING We would go through the villages looking for the enemy. I always said that to me, village and city is much more eerie and scary than the jungle. When we would sweep through the villages, we would move incrementally. It's just even more unnatural than watching out for or looking for people to kill in the jungle and brush. It was minutes of incredible terror, and then hours of boredom.

I was hit first on January 6 and it wasn't any big deal. I got hit with shrapnel. Things started to become more active, and we started getting called out to come in on behalf of sister companies or battalions. That was leading into Tet. On February 2 I was hit twice and airlifted out of there, so I missed a good part of Tet. That was total turmoil. I mean people didn't know what they were doing, where they were going. It was bedlam. A lot of people killed, a lot of people killed. I was taken to [a medical unit in] Dong Tam [and later Japan]. The whole place was chaos.

Ted Fetting, far right, with fellow soldiers Elroy "Steve" Le Blanc and Fred Jansonius. Le Blanc and Jansonius were killed in action on February 2, 1968, just three days into the Tet Offensive.
Ted Fetting

I got hit in the arm with [something like] a railroad spike in an explosion. You could easily drop a half dollar right down to the bone. And it was ugly. And there was a question for a while whether I was going to lose the arm. I was incredibly lucky. I got to Japan and saw some others from our area, some I recognized. One guy, nineteen years old, lost a leg, lost an arm, lost an eye. He's telling me how thrilled he is that he's going to be home for his birthday. I lost it. I just, I couldn't...what do you say? He'd only left the U.S. not even two months before. I was lucky all the way through.

JOE CAMPBELL We look ahead and Vietnamese police were there. They had barbed wire across the road and they just pulled the barbwire aside and waved us through. No sooner did we get past the barbed wire [than] we come up to Newport News dock. It's right as you go into Saigon from the outskirts. There's a bridge and a Vietnamese police station and it had just been blown up. Obviously, we got there shortly after it happened. There was some firing going on and it was like, "What the hell do we do?" The gospel truth, the first thing we did was hit the ditch. The person I landed next to was my first sergeant from basic training, Sergeant Matos. You never forget your first sergeant from basic training. I'm looking at him and of course he

Joe Campbell on guard duty in Trang Bang, South Vietnam.
Joe Campbell

doesn't remember me. But I said, "Sergeant, what do we do?" He said, "I don't have the faintest idea. Where'd you come from?" I said we'd come from Dion. He said, "Well, do whatever you want to do." And the warrant officer said, "Let's get the hell out of here."

We headed back, and I thought we'd go to Bien Hoa, which is about twenty miles north of Dion on Highway 1. It was a major Air Force base. I thought, "Well, we can get him to Bien Hoa." We're driving down 1A again with nobody on that road. The military police pull that barbed wire back and let us go through again. But we knew something obviously was up, but still no clue what. We get to the outskirts of Bien Hoa and the Air Force military police were there. "Get the hell out of here! We're getting attacked all over the place." They said, "You ain't staying here and you ain't going in there, so you might as well try and get back to your unit." So we just drove like a bat out of hell back to Dion.

Base camp was probably about a mile in, and it was through the jungle. I was just not going to stop. I [lost track of] my warrant officer. I'm sure he left. I know we were on guard duty. It was a constant guard duty, because that was one of the headquarters of the First Infantry Division. I don't remember anything until the company commander said, "You're out of here. You've got two hours." I was just in shock.

ROGER TREECE Tet of '68, I was there. I was in the bunker when the sirens went off. Between our barracks and the flight line was the ammo dump. They hit the ammo dump going up and then the east gate, which was 250 yards in front of our barracks, towards the wire. It was a pretty hairy night with a lot of the ammo dump cooking off. They hit a fuel bladder and it was burning, so it lit everything up like a torch. I'm in that bunker and of course with everything blowing up, the bunker was shaking. You're just sitting there. No weapon. Those bunkers were just full of rats. You're sitting there in the dark and the rats are running over your legs and your skivvies. Ugh. I didn't think I'd make it through that night. The helicopters kept them off of us and we did OK. I got out the next day and found the nose drag off a 250-pound bomb where my bunk was. It's a lead weight shaped like a cone and they screw it on the nose of the bomb to make the bomb go down nose first. That was my good luck piece. It weighed about seventy-five pounds, but it was my good luck piece. [Laughs.] I carried that thing with me the rest of my tour of duty in my sea trunk. I left it over there when I came home. I figured they weren't going to let me take pieces of ordinance through.

TED FETTING [It] was late in the day on the other side of the main village that we had come through. We were pinned down for a while right at the edge of that town. There was a lot of activity there. We did not move very much in one day's time there and lost a lot of people that day. There were a couple of people killed together. A guy tried to throw a grenade and the thing bounced back and actually killed him. It was just unlucky.

I don't think anybody expected Tet was going to be quite as extensive and horrible as it was. I am sure that we took them too lightly. If people suspected it they did not get the word around that much. It just seemed like it was getting worse and worse. Areas that we could go through normally all of a sudden, there were all kinds of enemy in them.

DON JONES The morning of Tet, we got awakened about 4:30, and there were definite movements going on in the area. There was a small South Vietnamese Communist unit moving up on the south side of the I Corps compound. About a week before it happened, there was a pretty good indication that some pretty heavy movements were going to take place. And the commander of Da Nang got permission to call in the National Police from out in the countryside. The Rangers [were brought] in from various locations into Da Nang as a scouting force. We saw the very first of the Soviet PT-76 tanks,

U.S. Army and Marine fire bases getting attacked, and nighttime attacks. There was a lot of activity going on. They overran a number of the fire bases. There were a lot of Marines and Army stories, confirmed, where they actually called in friendly fire on their own position, because they were the next thing to hand-to-hand combat with NVA forces.

The first thing that I noticed when I got to the compound was that there were South Vietnamese Army forces up on the back wall. They were firing off of the back wall with rifles and machine guns. I figured that was not something that they were doing for practice. It was loud. It was just like being in a bowl of Jell-O. If you've been in an earthquake, you know how plastic the earth really is. It just rolls and rocks. We were familiar with the rockets when they hit Da Nang. This was small-arms and mortar fire, and it was much different and much more threatening because you know that it's all short range. It's aimed pretty much at you. We were in bunkers, so we could perceive the ground shaking and some very loud noise. It was devastating.

TED FETTING I don't think anybody had any idea it was going to be that bad. Because I think they would have been better prepared and dealt with it better. I think the greatest ally the enemy had was the surprise. People were just incredulous that anything like that could be happening. We had people on R&R then. If you figured something like that was happening, you weren't going to be sending people away. You act with reckless abandon. You are feeling miserable, so to hell with the rules. I think part of the time you are really better off after a while. When you are at a point when you really don't care, you think, "I've got seven, eight, nine months left of this stuff." It was an attitude of, "If it happens, it happens — to hell with it. I am not going to be responsible or careful. I am going to be as comfortable as possible." We would be on ambush or roving patrols all night where you basically are moving, trying to find enemy. You are trying to draw fire. The ambush patrols are miserable. You sleep so little and when you are sleeping your welfare and your life are in the hands of those on guard. Sometimes people aren't that careful. Of course they are also horribly tired. You'd hear the horror stories where some NVA unit, or Vietcong [NLF] unit, would come in and find the guards asleep and you'd find throats cut and people killed en masse.

ROGER TREECE I'd made my peace. I was ready to go. I didn't think I was going to be getting out of there. The next morning I had the best thing I ever ate in my life: a can of peaches. [Laughs.] There's no describing those

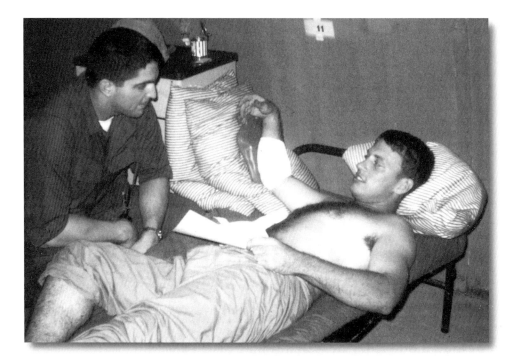

Pittsburgh Steeler Andy Russell, left, visited Ted Fetting in a Long Binh hospital. *Ted Fetting*

peaches. They were the best thing that anybody could ever eat in the whole wide world, because you never thought that you were going to eat them.

After Tet I didn't go back in a bunker. I'd find a ditch. I'd find anything. I would not go back in a bunker the rest of the time I was over there. I don't know how many times I got my butt chewed by an officer, but I wouldn't go back in a bunker. I didn't want to be trapped again.

We have no pets because anything furry in the dark freaks me out. When I first met my current wife, she had a cat. He learned very quickly not to get on the bed at night because I would fling him against the wall as soon as he touched me. It's just an instinctive reaction. According to the professionals whom I have talked to about going through the PTSD, that kind of sustained stress physically changes the way your brain is wired. It changes the shape of the medulla oblongata, so it's now hardwired for that combat situation and it never unwires. If there's a loud bang close by, I still hit the ground. It takes me a lot longer to get up than it used to, but... [Laughs.]

JOE CAMPBELL I left Vietnam on February 7, and I was due home February 12. I had my uniform on in the Oakland airport, carrying my duffel bag, and some hippies started harassing me as I was by myself walking down the stairwell; pushing and swearing and calling me…I didn't have a clue. We never saw TV. The little papers we got, the Army's *Stars and Stripes*, was all edited. I really wasn't aware about the big protests that were going on and how the troops were becoming the enemy. Man, I got out of that goddamn uniform as quick as I could.

ROGER TREECE   I don't regret one bit volunteering for Vietnam. I don't regret one day of service over there. I still believe that what we were doing as troops, we did the very best job we possibly could. There were a few no-nos here and there, and that's in any environment in any situation, but the majority of guys who I know served their country admirably. We served each other.

JOE CAMPBELL   I used to rack my brains out trying to recall things. It doesn't mean I don't care, but I'm not going to try and figure it out. One thing that I think is important to share — and it took my PTSD counselor to really get it out of me — is that I truly believed, and it had all the logic in the world,

On the back of this photo, Joe Campbell wrote: "These children now have a very good chance to live without constant fear." *Joe Campbell*

the only two months that bothered me over there were the first and the last. The time in between, I didn't give a shit. I'd say that, and I believed it. The first [month] because you're going into the unknown and the last [month] because you've got the known. The ten in between? Who cares? [But] it was the ten in between that did me in. It took about a year and a half of going to these groups and sharing privately with my counselor. I was not good at expressing my feelings. The one thing that I didn't want to get too much was too emotional. It just felt like, "You weak son of a bitch, all these other people have given so much. You little baby, shut up and get on with life." I started realizing that [with] the ten in between, I did care. A lot of things happened in that ten in between. A lot of people killed, a lot of seeing them come in on those helicopters and get off. It hurt like hell. I was totally numb. Now I definitely go to the funerals of our fallen and support the families of our fallen. Realizing [the importance of] that hug and that embrace.

Battle of Hue

"They overran Hue City, took it and dug in, and we had to go in and dig them out. We literally dug them out; out of the holes, out of little bunkers."— Sam King

The battle of Hue, which began in January 1968, was a central conflict of the Tet Offensive and one of the war's bloodiest, most exhausting battles. Located sixty miles south of the demilitarized zone in I Corps, Hue was what historian James Willbanks calls an "open city," an area that "had been relatively peaceful and secure prior to 1968."[1] Indeed, prior to the battle, the U.S. military presence in the city was limited to a MACV (Military Assistance Command, Vietnam) compound, staffed by two hundred U.S. soldiers. The South Vietnamese Army (ARVN) also had an infantry division headquartered in Hue; however, most of its troops were scattered along Route 1 to the north of the city. National Liberation Front (NLF) forces were thus able to infiltrate the city prior to the battle — many hidden among people visiting the city to celebrate Tet — and gained extensive knowledge of the city's layout, bringing in weapons and supplies to prepare for the fight to come.

The former imperial capital of Vietnam and a major cultural center, Hue had two distinct sections, divided by the Song Huong (Perfume River). The southern section, the site of the MACV compound, was more modern and contained residential and administrative districts. In contrast, the northern half was the site of the old city, also known as the Citadel. The Citadel, which included the Imperial Palace compound, covered three square miles. Surrounded by an outer wall up to forty feet thick, it was packed with shops, villas, and row houses. According to one observer, the Citadel and the Imperial Palace were a "camera-toting tourist's dream" but "a rifle-toting infantryman's nightmare."[2] Indeed, the nature of Hue's architecture would lead to some of the most intense fighting of the war, hand-to-hand combat that went block by block, building by building, and even room by room.

As part of the Tet Offensive, the battle of Hue began at 3:40 a.m. on January 31, as NVA/NLF troops assailed the city with rockets and mortars. Joining with NLF infiltrators, NVA/NLF forces quickly took control of the majority of the city, and by sunrise the same day, the NLF flag flew over the Citadel.[3] These enemy forces sought not only to deny U.S./ARVN forces control over the city but also to transform the city itself by establishing a "revolutionary administration."[4] In the aftermath of the attack, NVA/NLF forces rounded up key figures such as city administrators, intellectuals, religious figures, and foreigners; a mass grave of 2,800 people was later discovered on the outskirts of the city.[5]

Due to the ongoing siege at Khe Sanh and the coordinated attacks and confusion of the Tet Offensive, it was difficult for the U.S. military to dispatch forces to Hue. U.S. forces began their counteroffensive by working to retake the southern section of the city by foot — a task that proved difficult and deadly. NVA/NLF forces were so entrenched in the city that after reaching the MACV compound, Marines were unable to cross the Nguyen Hoang Bridge to the Citadel. It took more than a week to fight through eleven blocks of southern Hue. Originally, the northern part of the city was the responsibility of ARVN forces, but Marines were sent to assist after ARVN was stymied by NVA/NLF forces "who had burrowed deeply into the walls and tightly packed buildings" of the Citadel, making it a "defender's paradise."[6] Working in small teams and enduring harrowing, bloody combat, Marines worked their way through the Citadel, and on the night of February 23, ARVN forces captured the Imperial Palace. By March 2, the battle was over and the city itself was destroyed. In more than three weeks of intense fighting, approximately 10,000 of the 17,000 houses in the city were ruined; in the words of an observer, "the beautiful city…was a shattered, stinking hulk, its streets choked with rubble and rotting bodies."[7] The Marines lost 147 men, with another 857 wounded, while ARVN's casualties reached 384, with more than 1,800 wounded. Exact battle statistics for NVA/NLF casualties are unknown but are assumed to be high based on the intensity of the battle.[8] Hue encapsulated the shock and brutality of the Tet Offensive as enemy forces managed to occupy a city in the heart of the U.S. military presence, one that had previously been largely untouched by war.

Charlie Wolden, Amnicon Falls State Park (Marines, First Marine Division)
Sam King, Plum Tree, NC (Marines, Fifth Marine Division)

CHARLIE WOLDEN I'm from Amnicon Falls State Park, about fifteen miles outside of Superior. We had a round barn. The joke when I was a kid was, "All those Wolden kids are crazy, they don't have a corner to piss in." The joke ain't even funny. I got so sick of hearing it. I had twelve brothers and sisters. We were very, very poor: outhouse-type poor. I didn't have a military tradition or family, other than my brother had been drafted and my older sister joined the Army for a little while. My other brother had joined the Army. I joined the Marines very impulsively. I was damn near dropped out of school. I was just doing really poorly. I had the brains to do it, but I just didn't have the motivation. I was having fun. I had a '57 Ford convertible and was going steady with this girl. I cut wood — we called it cutting pulp — and I worked about three days a week. I showed up at school whenever I felt like it. I was sure I wasn't going to graduate. I went out drinking one night; my brother bought a twelve-pack of Schlitz malt liquor for these two guys, and me and this one guy named Dale said we all ought to join the Marines. The next morning, we were hung over and we went down and joined the freaking Marines. Tim Nevins's dad stepped in and said, "You ain't doing it." My dad said, "Whatever." Dale joined on the buddy plan. He didn't go. He broke his nose beforehand, so I was the one that went. He ended up going to Okinawa his whole tour. He never did go to Vietnam.

Sam King cradles an M-79 grenade launcher. *Sam King*

SAM KING [I've lived most of my adult life in Wisconsin, but] I grew up in the western part of North Carolina, right on the Tennessee-North Carolina-Virginia border. I came from a family of Marines. My dad was a Marine in World War II. I had an uncle who was a Marine in Korea. When it came time, when I got out of high school, I was going to go. It wasn't a question of if I was going to be drafted into the Army. It was just a matter of when I decided to go into the Marine Corps.

I went through boot camp at Parris Island in 1967. I went to Camp Geiger for infantry training, then from there to advanced infantry training.

Two of Sam King's fellow Marines, J.D. Ply and S.O. McCorie, at ease before night patrol. *Sam King*

Boot camp was something else. I'd never been anywhere or seen anything. The first time I had an indoor toilet was when I went to boot camp. Everybody talks about the stress. Being in a Marine Corps boot camp in 1967, that was stress. That's like being a goldfish in a blender. The least little thing you do, you get whacked. But at the same time now that I look back on it, it was the best training because it developed the teamwork that the Marine Corps is famous for. It has affected my life ever since, having that personal discipline that I learned with those DIs [drill instructors].

CHARLIE WOLDEN It was July 1967 when I went in the Marines, right out of high school. I didn't have an aversion to going to Vietnam. I didn't know anything about it. It was on the news and I didn't pay much attention to it. I didn't think much about it. It was very sad leaving my girlfriend when I went to Vietnam. I got there in December. It was raining....I got to my unit late because they were out on an operation and they sent me through land mine warfare school and demolition school for two weeks. I got to my unit and there wasn't much going on. We were in Quang Tre. We did patrols, didn't see much action, and didn't really get shot at. One burst of AK [47] fire one time. It was nothing.

There were a lot of rumors about NVA buildups. We went on a squad-

The words penned by Sam King on the back of this photo tell the story: "Our kid who has been with us since I have been here. 14 years old and fighting a war." This child interpreter was later killed in a mortar attack. *Sam King*

sized patrol outside Quang Tri. Up on top of a hill there was an old bombed-out Catholic Church. I was still a tourist. I started looking around. There were a bunch of claymores [mines] set up in there. I told the squad leader and he kind of flipped out and did a big sweep around the hill. We found the wire going down off the back of the hill. We found these mines and then a couple Bouncing Betties, Walker and I did, just walking around looking. We blew up everything and got out of there. There was a policy in our company to send people who did something for in-country [to] R&R because the morale was real low after this hell-ish fight they were in. The company commander sent Walker and me. We'd only been there three weeks. It really angered the sen-ior guys and they were very resentful. "Who are these new guys going to R&R?" We didn't know the difference. We just went.

[When we returned] we got sent to Phu Bai, south of Hue. When we were going into Hue in a convoy, people were coming out of Hue, just streaming. It was like the parting of the Red Sea. These peo-ple were just getting out of our way and we were smoking into Hue. We got in and there was a roadblock. We started going around the roadblock and started seeing stuff. The first thing I saw was a tank jammed up into a build-ing that was all burned out. There was a jeep that was all burned out with a

Soldiers traveled by convoys — sometimes stretching for miles — to ensure safety. *WHi Image ID 33296*

Refugees flee across the Perfume River during the battle of Hue. The bridge was destroyed soon after by NLF insurgents. *National Archives (306-MVP-22(6))*

body hanging out of it and I think it was an ARVN, I don't know. Alpha Company fought their way in that morning. It was not good. The shooting started and the dust started. The billows of dust were coming up and you couldn't see in front of you. The trucks were just smoking down the street. The people started shooting. It was just deafening. I'd see flashes coming out of the buildings around us. I have no recollection of what happened next. Next thing I remember I'm laying on the ground. Boxes of ammo all over the place, the mortar rounds we were sitting on. The truck was on its side. It hit a bomb crater and it just went over. When a bullet goes near you it's "snap," but this was hitting the ground so it was like, "crack, crack, crack, crack, crack." They were hitting dust all around me. I thought, I'll just lay here and they'll think I'm dead. The thing that became really apparent right then was there was no background music. Man, this is real. As simple as that is, this is real. A guy starts peeling back out of the building to get me and I can't lay here. He's going to die trying to get me. So I got up and ran to the building.

SAM KING I did two tours over there. The first tour after we got done with training, I reported to Camp Pendleton, went through staging battalion, and flew to Okinawa. I fooled around there, got shots and gear. Then it was on to Da Nang and to a gulf company, Fifth Marines. I got there January 28, 1968. I got there just in time. We'd been on patrols, but it was nothing until Hue City. That was the first time I saw what I consider combat. It's hard to describe that. In a way it was kind of like controlled chaos. The enemy, the Vietcong, was dug in all over the place. We couldn't get across the Perfume River on the bridge. They had built a pontoon. I went in to Hue City, with a full squad. I was the low man on the totem pole. Fourteen days later, it was only me and one other guy who'd gone in originally. The rest were either killed or wounded.

It'd take us a day to go a hundred yards if we were lucky. It was fighting inside buildings, in hedgerows and behind buildings. I learned a lot in those weeks. I learned a lot about myself. It was tough. During Tet, New Year 1968, the Vietcong massed and conducted simultaneous attacks against the major cities in Vietnam all across the country. It caught everybody off guard because no one in the higher-ups thought that they would be able to coordinate an attack like that. They overran Hue City, took it and dug in, and we had to go in and dig them out. We literally dug them out; out of the holes, out of little bunkers.

CHARLIE WOLDEN The next morning [after arriving at Hue], we formed up and went on this patrol. It was a mad dash out to the stadium to get a couple guys who were left out there from the fight the day before. We found them. They were dead. I think we took one or two dead and some wounded. We were dragging them back in and [the NVA] were shooting all the way through it. They were all over the place. They were on streets, they were in alleys, and they were in buildings. They were all over the place. I found out much later that nobody knew how big a unit it was or anything. They started sending Marine companies in and they were just too little. Gulf and Fox 2/5 and Alpha 1/1 and our platoon that was attached to 1/1 were made up of about half rear echelon guys and half infantry. Half of the infantry were new and half of them were being held over from going home. We had some lieutenants, some squad leaders, and some NCOs [noncommissioned officers] from the different companies they just scrounged up real quick and threw them in there. Thank God we had them. I had no idea what I was doing.

I was carrying the radio for this black guy named Livingston. He was a big, big guy. All he did for the first few days was hit me and "bang, bang, bang, bang" me with the headphone. He'd hit me in the head, "You dumb son of a bitch. Geez, where the hell were you born? Kentucky?" I just got sick of it, but he kept me alive. He would grab me and throw me this way, "Don't do that!" One day he hit me so hard in the back, I went on the ground. I remember thinking, "I've freaking had it." All of a sudden, "wham, wham, wham." Three RPGs [rocket propelled grenades] came in. It really screwed up [the] four people right in front of us. But [Livingston] heard them coming!

We kept going out a little further every day. It was every day. Every day we were making contact. Every day we were taking casualties. Every day we were going through houses and running across streets that had snipers. You'd go block by block to a building, then you'd pull back at night to the other side. It was a cluster fuck. Nobody knew what they were doing. Marines were not trained for this. These guys that we were fighting [with and against] had a lot of experience in the triple canopy jungle, in the bunker complexes. We were learning by doing.

SAM KING It amazed me many times how many bullets each side could fire at each other and nobody would get hit. It was just amazing. You couldn't figure it out. That's where I saw my first man die. My first Marine. I was totally baptized. That changed me.

The guys who had been there a long time had never been in something like the fighting in Hue City. I remember when we finally took the Citadel it was kind of over. I think some of the bravest people did the bravest acts I [have] ever seen and never got any credit. They didn't really want any. There was a lot of that in Hue City. There were racial tensions that were pretty strong in the service. Dr. King had been killed but in that battle in Hue City it didn't make any difference what color you were. Everybody was covering everybody's ass. Marines didn't have as many problems [with race] as some of the other units.

CHARLIE WOLDEN To talk about Vietnam, and a one-year experience in Vietnam, it's impossible to pick out one piece without my mind going to another piece to another piece because like the whole war itself, it's fragmented. It's hard to make sense out of it all. I try my best to put it in a linear way: this happened, this happened, this happened. If I was going to sit here and tell you that, it would take a month.

The North Vietnamese were very ruthless. I don't hate them. In fact, I respected them. But one of the things that I learned in Hue is how ruthless and how dedicated and how hardcore they were. We were fighting an army that was very dedicated and would die for this. They didn't mind killing civilians. They had no qualms about shooting from a house that had civilians in it and putting you in a position…a nineteen-year-old and if you're going to save your own life and your own ass and everybody else's ass around you, you'd have to put a rocket in that building and kill the civilians. [But] our unit did not commit atrocities. The NCOs and officers just wouldn't allow it to happen. When it got real close one time, they stepped up. I remember the radio call coming across to the squad leader. "All units, this is Charlie 6, hold your position, hold your position." People were throwing Vietnamese civilians into the wells and throwing hand grenades down. I know that happened, [but] I didn't see it happen.

There was a French guy that came up to me in Hue. He talked very good English. He looked French Vietnamese and he said he was a university professor. Most of those guys had been killed. The North Vietnamese, when they got in there, killed hundreds of them. They found the bodies in big graves after the battle was over. They killed the intellectuals. This French guy told us, "Don't wreck the walls. These things are beautiful, they're hundreds of years old. Don't wreck the courtyards." In Hue, we were only allowed to have direct fire weapons. We didn't have any rockets, any mortars or artillery [for the first two weeks]. They didn't want to destroy the city. The irony of it was that before we were done, the city was in rubble.

SAM KING During night fighting, your sense of smell and your sense of hearing become really good because you can't see anything. You listen for certain sounds: bushes scraping against uniforms, half an empty canteen making a splash. Maybe everything's not taped down well and there's a dog tag rattling. You listen for animals that are disturbed. Birds that are disturbed in the night make a lot of noise [when they] fly away. When someone's close, especially when you're in ambush, there's a lot of nightlife, night sounds. As people come through, the critters sense them and they quiet down. You listen for things to get really quiet. You learn, it's just one of those things.

I look at photos….Was I ever that young? Jesus, look at this. It brings back memories. But not all of them are bad memories. The traumatic memories and stuff like that are easy to remember because they're just…But then there were other times. One time we were on patrol and we break out of the edge of the tree line and there's this pond and it's covered with lotus flowers. They're blooming everywhere and the whole clearing is full of butterflies. All kinds. They were so bright, those tropical butterflies. They looked like stained glass. Here's this whole squad of old hardcore Marines on patrol standing there looking at it. There were moments of beauty. I helped the corpsman deliver a baby one night because the midwife couldn't get out because of the weather. He did the work and I just handed him things and did what he told me to. Well, the woman did the work and we were there.

CHARLIE WOLDEN One of the four or five worst days in Vietnam was the 9th, 10th, or 11th of February. I'd been there about eight days and by then we were getting better [at it]. Livingston had his legs blown off. He wasn't a squad leader anymore. Cole was. I barely knew Cole. He was a squad leader from Charlie Company. He was a very good guy. We were down from a squad of maybe a dozen people to five. They sent our squad out on a kind of a recon. Nobody had been in this one part of the south side. That area coming off the causeway, the street forked at the causeway and went straight east three-quarters of a mile. There weren't clear blocks. They had city blocks off to the right and then there was the river that meandered through there. They had very nice houses and very ancient courtyards.

We were walking along this wall. There were five of us. I knew the difference between an AK-47 and that Chinese machine gun they had. We heard a real quick burst of machine-gun [fire], just about six rounds. Next thing you know we start running to get up there. While we're still running, Denim calls for a corpsman up. The grass was about eighteen inches, just enough high where you could lie in it. I didn't see Denim right away. I saw Cole hit the deck and then I hit the deck. Nobody shot when we came around the corner. All of a sudden, all hell broke loose. It was just "Shoop, shoop, shoop, shoop!" all over us. I had a sharp pain underneath my arm. I said, "I think I was hit!" Cole looks at me and he's over top of Denim; he says, "On the count of three we're out of here. One, two, three!" I got up and Denim got up and right then, just "poof" out of his back, right between his shoulder blades. It was instantaneous but it is entrenched in my mind. He fell forward. We got back around the wall. Cole looks at me and says, "Where's Denim?" I said, "Man, right behind [us], right in the back." He said, "OK, we're splitting up." I don't know why he did this. I don't know why, you just do it. He said, "Wolden, you go down by the river. I'm going through the middle. Merincel, you get up on the road and we'll meet back at the pagoda." The pagoda was about two-thirds of the way back to where

Soldiers take cover against a Hue City wall, performing makeshift medicine. *National Archives (127-N-A3719)*

we started. I go down by the river and I'm running, I'm running. This guy in a tree is shooting at me. It was "crack, crack, crack, crack, crack, crack." I'm trying to keep away from [the shooter], trying to get going. I felt this thing like a bullwhip hit me in the face and my helmet fell off. I hit the deck and I grabbed my helmet and I'm thinking, "God damn it, I'm shot," but there was no blood.

I'm kind of half-crawling, half-running and he's still shooting at me! I get behind this little wall. I'm crawling and I kind of peek around the corner because he couldn't see me. I peeked around the corner and I could see the tree. I put a magazine, the whole eighteen rounds, into that tree. I got up and hauled ass straight back to the road. When I got back to the road and looked at my helmet, they'd shot my chinstrap off. A bullet had gone through my field jacket, hit my flak jacket, and chipped into my [left] underarm. I pulled it out. It was not a big deal. The radio didn't work. I had two bullet holes through my radio. We start running back up to where the platoon was. They'd heard shooting down there, so they were already getting ready. [Cole and the lieutenant] built a plan of what we were going to do. Cole came back and said, "Wolden, I'm going to go out and get Denim. You go get Burgess. We got these two guys going with us. [The platoon are] going to get behind the wall. The wall is six feet high. They can't shoot over the top of that wall."

We got down there. I saw people kneeling down. These guys were just hosing down that tree line. It turned out we bumped into the North Vietnamese regimental headquarters. We just walked right into their perimeter. I'm running out there to get Burgess. All this noise! I couldn't tell if they were shooting at me or not. I was waiting to die any minute. I saw the machine gun before I saw Burgess, and there was nobody manning that machine gun. We ran right out there. It was about ten feet in front of the machine gun and we grabbed Burgess by both legs and were running and hauling him back. He was heavy. They call it dead weight for a reason. He was dead and he was heavy. We were just trying to get him back. You could hear the snap right over the top of everything else. That machine gun opened up on us. I felt a real sharp pain in my buttocks. I fell forward. I don't know if I tripped or what. The other guy that was holding Burgess dropped his leg. We dropped Burgess. He was reaching down to get him and I saw his finger was hanging off. He was shot in the hand. I think Burgess's body took a couple rounds. I looked up at the kid and I just said, "Fuck him. He's dead. Let's get out of here." We took off. This all happened in seconds. I kind of spider walked. My helmet goes off again. I heard this "wank!" I found it the next day. A bullet had gone through the top of it.

We got around the corner into this little building. Cole had Denim's body. People forming around, they said, "Where's Burgess?" I said, "We didn't get him." The look on their faces was like, "You guys didn't do it. Now I'm going to have to go out there." Right then a rocket hit the top of a tree. All the shrapnel from it hit the tin roof on that building. It was just chaos. Everybody started hauling ass out of there. It was almost like a retreat, unorganized. Cole grabbed a hold of me and a couple other people and he said, "OK, here's what we're going to do. There's about five of us. We're going to set little fire teams up and kind of leapfrog back." They were coming. There were a few times I saw North Vietnamese. I can clearly remember where they were. They're quick and they're quiet. We saw six of them heading down toward the river. Cole said, "They're going to cut us off. Get the fuck out of here." We got back to the pagoda and set up. I didn't see them, but Cole started shooting. We all just started lying down in the base of fire and it stopped them. Then we got back up to the compound.

When I got back to Burgess's body [the next day], Denim's pack was there. He had an oddball pack that he had. It was kind of a canvas satchel pack that he made. He sewed it together. He carried all of his stuff in it. I opened it up. I found a can of C rations where the bullet had gone through the cracker part, but the jelly was OK. The bullet that killed him. I sat down and I methodically ate it. I have no idea why I did it. I just did it. I ate it. I'm sure that I was just ceremonially saying, "He's gone, he's dead. Move on. Suck it up. Eat his fucking crackers. They've got to be good for something. They didn't stop the bullet." I've always felt guilty about doing that. Ashamed, I should say, of doing that.

SAM KING You'd get set in for the night, but there were times when you couldn't have slept if you wanted to. The tension and the noise and heat and smell. The smell was something else. The smell in combat, the smell of war after a battle that went on for days, is just something else. It smells of things burning, bodies turning putrid, especially in Asia where it's so hot and bodies start to deteriorate pretty quickly. It smells like dead animals, fumes, gunpowder smoke, and dust. It's a smell unlike anything else. Blood has it's own smell. It smells like hot copper. To this day if I'm driving down the road on my motorcycle and I go by a dead deer and I get a whiff of the carcass, those memories snap right back to me.

CHARLIE WOLDEN The one common theme for me is corpses in Vietnam. Bloated, rotten corpses, both American and NVA. I saw a deer today and I'm still a little bugged by it, that smell of rotten flesh. After we got up on Hill 689, we couldn't get off. We couldn't get our dead out of the wire. The bodies were stacking up inside the wire and they were bloated. My platoon was trapped out with the NVA. There were only six or seven of us left in my platoon. I went from a rank-and-file Marine to squad leader right away. We had to pick up dead NVA bodies that were inside the wire now for a day or two and they were stinking. We'd put them in a bomb crater and piled fifty or sixty of them up. They stunk. We were told to burn them because the flies were terrible and the stink was terrible. I was hard. I got real hard in Vietnam, real hard. I poured the Gerry can all over myself so I wouldn't smell so bad. I can still smell it. When I smell diesel or fuel oil, I still get intrusive recollections from that.

SAM KING That was the most intense period of combat that I was ever in over there. I finished my tour with the Fifth Marines. I came home. I was so young but didn't fit in with anybody but military. After Tet 1968, the war

Sam King signed on to another tour after he returned to the United States. Here he is pictured with his new unit. *Sam King*

got terribly unpopular among the people. The guys coming home were not the people who planned the war, but we were the ones that got all the abuse and the apathy. That was a hard thing to go through. We had protesters at the airport in L.A. They told us maybe we shouldn't wear our uniforms. That's a terrible thing to say to a bunch of Marines. There had to be police officers to separate us from protesters at LAX, who were screaming, "Baby killer!" and, "You should have died in Vietnam!" They were our age, our contemporaries. It seemed like there was total indifference from World War II– and Korean War–era veterans. They let us come back to that kind of thing. I've never gotten over how the country treated us when we came back, how they treated us then and still do to a certain extent today. I came back, spent my time at home, and was here for about two and a half months and I just couldn't take it. It was too spit and polish, but I was a sergeant, so it wasn't too bad. You couldn't go anywhere outside the military areas because if you went to a bar in another town, it was pretty obvious you weren't fitting in with the crowd with that Marine Corps high and tight haircut. It was just not a good place to be. I hate to say that about my country, but at that time it was not a good place to be if you were in the military.

So I put in for orders back to Vietnam and I got them. I went back to Camp Pendleton, over to Okinawa, and then onto Da Nang.

CHARLIE WOLDEN I was alone, very alone. Vietnam is a very lonely experience. You are very close to the people you were around, but it was very lonely. You went through alone, you came home alone, and your experiences were alone. If you had sympathy for the Vietnamese, you kept it to yourself. The last thing we wanted was a "gook-lover" in our unit. We all had showed compassion and sympathy, but we never talked about it.

I had stopped writing everybody at home. I'd stopped writing my girlfriend. After Hill 689 and burning the bodies and getting overrun, it wasn't just a joke. It was a big deal because these guys were real. This isn't how I figured it would be. And it was shocking. I was lonely, not homesick lonely. I quit being that. I didn't think I was going to live. I'd accepted I was going to die. I didn't want any letters. It makes me think about it. Just leave me alone. You cross a line. I don't mean a moral line, although we crossed every moral line you ever learned in order to do our job, in order to live. You cross a line of being human. I wouldn't say an animal, but more like a predator. You're still afraid. You're just automatic.

SAM KING The thing that was hardest about it was the way you were treated when you went to look for a job and stuff. These people would be interviewing you and talking to you as if you were a twenty-one-year-old kid. That was hard for me to take when just a few months ago I literally held life and death in my hands for men I loved and respected. That was hard. I had a problem with authority. I rebelled against everything I'd ever been taught. I just totally went against everything. I didn't realize it then, but years later I realized that I was just doing that to cover up the pain. Because I just couldn't deal with it anymore. I couldn't deal with seeing my friend's head go into a body bag. I couldn't see friends with legs blown off. By drinking, I numbed it. I did that for years. I moved everywhere. Two marriages kaput. I say today now that it's all over, "If they made it, I took it or drunk it somewhere along the way." I battled around like that for all through the '70s. I lived in California, I lived in Arizona, I lived in Tennessee, I lived in Colorado, I lived in Florida, and I lived in Louisiana. People would make me mad. If bosses yelled at me on the job, I'd just walk off. I couldn't hold a job. I just couldn't do it.

When you do things like that and you see things like that, you just don't forget them. They don't go away and they don't fade. Those guys, they'll never fade from me. They're as fresh in my mind as they were the day it happened. I mourn those guys just as much. I went to the Vietnam Veterans Memorial in D.C., and that was the most emotional time in my entire life. That includes the birth of my kids. I reached a little closure but I cried a whole lot. To look up those guys' names. I see them and they are nineteen years old. They're always young to me.

9 Brown Water Navy

"I treasure the memories: the travel and the shipmates. That was good. I don't regret that. But the Vietnam experience was bitter and the grief just eats at me to this day..."— Ken McGwin

From the early years of the conflict, South Vietnam's extensive network of rivers, canals, and inlets necessitated a central role for what was termed the "Brown Water Navy" — smaller patrol boats, troop carriers, and gunboats used by the United States to secure inland and coastal waterways. As Edward J. Marolda has noted, "Throughout the country the road and rail system was rudimentary while the waterways provided ready access to the most important resources. The side that controlled the rivers and canals controlled the heart of South Vietnam."[1] With Operation Market Time, begun in March 1965, the United States focused its early coastal efforts on interfering with NVA/NLF (North Vietnamese Army/National Liberation Front) supply lines, seeking to cordon off South Vietnam with minesweepers, destroyers, and patrol gunboats so that enemy troops could not receive supplies. The importance of Vietnam's inland waterways, however, made it clear that coastal operations alone would be insufficient. The United States thus expanded its efforts to include extensive riverine operations throughout the country via Operation Game Warden, establishing the River Patrol Force on December 18, 1965, to further disrupt NVA/NLF logistical support. By 1968, this River Patrol Force consisted of five river divisions, each composed of two ten-boat sections that operated from both fixed and floating bases in South Vietnam's major rivers. These divisions included river patrol boats (RPBs) and landing ship tanks (LSTs), along with helicopter air support units.[2]

U.S. river operations, however, did not simply seek to shut down enemy supply lines; with the creation of the joint Army-Navy Mobile Riverine Force (MRF) in 1967, U.S./ARVN (Army of the Republic of Vietnam) forces also focused on active river combat to destroy enemy troops. In particular, the MRF was well suited for combat in the Mekong Delta, which had little open

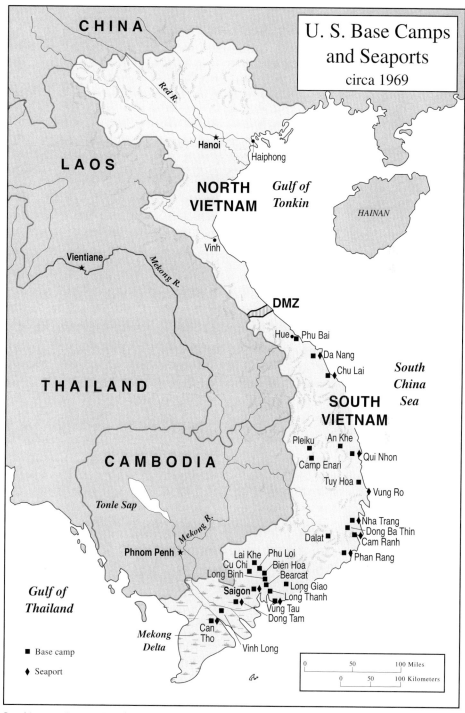

U. S. Base Camps
and Seaports
circa 1969

CHINA

Red R.

Hanoi

Haiphong

LAOS

NORTH
VIETNAM

*Gulf of
Tonkin*

HAINAN

Vientiane

Mekong R.

Vinh

DMZ

Hue Phu Bai

Da Nang

Chu Lai

*South
China
Sea*

THAILAND

SOUTH
VIETNAM

CAMBODIA

Pleiku   An Khe

Qui Nhon

Camp Enari

Tuy Hoa   Vung Ro

Tonle Sap

Mekong R.

Nha Trang
Dong Ba Thin
Cam Ranh

Dalat

Phan Rang

Phnom Penh

Lai Khe   Phu Loi
Cu Chi   Bien Hoa
Long Binh   Bearcat
Saigon   Long Giao
Long Thanh
Vung Tau
Dong Tam

*Gulf of
Thailand*

Can
Tho

*Mekong
Delta*

Vinh Long

■ Base camp

♦ Seaport

| 0 | 50 | 100 Miles |
| 0 | 50 | 100 Kilometers |

Patti Isaacs, Parrot Graphics

land and was laced with waterways. In the Mekong Delta, the MRF worked out of both a mobile floating base and the larger logistical complex at Dong Tam, which included barracks, mess halls, repair facilities, and waterfront facilities built especially for MRF forces.[3] MRF watercraft, which ranged from LSTs to smaller patrol crafts (PCF, also known as swift boats) and RPBs, included an air support component and carried both infantry and artillery to ground fighting, laid down gunfire to support land troops, and provided logistical and medical support.

In 1968, under Vice Admiral Elmo R. Zumwalt, the U.S. Navy emphasized and expanded its operations in the Mekong Delta area through Operation SEALORDS (Southeast Asia Lake, Ocean, River, and Delta Strategy). Working with the South Vietnamese Navy and U.S./ARVN ground forces, the U.S. Navy sought to extend its reach deep into the Mekong Delta to disrupt enemy bases and block enemy supply lines that extended into Cambodia.[4] SEALORDS focused on integrating U.S. and South Vietnamese soldiers and increasingly became the focal point of U.S. river strategy. Like previous operations, SEALORDS utilized both water- and aircraft, ranging from patrol and minesweeping boats to armed transports to armed helicopters. Moreover, PCFs took over patrol operations along the major rivers of the delta, freeing "the RPBs for operations along the previously uncontested smaller rivers and canals," and enabling penetration of former NLF strongholds.[5] River combat in Vietnam was exhausting and dangerous, as soldiers stretched far into enemy territory and faced enemy troops who were increasingly skilled at assaulting river forces. As veteran Ken McGwin notes, "It was very deadly work."

Mike Demske, De Pere (Navy, Coastal Division 11)
Michael Hoks, Menasha (Navy, River Assault Division 112)
Ken McGwin, Montello (Navy, Seventh Fleet Amphibious Force)

MIKE DEMSKE I was born and raised in De Pere. I went to school at UW–La Crosse for one year and decided that college wasn't for me. It was either be drafted or enlist, so I enlisted in the Navy [because] I wanted to be a gunner's mate. I wanted to be on the smaller boats. In swift boat school they taught us survival, evasion, resistance, and escape. They took us up into the Cleveland National Forest behind Camp Pendleton and dumped us for a week to

Engineman Ken Ehrhart and gunner's mate Mike Demske, March 1969. Ehrhart is pictured left, Demske right. *Mike Demske*

survive. All they gave us was a survival knife, a canteen of water, and a parachute to use as a sleeping bag. At the end, they captured us, put us in a prison camp, and tortured us for several days.

I arrived in Vietnam early February of 1968, right during the Tet Offensive. I remember listening to all the mortar rounds going off and rockets and everything in Saigon, wondering, "What the hell did I get myself into?" I mean it was just unbelievable.

MICHAEL HOKS Senior year of high school, 1966, I went to St. Mary's–Menasha. In April I was sworn into the Navy. I graduated in May. I was in boot camp in July, and I was assigned to a fleet tug in October after boot camp. I knew I was going to be drafted. I didn't have the money for college. My dad was in the Navy and I thought it would be nice to follow in the tradition. I also chose the Navy because I thought I would get three meals a day, avoid Vietnam, and end up with enough money for college.

I volunteered for Vietnam because they put me on a fleet tug for three months. They called it Building 100. It never moved and it was very repetitious and boring duty. I did not join the Navy to be stationed at Building 100. I was the first one to put my hand up when they asked for volunteers

Eighteen-year-old Michael Hoks rests near Vung Tau on the South China Sea coast. *Michael Hoks*

for Vietnam. I thought I was going to be stationed on an aircraft carrier or at Da Nang, unloading supply ships. We were the first river division over there, which is something I hadn't heard of, but apparently, that's what I volunteered for.

On January 2, at approximately 4:40 in the morning, someone came through and started tipping bunks over and telling us to get outside and assemble on the grinder for calisthenics. At 4:40 in the morning, I'm not too awake. We went out there and started doing jumping jacks and sit-ups and push-ups and we ran around the base for about forty-five minutes. They fed us breakfast and welcomed us for volunteering for river warfare, survival, and reconnaissance training. It was a real eye-opener at that time of the morning.

KEN McGWIN In 1967 in Marquette County, there wasn't much choice with the draft. The pool was not large up there and so it was inevitable that you were going to go. I had chosen not to go to college; I knew everything already. A friend of mine had gone into the Navy and I thought, "Maybe this would be a great thing to do." I had visions of the Mediterranean, France, Spain, and Greece. I was very wrong on that. I went into the Navy and took the basic training at Great Lakes, and I was assigned to my first ship out of San Diego, California. I remember the recruiter telling me that I should be in aviation, and I give myself credit — I was at least smart enough to realize that I wasn't going to be flying a plane.

After boot camp was over, I got assigned to a ship out of San Diego. It was the USS *Vancouver*, an LPD [landing platform dock], a big ship that could go into the beach, stern first, ballast down, drop a huge gate, and -unload tanks and troops. It also had a helicopter pad and I was assigned to that. I was transferred off the Vancouver early in 1968. I went to the *Westchester County* and then on to the Army-Navy Mobile Riverine Force. We were amphibious forces, so it was part of the persona that we would operate near the coast or on the coast. We were all young and it was differ-

Ken McGwin, left, enjoys a beer with his buddy. The men were allowed two beers during their break. *Ken McGwin*

ent and so we were apprehensive but still excited to be taking part. On the *Westchester County*, I decided that I was going to take the test for machinist's mate. I somehow passed the test and became a third class petty officer and then a machinist's mate. I went from the *Westchester County* to the *Tripoli*, which is a helicopter carrier. I was back out on the deep water, which was enjoyable, and I treasure the memories: the travel and the shipmates. That was good. I don't regret that. But the Vietnam experience was bitter and the grief just eats at me to this day and it's...I guess I struggle with the guilt that I survived when so many others didn't. I just cannot move beyond that. It just eats at me. It's gotten worse over the years. It's just my demon to struggle with.

MICHAEL HOKS Training was over and then we got a little bit of leave time, so I came back home and then we went down to San Diego, went up to Alameda, [and] hopped on a C-147 four-engine turbo-prop plane that looked like a peach crate the Wright brothers threw away. We proceeded across the Pacific, and every time we saw a piece of land we would stop for repairs to make sure that all the engines were somewhat in sync. One engine had a smoking problem, one had an oil leakage problem, one prop was just fluttering, and the fourth one was like a brand-new Pratt-Whitney. We were all praying for that one engine. We get over Saigon and a guy walks through the fuselage and says, "Put your head between your knees, we're taking a lot of flak and machine guns. They're going to take us in for a dive landing." I am thinking, "This is unreal." You could see the tracers and feel the effects of the flak going off, jostling the airplane around. I thought, "I'm not putting my head between my knees. I'm going to sit up and watch this, if I am buying it. I haven't even gotten in the country yet, and I am just about done in." The plane started coming down and making all this noise, and the flak picked up and [we] see the tracers outside the window. All of a sudden you could hear the screech of tires and brakes on the runway and everybody's

Gunboats debark on river patrol.
Ken McGwin

head pops up. And I'm looking around, and I'm thinking, "Well, we made it this far." That was my introduction to Vietnam, and to realizing that I volunteered for a somewhat risky situation.

We landed at Tan Son Nhat Air Force Base. From there, we went down to Vung Tau where we met up with the Navy fleet and they had our boats alongside the boats in the water. It was the first real time that we got to look at the actual boat. All of the training had been in the LCM-6s, which did not have the guns or the structure that we were introduced to in Vietnam. We had to paint the boat, mount the guns and a lot of the other equipment, and then get our supplies. The boat was void of everything that you would need to go out on a mission. The first few weeks were very intensified, with just making sure things would work.

We got the boats ready and for the first couple of days after things were ready, we just sat near Vung Tau. My first impression was this was a very, very poor, stinky country. The area we worked was called the IV Corps, which was the very southern part of Vietnam where the Mekong River had its tributaries and emptied into the South China Sea bay area. That was pretty much completely water. Ninety-nine percent of any movement was done on the rivers in the form of junks and sampans. And the Vietcong were running everything down through Laos and Cambodia and then getting on the rivers and transporting it back into Vietnam. It was our job to get the Army in place where we knew there was a heavy concentration of North Vietnamese. It was our job to get them there, to give them gun support, medical evacuation, [and] complete evacuation when the operation was over or if something went wrong. We also had communication with Army artillery. We could call in and pinpoint an artillery strike with the howitzer cannons. With all the firepower and everything we had over there, you'd think we would've been able to take care of business, but the majority of the fighting was in tunnels and jungles, where half the time you didn't even see what was there until hell broke loose.

A swift boat is an aluminum craft. It's fifty feet long, thirteen feet wide, and eleven feet high. It's got two Detroit 1271s to propel it. There were bunks on board. Originally it was designed to haul equipment out to oil rigs in the Gulf of Mexico, but they were modified. They put a gun tub on it and then set it up so you could have the mortar and the .50-caliber on the back. We were trained for all of the jobs because there were only five enlisted and one officer on the boat. If the engineman should go down, we all had to know how to get home. If the gunner's mate should go down, we all had to know how to repair and clean the .50s and the M-16s.

KEN McGWIN The LST is about 460 feet long, flat-bottom ship, quite slow. It was an old ship at the time. It was built in 1951 or '52 in Manitowoc. They were diesel powered, not steam-driven ships like the bigger surface vessels at that time. The LSTs had that unusual mission of being able to go up on the beaches or being able to navigate the waters of the Mekong, far up into the delta where other Navy ships could not go. The Mekong is a huge river and we traveled with the tides when the tides would allow us to move around. We supplied the armored gunboats, the Tangos, and the very heavily armored troop carriers. They operated on the river so they were pretty limited in what cover they could take, too. It was very deadly work.

PCF 94 cruising at top speed near An Thoi, Vietnam. *Mike Demske*

MIKE DEMSKE When we first got there, we got there as a crew and we stayed together. It was mainly just patrolling along the coast and inspecting junks. At night a lot of fishermen would be out there and we'd check them, make sure their papers were correct and stuff. My job specifically was gunner's mate, so I would take care of the guns. My responsibility was to make sure every gun on board worked.

When we first got there the main job was called [Operation] Market Time. We were supposed to patrol and prevent any infiltration of medical supplies, food, and ammunition to the VC. They would try and sneak it in via the ocean, and our job was to stop that. When Admiral Zumwalt took over as head of the Navy in Vietnam, everything changed in a hurry. We became river runners, looking for stockpiles of supplies that had come down the Ho Chi Minh Trail. If we found something, then we would try and set up an ambush and intercept it when it came into Vietnam. We were not allowed to go into Cambodia.

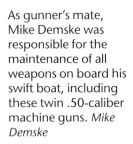

As gunner's mate, Mike Demske was responsible for the maintenance of all weapons on board his swift boat, including these twin .50-caliber machine guns. *Mike Demske*

Tango Boat 112-3 conducts a security patrol around barracks ships off the coast of Vietnam. *Michael Hoks*

MICHAEL HOKS They really had just a generalized idea of what we were. It's a seven-man crew; you had a boat captain, the coxswain that drove the boat, two gunners, a radioman, and two enginemen. This was the first type of a craft ever constructed like this. It was converted from an LCM-6, which is a Mike-6 boat. In World War II most people remember the boats going up on the beach, dropping a ramp, and the Army guys running off. That's exactly what we were on; however, it was totally refitted with .50-calibers and M-18 grenade launchers on each side and a 20-millimeter machine gun in the back. The well deck area, which was right behind the ramp, was covered with a urethane-coated canvas. We could haul a platoon of Army men in that well deck, get them where they wanted to go, drop the ramp, drop them off, and let them go off on their own.

KEN McGWIN We interacted with the guys on the gunboats all the time because they would tie up alongside the LST and they would come aboard for meals or to get some clean clothes. We would refuel and try to repair if they had engine problems. At night they would circle [and] drop grenades in the water to try to keep the Vietcong from being able to swim out there and do damage with mines or explosive charges. With the *Westchester County*, we were not entirely successful. They managed to get through anyway. On November 1, 1968, in the early morning hours there were two tremendous explosions. [The VC] had managed to get out there [and] fasten charges on both sides of the ship. The charges on one side did not go off. It was bad enough as it was. We ended up with twenty-five dead. It was a horrendous event. It just stays in your mind and you can hear, and you can smell it...

I was in the boiler room. I had the one boiler online and I was distilling water, making fresh water, for the ship. I think it was sometime after three o'clock in the morning as I recall. I had just about had my time in on the watch that night. I would have been back in my rack in a couple hours. There was this tremendous explosion and I did not know what had happened. I couldn't get anybody on the telephone between the compartments or anything. I waited for someone to come down because they had sounded general quarters for the ship: "Man battle stations." No one came down there to take over for me because I had a different battle station. I eventually decided, "Well, I have to see what in the hell's going on here," so I went out of the fire room onto the main deck. I just couldn't believe what was going on. It was dark and we still didn't realize the extent of what was going on. We manned our repair station and got ready to do whatever we would have to do, but the damage was on the starboard side [opposite ours].

MIKE DEMSKE You'd go in at night and put [the boat] up on the riverbank and sit there. We would not wear boots. We'd wear five pair of socks. Everything we wore was black. We didn't even wear dog tags because we didn't want the jingling noise. When you'd hear a motor running, you'd yell and turn the lights on and be ready to shoot if you had to. You'd intercept a lot of VC tax collectors. They would go into these villages and make villagers pay them with either food supplies or money.

The rivers made the job a little bit more hazardous. I think 75 percent of the people that were on the boats were killed or wounded. The jungle went right up to the riverbanks. A lot of times we couldn't even turn around. We'd have to back out of some of the streams that we went down. That's when Admiral Zumwalt ordered the use of Agent Orange. I don't know if it was actually Agent Orange, but it was one of the toxic defoliants. They worked real well. I remember the first time we went down the river after they sprayed it, you'd swear you were on the moon. There was nothing alive. It did move the VC back further, so it saved a lot of lives. Admiral Zumwalt's son was on swift boats and he ended up dying from cancer from exposure to Agent Orange. The Admiral said if he had to do it all over again, he'd still use it because it gave us all thirty more years to live. A lot of us suffer from diabetes because of exposure to it. Our immune systems were knocked down to next to nothing because of it. We were young and dumb and we didn't know what its effects would be. I don't think the Navy knew. We would tie our clothes on a rope and throw them in the prop to wash because it was the only way we had at cleaning our clothes. The river was full of Agent Orange and we didn't know it. But they had to shoot at us from much greater distance because of it and that was a godsend. It saved a lot of lives.

The U.S. government put out a notice that we weren't allowed to shoot unless we were fired on first. A lot of times we didn't know they were there and all of a sudden, "Whoom!" The day we were sunk, May 5, 1969, North Vietnamese regulars hit us. We were there for twelve hours before we got towed out. They were still shooting at us when we left. If the VC hit you, it was usually a thirty-second firefight and they'd disappear. They weren't well trained like the North Vietnamese were.

MICHAEL HOKS A general day when you had an operation would start at about 6:00 or 7:00 in the morning when you'd get up and make sure that everything was in working order. The engines, the guns, the radios, the ramp; you'd do a complete checkout on the boat. You'd make sure all your supplies were in place; all your ammo was fed into the machine gun properly. Around midnight or a little before, we'd go up to the barrack ships and pick up the Army men, load them on the boat, which at times could be extremely risky depending on how fast the current was going out. You had the pontoon going up and down, the ship going up and down, and you had the boat going up and down. So we would stand on the little bit of deck plate between the sidebar armor and the well deck and help these guys get on, because if they fell into the Mekong with their packs on, it was not a good situation because of the weight factor. We would get them on the boat, and then we would assemble with the rest of the boats. Then we would go single file into various river areas.

Sometimes the rivers were nice and wide, and sometimes they got so narrow, you could just about touch brush on either side of the boat. The boat measured fifty-six feet long and seventeen and a half feet wide. But with two engines and two rudders, you could make the boat go sideways down the river or stay in one place and make a circle. It was very, very maneuverable, but you had to have enough area to turn fifty-six feet around. Once the Army was on the boat, we would get to where they wanted to go. Before dropping them off, we would saturate the jungle area and the beach area with machine-gun fire and mortar rounds. Then we would go in and drop them off, drop the ramp and help them off the boat. We would just stay in the area, and when they confronted any enemy action, they would radio back to us, and if we could help with machine guns or the mortars, that was our immediate duty. Otherwise, they'd give us coordinates, and we would have the howitzers or the flyboys come in. On a lot of the operations we had helicopter coverage overhead. Overhead they could see a lot more than what we could. They could actually pinpoint some of the bunkers and some of the areas where they were dug in. There were times when we would be going down the river, and all hell would break loose, and we couldn't even see them.

I remember one particular time, we were last boat in line, and it was a heated situation, very occupied. I looked up through the slot in my gun mount, and I saw this [U.S.] helicopter dive straight down within fifty yards in front of me. All of a sudden he let go with four rockets, and a bunker right in front of me completely exploded. There was a massive explosion and ammunition and guns and bodies flying in the air. I never knew they were there. If it wasn't for that helicopter, I don't want to think about what might have happened. We were the target. We were very thankful for the helicopter coverage, many times in those situations.

KEN McGWIN We eventually decided someone had to go and find out what was going on. I went with one other guy. We got over to the other side [of the ship] and realized we were definitely under attack. We were taking fire at first, but the gunboats opened up and they were able to suppress that in a hurry. There were many, many dead and many, many people hurt. We tried to find them and get the ones that were alive out of there if we could. We couldn't get to some. They died, I suppose. We just couldn't get to them in time. We couldn't use torches to cut people out because of the diesel fuel; it was vaporized in the air. I was just choking with the steam, and then smoke, and the darkness. You could hear people struggling to get out.

Most of the senior petty officers were killed. Younger, lower-ranking petty officers had to take charge, and the crew was just magnificent. Everybody did what he was supposed to do. There was no running around blindly and no one lost his composure. Everybody stood and fought back with everything they had, and it was a hard thing to do. It was a tremendous explosion, just unbelievable. In those compartments that were affected by the explosion, there was no light. In the areas where men were trapped, there was no light there and we only had battle lanterns. Some of the battle lanterns worked but otherwise we had to use flashlights and be able to try to find them like that. It was time-consuming and much harder to get to people. We had one corpsman aboard the ship. He was a first-class hospitalman and I know that he got a Silver Star. I never saw him again after I left the ship. He was horribly wounded. He was in bad shape and he never stopped. He never stopped until everybody that he could help was helped. The Silver Star was not enough. He should have had a Congressional Medal of Honor for that. I guess it's all these years have gone by now and it doesn't matter any more. I hope he's still alive and I hope he's had a good life.

I can't tell you these things, what it looked like. I can't believe that humans can do that to each other. At the time, you just wonder, "What in hell has the world come to?" I felt myself just kind of spiraling downward into a black hole. "We're not going to live through this night. We're not going to get out of here." We did because everybody did his job. They did what they were trained to do. They did everything they could, as hard as they could, and we survived the night. To see people just torn to pieces… I just, I can't…

MIKE DEMSKE We were as far south as you could get on the southern tip of Vietnam. Admiral Zumwalt had the brilliant idea of building a base on barges in Ca Mau Province. On Easter of 1969, we went in, reestablished a base, and it became known as "Seafloat." That was right in the heart of Charlie's domain. They did not like us being in there. They weren't happy to see us at all.

It was early in the morning. We were the lead boat. We usually would hit the mouth of the river at dawn. That's what we tried to do. We were several miles up the river and all of a sudden all hell broke loose. We took two recoilless rifle rounds in the engine room. It blew out both of our engines. We took a B-40 rocket hit up in the bow and that started everything on fire. We were the only boat that day that really took any substantial fire. The first thing we had to do was get all the ammo off 'cause there were fires onboard. We got the fires put out and we had to work on damage control. When the rockets hit us, it lifted us straight up in the air. Other rockets hit under us, so we had holes mushrooming from the inside out and from the outside in. We had to patch all of those. We had wooden cones that you'd drive in as best you could to plug the holes. If they [the holes] were too big, we'd use mattresses and blankets. We were there for twelve hours.

We had some Vietnamese troops onboard, and they went out and set up a perimeter. And one of the guys from one of the other boats went with them, and he ended up getting killed. He was the only one that died that day. I had on a ceramic chest and back protector. It was the first time I ever wore one. I had five rounds slam into my back. I didn't know that the bullets had hit me in the back until well after the fact when we looked at my protector and it was all in pieces. I was pretty lucky that day. Some sniper had me in his sights and probably couldn't figure out why I wouldn't go down. Helicopters came in and brought us pumps so we could pump the water out. They took away the badly wounded. They came back and helped escort us when we finally got towed out twelve hours later. With no engines, we'd turned for the beach, and two boats pulled alongside of us and got us to the riverbank where we ended up sinking. It was a long, long day.

MICHAEL HOKS Sometimes when we were running along rice paddies, you could see quite a ways in. Then there were times where the banks were actually taller than us, and on top of the banks and along the river there was vegetation and tree growth. If we had to drop them off in something like that, that's when the machine guns really came into play, because you could do a sweep and knock over a lot of the trees and the brush. Another primary reason for saturating the beach and the bank was to detonate any mines that they had set up. They were very good with the mines as I personally found out on one patrol. We were running a patrol out of Dong Tam, going up the Xang [Canal]. Our boat was the lead boat, and we were the mine-sweepers. We proceeded down the river and came across a little village, and they were all sitting on the bank having a picnic lunch. I remember saying to the boat captain, I said, "This isn't good at all." We got approximately a quarter mile out of that village, and our boat was blown up. We were extensively damaged. We lost one .50-caliber with the Mike-18 grenade launcher on it. A gunner's mate in that particular gun mount was ejected over the side. The engine room was torn open completely from the bottom. Both engines collapsed, so we had no way of moving, other than with the current. Those village people on the bank, they knew what was going to happen. It was entertainment. It would be like us going to the outdoor theater and setting up and having our soda pop and our popcorn. I told the boat captain, I said, "Something's not right. It's not a good situation." And sure enough, our number was up that day and we bought it. The minesweeping gear was jammed into the bottom of the river, which held us up and acted like an anchor. The 20-millimeter ran on electricity and all the batteries were blown out. Out of the crew, seven were hurt, one was missing who went over with the gun mount, three were knocked out and unconscious. I, along with two other ones, managed to send a radio message after coming to from being knocked unconscious to let them know what happened.

The engineman got in the .50[-caliber] and I guarded the open part of the boat that was missing with our personal firearms: shotguns and M-16s. We thought for sure that this was going to be a rocket attack since we were the first boat, but we were so far ahead of the other boats. The gunner decided to surface and take his chances instead of drowning. The gunner's mate ended up going to the bottom of the river. He said later, he was at the bottom of the river, and he didn't know if he should just stay there and drown or come up and get shot at because we thought for sure it was an ambush. Everybody who was injured survived and came back to duty. The next boat that they hit with a mine was a Tango boat, and they had five hundred pounds of TNT. Out of seven crewmembers, six were KIA and one is a quadriplegic. I feel very, very fortunate to be the first boat to get mined. Maybe we were the test boat for them to see what they could do.

[Anyway,] the boat that came alongside [to assist us] was boat Tango 13 and my friend Lester Schneider from Milwaukee was on that boat. It was nice to see his boat and make sure that we were going to get back to Dong Tam for repairs. I thought for sure that we'd be eating some RPG B-40 rockets. I tied us to the other boat, and they pulled us back to Dong Tam. We spent two months in repairs. While we were in Dong Tam on a repair barge, we ended up every night getting a mortar attack. After the third night, I could sleep through them and not hear the siren to go into the bunkers. I would just sleep through them. That was a very big advantage, for obvious reasons, except for if the mortar landed where I was sleeping.

KEN McGWIN When daylight finally came, we were able to figure out what to do and how many were killed and how many were wounded. There were some who weren't found until later on. Their bodies had been washed away. We were able to use the tides to beach the ship way up on the bank, and the Seabees came in and welded patches as best they could. After a few days, they made it what they considered to be seaworthy and we got out of there. We steamed down out of the river and back and then all the way back to Japan. We got into heavy seas and patches broke off. For a while we thought we were going to lose it in the South China Sea, but again people did what they were supposed to do, and we made it. We got back to Japan.

So that was the *Westchester County* incident. Of all my memories of Vietnam, I can just focus right back in on that one night. We took it pretty hard that night. I hope that the ones who survived all have had good lives. There have been a number who have died of cancer, and I think that there is some evidence that Agent Orange was part of that equation. It just makes you wonder, "Well, they died over there and they didn't realize it." It just took longer.

MIKE DEMSKE It's really strange. It's like your soul leaves your body. And you're looking down and you can see everything that's happening. I think we were so well trained as a crew that we knew what everybody else was doing. It was like I could visualize it all. When it was over, it was as if your soul descended back into your body and you were back to reality. Sometimes you'd shake so hard you couldn't get a cigarette in your mouth after the fact.

That was the first time that we really ran into the NVA. That was different. They just kept hammering at us all day. Jets flying cover for us killed over twenty of them with napalm. They were dropping the napalm across the river from us, and we had to bury our faces every time they would drop it because we could feel the heat. The [South] Vietnamese Army was not quite as stable. They weren't as well trained. We didn't enjoy working with them as much as we did the mercenaries. You never knew what they were going to do. I remember we had some brand-new swift boats that came over that were turned over to the [South] Vietnamese Navy. One day we had gotten in a firefight up near the Cambodian border. We called them to come in because we were running out of mortar rounds, and they came after much chatter on the radio. We jumped onboard, opened up their mortar box, and it was full of fishnets. They had dumped their mortar rounds overboard and were using it as a fishing vessel, so we didn't have a lot of faith in them. We never called them for assistance after that. It just wasn't worth it.

The boats got painted darker and darker. After I left they actually started painting the boats green, so they blended in better. You can always hear a swift boat coming. I mean they made enough noise with those two Detroit diesel engines that you weren't going to sneak up on anybody. River water craft were a lot smaller. Most of them were just little wooden, one-man canoes with a putt-putt motor on the back. They'd use them as transport on the maze of canals. The canals were incredible. I don't know when they were built or how they were built, but they'd go on for miles. They were hard to navigate for us because they were so shallow. That's where the RPBs [river patrol boats] came in. They ran on a Jacuzzi system just like a Jet Ski today. The water shot out the back for propulsion. They could go through six inches of water if they had to. We couldn't do that. We needed at least two feet, preferably more.

MICHAEL HOKS The Army guys called us Navy guys river rats. I can see why because all I wore was combat boots and boxer shorts. It was ninety degrees out with 90 percent humidity. No laundry facility. No bathroom facility on the boat whatsoever. No toilet. No shower. When we would get alongside

Task Force 117's patch depicts a water dragon. *Michael Hoks*

the ship and think we'd have a few hours or a day or two to replenish, we'd try to go up there and take a shower, and the line would be really long. I think I had a total of three showers in the six months that I was in Vietnam off of the ship and maybe one meal cooked on a ship. One day we got very lucky. A supply boat came alongside the pontoons. Out of the front of the supply boat, they were unloading apples and boxes of chocolate milk. We hadn't had any apples or chocolate milk since we left the States. I went into the back of the supply boat and got a few friends in a line. I started throwing chocolate milk and apples out of the back of the boat and they kept yelling, "That's enough, that's enough." Well, once I doubled that amount, I figured it was enough, and we sat back on a pontoon, eating our apples and drinking our chocolate milk. Some officer came down. I truly am a meek, mild-mannered, shy, sensitive, cute guy. He asked me where we got the stuff. I said, "It was issued to us by the supply ship when it came alongside." I don't know whether or not he believed me, but he said, "Well, carry on, and clean up." "Yes, sir!" So we very happily drank our chocolate milk and ate our apples.

MIKE DEMSKE I came home for Christmas. It was about 120 degrees on the tarmac at Tan Son Nhat, and it was about 30 below with windchill in Green Bay when I got home. It was tough to get used to. I shook for thirty days. I looked forward to going back, but it was hard on my parents for me to go back. A lot of us extended and served eighteen months instead of the year. I extended partly because I wanted to be there and partly because my brother was in the Navy Reserve and he was called up. They were putting a lot of those people on the Mobile Riverine boats. I thought I was better equipped, and in the Navy they won't send brothers into the same war zone unless everybody agrees to it. He got to Treasure Island and they found out that he was missing a vertebra in his back, so he got a medical discharge. It didn't matter. I was with friends and was where I wanted to be. I don't regret extending at all.

MICHAEL HOKS I got there April 13, 1967, and I left October 15, 1967, so six months and a couple days. A normal tour was one year. When they brought the replacement division in to replace the whole division of boats, they realized that we run our operations by divisions. So, if they replaced Division 91 that would be thirteen Tango boats, two monitors, and a CCB [command communication boat] of rookies. What they did was they went to the first

Seaman Michael Hoks receives his Navy Commendation Medal from commanding officer Captain R. J. Norman. *Michael Hoks*

three boats of each division and asked if we wanted to go back to the States early. Being the somewhat intelligent individual that I am, I opted to go back to the United States. And I'm happy I did.

I [got a Purple Heart] for injuries I sustained, but the medal I'm really proud of is the Navy Commendation Medal with a "V." The *V* stands for "valor." The Purple Heart is actually a higher-rated medal, but to me, I was just in the wrong place at the wrong time. The Commendation Medal with "V" for Valor, that was me doing my job above and beyond what I was expected to do. So, that one to me personally rates higher.

KEN MCGWIN I always have a hard time on November 1, because I can't help but think about what happened that day. My wife said something about, "God will take care." I said, "Well, where the hell was God that night?" She said, "Well, he was with you." I guess he was, but I don't know, why me? That was the largest single loss of life for the Navy and I have often

Young seamen on Ken McGwin's ship, mugging for the camera.
Ken McGwin

wondered how on earth I ended up over there on that night. You think back to your life before that and the things that you did [to get there]. It's the same thing with all the ones who died. What strange twists and turns took them down that road to die on a jungle river on the other side of the world? There is not a more intense human experience. I've always told my wife that the Vietnam War was a horrible, horrible weight to put on the backs of teenagers. What did they do to a generation of people? I've tried to live a decent life to honor those guys who died that night. No matter how I try, I can't shake that guilt that I have. I thought when I was younger that as I got older, it wouldn't bother me anymore. But it does. It gets worse. I just think about how I've had the chance to have a good life and they never did. They never had a chance.

10 Brother Duty

"We got rocketed and mortared all the time. Imagine that happening and both of us were killed at the same time . . . The antiwar [protesters], especially in Wisconsin — what would've happened when the news got out?"— Marvin Acker

As David L. Anderson has noted, "there is no one description that typifies the experience of American soldiers in Vietnam."[1] The nature of the war within South Vietnam differed from region to region: soldiers in the 101st Airborne stationed in I Corps, like the Acker brothers whose story is told here, endured intense, almost trenchlike hill fighting against NVA (North Vietnamese Army) troops. Others searched for guerrilla soldiers in the low, flat marshes of the Mekong Delta, while the battles of the Tet Offensive were marked by intense urban combat.[2] The terrain in Vietnam varied from coastal lowlands and rice paddies to river deltas to mountaintops set amidst thick jungle canopy. Moreover, not all soldiers deployed to Vietnam saw combat. In 1967, only 14 percent of the troops in Vietnam were combat troops, while others served in a variety of support, intelligence, and leadership positions.[3] For example, after serving in combat doing dangerous reconnaissance work, Marvin Acker worked at Camp Eagle, the main base for the 101st Airborne in I Corps. Located near the city of Hue, Camp Eagle was still a part of Vietnam, yet life on base contrasted sharply with the daily grind, fear, and danger of combat. Large established bases like Camp Eagle served as an oasis within the war: in 1971, amenities at various installations included ninety service clubs, seventy-one swimming pools, twelve beaches, thirty tennis courts, and 337 libraries.[4] Six miles away from Camp Eagle was Eagle Beach, a popular site for in-country R&R.

Regardless of the chance to temporarily escape the fighting, Vietnam was a war with no clear front lines; the enemy had the capability to attack anywhere. Even large-scale bases were vulnerable to infiltration, booby traps, bombs, and mortar fire.[5] As one veteran later stated, "Complete safety was always relative in Vietnam."[6] Most combat soldiers spent months in the field, enduring together the common experiences of war — danger, fear, and pain, and often killing and death.[7] Fighting in Vietnam required a continued series of readjustments, as men were thrown from life at home into strains of combat among strangers. The average age of a U.S. soldier in Vietnam was around twenty, six to seven years younger than the average age in World War II.[8] Like the Acker brothers, many men entered the military directly after high school, thrust into war at the age of eighteen or nineteen. While the Navy allowed family members to request service on the same ship, the Army generally did not allow siblings to serve together, particularly in dangerous combat situations. Though many soldiers were critical of their commanding officers — many officers, but not all, used Vietnam as a means to build their military careers — they formed close bonds with the other men in their units. As General Volnay Warner stated, "soldiers fight and die for one another, not for country or even 'Ma' and 'apple pie.'"[9] The relationships that soldiers developed on the ground thus stood as a central element of each soldier's individual Vietnam experience, giving the war a sense of purpose that it often seemed to lack.

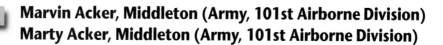

Marvin Acker, Middleton (Army, 101st Airborne Division)
Marty Acker, Middleton (Army, 101st Airborne Division)

MARVIN ACKER I grew up on a dairy farm in Middleton and did a lot of hard work milking cows every morning and every night. Instead of going to high school like average people, my twin brother and I decided we wanted to become priests. We spent all four years of our high school in a seminary. After spending all those years on the farm and all those years in seclusion in the seminary, we decided we needed action. We wanted to see the world. I volunteered for the Army because I always wanted to become a paratrooper. I wanted to get into the 101st. I went first because Marty wanted to spend the summer up in the Dells having a good time.

After I got my wings, I got sent back to Fort Campbell and we trained for Vietnam. They had openings for reconnaissance in E Company. I volunteered for that. It was a very dangerous job. You had your line companies who went out to the field to fight the enemy. Recon looked for the enemy. In Vietnam, a lot of our work was at night trying to find where the enemy was. Once we found the enemy, we would call in the line companies. In the

In the words of Marvin Acker, "What Airborne does best—jump." *Marvin Acker*

morning the choppers would come into that village and attack the group of Vietcong or NVA who we'd found.

MARTY ACKER Marvin was already a paratrooper. Two buddies of mine and I decided to join the Army together. So we got basic training together. We went to jump school at Fort Benning, Georgia. I knew paratrooper school was going to be a tough course, but I didn't know it was going to be that tough. You never walked to a class or walked to a training center. You ran. The instructors were very tough. Jump school was 1968, which was probably the worst year in Vietnam. They needed men and they needed men right away. Like Marvin, I wanted to be 101st Airborne Screaming Eagle. I didn't want to be the 82nd. I didn't want to be 173rd. It had to be the 101st. You didn't get to pick. When I did get the 101st, I was overjoyed. That was my dream. They sent me home for two weeks, then straight to Vietnam.

MARVIN ACKER Sometimes they would send us out in platoons, but a lot of times they would send us out in squads. You'd form an ambush in an area. You'd sit and you wait for the enemy to come to you. Sometimes that worked, and sometimes it didn't. Sometimes we found the enemy, and sometimes they found us. There was one very bad incident. I will never forget. We were in the middle of a rice paddy. There was a bamboo fence. You had the heavy woods to the left and a river to your right. It was a very narrow path maybe ten, fifteen feet wide. We climbed over this bamboo fence because there was no gate. We got to a second bamboo fence and we climbed over that. Then we got to a third one, and that was the scary one because in the middle of this bamboo fence was a woven NVA star. We knew we were in an NVA base camp. It was dark. We walked a couple of feet when somebody yelled out. For a split second there was silence and then we opened up and they opened up. It was a mad scramble backwards to get out of that area. One of our soldiers got hit in the lungs. He was right behind

Soldiers training at Fort Benning, Georgia. *Michael Chamberlain*

Marvin Acker outside his barracks, January 1968. *Marvin Acker*

me. He was in very bad shape. We couldn't go over the river. We couldn't go into the tree line. We had to go back over these fences. I remember just praying. Meanwhile they're shooting everywhere. We dragged this gentleman. We finally got into the rice paddy. The choppers came. We thought they would take us out, but instead they just took the wounded soldier out. We had to find our way back by foot. Of course, that was our job. The next day the line companies came in and attacked that base camp. But it was a very bad experience. Very scary.

We lost a lot of men in recon. I can't remember the numbers, but I think after two months there were only three of us left of the original group. You start looking at the odds. When is it going to be your turn? I kept thinking to myself, if I am going to die, I want to die looking up at the sky, and at the sun. I don't want to die in pitch darkness. That was my biggest fear. We got a new lieutenant, a "shake and bake." A shake and bake is an officer that goes to officer candidate school for a month and they send him to Vietnam. We'd been in Vietnam for three months. We had three months' experience and this guy knew nothing. We went into this small village. He didn't know if we should bring in food by chopper at this end of the village or the other end. He told me to go down the path and pace the distance between where we were and the end of the village. I looked at him, and I said, "You want me to go by myself down that path and just to do a foot count?" He said, "Yeah." I said to him, "You will never see me again." Sergeant Bruce had three or four South Vietnamese soldiers go with us. As we went down this path, we saw spider holes on each side where the Vietcong and NVA would hide. If they saw helicopters or if they [were] attacked by the air, they would go into the spider holes. So right away we knew this was enemy territory.

I remember going down the path and as I was ready to take a right because the path was going to take a sharp right-hand turn, a bullet went over my head. [My buddy] Lane had a rucksack on his back and he was trying to get into one of these spider holes. I couldn't stop laughing. I said, "Lane, your whole body is showing. Get out of that spider hole. Get behind me." I had an M-79 grenade launcher. And I was very good even though it was across the river about two hundred yards. I landed two grenades into the hooch. By that time the rest of the platoon caught up with us. We strung out across the river. There was a bamboo bridge. I hit this tree firing across the river. They are firing back. I had an M-79 grenade launcher and they had an M-79 grenade launcher. He is shooting at me and I am shooting at him. I am plunking grenades at him and he is plunking grenades back at me. One of his grenades hit the tree that I was under and I got hit by a piece of shrapnel from the down blast. This green lieutenant comes up to me and says, "Take your squad across this bridge." I said, "What!?" They had an RPD, a rapid people destroyer — a machine gun. I said, "If we cross this bridge we are going to be sitting ducks. We are wide open." He says, "Cross the bridge." I said, "I am not going to do it." Some of the men started to cross the bridge and the machine gun opened up. Two of them fell in the river. I told the lieutenant that there was a big stone wall behind us. I said, "Let's go behind that wall, and let's send in artillery." That's what we did, and then we start walking out. I didn't notice the wound in my thigh. I walked maybe a hundred steps and I fell down. I couldn't get up again. They brought in a chopper for me to take me into the medevacs to get the shrapnel out.

At that time the Second Brigade had a rule that if you got wounded twice you got taken out of combat. I said, "Great, that's fine with me." I had my commander write a letter requesting that I get out of combat duty.

When I got to the First Brigade, they said, "You're kidding. You're going out to the lines." I said, "No, I'm not, I've got this letter and I'm not going to do it." And they said, "Oh yeah, you are." So, for about a week I was on pots and pans duty. I was on guard duty, while they decided what to do with me. I got sent to the sergeant and he said, "Get on the next chopper, you're going to A Shau Valley." I looked at him; I said, "You're kidding." He goes, "No, I'm not. There's the chopper." So, I grab my rucksack and I grab my rifle and I got on that helicopter. It still bothers me today [that] that chopper was about ten feet off the ground when all of a sudden a clerk came out, going like this [motions to land]. He asked, "Is there an Acker on that chopper?" And I said, "Yes." He said, "The platoon sergeant wants to see you." I jumped out of that chopper to see him. He was testing me. That chopper got shot down. It took months before they found the chopper and the bodies. I always think about that two- or three-second delay, if it would have made a difference for those men in that chopper.

Marty Acker poses on the truss of a bridge.
Marty Acker

MARTY ACKER I didn't keep in touch with Marv at all. He wrote a couple letters here and there but was in recon so he didn't get a lot of chances to write. I knew he was in the 101st Airborne, and I knew he was at Camp Eagle.

I found out I was going to be with the Second 502 Infantry, which I was very happy [about] because it is a very proud unit from the World War II days and it was a proud unit in Vietnam. I got to Camp Eagle and first thing, a sergeant came over and said, "Fill these sandbags." I said, "I don't think so. My twin brother is somewhere in Camp Eagle and I'm going to find him." He said, "No, you're not. You're going to fill those sandbags." A captain comes by, and I explain the situation. He said, "Son, go and find your brother."

It turns out that that captain was my future commanding officer, [but] he didn't know me and I didn't know him. I'm tooling around Camp Eagle. It's a huge base. I ask[ed] everybody if they knew who Marvin Acker was. "I think he's over there," [they said], and "I think he's over there." This went on for about forty-five minutes, an hour. Finally one guy says, "He's down in that hut."

MARVIN ACKER I became noncombat at Camp Eagle and ended up becoming the brigade commander's driver, and that's what I did for the remaining part of my tour. They had a hooch gazebo and one of my jobs, around five o'clock at night, was bartender. And I would serve all of the officers of the First Brigade and they would go over the details of the operation for the next day. I got to know many officers. I'm making drinks one day and I look out the window and I see this guy walking down the hill towards me. At first I didn't think anything of it. All of the sudden, I thought, "I know that walk." It was my identical twin brother who I had no idea was in country.

Marty and Marvin Acker together at Camp Eagle — proof that both served in Vietnam at the same time. *Marvin Acker*

MARTY ACKER I go tooling down the hill towards the hut. I have no idea what to expect. I walk in the hut and sure enough, there he is, behind the bar, serving drinks. And I'm going, "Serving drinks?" I gave him a hug. I didn't notice the rest of the crowd in the hut because I was so overjoyed to see Marvin. One of the majors notices my 101st Airborne patch and goes, "Are you in the 101st Airborne?" I said "Yes, sir. Second 502 Infantry." "Here?" he asks. I said, "Yeah, here." And then everything went quiet. The colonel says, "Take care of this." That was the end of the party. So I walked out and Marvin told me to meet him later on.

MARVIN ACKER All we did was hug each other and jump around behind the bar and I started introducing him to everybody. One of the officers said, "Where are you stationed?" And he said, "Here at Camp Eagle." "With the 101st?" He goes, "Yup." And then it hit the fan. Two brothers in Vietnam at the same time in the same division in the same area. Two identical twins! So, of course there was an uproar about how this could have happened because you couldn't have two brothers in Vietnam at the same time. We had two identical twins in the same division in the same base camp at the same time. We got rocketed and mortared all the time. Imagine that happening and both of us were killed at the same time, during the turmoil of the Vietnam War. The antiwar [protesters], especially in Wisconsin — what would've happened when the news got out? That was it.

MARTY ACKER The next morning we had a meeting with the sergeant major. Sergeant majors are the hardcore of the Army. He asks, "What are you doing here? You're not supposed to be here." Marvin was with me. We went back and forth, back and forth. He said, "We're going to send you to Korea. When Marvin leaves, you're going to come back." I said, "No, I'm here now. I've already got my two days in, out of 365. I'm not leaving for Korea and coming back here in five months. I'm here now, let's get it over with." There was more back and forth, back and forth. Marvin knew Sergeant Major very well, and that's why I ended up in Echo Company, 81 Mortars, which is what I was trained for.

Marvin Acker visits Marty at his mortar position, summer 1968. *Marvin Acker*

MARVIN ACKER Marty was a mortar man, but you had to spend six months on the line before you got into mortars. I made a deal, because I knew all the brass. They wanted to take Marty out of Vietnam and put him to Korea and when I left Vietnam, they'd send him back to Vietnam. Marty was already there, though, so we made a deal that he would go straight into mortars. That's what they did. They kept that deal and they kept him in Vietnam, but they didn't have his name on the roster while I was still there. He didn't exist. As a mortar man, he was out in the mountains all the time. I didn't get to see him much. With the time I had left, maybe three or four times, but it was great to see him.

MARTY ACKER I didn't know about the brother thing. It didn't even cross my mind. The chances of both Marvin and I ending up (a) as paratroopers and (b) with the 101st Airborne was so remote. It was a big screw-up. I was told, "Take your last look at Camp Eagle. You're going to be on mountains the rest of the time you're here." It was one mountain after another. We would land on the mountaintop. Bulldozers would knock down the trees and we'd build a fire support base: bunkers, concertina wire, set up the 105s. That's where we stayed, normally about a month at a time on each mountain. It was cool to be on top of these mountains. You'd wake up in the morning and with a whole sea of clouds below you. You were a hundred feet

The ocean view made Firebase Roy a favorite of many American mortar men, including Marty Acker. *Marty Acker*

above the clouds having coffee. It was quite a beautiful sight sitting on those clouds. The bad thing was when the clouds came. It would be weeks on end that you'd be living in the clouds. It got cold. It was hard because you'd have wounded soldiers on top of your firebase and helicopters couldn't come in to get them out because it was so foggy.

I always had my rucksack filled with C rations. Everybody always made fun of me because I humped all these extra C rations. I said, "Some day, knowing the Army, we're going to need this food." Sure enough, we were socked in for three weeks and they couldn't get food and water in. We ran out of food. It was mutiny down below us with A Company. They said, "Feed us, otherwise we're coming on top of the mountain with you guys and nobody's going to be below you. You better feed us." I didn't tell anybody about the food in my rucksack. I was saving that for my squad in the last days. One day a sergeant came into our bunker area with two privates with M-16s. They made everybody stand outside by the mortar pit. He went inside, took all our rucksacks, dumped the food out. They took all my food, every bit of it. I humped that for eight months. He took it all just when I was saying, "OK, it's time to go into those emergency rations." Why didn't I hide a few cans? Of course you get the other troop some food, but you're always worried about your squad. Your squad comes first, then the platoon, and then the company.

The biggest coup the NVA could accomplish was to overrun the base camp. That was the worst possible thing that could happen because it would demoralize everybody: the infantry, all the other firebases, everybody. It was such a morale sinker to have a firebase overrun. You'd have a company of infantry manning the bunkers. You had the 105[-mm] howitzers, 4.2[-mm] mortars and 81[-mm] mortars, and a command center. When the enemy would mortar you and the firebase, everybody would go into the bunkers and foxholes and hide except for the 81[-mm] mortar men. It was a badge of honor. You had to stay out in the open and man your mortars and try to find where the enemy mortars were coming from and silence them. You had to sit out in the open and ask, "Where should we fire?" You had to wait for the Fire Director's Center to tell you, "OK, aim that way, this elevation, start firing." It was very scary being out there because you could see these mortar rounds walking towards you. You just hoped they'd go alongside of you and not right over you.

After [Hamburger Hill] they put us on Firebase Bastogne, which was one of the biggest firebases I was ever involved with on a mountain. I remember the helicopters took us out of the valley and they put us on Bastogne. I wanted to be by myself 'cause it was...I had to clear my head. I went over by the side of a hill. I saw all these rucksacks and helmets lying there. I just

One of most dangerous jobs on mountaintop firebases belonged to mortar men like Marty Acker, pictured at Firebase Boise in April 1969. *Marty Acker*

sat down and had a cigarette trying to get myself together. I'm looking at all these rucksacks and helmets and I notice the bullet holes and the blood. I'm going, "Huh, crap. All these rucksacks and helmets belong to guys who were killed or wounded. Look at them all." There were at least fifty of them. Helmets with bullet holes, shrapnel holes, helmets cut in half, rucksacks shredded. A lot of blood. I'm going, "Christ almighty. I've got to get out of here." That's when I noticed one of the rucksacks had an open flap and there was money sticking out. I grabbed the money. It was in an envelope. I said, "They are going to take these rucksacks to the rear and some guy is going to take the money." There was a picture of a girl in the envelope. He was from Spooner, Wisconsin. I still know his name. I always wanted to see if he made it. There was a letter from his girlfriend from Spooner, Wisconsin. I took the money and gave it to my lieutenant and said, "This belongs to so-and-so. Make sure he gets it."

I got out of there and went back to my main squad area, and waited for the end of my tour. I only had two months left to go. You realize it's just sixty more days. "What do I have to do to survive sixty more days?" I felt very safe at Firebase Bastogne. It was just so, so big. Two weeks after I got back to Madison, I read in the paper, "Firebase Bastogne Overrun." I went, "We're going to lose the war." How could they overrun Bastogne? It was so big with well-built bunkers. It was impossible to overrun. I went, "We're not going to win this war if they can take over Bastogne." In '68, we thought we could win the war. Every soldier over there thought we could win. People in the United States have the feeling a lot of Vietnam soldiers were lackluster, not real military. There were very, very brave men in 101st Airborne and in other divisions. We wanted to win. I saw acts of bravery. Unbelievable. But I was glad to be out.

MARVIN ACKER In my eyes, I was a patriotic American doing my job. I was not for the war. When you were in Vietnam and you saw a dead friend, you'd ask, "He died for this place? This place?" That's one side, but you are there to do a job. That's what I was sent for. You've got only you and your buddies, because no one else cares. As long as you've got your buddies, you just get through that year.

MARTY ACKER [Back in Madison] I was amazed how nothing changed. [Shakes head.] All my friends did the same things they'd done a couple years [before]. They all had sundaes and nothing at all changed. Everybody had the same talk. They talked about going to dances and going to movies and it was just like I'd left yesterday. My way of thinking had obviously changed tremendously. I went from being a kid to a veteran. They were just the same nineteen-year-old kids talking about having fun, going to the Dells and screwing around. I'm going, "Don't they know what happened?" No. They didn't know. They didn't care. If you're not in it, you don't care.

Hamburger Hill

"Whether we actually ever took it I can't really say. I can say that we were up there, but I can't ever say whether we took it because I don't think we spent ten minutes up there the whole damn time."— Ed Hardy

The battle for Hamburger Hill, which lasted from May 10 to May 20, 1969, was one of the bloodiest, most brutal battles of the Vietnam War. Though the actual name of the hill was Dong Ap Bia, it earned the more graphic name Hamburger Hill for the way it "ground up" men throughout the battle. Also known as Hill 937, Hamburger Hill is located in the A Shau Valley, a part of I Corps close to the border with Laos. Determined to take the war to this remote area, on May 10, 1969 U.S./ARVN (Army of the Republic of Vietnam) forces launched Operation Apache Snow, designed to destroy enemy bases and communications in the A Shau Valley, which NVA (North Vietnamese Army) forces had been using to move supplies, stage attacks, and escape into Laos. Calling on U.S. soldiers to redouble their efforts against the NVA in 1969, General Creighton Abrams, the commander of U.S. forces in Vietnam, emphasized the necessity of continuing "unrelenting pressure on the VC/NVA main force units. We must carry the fight to the enemy and complete his destruction."[1] As allied forces — three battalions of the 101st Airborne, along with an ARVN regiment — moved through the valley, the extent of the NVA presence became clear. Andrew Weist writes, "The rapidly rising ground was dotted with numerous spider holes, bunkers and even communication cables, suggesting the presence of an enemy force of great size."[2] Still, U.S./ARVN forces pressed forward and soon encountered fire from NVA bunkers guarding the slopes of Hill 937.

Hill 937 was ill-chosen as a site of battle. The terrain of the hill was unforgiving: steep slopes, covered with bamboo and elephant grass, surrounded by thick layers of jungle canopy. The NVA was fully ensconced on the hill, in an extensive system of concentric bunkers and tunnels that extended up to the summit. As U.S. forces sought to reach the top of the hill,

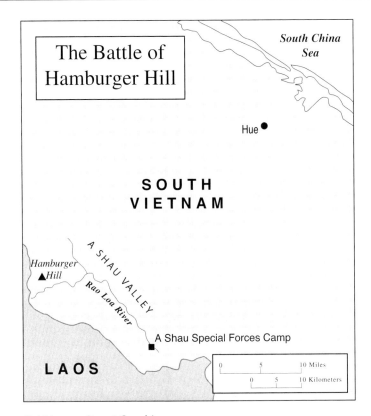

Patti Isaacs, Parrot Graphics

the fighting fell into a devastating pattern, where U.S. forces spent their days fighting uphill against a heavily entrenched enemy, pushing through difficult terrain, only to have to retreat at night to safety. Meanwhile, NVA forces used the hours of darkness to reinforce their positions, with the battle to begin again in the morning, "yielding similarly bloody and indecisive results."[3] Indeed, on May 14, U.S. forces reached the top of the hill but were unable to hold it as NVA reinforcements moved in to encircle them.

As U.S. airpower attacked Hill 937 from above, the terrain became increasingly bleak, with destruction of both NVA bunkers and surrounding jungle foliage creating further obstacles. The commander of the Third Battalion, 187th Infantry (3/187) of the 101st Airborne, Lieutenant Colonel Weldon Honeycutt, was particularly determined to confront the enemy at Hill 937, pressing U.S. forces forward into an increasingly bloody assault. Though Honeycutt hoped that the 3/187 could take the hill alone, reinforcements of U.S. and ARVN troops were called in, including the Second Battalion of the 506th Infantry. Ultimately, U.S./ARVN forces took the hill on May 20, 1969, only to abandon it two weeks later. The 3/187, which had battled for the hill for ten days, suffered heavy losses, with some companies reaching an 80 percent casualty rate.[4] Commander of the 101st Airborne, Major General Melvin Zais, later explained that "the only significance of Hill 937 was the fact that there were North Vietnamese on it. My mission was to destroy enemy forces and installations. We found the enemy on Hill 937, and that is where we fought him."[5]

The battle for Hamburger Hill received extensive press coverage in the United States, becoming emblematic of the seemingly senseless, brutal nature of the war in Vietnam. On May 19, the Associated Press described the battle in what Rick Perlstein called an "evocative dispatch": "The paratroopers came down the mountain, their green shirts darkened with sweat, their weapons gone, their bandages stained brown and red — with mud and blood."[6] The battle was also part of a striking photo essay in *Life* magazine, which showed 241 U.S. soldiers killed in Vietnam in one week. On May 30, 1969, *Time* magazine noted that "the battle for Hamburger Hill set off tremors of controversy that carried all the way to Capitol Hill."[7] Indeed, Senator Edward Kennedy, assailing the strategy that had led to such a battle, called Hamburger Hill an example of "cruelty and savagery," "senseless and irresponsible," "madness," and "symptomatic of a mentality and policy that needs immediate attention."[8] Ultimately, Hamburger Hill reignited public debate over the war, placing pressure on newly installed President Richard Nixon to change the United States' approach to Vietnam and move away from the costly approach of placing maximum pressure on enemy forces. It thus played a key role in tipping the strategic balance toward Nixon's policy of "Vietnamization," in which U.S. forces focused on training ARVN forces to take over the fighting, accompanied by the withdrawal of U.S. troops.[9] Though Hamburger Hill would be one of the last battles of its kind, U.S. combat troops remained in Vietnam for several more years, demonstrating the difficulty of ending what had become a two-decade commitment.

Cletus "Ed" Hardy, Fennimore (Army, 101st Airborne Division)
Roger Harrison, Racine (Army, 101st Airborne Division)

Ed Hardy in his combat fatigues. *Ed Hardy*

ED HARDY The way I actually got into the military was there was a judge by the name of Orthouse who decided the military was probably a better place for me than the streets around Fennimore, Wisconsin, at that time. It was inevitable. I was going nowhere. I was just having a lot of fun. That was back when we had the eighteen-year-old beer-drinking laws in the state of Wisconsin. I got myself into a little trouble, nothing serious, but he suggested it would be good to pray that I pass the physical. I went in on the 19th of September, 1967. I was actually inducted. There was no such thing as a lottery or draft. Unless you had a student deferment or a medical deferment, you were going into the service. You might not be heading for Nam, but you had a pretty good chance of doing that too. I took my physical on a Wednesday and on a Friday I was in Fort Campbell, Kentucky, a soldier. It happened very fast.

I remember they said, "Count off 'One, two, one, two.'" If you were a "1" you would go into the Army and if you were a "2" you were drafted right into the Marine Corps. I got a "1," thank God. I guess it wouldn't have made much of a difference. We got attached to the Marines when we got there. That wasn't exactly the good place to be either. Those guys that got drafted for the Marine Corps, it was not their lucky day. They were not having a good day at all. They went onto those buses kicking and screaming some of them, but they went on the buses. It didn't matter how. They were going.

I had actually gotten orders to be shipped out to Korea. I said, "To hell with that. If there's a war going on I'm not going to miss it." I raised a fuss. I wrote our senator a letter and said I couldn't see why if Vietnam was going on I couldn't go to Vietnam. He wrote me back and said he had advised the military of my desires and he was sure I was going to be hearing from them really soon. I did.

Before departing for Vietnam, Roger Harrison was given leave to visit his family at Christmas. *Roger Harrison*

ROGER HARRISON I graduated in June of '68. On my eighteenth birthday in September I just went down and joined the Army to get it over with. I figured I was going to get stuck getting drafted and have to go anyhow. We kind of figured there was no getting around it because none of us were smart enough to go to college and beat it that way. I was about 210 pounds when I went [to basic]. I had a pretty good belly on me. [Laughs.] When I got through basic I had a thirty-two-inch waist. I didn't lose much weight, but I lost a lot of gut.

I had thoughts of making [the military] a career, but then again I didn't want to come back to Vietnam for a second or third tour. After AIT [advanced infantry training] it was straight to Vietnam. It was March of '69. When I got to Cam Ranh Bay, they gave me my orders for 101st Airborne Division. The first sergeant I saw, I said, "You can't put me in the 101st Airborne Division. I've never jumped out of an airplane." He said, "I don't give a shit, that's where you're going" [Laughs.] They don't care. It took three and a half weeks altogether from the time I stepped off the plane in Cam Ranh Bay to be out in the jungle with my company.

ED HARDY We flew out of Colorado Springs, Colorado, at about three o'clock in the morning around the 18th of July, 1968. We went from Fort Carson in combat fatigues and full dress. We had everything but ammo. It took us twenty-six hours. I didn't know you went through Alaska to get to Vietnam. They dropped us in Da Nang. Da Nang was a pretty hot spot at that time. We're just all standing around looking at each other, like, "What the hell are we going to do now?" We're all just green as grass. I had my wish. I was in Vietnam.

I think the first thing that I remember was the ungodly heat. I was like, "Oh my God, I'm not going to be able to breathe here. There's just not enough air." The heat and the stench. Vietnam in all its glory. There were a certain number of people who got stuck burning feces every day. I think at that time we had half a million troops on the ground. Twenty-four hours a day, seven days a week, they were burning shit. We spent about three or four nights there getting processed in. They attached us to the Fifth Marine Division and put us in trucks and took us up to Quang Tri, which is in I Corps in northern Vietnam. From there we basically took over. The 101st Airborne Division and the First Cav[alry] were changing places. One was coming out of the [Mekong] Delta and one was going in. Then the Marines took us up.

We landed at Dong Ha. From there they gave us orders one morning to move out north three clicks. That's 3,000 meters, about a mile. Everybody's going, "Where the hell are we going?" We went to Con Thien and that's when we got indoctrinated with what Vietnam is all about. If you didn't have mortars incoming or artillery you'd have B-40 rockets going through the base camp constantly. You literally lived underground. You ate C rations. We were eighteen-year-old kids. We didn't know much. I remember we'd get hit every night. They called them "human wave" attacks. You wouldn't think there were that many people in the world. Some of them didn't even have weapons. They'd run at the wire every night with satchel charges and blow themselves up trying to get into the wire. I remember it getting bad enough that one of the duties became setting up a perimeter for trying to get the napalm in close enough to burn the bodies off the wires because they stunk and bloated up so bad. Patrols went out and doused bodies with diesel fuel and burned them on the wire to prevent disease. It was bad. There wasn't a morning that you wouldn't have 150 or so dead bodies lying around. Had we been twenty-five, they wouldn't have gotten anybody to do it. You have to fight wars with kids because they don't ask any questions. They just do it. It was tough burning the bodies.

I spent quite a bit of time there. The Fifth Division started getting their feet on the ground and building some base camps. There was a place called LZ [Landing Zone] Nancy and Linda. [LZs] were about every four or five miles. They were just mesas on top of a hill. We would land a company and they would dig in. We'd spend maybe four or five days on top and then we'd run recon off of those. We called in a lot of artillery and air strikes off the top of those things. That went on until around Christmas 1968. Things in the Fifth Division were really bad. They just had the snot knocked out of them. There wasn't much left of them. They took a whole bunch of new guys into the Fifth Division. They called it an infusion program, I think. I had wanted to be in the 101st. Around December I got my wish. I got an order to go to the 101st Airborne Division at Camp Eagle, which was closer down by Phu Bai. These people ate hot food and had cold beer. It was unbelievable. I had

Roger Harrison sets up camp for the night, using his poncho as a tent, July 1969. *Roger Harrison*

never seen anything like that in the six months I had already done. We didn't walk much of anyplace. We were all mobile at that time. [The 101st] had done a couple of actual jumps. We got new socks, new fatigues once a week. Life changed a lot. Life got a lot better in the 101st.

ROGER HARRISON We were close to a firebase called Bastogne, [doing] platoon-sized patrols. I would say about my sixth or seventh day out there was contact [with the NVA]. One of our guys got killed, and a couple were wounded. They were shooting real bullets at you. I was in the back end of a platoon, so I really didn't get to do any shooting. The guy next to me got hit with a piece of shrapnel, so I got to carry his machine gun after that day. I wanted to carry it until I found out how heavy it was carrying it out in the jungle. [Laughs.] [It was] somewhere around twenty-six pounds with one hundred rounds of ammunition on it besides. After that, there was nothing until they sent us into the A Shau Valley. I'd never heard of it. I was only with my company a month when they sent us in there. The only thing I ever heard before that was people saying that the NVA were supposed to stay away from the 101st Airborne Division. I don't know why [but] to avoid us if they could.

ED HARDY The first few [helicopter rides] scared the hell out of you. They never closed the doors. You had a door gunner. He might have [the gun] on a tripod. He had his canvas seat and then there would be three or four sitting with their feet hanging out the doors. You sat like that with your M-16 ready to go. On the other side you had the same situation. There'd be a crew chief up between the two pilot seats. Then there would be one or two more. We tried to get ten on so there would be four on the sides and two in the middle to ride. Depending on how heavy the chopper was on fuel and ammo and how high it was in terms of the altitude, you couldn't get them off the ground sometimes. They wouldn't fly.

A Huey brings troops to the field for a combat assault. *Richard Berry*

You'd basically go along. You've probably seen the classic pictures of them flying five or six at a time in a trail. They're up on frequency, but you're not on frequency. You don't get to hear what the hell they're talking about. You don't know if the LZ is hot. It always seemed to me that when they said, "This going to [be] bad," you didn't get anything. When they said, "This is going to be a piece of cake," you'd better hang on because it was going to be really bad. They'd maybe circle twice and call an air strike or two on it. Then the Cobras [helicopters] would work it over a little bit. I think they used to step them in 1,000- or 1,500-foot intervals. You had five circling in a racetrack down here and five above. You had sixty combat troops ready to come off. When they said you were going in, they just basically laid them over, and then you went right straight down. The grass on most of the LZs would be very high. The choppers would fan the grass off and when you got down to within ten feet of the ground, your feet better be on the skid and you better head out or you're going to get pushed out because they're not going to wait. I've gone out of them at least ten feet. You roll. You've got at least four days of ammo, four days of food, and at least three gallons of water depending on where you were going in. You had all of this in your rucksack. Everything that you were going to need for the next five days; if you didn't bring it with you, it wasn't going to be there. You would set up a perimeter. Usually the assaults would go early morning or late afternoon because as you landed, that landing zone would be zeroed in with mortars. Charlie watched you all the time. There was never a time where Charlie didn't know where you were.

We would set up a perimeter by digging in foxholes. You'd crawl in there with your buddy and there'd be two to a foxhole. There was a buddy system. You dug in and you had the biggest treat of the day. It was a can of "beanie weenies." You'd use some heat tabs to heat those up. If not, you'd just scrape the grease off the top, eat them the way they were. You'd lie there and talk to each other. You became really good friends. As it got dark, we'd have a briefing with the platoon commander and/or sergeant and figure out how many ambushes we were going to send out and what the code words would be for getting back in. We'd set out our claymore mines around the perimeter and that was the evening. Then until you got extracted, you'd stay pretty much in a 40-man to a 160-man unit and you'd walk [at least] 3,500 meters a day. I saw a lot of interesting things. I wish the situation had been different because it was just an absolutely beautiful country. It had a quadruple canopied jungle and unbelievable wildlife: small deer, monkeys.

Prepared for a combat assault at Hamburger Hill, Roger Harrison, right, and a fellow soldier pose for a picture. *Roger Harrison*

ROGER HARRISON On May 10, they sent us up on Hamburger Hill. Our battalion was dropped off on the west end between Laos and Hamburger Hill. We were circling around and seeing all the artillery going off on our landing zone. You didn't know what to expect. I'm thinking, "Oh, something's wrong here." After everybody got there, we started moving out. First, you heard all kinds of shooting around us that first day because everybody [was] dropped all around the hill. The hill we were on was west of the actual Hamburger Hill. We were pretty much working on flat ground.

ED HARDY The Third of the 187th, our sister battalion, had a commander named Honeycutt [who] got in his head that he was going to take [Ap Bia] mountain come hell or high water. He was going to go up there, and he was going to take those people off the top of that mountain. We were out in terrifically mountainous terrain; steeper than any hill, probably including Granddad's Bluff. The Vietnamese had a hell of a base camp up on top. They were actually driving trucks and tanks into the base camp. Honeycutt decided he was going to come up the front side and take it away from them.

It was somewhere around the 10th of May. I remember the dates fairly well. We had gotten kicked around pretty bad. We'd been in firefights about every day for maybe a couple of weeks. Not big things but skirmishes, losing a couple guys a day, and things like that. They decided that we would go to China Beach. You were allowed one in-country R&R. Finally our turn came around and they said, "You guys have been kicked around enough." They flew us directly off of the firebase directly to China Beach down by Da Nang. We had hot chow, cold beer, and no guard duty. We were supposed to be there for seven days stand-down. I think we arrived there on the 12th of May, and on the 13th or the 14th, all bets were off. They said, "You've got a sister battalion in trouble. You're going to high alert." We were going, "We just got here. We just got out of that place." They said, "Well, you might have to go back up." Of all of the people that could have gone back up there, [Honeycutt] only needed one more company to take this mountain and that company happened to be A Company of the Second Battalion of the 506th Infantry. When the time came, [they] flew us directly out there. We had new fatigues, and our bellies [were] fairly full. We were there for four assaults on the mountain. I've never understood it. There was a July 1969 *Newsweek* where [Senator Edward] Kennedy gave them holy hell for it, saying, "You got to get this over with."

ROGER HARRISON We fought every day, sometimes two or three times a day. They'd pull back and we might make one hundred yards or so, and they'd contact again. One day our point man got killed. I don't think he made ten yards. We'd fought all day in that one position. He took off and he was walking point. He got killed, shot right away. We stayed there for two days and never moved.

I went back to carrying an M-16 when we went up on Hamburger Hill. I was too scared to really think. In my company, we started out with 115 guys and after we took the hill, there were 37 of us left. Six were killed, one was missing presumed dead, and the rest were all wounded. There were a couple of us that had shrapnel, but you just grabbed the eyebrow tweezers and pulled it out and slap[ped] a little salve and a Band-Aid on it.

Supplies were coming in off the helicopter and they were kicking them out over us. No food, no water. What we took up there was pretty much what we had to eat. Why have the pilots jeopardize their life just to bring

Roger Harrison eats a can of C-rations in the jungle near A Shau Valley, August 1969. *Roger Harrison*

us food? We need the ammunition and the grenades to stay alive. We need that stuff. Forget the food. When it's all over with, then bring us something to eat. We went a couple days without food and a couple days without water. I know I was thirsty because when we came across the bomb crater there was some real nice clean water in there. A couple iodine tablets and it stunk so bad you had to plug your nose before you could drink it and push the slime off the top of the water.

You wondered how you made it. I remember hearing reports and reading in the *Stars and Stripes* about Delta Company. I was told they were dropped on top of the hill itself. After three days they were down to fourteen guys. They got up during the day and at night they got kicked off to their position, and they went back and after three days [the NVA] just took them out, the fourteen guys. I don't know how true that is, but there were rumors. We were one of the lucky [companies] because it is dark out there. [Laughs.] You can't see shit.

Hamburger Hill is one of those things from Vietnam. It's like Normandy. It's like Hiroshima. They said it was the worst battle since Pork Chop Hill.

Up there [the NVA] weren't leaving. They were dug in. There was shooting twenty-four hours a day. We were lucky. We didn't have fighting at night-time.

ED HARDY When you thought it couldn't get any worse, it would get worse. The Vietnamese bodies never got cleaned up much. We would drag some of them back down or roll some of our own back down. They went down the hill real easy. It was steep. Each unit tried to get their own, but some of them were blown up so bad they were beyond recognition. There's not much that's publicized about that. I don't think anybody will ever know how many died up there. I think we went up four or five times; hanging onto tree roots to pull yourself as you went up that damn thing. It was so slick when it rained, and the air strikes had stirred the mud up. I don't know how the hell many Vietnamese were dug in up there trying to kill you. They were sitting in a pretty good bunker line. Whether we actually ever took it I can't really say. I can say that we were up there, but I can't ever say whether we took it because I don't think we spent ten minutes up there the whole damn time. We went down and they started airlifting people out, and that was the end of it. That was about the 19th or the 20th of May, 1969. If we had gotten up there and said, "Hey, now we can build the Taj Mahal" or whatever reason we went up there for, you might have understood it a little bit more. [It] ended up, "Hey, we're up here. We made it. Now let's go do something else." That's what it felt like at the end of it.

I never had any respect for that man afterwards. Honeycutt. I can remember him coming across the radio. We were all on the same frequency and people were going, "You're going to get us all killed. You've got to get us the hell out of here." He said, "You're getting paid to fight a war, not make decisions." He's up there riding around in a helicopter for Christ's sakes, two thousand feet above us. It was for his ego. He was a lieutenant colonel looking for colonel.

ROGER HARRISON We went back to the one place where I was walking point and I walked into an ambush. I realized how close the machine gunner was to me. They left the RPG [rocket-propelled grenade] launcher and all the little belts from the machine-gun belt in the foxhole. I don't know how I survived. They must've been shooting with their eyes closed because there's no way I would've missed. I was probably somewhere between twenty and thirty yards. It was pretty open. I was just coming out of the thick stuff, and

I was the first guy to move up. I never heard the explosion. When I hit the dirt, all hell broke loose. I could feel the dirt hitting my helmet and my back, and I couldn't get one shot. I was pinned down. I don't know if what hit the M-16 was a piece of grenade or a bullet. But something hit it, so we both went over. I couldn't reject the empty and I couldn't get another one in.

When I got out of there to get the rest of my guys to come up and lay down a base of fire, I just stood up and took about two steps and dove and started doing low crawling. I got back into the middle of the company. This was on May 16. Some of the guys were wounded earlier that morning and we couldn't get them out on the medevac. They were carrying all the extra weapons, so I went back there and I grabbed an M-60 machine gun, [and] as much ammunition as I could carry. All of a sudden I heard my guys hollering for the medic from my squad. I grabbed him and then grabbed another guy from another squad to come up with me to be my assistant gunner. I went up there and helped the guys out. Everybody in my squad but two got hurt. One guy lost his eye. One guy got shot in the leg. One guy got shot in the back. A lot of guys got hit with shrapnel.

The next day after that, they took us down. We left that ridgeline and we went to another ridgeline to meet up with another company, which we didn't do until late at night. But in the afternoon we came across a nice trail on that ridgeline and they had me and the other machine gunner walking on each side of the trail with one guy walking point in front on the trail. Then all of the sudden we just came to a real wide-open area and stopped. We decided to sit there for an hour, look, and watch. Nothing happened, so then my lieutenant wanted me to walk point with the machine gun. And my squad leader said no. And they were fighting over it. They were afraid that if I got shot, they would be without a machine gun. I said, "If you get somebody else to carry the machine gun, I'll walk point." Nobody wanted to carry the machine gun, so that was out. Finally they convinced the lieutenant that I wasn't walking point with the machine gun. Nobody would walk point, so my squad leader decided to walk point. He got about ten yards out in the open and got shot. I laid down. I couldn't shoot because I had a guy right over there [and] I would have been shooting right over his back. We were going up a little hill and waiting, and all the sudden something comes rolling down the hill. For the life of me, I could never say what it really was except that it just scared the hell out of me. I got up and I jumped behind a tree. I left the gun there. All of a sudden it [the rolling thing] exploded and I don't know if that's what killed my squad leader. He

Roger Harrison at Camp Evans, September 1969.
Roger Harrison

was killed by shrapnel. He didn't even get maybe ten yards. I just broke the brush with the machine gun. It was like three guys in front of me. I couldn't do anything. Then later on that night, we met up with the other company. The next day, there was some fighting going on. The following day, we finally took the hill. It took a toll. On the 20th it just seemed like [the NVA] were gone. We walked in there and took a couple prisoners and just started searching the bunkers. I went back to the place where I walked point. They just came and picked us up after about a week of being up there.

ED HARDY It was the biggest battle of Vietnam. We didn't know what the hell we were getting ourselves into. We were kids. We didn't have a clue how bad it was going to get. I can remember when the action reports got filled out; squad leaders would come around and say, "All right, we had contact today. What did we get for a body count?" We'd say, "Well, what do you mean, what did you get for a body count? We didn't have any bodies." They'd say, "We think we hit some, didn't we?" "Well, yeah, I think I might have hit one." "OK, well, they never travel alone, so you must have got two." Before it was over, you had a ten-man body count and I'm not sure anybody ever saw anyone get hit. Our body counts were run the other direction to make them as small as possible. The body count was everything.

I think [Hamburger Hill] was about Honeycutt's ego. Our company got to the top of the mountain first. He would not, just could not, have that. We were out in the middle of just…I think that's what hell must look like. It was raining and there were mudslides and dead bodies everywhere. The stench is unbelievable. He wanted our company to hold up so he could get a company moved up onto the limb to pass us up to that mountaintop. And I'll never forget that I thought, "What the hell kind of game are we playing here with all these lives?"

12 The Price

"People want to fight war in a nice, neat, moral box. You can't do it. It's all immoral. The bottom line is you kill and destroy and kill and destroy until one side or the other says, 'OK, that's enough.' And then you stop."
— *Linda McClenahan*

Perhaps the most enduring symbol of the Vietnam War is the helicopter. Helicopters conducted reconnaissance missions to identify enemy troops and transported U.S. troops into combat. They resupplied isolated troops and firebases. Armed helicopters participated in air assaults. Building on a policy first begun in the Korean War, helicopters reached their "fullest potential" in Vietnam when they pulled wounded men out of battle.[1] Staffed with medical corpsmen such as Andy Thundercloud, helicopters were especially well suited for Vietnam's varied terrain; able to transport soldiers from battlefield to operating table in as little as an hour, they were "critical to survival."[2] In 1968, for example, for every one hundred wounded Marines, forty-four were treated in the field and fifty-six were taken to the hospital; ultimately, only 1.5 percent died of their wounds.[3] The Army also ran an extensive medevac program, and between 1965 and 1973, Army air ambulances evacuated approximately 850,000 to 900,000 soldiers and Vietnamese civilians.[4] Key to these soldiers' survival were Navy medical corpsmen and Army medics who often treated men in the midst of combat, seeking to clear airways, stop bleeding, reduce pain, and prevent shock. As Thundercloud notes, "I saw everything imaginable from head to toe...I always did my best. I did my damnedest." Medical care in the field was vital but dangerous. Over 1,100 Army medics were killed in action, and countless more were injured. Out of the 5,000 medical corpsmen who served in Vietnam, almost 700 lost their lives.[5]

After evacuation from the battlefield, women played a central role caring for wounded soldiers. The Department of Veterans Affairs estimates that between 1962 and 1973, 11,500 women served in Vietnam, and approximately

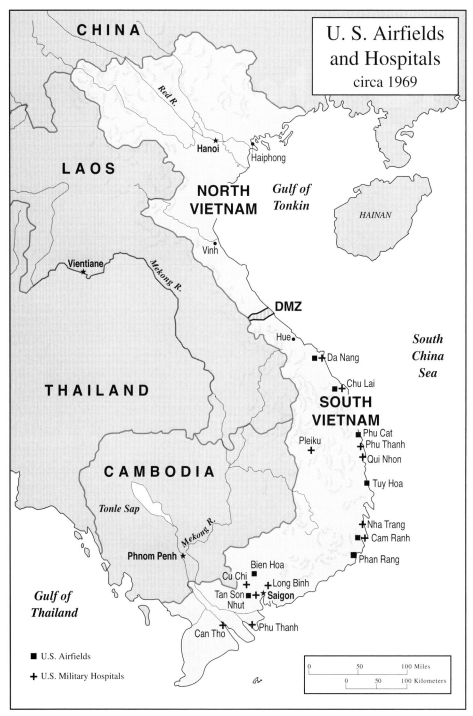

Patti Isaacs, Parrot Graphics

90 percent were nurses.[6] Many of the rest, including Linda McClenahan, served as members of the Women's Army Corps (WAC), first created during World War II and expanded in response to the United States' escalating commitment to Vietnam in the mid-1960s.[7] Though WAC members had been in Vietnam since 1962, their numbers increased in late 1966 and early 1967 when more than eighty women arrived to serve at U.S. Army headquarters, later moved to Long Binh. In 1970, the WAC unit at Long Binh reached its peak strength of 139. Although the majority of WACs worked in clerical positions, others held a variety of jobs, ranging from personnel to intelligence to communications.[8] Still, women in Vietnam were scarce and often confronted the difficulties of living in a combat zone where "war was still largely a male prerogative."[9]

Despite their different wartime duties, both Thundercloud and McClenahan had to face the deadly consequences of Vietnam on a daily basis, whether it was treating wounded men in the field, listening helplessly to besieged men calling for reinforcements, or processing casualty reports on base. According to the records of the National Archives, between 1956 and 1998 58,193 U.S. soldiers died in Southeast Asia, more than half of them less than twenty-two years old.[10] Of these, eight were women, five of whom died of combat-related causes. In the words of Robert Schulzinger, the war in Vietnam was a "national trauma," depleting a generation of young Americans.[11] The extensive use of helicopters combined with advances in medical care meant that compared to past wars, more wounded soldiers survived. Yet for many, the wounds of Vietnam lingered far beyond the battlefield.

Linda McClenahan, Berkeley, CA (Army, Women's Army Corps)
Andy Thundercloud, Tomah (Marines, First Marine Air Wing)

LINDA McCLENAHAN I grew up in Berkeley, California. I went to a Catholic grade school and high school, and it was my intention to become a sister after I graduated. In 1967, the Vietnam War was hot and heavy and the protests were hot and heavy. Coming home from school my senior year, the bus was going down College Avenue. We had to turn and do a detour because they were rioting at the UC–Berkeley campus. Down Telegraph Avenue, I could see a police car overturned and on fire. It moved me. I was tired of the people in the street telling me how to think. At that moment I

Linda McClenahan with fellow graduates of the Women's Army Corps. *Linda McClenahan*

Linda McClenahan, center, receives her sergeant stripes. *Linda McClenahan*

decided I'd give three years of my life to my country. When I graduated in June, I joined the Army. I was a 72 Bravo, which is a fixed station in communications. I accelerated promotions, so I was never a PFC. I went very quickly from Private E-2 right to Spec-4 and then was a sergeant. I got my orders and went to Vietnam.

Linda McClenahan's War Poem

War is hell, a wise man said,
And those who knew so nodded.
War is hell, a young voice cried
And with his friends he plotted

To lead his troops of neighbor chums
Against imagined foes;
To charge and die a thousand deaths
Up and down he goes.

Charging bushes tall and green
Around his father's yard.
Collapsing upon the soft green grass
after fighting brave and hard.

Then gather round and re-choose sides
New strategies to form
Then charge and fall and rise again
No losses do they mourn.

But suddenly the boys grow up;
The game's no longer fun.
Their friends, they die and don't get up
And they're not sure just what they won.

And the neighbor girls who couldn't play
With little boys at war
Become nurses and support troops
Who give them care and more.

And soon they find what others know;
They learn the lesson well.
It's just as the wise man said.
Truly, war is hell.

ANDY THUNDERCLOUD In my life I had heard [Ho-Chunk] warriors tell their stories. I listened to them and never gave it much of a thought. It was just something that I accepted: "One day, I'm going to be doing that." I remember going to Winnebago, Nebraska, and the head man dancer is always a combat veteran. I remember thinking back then, "I'd like to be able to be the head dancer someday." My dream came true in 1992 when I was the head man dancer at Winnebago, Nebraska. I was very proud to fulfill one of the dreams that I had had when I was younger.

LINDA McCLENAHAN I arrived at the 93 Placement in Long [Binh] area. I thought war would be kind of a glorious, grand adventure. I even wrote a poem about that at one point, but of course I get there and find out, "What the hell was I thinking?" [Laughs.] I was sitting on the benches waiting to be assigned and all of a sudden, "Boom!" Somebody yelled, "Incoming!" and everybody was on the ground. I was flat as I turned to the captain next to me and asked, "Aren't we behind the lines here?" He said, "Lady, this is Vietnam. There are no behind the lines here."

ANDY THUNDERCLOUD I joined the service in January of 1963. I had an ambition to be a pilot, but unfortunately when I took my physical, I flunked. I had a bad left eye which I was not aware of and you had to have everything perfect. I still had an obligation since I had signed on the dotted line. They wanted me to go into nuclear-powered subs as an officer and I told them, "No, I don't think I'd like to go aboard nuclear-powered subs." They offered to make me a line officer and I didn't really like the idea of being an officer at all. I said, "I want to be a corpsman." I'd always had an interest in medicine. My grandfather was a healer. He'd taught me a few things when I was younger and talked to me about the body and the mind and how to do certain healings. My mother always wanted to have a doctor in the family. My father had been a Marine during World War II. When I enlisted in the Navy, my dad was a little disappointed. My father had been wounded in World War II and he often credited corpsmen for saving his life. When I got attached to the Marine Corps, my father was very proud. I often heard that he'd go around and tell people, "My son is a corpsman with the United States Marine Corps." I finished [college]. I got my orders [in December of 1966].

LINDA MCCLENAHAN I got assigned to the WAC [Women's Army Corps] detachment. On the way in, I saw rockets come in and saw bodies on the side of the road. In my head I figured soldiers got killed, but not civilians. Naïve. The WAC detachment on Long Binh had about 120 women. I was in communications. My assignment was at the U.S. Army in the Republic of Vietnam (USARV) headquarters. It was about fifty thousand people. It was a huge base. I was at the center of the communications facility. There were two twelve-hour shifts, from six at night to six in the morning and from six in the morning till six at night for six and a half days a week. We got half a

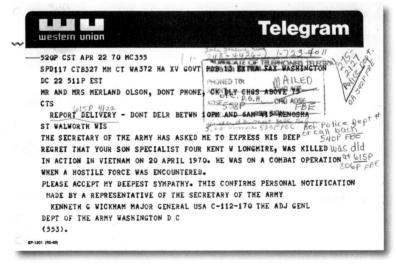

Death notices like this one for fallen Wisconsin soldier Kent Longmire originated from the office of communications where Linda McClenahan worked.
Courtesy of the Wisconsin Veterans Museum

Some of Linda McClenahan's fellow workers, whom she fondly termed "my guys." *Linda McClenahan*

day off a week. At that point I was still a good Catholic kid, and I asked for Sunday morning off so I could hit mass.

ANDY THUNDERCLOUD I remember [coming into Vietnam] you took a look at those guys and they're pretty scruffy looking. Their fatigues were all worn and faded. They looked like veterans. I remember some of the things that they were yelling at us: "Oh, new meat is here." "You guys are really going to regret this." "I'm going home." I remember thinking to myself as I was walking along, "When it's my time to go home, I'm not going to do that. I'm not going to do that to them."

I never talk about the first six months that I was in Vietnam. I absolutely refuse to talk about it. I will not. It's in me. It's part of me. I will never share that with anyone. I don't care how much I love a person. I don't care. I survived. That's all I'll say.

LINDA McCLENAHAN On my shift, there was me with fifty-some guys at night. We handled the messages that came through: surveillance reports, troop movements. Everybody was included. That part was kind of nice. The guys that I worked with were really great. They were like brothers. We worked together well. We had a job to do and we did it. The casualty reports went out of our office to the various [branches] so that a soldier's hometown could be notified. We saw everything from a sprained ankle in a parachute jump or getting out of a jeep to pieces of remains not positively identified.

ANDY THUNDERCLOUD The Marines have a lot of respect for corpsmen. I understand that. The Marines took really good care of me. I did my best to take care of them to the best of my ability. If someone mentioned my name, the thing I wanted to be remembered for is that I was a good corpsman. I hoped somebody would say, "Doc Thundercloud. I remember him. Damn good corpsman."

In Linda McClenahan's words, "I think just about every unit over there adopted some orphanage somewhere." *Joe Campbell*

LINDA MCCLENAHAN I had traumatic things happen in a very short period of time in the summer of '70. I lost God over there. My idea of being a sister after I got out was out the window. [Laughs.] [In] the messages I processed, including the casualty reports, you'd read about a battle that was going on. We'd lose eight, ten, twelve guys. We'd take real estate and then go away and leave it and back and forth. It was insane. I was drinking pretty heavily by that time.

At the comm center in the tech control area, we had these patch cords and we would patch in a different signal for different lines to make sure everything was OK, or tune in the radios to different things. We'd make sure the frequencies were working because we might have to change an antenna or something. I didn't do that stuff, so I didn't fully understand it, but I'd be hanging out with the guys who did. One day on the radio, we picked up a squad that was under attack and was asking for help. They didn't get it. To sit and helplessly listen was tough. Another time we were working with a group of orphans. I think just about every unit over there adopted some orphanage somewhere. I saw this one little girl who looked like she'd had her throat cut. That just hit me badly. I don't know if it severed her vocal chords or what, but she really couldn't talk. Who would slit the throat of a three-year-old?

ANDY THUNDERCLOUD   It was either late July or early August that one of the chief hospital corpsmen from MAG-16 came to our unit and was looking for corpsmen to volunteer to go fly medevacs. It was the only time in my entire military career that I volunteered for anything. [Laughs.] I volunteered to go to the Air Wing to fly medevacs.

Like the medic pictured here, Andy Thundercloud treated wounded soldiers during transport from the field. *Courtesy of the United States Army Aviation Museum*

The helicopters that I flew in were UH-34s. They had some CH-46s and CH-53s, the great big guys. When they'd fly medevacs they would either use the CH-46 or the UH-34. We didn't have any nurses like they had on the TV series *China Beach*. [Laughs.] We flew every three or four days from 6:00 in the morning to 6:00 in the evening. Then another corpsman would come in and fly from 6:00 p.m. to 6:00 in the morning. Phu Bai and Dong Hoi were covered by our units. We were just down in Chu Lai. We covered quite a lot of area.

Flying at night was a real experience. I always give the pilots a lot of credit for getting us in and out of where we were supposed to be going. When we got shot at, that was exciting. Once we landed and started picking up the WIAs or KIAs, I got busy taking care of the wounded. I tried to ignore anything else that was going on. I guess I was concentrating more on them, their well-being and what I could do for them, than worry about what was going on outside. We let the pilot and gunner and the crew chief worry about that. My mind was set on what I had before me.

LINDA MCCLENAHAN In August, I was at Annex 11 with some friends, and we met this guy named Tony. He had been with the 212 MPs, the dog group on Long Binh. They had pretty much shut down in June or July of that year. I met [up with] him and some other people and we danced a little bit. About the third time I saw him, I was by myself and he said they were going to have a party down at the old location because it was empty. They could make all the noise they wanted. He asked me to join him. I had no reason not to so [I said,] "Sure, I'll go with you." I got in the jeep and when I walked in the door, there were two people I had never seen before. There was a reel-to-reel tape playing Elvis's greatest hits and a bunch of beer and a cot, and that was it. By the time I realized what was going on, it was too late... I was devastated by that because it was pretty brutal with all the guys — not only physically. I was getting short [on my enlistment]. I spent a week in a fog. Part of it was that the guys I knew over there were really good guys. I trusted them all. They were brothers. To add insult to injury, when Tony was driving me back to the WAC detachment, he just stopped the truck right after USARV and told me to get out. I did and off he went. I felt like garbage dumped on the side of the road. It was probably a good thing that I didn't have a weapon because if I'd had a weapon at that point, we wouldn't be having this interview.

ANDY THUNDERCLOUD I saw everything imaginable from head to toe. I saw dismemberments, disembowelments, chest wounds, traumatic amputations, and burns. I always did my best. I did my damnedest. I don't ever recall losing anybody on the helicopter. If they came aboard alive, they left my helicopter alive. There were times that we had to haul KIAs out of there, you know.

I won't say it was an everyday thing but I do remember civilians who we had picked up from hitting a land mine [or] having their village attacked.

An extraction team rushes a wounded soldier to a waiting medevac. *Courtesy of the United States Army Aviation Museum*

Medevacs transported soldiers to a number of evacuation hospitals in South Vietam, including the 24th Evacuation Hospital in Long Binh. *Linda McClenahan*

I remember one pregnant young lady coming aboard who was about ready for delivery and I kept sweating, thinking to myself, "Oh my god, I'm going to be delivering a baby here pretty soon." Fortunately, I didn't deliver her.

LINDA McCLENAHAN It took me a long time to walk home. I was late for curfew, obviously. I was in a world of hurt. I tried to go to work the next day after I got . . . after the gang . . . after I was attacked. Somebody came up behind me as they did a million times to show me something. He put his arm around me and I slammed his arm off and told him to get the "F" away from me. They had never heard me say that stuff, so the whole place got quiet and I just got up and walked out. I notified the CO [commanding officer] and we tried to do something, but in those days, it didn't work out. The CO basically said that the guys said that it was my idea and [that] they'd paid me and, "Besides, what did we women expect putting [our]selves in a man's world?" The CO reminded me I was short, and to go through all this would probably just make it worse, so if I could just forget about it as best I could and whatever. I did, as best I could.

I lost God after that. The concept that I had of God was that if you do all the right things and follow all the rules, then God takes care of you. I'd kept my end of the deal and God didn't keep God's end of the deal. Years later I was able to put all of that into the proper perspective. God doesn't start wars. I think one of the greatest gifts God gives us is the gift of free will, and no matter how badly we abuse that gift, God won't interfere. I really have come to believe that there are times when God cries with us over some of the choices that are made. That's part of my own concept. I am in recovery [now]. I've been sober now by the grace of God and a few good friends for about fifteen years. You get into AA [Alcoholics Anonymous] and you get into the God of your own understanding. I was able to make peace with God, but it took years.

ANDY THUNDERCLOUD I flew a couple hundred medevacs. I didn't have as many as some of the guys. There were a couple younger guys who had come to the unit. They were enlisted for a couple of months before I finally came home. I found out that both of them had wanted to fly more medevacs than any other corpsman. Their goals were one thousand medevacs. Both of them extended. [Both] of them got in the eight hundreds and [were] killed.

I wanted to stay because I was thinking, "Who can take care of these guys better than I can?" I kept thinking to myself, "Nobody can take care them like I can." I considered myself a good corpsman and I thought, "I want to stay."

LINDA McCLENAHAN It would get to the point where a lot of choppers would be coming in and I would say, "It's going to be a busy day tomorrow. We're going to have a lot of casualty reports." [I thought] of the people coming in as work rather than people because it got too hard. [Long pause.] Yeah. Got too hard. That was what hit me about the Wall. I'd processed names all the time and here are all these names. That's when I lost it the first time. I had a few names to look up and I found them. I'm walking along and it's like, "OK, there's that person," and, "There she is," and, "There he is." [Then] I was standing up at the other end of it. I was looking down at all these names. I'd worked with names. I'm watching people touch the names and do rubbings, leaving things. Suddenly every single name was a person. I just lost it. I started sobbing. All of a sudden I had my head buried in [someone's] fatigue jacket. I don't know where the guy came from. I was sobbing and sobbing and sobbing. I finally came up for air and I'd slobbered all over his jacket. I thanked him and asked who he was. I had my boonie hat on to identify me as a vet. He said, "I'm just a brother vet." I asked, "How can I thank you?" He said, "Just pass it on, sister. Pass it on." I did. Later, we had a candle-light ceremony, and I saw another guy by himself and he was crying and I did the same thing. So, it was good.

ANDY THUNDERCLOUD I had everything packed, so I just grabbed my bags. They threw me in a jeep and drove me over to the airbase. It was our turn to leave. I saw these guys getting off the planes and I kind of looked at them. I said, "God, did I look like that at one time?" You could see the fear in their faces. There were these guys standing on the side [saying], "New guys. New blood. New meat." All these obscenities. I kept my promise to myself and I didn't say anything. I was just thinking, "Poor guys. I'm going home."

I came home at the end of March 1968. It was good to be home, to see the people. I remember, [my parents] told me, "We're going to have a dance for you. It's going to be in celebration for your coming home safely." They had that celebration and there were hundreds and hundreds of people there. They got the drum out and there was a song that was sung in my honor. My father gave me regalia. He said, "These are yours. You have earned these." It's similar to the ribbons that are worn today. [It was] one of the dreams [I'd had that] I had to wear the two feathers of a veteran. After I returned and I would put on my regalia and I could dance, I was able to wear two feathers. I was proud of that. There were items that I was given by my grandfathers, grandmothers, aunts, and uncles. They're invaluable. If you were to ask me their monetary value I'd say, "You don't have enough money." When I leave this world, that's what I'm going to be dressed in.

LINDA McCLENAHAN It's hard to explain to people. Normally when you meet people, you sort of talk a little bit, see what you have in common. In a war situation, you don't have time for all that surface nonsense. You get down to the basics of human existence. [They're] the closest people you'll ever have. When you're in that kind of a life and death [situation] every day, you get pretty close. My best friend over there also happened to be [named] Linda. I would've died for her. I know she would've died for me. It was no question. After I came back, it took me sixteen years before we found each other again. We reconnected immediately. We discovered we really didn't have anything in common, but it didn't matter. We didn't like the same kind of movies and we didn't like the same kind of books. We did continue the [card] game we started in Vietnam for a penny a point. [Laughs.] We started it in a bunker one night under an attack. We kept it going. She kept the scorecard. I couldn't believe it. She died a couple years ago in June. I put in her coffin the 722 pennies I still owed her. That was the score at that point.

ANDY THUNDERCLOUD Who knows where the next place will be. I go back to my ancestors and I take a look at what they've gone through. I had grandfathers who participated in World War I with the Red Arrow, 32nd Division. I had relatives who participated in World War II, you know, my "fathers." I had relatives, some of my younger fathers and my uncles, who participated in Korea. I participated in Vietnam. I've got nephews and sons who have been in other conflicts since. I've got sons and daughters who are in the conflict now. In the future, I don't know. I don't know what's going to happen but it's something that will continue. It's a responsibility that we as Ho Chunks will not shirk. We will not shirk the responsibility that's been placed upon us. It's something that we try to do as honorably as we can. We instill these values in our younger people, and they try to carry on what our ancestors have foretold.

LINDA McCLENAHAN War's insane. It brings out the best in people and the worst in people, sometimes in the same person on the same day. I saw too much of that. It's all insanity because anything goes. I think that was part of the problem with the Vietnam War. People want to fight war in a nice, neat, moral box. You can't do it. It's all immoral. The bottom line is you kill and destroy and kill and destroy until one side or the other says, "OK, that's enough." And then you stop.

I think it's important for everybody to tell a story. The only thing we can truly give each other is our stories. Everybody has a story and we need to share those. It's important. This American attitude [that] men aren't supposed to cry [is] B.S. I think we're the only country in the world where [it's not OK] for men to cry. Every other country in the world, they get it. There's plenty to cry about, so what's the issue here?

Firebases

"Every five seconds an explosion would go off and just shower you with shrapnel, and white phosphorous would start burning you... Trying to get up and run anywhere was out of the question. We just stayed and kept fighting."
— *George Banda*

After Richard Nixon won the 1968 presidential election, he sought to change U.S. policy in Vietnam. Elected after promising that he had a "secret plan" to end to the war, Nixon was determined not to allow Vietnam to consume his presidency as it had Lyndon Johnson's.[1] The Nixon administration pursued the Nixon Doctrine, or "Vietnamization," a plan to shift the burden of the fighting to ARVN troops, supplemented by U.S. supplies, training, and air power. With this policy in place, Nixon announced the first withdrawal of 25,000 U.S. troops in July 1969; in April 1970, he announced the withdrawal of an additional 150,000 U.S. troops.[2] In an attempt to diffuse increasingly visible and widespread antiwar activism, Nixon articulated his policy in a speech televised on November 3, 1969. Calling for support from the "great silent majority" of the American people, Nixon argued that the stakes remained high and that the global "survival of peace and freedom" depended on whether the "American people ha[d] the moral stamina and courage" to continue aiding South Vietnam in the "right way," that is, through Vietnamization.[3] Despite the drawdown of troops, Nixon argued that it was imperative that the United States remain committed to winning the war.

Based on the conviction that "the way to end the war in Vietnam was to expand it," Nixon also widened the war to surrounding countries, including Cambodia.[4] Nixon had begun secret B-52 bombing raids on Cambodia in March 1969. On April 30, 1970, he announced that he was sending troops into Cambodia. Throughout the early years of his presidency, Nixon had publicly presented his policy as the pursuit of peace. The further spread of the war was thus met with a wave of protest "that swept college campuses, professional circles, Congress, government agencies, even the Cabinet."[5] In the most shocking incidents of the antiwar movement, National Guard units fired on protesting students at Kent State University on May 4, 1970, killing four. Police similarly shot and killed two students at Jackson State College (Mississippi) two days later. Nixon had campaigned as a president who would restore law and order to American society, yet the war seemed to be ripping America apart.

Against this backdrop of protest at home and military expansion abroad, U.S. troops continued to experience fierce fighting in Vietnam. The withdrawal of U.S. forces, especially from I Corps (the northernmost region of South Vietnam), placed the burden of the fighting on the 101st Airborne and ARVN (Army of the Republic of Vietnam) troops who remained.[6] Seeking to maintain the U.S./ARVN position in I Corps, and push back NVA (North Vietnamese Army) troops in the A Shau Valley, allied forces focused on a series of fire support bases (firebases) throughout the area to prevent NVA infiltration. Widely used in Vietnam, a firebase was a camp designed to provide artillery support to surrounding infantry units and usually included long-range infantry weapons such as howitzers and mortars, along with bunkers, medical support, and a command center. Often isolated and resupplied only by air, some firebases were permanent while others moved with their infantry units. As veteran George Banda notes, firebases that were less fortified made easy targets: "I was coming from Firebase Bastogne with a hundred feet of concertina wire, claymores, no vegetation at all for a mile. With [Firebase] Henderson, anybody could sneak up real quick. You wouldn't see them until it was too late." Surprise attacks by NVA like the one at Firebase Henderson in the early hours of May 6, 1970, meant that casualty lists continued to grow in Vietnam.

The NVA reacted strongly to the renewed U.S./ARVN push into I Corps and the A Shau Valley, and on July 1, 1970, they attacked the 101st Airborne at Fire Support Base Ripcord, starting a twenty-three-day siege on the base. The ensuing bloody, hilltop battle was one of the last major ground conflicts of the war and ended with U.S. withdrawal from Ripcord. Though Nixon claimed to be drawing down the war, Vietnam remained deadly; between 1969 and 1972, 15,315 U.S. troops, 107,504 ARVN troops, and countless NVA troops, NLF [National Liberation Front] fighters, and Vietnamese civilians died in combat.[7]

George Banda, Milwaukee (Army, 101st Airborne Division)
Charlie Lieb, Minneapolis, MN (Army, 101st Airborne Division)

GEORGE BANDA I was drafted in January of '69. I was in Milwaukee having a good time and I got a notice. They said, "Come on down." I said, "Oh, OK. Do I have a choice?" I was hoping maybe I'[d] get there and it [would] be all over with. That wasn't the case, unfortunately. I got through twelve weeks of boot camp at Fort Campbell, Kentucky, and then went on to advanced infantry training. For me, it was medic training at Fort Sam Houston, Texas. I enjoyed that training quite a bit. I like to help people out. I like to give to people. I fell right into that. I picked up on the medical aspect of it quickly. I said, "Oh, this is good. Maybe they did pick me for the right reasons."

After he completed basic training, George Banda spent twelve weeks training to be a medic at Fort Sam Houston. *George Banda*

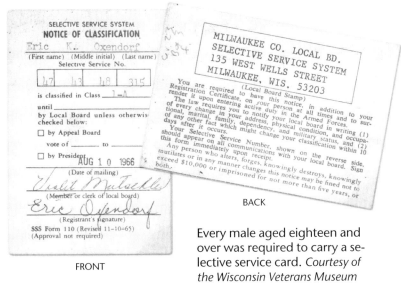

FRONT

BACK

Every male aged eighteen and over was required to carry a selective service card. *Courtesy of the Wisconsin Veterans Museum*

After jump school, I got orders to go to Fort Ord, California, Big Sur. Beautiful. Again, I'm lucking out. I'm thinking to myself, "This is really good. I'm drafted. I've only got two years to serve. I'm already into October." I said, "The Army probably forgot about me." It was just fantastic, an excellent place to work. November of '69, I got my orders for Vietnam. I'm like, "Damn it, they got me." You get thirty days off before you go. I went back home to say, "I'm doing good. You know I'm going to go to Vietnam, but don't worry. I'll be back. Everything's fine." My mom and dad, they're seeing all this news on TV about Vietnam and all the terrible things that are happening to the troops being wounded and killed. I said, "Hey, I'm fine, Mom. I'll be back. Don't worry about it."

CHARLIE LIEB I was born and raised in Minneapolis. A very good friend of mine in high school wanted to go to West Point. I went down with him and took the test for a congressional appointment. They took me down to Great Lakes Naval Training Station near Chicago and I had a physical aptitude test. I failed my physical, so I thought, "OK, that's over with." I went back

to my doctor in Minneapolis and he went through a series of tests and said, "Nah, there's nothing wrong with you." I had accepted a scholarship [at another school] to go play football. On June 27 I got a telegram saying, "You've been accepted to West Point as a qualified alternate." I said, "What? I thought I was medically disqualified." They said, "Well, you've got forty-eight hours to tell us if you're going to come and then you have to show up on the 1st of July." I thought, "I'll go and give it a try and see what it's like. As long as I quit by mid-August, I can still make my other commitments." I stuck through four years of West Point and graduated.

During senior year I had to choose a branch and I chose to go into the infantry knowing full well that by that time, 1968, I was going to end up in Vietnam a year or two after I graduated. I went to the 82nd Airborne

From left to right, Bob Wallace, Jim Campbell, and Charlie Lieb, all lieutenant platoon leaders in the 101st Airborne, pose during a stand-down at Camp Evans. *Charlie Lieb*

Division at Fort Bragg, North Carolina. I spent six months there. Then I got orders for Vietnam. I showed up in Vietnam and reported to the replacement depot at Bien Hoa. I was assigned to the 101st Airborne Division, Charlie Company, Second Battalion, 506 Infantry.

GEORGE BANDA I got to Vietnam about the 10th of December, '69. I landed in Cam Rahn Bay. I remember getting out of the plane and the first thing that hit you was the smell: heat, humidity, animal urine, and people cooking food that I was not that familiar with. [I thought,] "I'm not in Kansas anymore. This is Vietnam." I was scared. I was like, "You're in Vietnam. Now what? Just follow orders. Latch onto somebody who's been here a couple months or longer who can tell me what I have to do to stay alive." For me,

Tommy Wilkenson, John Eaves, and Charlie Pentecost, pictured left to right, were praised by fellow soldier George Banda as "born survivors" who "seemed at home in the hot steamy jungles of Vietnam." All three survived the war.
George Banda

that was Sergeant John Eaves. He was an Airborne Ranger. He had been with Special Forces. John Eaves was an incredible soldier, an incredible human being, too. You could just see there was so much leadership in him and confidence. Whatever he did or said to you, that's what you did. He had been there six months. He knew the lay of the land. I'd follow him into hell. I knew he'd bring me back. He was that good. I mean he was just tremendous. I think about him now. We lost John. John Eaves passed away a few years after he got back from Vietnam. He was killed in a logging accident.

CHARLIE LIEB [When I got to Vietnam] I was an Infantry Platoon leader. In early October [1969] we were operating in platoon-sized units, trying to ambush enemy and establish enemy contact. We had encountered some small VC a couple of times, nothing major. We were out in the boonies, and we spent the whole year I was [in Vietnam] there. I was never in any villages. One night we were out on patrol and we ran into some enemy fortifications. We got into a gun battle and I got wounded for the first time by enemy grenades. My elbow was pretty screwed up. I got to the 85th Evac Hospital and they wanted to send me to Camp Zama in Japan. I didn't want to go because I wanted to go back to my unit. I had formed some very good bonds there and had a good unit and enjoyed it. Luckily the monsoons came and for three days they couldn't get any planes in or out. By the end

While recovering from his second injury, Charlie Lieb met Ron Ely, the actor who played Tarzan, at the 85th Evacuation Hospital in Da Nang. Lieb is pictured far left, Ely far right. *Charlie Lieb*

of the three-day period I had shown enough improvement that they decided I didn't have to go, and a few days later they released me back to my unit.

GEORGE BANDA I think I feared ambushes the most. We were a small team. In recon we went out with seven or eight guys. We were ambushed frequently. They knew we were coming. We lost a lot of guys through ambushes. Our first firefight casualty was a young guy named Jackson. He always had a smile on his face. He loved to dance. Me and him would dance together when we got back to Firebase Bastogne. Jackson was our cool guy. We'd have a few beers — maybe two or three or eight or nine — and turn on the music. We just loved dancing and laughing.

He had gone out and was walking point, and he ran into an ambush. He was shot and killed instantly. He was probably dead before he hit the

The area around Fire Support Base Bastogne was devoid of vegetation as a result of Agent Orange, napalm drops, and "mad minutes" in which all firearms on the base were shot simultaneously toward the perimeter. *George Banda*

Few moments in Vietnam brought smiles to the soldiers' faces. This day, however, did—George Banda's fellow troops display their "catch of the day" after frag fishing.
George Banda

ground. That was the first time that I had experienced someone dying. I felt like I was just talking to him an hour [before] about home and what we were going to do when we got back. Now he's dead. It's terrible. You carry the body bags with you. You get a body bag out and you unzip it and you put the body in it and zip it up. You call in a helicopter and then they come and take the body away, and then you never see him again. People try not to talk about it. [They say,] "Let's move on. Let's not let it happen again. Let's be a bit more alert." That was painful. I know John Eaves took it hard. We all did.

CHARLIE LIEB We got a new captain, Captain Vasquez, who'd been an enlisted man in the Korean War. He was Puerto Rican, very thorough, very seasoned. Captain Vasquez ensured that the discipline was followed, and he was actually the one who constructed Fire Support Base Ripcord. He went in and built a pretty impenetrable firebase up there. Toward the middle of March after about seven months as a platoon leader, they brought me back into the battalion staff and they made me a battalion liaison officer. They picked lucky Second Battalion, 506 Infantry to establish a firebase on Hill 935, Fire Support Base Ripcord.

In mid-March, we made our first combat assault to try to establish the firebase. I was assigned to a battalion of the First ARVNs, and they went out and established Fire Support Base O'Reilly, which was a little farther from the A Shau Valley but was there to support Ripcord once we got Ripcord established. We were taking mortar rounds and recoilless rifle rounds from the first day we were there. I was supposed to leave for R&R in four days. I'm out there and the monsoons strike again. We continued to take incoming fire, but we couldn't get any resupply helicopters in or out of the base.

[To establish a firebase] you go in and you secure the ground. Usually you go in with aircraft first, do some bombing missions to try to clear the area, then you combat-assault in. You secure the perimeter. Then you start bringing in concertina wire, digging foxholes, clearing fields of fire, clearing a place to put the artillery batteries on top of the firebase. The size of the firebase and what your mission is and how long you expect to be there [determines] how extensive the preparations are. It's a time-consuming process because you have to sandbag and build bunkers for the mess hall and that kind of stuff. You're out far enough that your only resupply was by air, so everything was in and out by air.

In late March, [the Second Battaltion 506 Infantry] tried again to get on Hill 935 [by helicopter] and got hit with another assault. They took casualties and weren't able to do it. Finally in mid-April, we did a ground assault and took over Hill 935 and were able to start building Fire Support Base Ripcord [on the edge of the A Shau Valley]. It took thirty days before [Captain Vasquez] was happy with [the defenses established] on Fire Support Base Ripcord.

GEORGE BANDA I was transferred out to Firebase Henderson. Henderson was up at Quang Tri, about twelve miles south of the DMZ [demilitarized zone]. I never had heard of it. We were up there pretty close to all the activity and the trails that were coming from the north resupplying the North Vietnamese soldiers. We were always making a lot of contact with the enemy. At the time, I'd say, "I'm in I Corps. OK, what does that mean?" Later on when I got home and started reading about it, I was like, "Oh my goodness. That was not a good area."

William Hawley was our lieutenant. He was a good guy, a West Point grad. Henderson was one of the worst firebases I had ever seen. There was no protection there. There was just one or two strands of concertina wire. I said, "We're in the jungle here and there's enemy around us and this is all we got?" Lieutenant, he saw it first. He said, "OK, we have to dig in. We gotta dig deeper. Get more sandbags." We got there on the 5th of May. We worked all day long, digging in deeper foxholes, putting up more sandbags. We were right next to the ammo dump. The ammo dump had almost one thousand rounds of 155 [155-millimeter howitzer ammunition]. I said, "When the enemy comes, that's what they'll go for." They'd want to get rid of the artillery. That's what was hurting them out in the field.

We had fourteen or fifteen recon there. Alpha Company and the ARVNs were there, plus the artillery people with the 155s. Supposedly it was a temporary base. We were just coming in to give support, and then we were supposed to go. The jungle was right there within a few feet. It was not a good place to be. It was very insecure. I was coming from Firebase Bastogne with a hundred feet of concertina wire, claymores, no vegetation at all for a mile. With Henderson, anybody could sneak up real quick. You wouldn't see them until it was too late. That's exactly what happened. I was like, "OK. Tomorrow morning we'll get up early and start making it a little bit more secure." We never got the chance.

CHARLIE LIEB On July 1 things really started to heat up, and the companies we had out in the field started taking significant casualties and meeting significant enemy opposition. The most damaging was my old company. Charlie Company was on Hill 902, and Captain Vasquez had left and they had a new company commander come in, Captain Hewitt. Captain H was on his second tour. During his first tour he'd been an ARVN advisor, and he was not nearly as strict and tactical as Captain Vasquez had been. He set up on Hill 902 for one night and they'd had some enemy contact. He stayed on the hill for the second night, and they didn't really dig in. They got hit that night by a sapper attack. At that time there were only two platoons there and probably only forty-five people.

It was a pretty devastating attack. There were eight killed including that company commander and quite a few wounded. The next morning we had the Third Platoon of Charlie Company on Fire Support Base Ripcord. I led the combat assault out there to see what had happened and to evacuate the wounded and dead. One of the soldiers had been in my platoon not that many months before. All you could find was his boot with his dog tag on it. It was pretty brutal. A lot of good people were lost during that time.

GEORGE BANDA I was on watch that night. I remember sitting there by the foxhole and looking at my watch and thinking, "My watch is almost over. It's getting light out. It's about five minutes to five o'clock." There was a heavy fog. I thought maybe I should wake one of the guys up to shoot the breeze with him. Just then, I heard an explosion on the west side of the hill. It didn't sound right. I was like, "OK, what is that? Was that a claymore going off?" Ten seconds later, a trip flare goes off maybe fifty feet in front of me. We had the concertina wire, so we had put trip wires out just in case the enemy tried to come through. The trip flare goes off. I hit the claymore. It blew. To my right, there was a tower with some guards from Alpha Company. They just opened fire over that whole area. I turned to my left and said, "Hey!" to the guys that were asleep. (I'm on watch, so they're asleep.) I turned and yelled, "Something is happening!" An instant later, I saw a flash out of the corner of my right eye, and an RPG [rocket-propelled grenade] hit five feet away from me. It exploded. I went flying up in the air. I landed on my head and rolled over. I got up real quick. I was deaf. There were tracers flying through the air. I could see explosions but I couldn't hear anything. It was surreal. Slowly, my hearing started to come back. The adrenaline started to rush. I looked at myself: "OK, I'm fine. I'm not hurt. I'm not bleeding." I picked up my rifle and started shooting. I ran out of ammunition.

There was a box of hand grenades. I tore the box open. The other guys came around. One of the guys had half of his left foot blown off from the RPG explosion that hit the bunker. You could just see smoke coming out of his boot. There was very little bleeding because it was an explosion. It cauterized it. It was a lot of pain for him. My first aid bag was blown to smithereens. The other guy wasn't wounded. I said, "Well, two of us weren't wounded." He still had a rifle. He started shooting. We were throwing frags and rocks, whatever we could find. He turned around. There was a gook. We called them "gooks" back then. He shot and killed one and the guy fell right into the ammo dump. Five seconds later the ammo dump starts exploding. You've got one thousand rounds of 155, white phosphorus, claymore mines. You've got highly explosive stuff up there.

Every five seconds an explosion would go off and just shower you with shrapnel, and white phosphorus would start burning you. We stayed in our foxhole because that was the safest place to be. Trying to get up and run anywhere was out of the question. We just stayed and kept fighting. Their purpose was to get over to that ammo dump and cause as much damage as they could. They did. It was horrible. We stayed in that position for as long as we could. The explosions were getting too powerful and too scary. Every explosion was louder and closer. I said, "We can't stay here. We're going to get killed for sure. We need to get away. Come around the hill." We went about ten or fifteen feet down toward the bottom of the hill. We had only one guy with an M-16 and he was down to one clip. I said, "We have to get around to the north end of the hill and then come back up to get away from these explosions. We'll get over by Ed Veser, Kenn Schutte, Doc Diller, Doc Bowman, Lieutenant Hawley, and Sergeant Snyder." We came around to the north end of the hill, and we managed to get up to the guys. I thought we were going to be safe, but most of them were dead already.

CHARLIE LIEB The sappers, whether they were North Vietnamese Regulars or Vietcong, stripped down under cover of night and painted themselves dark. They had something called satchel charges. They attacked on Hill 902 at four o'clock in the morning. It proved to be the ideal time because you'd been in a defensive position since nine o'clock. You hadn't seen anything, heard anything. Things were quiet. People were lulled to sleep and not paying close attention. They penetrated the perimeter. The battle for Hill 902 started when Charlie Company discovered the NVA had already penetrated the perimeter. As they started firing down, they were getting satchel charges from behind them and firing from behind them down into the foxholes. They didn't have good security. They didn't have listening posts out. They didn't dig good positions. It was a travesty because it had been a very good unit under Captain Vasquez and he'd only been gone for a month and a half. It shows that leadership is pretty important. Captain Hewitt was lying in a hammock. He took an RPG. They found an arm here, a leg there. He was supposed to be back in the center of the perimeter. They knew better. Some very good soldiers were needlessly killed because of a lack of security and a lack of discipline.

GEORGE BANDA Kenn Shutte was wounded. He had been shot and then I think he had lost one eye. He was throwing hand grenades out because he had run out of ammunition. The machine gunner had been killed. There was still shooting and explosions. I said, "I've got to check on these guys just to make sure they're OK. I'm a medic. I need to help these guys." I went to Doc Diller. Doc Diller was just laying there on his back. He looked like he was asleep. I said, "Hey, Doc, get up." I tried to pick him up. The back of his head was gone. His head was full of sand, which freaked me out. I'm like, "How can that be? How can his head be full of sand?" I laid him back down and I went over to Lieutenant Hawley. He was dead. Sergeant Snyder was dead. Our lieutenant and our sergeant. Our leaders were gone, both dead.

I caught a round on the left side of my head, which severed an artery. Being a medic, knowing an artery had been severed, I knew I was bleeding to death. I couldn't stop it. I didn't have any bandages, so I was taking whatever I had to wrap around wounds. Every time I moved around, I would squirt five feet of blood from that artery. Your adrenaline is going. Your heart is pumping. Every time my heart pumped, that blood shot out. It slowed down a little bit. I said, "OK, I can handle this. Start taking care of Kenn Shutte and everybody else." I tried to get them into a safe area so the explosions or the shooting from up in the jungle wouldn't get them.

I went over to see Tommy Teran and I couldn't find him. I found out later that he was MIA. His body wasn't found until 2001. I went looking for bodies and survivors, and there was nobody left. I looked for Ed Veser and I said, "Where the hell is Ed?" There was a pile of debris from the explosions. Somehow he either walked down there or was blown down the hill. I don't think I've ever told this to anybody but I hesitated to go down there. I was scared. You get so scared that every cell in your body is just terrified. I just wanted to stay where I was. I was thinking, "I'm bleeding to death. Ed's way down there. What good can I do?" I was scared because there was no protection down there. He was in an open area. I said, "If I go down there, I'm going to get killed. I know it." I hesitated. I was scared but he was my friend. I finally said, "I can't leave him down there." I tore a little piece of my T-shirt and balled it up and pushed it into the hole in my head until it hurt. I said, "OK, you feel pain. That's good. You're all right." I tied the rest of that T-shirt around my head. I crawled down there. I got to Ed. The thing that I'll always remember: he said to me, "I knew you'd come." Terrible. I feel guilty about that. I still do. He was horribly wounded. Horribly. I'[d] seen wounds before because I'd been a medic all the way up until then, but I was shocked that he was still alive. The wounds he had should have killed him instantly. He was strong, young, and he had a wife. He'd just gotten married in Hawaii. He'd just gotten back from R&R, and he comes back to this?

I said, "We've got to get out of here. We're going to get killed down here for sure." I could see dirt kicking up around us, so I knew people were shooting at us. I said, "We've got to get you back up there." He couldn't. He was too badly injured to help himself. I can't remember how I dragged him up to the hill. I got him up to the sandbags and laid him down. I said, "Ed, the helicopters will be coming." He said, "OK. Don't leave me." I said, "I won't, Ed."

He grabbed a hold of my dog tag. He grabbed it real tight. I said, "Ed,

I've got to go. I've got to check on the other guys. They're hurt too." He said, "No, I don't want you to go." I said, "Ed, I don't want to go, but I have to." I started pulling away and he pulled one of my dog tags out. He held onto that. I said, "Ed, I'll be right back." I went in to check on Kenn and the other guys to make sure they were OK, that they weren't bleeding out or going into shock. They seemed to be all right. I turned around and started coming back. That's when Alpha Company Team came from around the corner to rescue us.

Soldiers patrol Fire Support Base Henderson looking for survivors after the May 6, 1970, early morning attack. *George Banda*

They couldn't get to us because the ammo dump was exploding. Cobra gun ships that were coming to give us support were flying around us, shooting at everything that was coming. They had called artillery in on us, but they couldn't land because they were still taking a lot of fire. You could see the medevacs flying around, but they couldn't land. It was real frustrating because I knew Ed was dying on me. I would move back to him and start talking to him, trying to keep him conscious. I said, "Hey, your wife, Connie, is waiting back there and we're all going to go home, Ed. Just hang in there. The medevacs will be here soon and they'll be able to land and get you out of here."

The medevacs finally were able to land. They came in real quick and loaded him up. I'm thinking to myself, "Maybe they might be able save him. Maybe he's just unconscious. Maybe he'll be OK." The helicopter took off. I did another walk around to make sure that I hadn't missed anybody, but everybody was dead. Another helicopter came in and got everybody else, and I jumped in and flew out of there. I wound up in the Marine hospital because our hospitals were so full that day. There were thirty-two Americans killed that morning. I knew ten of them personally. At the hospital they put me on a stretcher. I jumped up because I saw Ed on a stretcher. There was a doctor and a nurse looking over him. I remember running over to them and saying, "Doc, you've got to save this guy 'cause he's got a wife and he's going to have a kid and he needs to go home." A nurse grabbed me and put me back in a stretcher and I laid there and all of a sudden, I just got drained. I became weak as a kitten. I couldn't move.

I remember lying in the hospital where they took me by helicopter. I was still bleeding. A priest came up. My eyes were closed, my head bandaged. I could hear somebody speaking Latin. I thought, "Am I dreaming?" I had to force my eyes open. I was so weak. I could not believe how weak I was. There was a priest there and he was giving me the last rites. That was a shock and it angered me. There was a time when I was so weak and tired and exhausted and I'd seen so much and all my friends were dead, I felt like, "Just give up. Just go to sleep. It will be all over." Hearing that priest, I couldn't see him so much as I heard him, speaking Latin. [In my head] I was saying, "No, no, no, no. I've made it. I'm going to make it now. I'm not going to give up." I opened my eyes. I don't think there was any expression in my face, but inside of me, I was like, "No, no. I'm not going to die here. I'm going to go home." Here I am.

Charlie Lieb calls in an airstrike on enemy bunkers using his PRC 77 Radio at Fire Support Base Ripcord, June 1970. *Charlie Lieb*

CHARLIE LIEB Everybody [who was with me that morning] came back. There were forty-five people there. Eight of them were killed, twenty-some were wounded. Some were claiming hearing loss because of the satchel charges. It effectively wiped out two platoons of Charlie Company.

We had a 105 and a 155-millimeter howitzer battery on top of the firebase. On July 18, a Chinook helicopter was bringing in artillery ammo to resupply our 105 and 155-millimeter howitzer battery on top of the fire support base, and the helicopter was shot down. It crashed into the ammo dump and [burned, setting off all the artillery ammunition]. We started taking some heavy casualties. Two days later, on the 20th, several recoilless rifle rounds came in and actually exploded close by; I got wounded for the third time. I got evacuated again to my favorite hospital — the 85th Evac. The next day, Captain Don Workman [my roommate at West Point] got killed. When they were trying to extract [his unit the NVA] shot down the Huey that was coming in to lift them off. As it crashed, the blade came and decapitated him. That was a big loss because he was a tremendous soldier. He [held] one of the four top positions they have there. He was a heck of a guy and that was a gigantic loss to me.

Two days after that, on the 22nd, they decided that they were going to evacuate Fire Support Base Ripcord. They [started evacuations] on the 23rd. Some very brave pilots made many trips. [Two artillery batteries] started firing off all the ammunition. They knew they weren't going to be able to get the howitzers out, so they blew those up on top of the fire support base. They brought in a pathfinder team [and] started evacuation of all the units in the field plus the fire support base. It was a difficult evacuation both because of weather and because of heavy enemy fire coming in. They had one Chinook shot down and several helicopters took a lot of rounds, but most of them managed to limp back to their bases. The evacuation was completed that day.

GEORGE BANDA I was in the hospital for a little over two and a half weeks. In the meantime there was all this chaos and nobody knew who was killed or who was wounded or where they went. I was reported MIA. When that happens, they make a phone call to your parents "Mrs. Banda, your son is missing in action and we're still looking for him, but we're hopeful." My poor ma was just freaking out, I'm sure. She told me later.

Once they let me go from the Marine hospital, I had to catch a C-130. I felt all by myself; all alone. I asked, "Is somebody going to give me a ride over?" "No, here's your discharge from the hospital. You've got to find your way back to your base." I'm like, "OK. Where do I get a C-130?" "Oh, you've got to talk to that officer over there." It's surreal. Everybody's got their own thing they're doing. They don't know what you just went through. They say, "Just sit over there and wait. There will be somebody here." You wait a few hours and then you get up and say, "Hey, what's going on?" "Oh yeah, yeah, that's right. They're not flying out today. Maybe you can catch one tomorrow." "Well, now what? Where do I go?" "Well you can stay right here and nobody will care."

Waiting there for the C-130, I told myself I was never going to talk about it. I came back to the base. Everybody was shocked to see me. The first thing they said was, "We thought you were dead." I'm like, "No, I'm still here."

Weak from injuries sustained at Firebase Henderson, George Banda steadies himself with the back of a supply trailer at Camp Eagle.
George Banda

"What happened?" "Nothing. Firefight. I'm here. What do you want me to do next?" I didn't talk about it. Once I got back to the world, I didn't say anything to anybody about it. My brothers, my family, would ask and I would say, "Well, it was bad. And that's that." They didn't press me. Years would go by and then some people would ask. Again, it was, "Oh, Vietnam was Vietnam. Shooting. I'm here."

CHARLIE LIEB During the evacuation, the battalion commander, Andre Lucas, and his XO got hit by an incoming mortar round and were killed. He received the Medal of Honor for his operations at Fire Support Base Ripcord. There were three Medal of Honor winners associated with the battle of Fire Support Base Ripcord. Two were awarded posthumously. There were 247 U.S. troops killed in action from March 1970 until the end of July 1970 in and around Fire Support Base Ripcord. I lost a lot of good friends, and a lot of good people were either killed or wounded there. The battle for Fire Support Base Ripcord was actually the last large battle that the U.S. was involved in during the Vietnam War.

Since I was three-time[s wounded] they volunteered to let me go home early. I said no. I went back to my unit after I got out of the hospital the third time. There was a new battalion commander. There was just nobody left. That was sad because there were a lot of very good people who had served very well, and they were either dead or wounded or just weren't around anymore.

GEORGE BANDA I see them, those young kids. I'm almost sixty-one years old now. Those guys were nineteen, twenty, twenty-one. I look at the photos that I have and we were kids. What a thing to witness. It never goes away. I see their faces. I remember the sounds of their voices and their laughter and

Sergeant John Eaves addresses his men "at ease." Ed Veser is pictured front row center, across from Eaves and next to the soldier with sunglasses. *George Banda*

the jokes we used to tell. When I first met Ed in Vietnam, this new guy coming into the platoon, I asked, "Hey, where you from?" This young kid, blond-haired, freckled face: "I'm from Wisconsin." I'm like, "Wisconsin? Where?" "Milwaukee." "Milwaukee! Me too!" We got to be real good friends. We had a lot of plans. He was going to buy a GTO and I was going to buy a Mustang, and when we got back we were going to drive up and down the street and have a good time. He was going to come to my cookouts, and we were going to go to Packer games. We were going to visit each other's families and have a good time afterwards.

It never happened. He died at 7:40 a.m. on May 6, 1970. I tell people, "Ed got back earlier than I did. He was here, waiting for me, when I got back." [Tears up.] Ed was there when I got married. He was there when I started my first job. He was there when I got divorced. He was there when I got married again. We had a few drinks together. Whenever I go somewhere, he's there. I talk to him.

When I got back from Vietnam, I got a chance to meet Ed's family and his wife, Connie. They were very nice and kind. We'd talked about his mom and dad. He'd said, "Oh my, my dad's a plumber and my mom's a good cook. My wife, I just love her to death." He couldn't wait to come home. He wanted to do his duty, get in and get out, survive it. His wife took it really, really hard. She never remarried and they had a son, Eddie Jr. He's had a hard time with life, without a father. That's what happens when a life is lost. It ripples, and it affects a lot of people, family and friends. It affected me and everybody that knew Ed.

I picture them smiling. That's the way I try to remember them from those dear, happy moments when we were all together, having a beer and laughing and talking about things we were going to do when we got back to the world, passing photos around saying, "Oh, this is my fiancée," or "This is my kid." Happy times. Every time I go up to the cemetery where Ed is buried, it's a pretty day. I visit his place of rest once a month. He just happens to call and I go there and hear birds singing. I tell him, "Hey, the sun is shining and the birds are singing, and it's good to see you again." I tell him what's happening. I'm jealous because he's still young. I'm old now, Ed.

I remember Ed and me, after we'd been through a number of firefights, looking at each other and promising, "If we get back to the world, everything's going to be gravy. We're never going to complain about anything again. Every day is going to be gravy." I made it back from that. It's gravy. You tend to forget that once in a while. I have. When I've forgotten it, I start feeling sorry for myself. I remember Ed. Ed says, "Wait a minute," and I say, "Right, Ed. It's good to be alive." He reminds me.

14 Secret War

"You're just a kid. You don't know. You're not scared of anything at all. You're just willing to fight"— Nhia Thong "Charles" Lor

Though the United States' military intervention in Southeast Asia is commonly referred to as the Vietnam War, the fighting was not isolated to Vietnam itself. Concerned about the spread of Communism to other Southeast Asian countries and seeking to destroy enemy supply lines and refuges in neighboring Laos and Cambodia, the United States extended its combat efforts far beyond Vietnam's borders. In the 1960s, Laos was also undergoing civil conflict as the Communist movement Pathet Lao, an ally of North Vietnam, sought to overthrow the royal Laotian government.[1] Though Laos was officially a neutral country, in what is now known as the "secret war" the CIA began organizing and training an army of Hmong, an ethnic minority in Laos, to attack both Pathet Lao and North Vietnamese forces in the early 1960s.

Because of their relative invisibility in the West, there were few restraints on U.S. activities in Laos; as one U.S. official commented in 1960, "This is the end of nowhere. We can do anything we want here because Washington doesn't seem to know that it exists."[2] Along with training Hmong forces, the United States also dropped thousands of tons of bombs on Laos, bringing widespread destruction. The bombing of Laos began before the passage of the Gulf of Tonkin Resolution in 1964 and escalated alongside the war in Vietnam. Though the bombing initially targeted the Ho Chi Minh Trail — the major enemy supply line between North and South Vietnam that also crossed into Laos — it expanded to destroy Laotian towns and villages.[3] The Plain of Jars, a region in northeastern Laos dominated by the Pathet Lao, became the central target of U.S. bombing efforts, and from 1964 to 1969, between 74,000 and 150,000 tons of bombs were dropped on the area.[4] As a United Nations worker stated, "The bombing climax reached its peak in 1969 when jet planes came daily and destroyed all stationary structures.

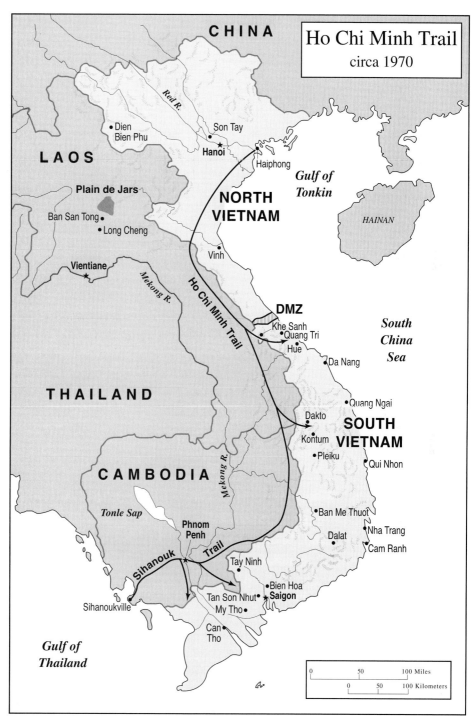

Patti Isaacs, Parrot Graphics

Nothing was left standing. . . . In the last phase, bombings were aimed at the systematic destruction of the material basis of civilian society."[5] By 1970, more than 25 percent of the Laotian population had become refugees.[6] In December 1969, the U.S. Congress passed a resolution banning the introduction of U.S. ground troops to Laos, but it did not address the bombing or U.S. support for South Vietnamese and Laotian forces. Bombing and fighting in Laos continued into the 1970s.

Much as the war itself radiated through Southeast Asia, the United States' withdrawal from Vietnam in 1973 and the subsequent victory of North Vietnam in 1975 also had grave consequences for surrounding nations. The Khmer Rouge, led by Pol Pot, took control of Cambodia, leading to large-scale genocide. In February 1973, the Laotian government and the Pathet Lao signed an agreement that strengthened the Pathet Lao, giving it control over important territories.[7] In 1975, with North Vietnam's victory, the Pathet Lao took power in Laos. Seeking revenge on the Hmong who had fought against them, the Pathet Lao hunted down and killed approximately 100,000 Hmong.[8] An equal number were able to immigrate to the United States, often through Thailand, and many, like Nhia Thong "Charles" Lor, who tells his story here, settled in the Midwest. Ultimately, the war in Vietnam consumed not only Vietnam but also surrounding nations, leaving a trail of devastation that changed the course of history throughout Southeast Asia.

Steven Schofield, Chicago (First Special Forces Group and Studies and Observations Group)
Nhia Thong "Charles" Lor, Long Cheng, Laos (Military Region II Special Guerilla Unit)

STEVEN SCHOFIELD I [finished my] sophomore year in college. I was out in New Jersey with some friends, fooling around, and my mother called and said, "You've got a draft notice." The dean of my college had called the draft board and said I was eligible. I'd left under a cloud. It didn't take very long. Rather than being drafted I just enlisted. In basic training, the Special Forces recruiter came by, and I said, "What the heck." I went down and took all the tests and out of about two hundred guys who went down and took the two days of exams, only two of us passed and were accepted. I just signed up right there, in basic training.

I went in February '66. I became a medic and I went to basic medical training, then went to jump school, then went to Special Forces training. Jump school was tough in that it was in Fort Benning, Georgia, in July. It was 100 degrees and 100 percent humidity almost every day. Out of, again, about two hundred in my class, I was up for what they call "Mr. Airborne," the honor graduate. [Before] the last inspection they had us take our T-shirts off. I had a little bit of a gut and it was hanging over my brass belt buckle. It left the top half of the brass buckle sort of green. They saw that and they said, "What the hell kind of airborne troop would have a buckle like that?" I was number two, not the honor graduate.

After training in the fall of 1967 I went to the First Special Forces group in Okinawa. First Group had responsibility for all of Southeast Asia at the time. I was there off and on for two years. I first left Okinawa to go to Taiwan to train Chinese Nationalist Special Forces, [then] came back to Okinawa. I did a medical civic action mission. Then I did the Taiwan mission. Then I went to Vietnam, came back from Vietnam, then I went to the Philippines to train Filipino special forces and also work counterinsurgency against New People's Army in Northern Luzon.

NHIA THONG LOR My name from my country is Nhia Thong Lor. When I [be]came [a] U.S. citizen, I changed to Charles. I still use my middle initial, T., for Thong, so people remember. We lived in Laos, close to North Vietnam. I lived with my parents in the [Phou Pha Thi] camp because my father was a soldier. My father and my father's older brother and uncle, they were all soldiers. They all got killed. In my culture we called my father's older brother's son "brother." In America they are called "cousin." He got killed too. They lived on the front line. They lived in the fighting and they got killed. I'm really lucky. We got [the] fighting three or four times. One time I had one person in front of me and two after me; they got killed. I [was] really lucky that time. I joined the Army [in 1969] when I was twelve years old. I joined to protect my family and my country.

STEVEN SCHOFIELD I went to Vietnam as a replacement for a junior medic who was wounded at Khe Sanh. My team had gone to FOB4 [Forward Operations Base 4], which is Marble Mountain, near Da Nang. They were already back from Khe Sanh when I joined them at Marble Mountain. [As part of]

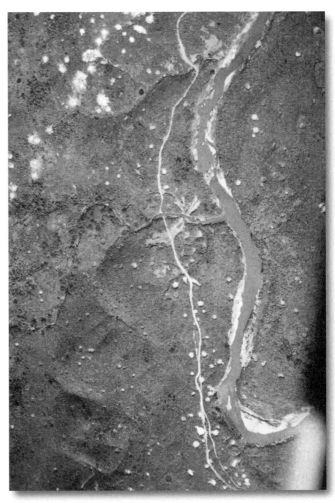

Above: Steve Schofield outside the barracks at Marble Mountain in Vietnam, preparing for a training mission with the Studies and Observations Group. *Steven Schofield*

Right: Circular bomb craters line the Ho Chi Minh Trail in Laos. *Robert Curry*

the Studies and Observations Group, also known as Special Operations Group, we did cross-border operations into Cambodia, Laos, and North Vietnam. We went across into Laos with no ID cards, no dog tags, and mixed uniforms made in Korea or the Philippines, indigenous rucksacks, no U.S. gear other than our weapons.

There were several missions. One of them was to wiretap or interrupt the communication of the North Vietnamese along the Ho Chi Minh Trail. One was to identify weapons caches for the bombers. Another was to do bomb damage assessment, and [another] was prisoner snatch. When I was assigned to Hatchet Force, we had a company of indigenous troops in the camp at FOB4 who were mostly Chinese ethnic troops with a few Vietnamese. The Hatchet Force would go into Laos, near the Ho Chi Minh Trail, to either assist in the recovery of a team or extraction of a team or to exploit a target that a small team had found. The small team would just do recon. [Then] when the Hatchet Force went in it was combat, all the way. We took the Hatchet Force into Laos.

Probably within three weeks of my arrival we did the first operation and we went in with a 140-man group near the Ho Chi Minh Trail, about thirteen miles into Laos, and stayed for five days. We landed on a grassy slope of a hill in broad daylight and dug in there. Next day we moved out and found the area that had been bombed, and we did the bomb damage assessment. Then we spent the night right in an area that had been an NVA camp. [The next day] we moved further up to the top of the mountain and started digging in. The idea was we were to draw the North Vietnamese so the bombers could bomb them. That's what happened. We started clearing the LZ as soon as [choppers brought in supplies]. I had a rope tied on me and a chainsaw, and I started cutting trees. No weapon, of course. I was just going down the slope cutting trees. Right after they pulled me up, I moved over to my hole and we got hit pretty good. I was wounded right away. The guy next to me was wounded and the guy to my right, his rucksack strap was cut off. These were Chinese. I was amongst my squad of Chinese.

It wasn't much of a wound. I got hit across the nose and the cheek with a bullet. It broke my nose. I looked over to my machine gunner squad leader, a Chinese guy; I asked if he was all right. He was lying on the ground, and I said, "Are you OK?" He's going like this. [Uses hand to gesture.] "Yeah, I'm OK." I could see him laying on his stomach and his toe was pointing straight up. We didn't know if the enemy was still in the area, so I crawled over there and saw that he had been shot right through the knee and it turned his leg around. That was my first combat wound. I had to turn his leg around and set his leg. I gave him morphine first and then turned his leg all the way around and splinted it up with branches and my T-shirt and some bandages. We had about twenty other wounded men in the three days we were surrounded. [One] American was killed out of the fourteen and another was KIA when a medavac chopper was shot down.

NHIA THONG LOR We [were] train[ed] how to shoot a piece of paper. The gun was still heavy for me. The carbine was still heavy. We trained [for] many, many things: to dig holes to protect you [for when] the enemy came. They trained you when something happened, you had to lay on the floor.

Like many Hmong boys, Nhia Thong "Charlie" Lor, pictured center, joined the army at a very young age. These young soldiers supported American troops during the Secret War in Laos.
Nhia Thong Lor

Also, in the evening time you didn't use the gun because if you used a gun, then [the enemy] would see the spark and know where you [were] and that's not safe for you.

I [knew] that one day I w[ould] grow up. In the beginning, they [did] not put me right [on] the front lines. They put me in the meat cent[er] for packaging food. One year later they sent me to the front line. You're just a kid. You don't know. You're not scared of anything at all. You're just willing to fight. A couple years later all my friends in my group, they got killed. The enemy was the North Vietnamese. The United States asked our Hmong people because [we were] close to North Vietnam. We protect[ed] that area.

STEVEN SCHOFIELD My term was up. I'd gotten a letter from my senior medic, who was on the operation with me in Laos. He was getting ready to retire and had been contacted by another medic that was his age, an older guy in his forties, who wanted to recruit him to go to work in Laos. He found out both his mother and his brother came down with brain tumors and he had to go back and take care of them. He couldn't go to Laos, so he recommended me to his buddy, Don Dugan. That was the start of the process of recruiting me to go to work for U.S. Agency for International Development (USAID). It was part of the State Department. In order to go to work for USAID, I had to get out of the Army. But I just wasn't quite sure. I'd met my wife at a beach party. I wasn't sure I wanted to get out of the Army and go to Laos. I'd extended for four months, and that was when I went to the Philippines. I spent two months out of those four months in the Philippines. Yasuko said she wouldn't marry me unless I got a real job and got out of the Special Forces. I told her USAID was a real job. We've been married thirty-nine years.

[My job was] running the field medical operation and the dispensary program in Northern Laos. I said, "Well, sure, I can handle that." I was sent to Washington for State Department training. They pulled me aside, out of

Steve Schofield, chief medic Lu Chay, right, and a Lao Theung veteran pause while traveling between villages in the Xieng Khouang Province in Laos, November 1973.
Steven Schofield

the class, and said, "Your cover story is that you will be the public health advisor for Military Region 2 [MR2], but your top-secret duties will be running search and rescue for American crews that are shot down in Laos." I got to Laos, [spent] three days in Vientiane, and within three days I was up in Sam Thong, Laos, working. We did a few search and rescues. Most of the time we picked up dead bodies. Once or twice we got a couple of live ones. The real day-to-day mission was to supply and train the medics that were out in the field dispensaries [in] villages, [usually] with a military camp nearby.

We would go into these villages in the mountaintops where the Hmong [had outposts], and they would always take their families to the outposts. There'd be a military outpost, maybe a military medic or maybe just a civilian medic, and I would go in, bring them supplies, bring their pay every month, and give them on-the-job training. I'd look at their patients and see how they were treating them. I'd look at what little records they kept to make sure that they had enough supplies. Then I'd go on to the next. When I first started in Laos, I'd go to probably sixteen villages a day. [That was] sixteen take-offs and landings in a single-engine aircraft on a mountaintop strip. I'd bring patients back to the hospital in Sam Thong. I'd do maybe three of those trips a day. [I'd go] from first light to last light. That was my daily routine.

Laos was always a sideshow to Vietnam. Whatever happened in Vietnam affected us in Laos, of course. The war in Laos was primarily a CIA operation. What the CIA had done was organize the Hmong tribal people, in 1960, to be a guerrilla force to fight North Vietnamese encroachment into Laos. In the area of MR2, where I was, it was primarily the movement of North Vietnamese into the Plain de Jars, which was the axis from [Hanoi through] the Xiang Khouang right through to Vientiane and of course Thailand.

NHIA THONG LOR I served [from] '69 to '75. [I met] Steve [Schofield] in 1969. Back in Laos, I saw him, but at that time, he was young. He was a little kid, too. He was tall. I watched him like this. [Looks up.] He didn't tell me his name, "Steve." I didn't talk to him. He just s[aw] me with my friends and want[ed] to take a picture. I didn't know him well. He got my picture. My friend [in the photo], we were in [the] same group. He got killed in 1972.

Steve Schofield snapped this shot of Nhia Thong "Charles" Lor in Sam Thong, Laos in 1969. Lor, age twelve, is pictured right holding an M-16 rifle. *Nhia Thong Lor*

Steve has another friend. I don't really remember his name. He tried to bring me to the United States in 1969 because at that time my parents [were] gone. There was only me. I stayed with my father's older brother's family. He tried to bring me to the United States, but my family [didn't] let me come. I think [Steve] look[ed] for me after [the war]. I met him [again] in 1998 between Manitowoc and Sheboygan. He saw my picture. I'm not really different from my picture. I still look like pretty much the same. He helped me; if [I had] a problem or questions or something, he helped me a lot. He's a very nice friend of mine.

STEVEN SCHOFIELD The Hmong were primitive people. They traveled by foot. There were a few horses. No carts, no wheels. They used grinding wheels for tools and flintlock muzzleloaders and crossbows to fight the North Vietnamese. They had very little education, no knowledge of astronomy, no knowledge of science, no knowledge of math, and no written language except one that was developed in the 1930s. They had an oral tradition. Nhia Thong said he had three years total education where he barely learned to read and write his own language. I have tremendous respect for these guys who have come over here and made it in this country and for their kids, who have done fantastic.

I'd only been in Sam Thong probably a month or two and I saw this little guy walking by and I stopped him and said, "I'm going to take your picture." I posed him over by the jeeps. I had him exchange weapons with his cousin. He had the M-16 and [you could] really [see] how short and small he was. I took the photo and he was on his way. That was the last I saw him until 1998.

I always thought it was a great picture. I'd looked at it a lot over the years and always wondered what happened to that kid. I had some Hmong over at my place and I was showing them pictures. They love to look at pictures. Those Laos kids had so few. They obviously couldn't carry things like that [when they fled]. I was showing them slides and I had maybe 500 or 600 slides I'd taken in Laos. I'd put up the slide of Nhia Thong and one of the guys says, "I know that guy. That's Nhia Thong. He lives in Milwaukee." I said, "Well, shit. Bring him up here!" [Laughs.] Within a week, they brought Nhia Thong and we had a little reunion. It was great to see him. We've become good friends since. He's got a great family. His kids are all well educated. They're smart, polite kids. His oldest son runs a dental lab in St. Paul. He calls me Grandpa and calls my wife Grandma.

[The Hmong] weren't fighting just for us. As early as 1952 they were fighting Vietnamese encroachment into their territory. The North Vietnamese would come and treat them as ethnic minorities, as subhumans. They used them as pack animals to carry their supplies and do their dirty work. The Hmong resisted then. They're very independent, self-reliant people who moved out of China because of persecution by the Chinese who wanted to force them to assimilate. The Hmong would not assimilate. The Hmong were great fighters. They were loyal and honest. You could trust them. They suffered greatly. The total population of Hmong in Northern Laos in MR was about 250,000 and the estimates are they lost 25,000 to 35,000 during that ten-year war. They were just wiped out. When I took that picture of Nhia Thong in 1969, it was because he was unique: a small, young soldier. There weren't that many of them in Vang Pao's army then. By the time '72/'73 came around, there were whole platoons of ten- and twelve-year-olds because the Hmong were just wiped out. The older guys were either dead or in high leadership positions and so they could strip these kids right from the villages to go in and fight on the front lines.

Nhia Thong "Charles" Lor patrolling in Phou Kae, Laos in 1972 during a recon mission for the Special Guerilla Unit. *Nhia Thong Lor*

By '72/'73 the Hmong had really been decimated. They started bringing in Lao troops. These were Lao SGUs [Special Guerrilla Units] trained by the CIA. They stayed almost a year. They were being used badly by General Vang Pao. He'd put them out in the worst positions and the front lines and they were getting wiped out. Finally they revolted and walked out of Long Cheng. They were put on airplanes and flown back south. Then right after the Lao, the Thai volunteers came in. They went up in front-line positions, artillery positions, and again they were wiped out. My office turned into a front-line dispensary, like a MASH. All day long during the dry seasons of '72 and '73, chopper load after chopper load of these wounded Thai soldiers came in. My medics and I would stabilize them, put IVs in, lop off legs if they were just hanging there, do whatever it took to keep them alive until we could get them on a C-123 or C-130 back to Udon.

It went on all morning up until midafternoon, then we'd take a break. I'd usually have a half dozen beers, take a shower, get all the blood off me, and go home to Vientiane where my wife was. By this time, my son was born. I'd go back and have a steak and bottle of wine. I'd get up in the morning, fly back up, and do it all over again. Just blood and gore. We'd hose down the office every night after we'd had all the wounded in there. We'd have a pile of weapons in the corner. We were supposed to send those back to Thailand, but I'd give them out to all my medics. That's what we did for five months. We did it again in '73. So the Hmong had already been wiped out. Now the Thai were being wiped out. It was grim. The North Vietnamese were at the gates of Long Cheng, basically firing down into the valley with tanks, with rockets and artillery. It was not looking good.

In '73 the peace [agreement] was signed. The CIA, air support left. Congress mandated, basically, that there were no more supplies for the Vietnamese and the Lao. They just were wiped out. They had nothing to fight with. No supplies. We'd made them dependent on us, on our air power, on our resupply. They couldn't even farm because as the families moved with the soldiers, they'd given up farming. We fed them and made them dependent and then left them. Just like that. In '74/'75, the Hmong were on outposts. It was sort of lock-in-place, "Stay where you are," no aggressive actions. The North Vietnamese didn't [adhere]. They consolidated their forces, and the Big Push occurred in the spring of '75. They took out the rest of Vang Pao's troops. Vang Pao first was evacuated to Thailand with many of his officers and close allies [and the rest] were left to fend for themselves.

NHIA THONG LOR [In 1974 and '75] we didn't know [the war was coming to an end]. I think General Vang Pao, he knew. I think [he knew] the Americans were pull[ing] out, but we [were] still in the field. Later we got the [radio] call: "You need to pull out, to come back." General Vang Pao and other Hmong leaders, they [had flown] to [Udon] already. That's why we just came back to Long Cheng and tr[ied] to find a way to come home with family.

Some Hmong leaders [with the Pathet Lao], they knew that you served for the United States. They [tried] to catch you. They said they had a new rule, "You need to train." They still want[ed] you to be a soldier but want[ed you] to train. But you [went] and you never [came] back. We knew we c[ould] not let them take us like that. We had to move the village to the jungle from '76 to '79. I lived in the jungle. We found something to eat from tree[s] — whatever you c[ould] eat [so] you didn't die. I tried to find a way to come to Thailand. Most people did that.

[There were] more than three thousand [people]. We used the banana leaf for a house. The rainy time was very difficult for us. The old people and the young, they died [of] hunger. There was no rice, so they died. [Those between the] age [of] fifteen to forty-five, they were still strong. They were OK. We tried to find a way to come to Thailand, but we didn't know where we [should] go. We didn't have anything to show which direction to go to Thailand. We moved one place to another place until [we were] closer to Thailand.

STEVEN SCHOFIELD No one got word to [people like] Nhia Thong that he was not going to be evacuated. He had to figure out what to do on his own. Tens of thousands of Hmong fled to the jungles. He talked about how the Vietnamese and then the Pathet Lao said, "We're going to put you in the army and train you." What he meant to say was "reeducation camps." Nobody came home from a reeducation camp. Any military officers or soldiers that went to a camp never returned. [The camps were] in Sam Neua province. They'd send them up there and work them to death or kill them. The king and queen were killed in a reeducation camp. The king and queen of Laos! It was very brutal. The Hmong were bombed from the air, hunted like animals, by the North Vietnamese Army because they had done such an effective job working for the U.S. government against them. They lived in the jungle until they could get across the river to Thailand. Many drowned in the [Mekong] river after all they'd been through.

Vietnam fell first and then Cambodia. Right after Cambodia fell, I was in Vientiane. We had a nice townhouse in KM6, which was the American compound. We had a big party. Dr. Kirkley was leaving with his wife and kids. It was catered. A political officer for the embassy was there and he got up and gave a little speech. He said, "Well, even though Vietnam fell and Cambodia fell, don't worry about it. We're going to be fine here. This is different." It fell so quick that I never got the bill for the party. [Laughs.] I had not been up country for the last month when things got bad. The reason [for this] was I had gotten a bullet letter. A bullet letter is a cartridge in an envelope with a note in it. It means, "You're going to die." A Hmong had sent it, probably one of my medics because he was unhappy with something I had done. In the letter he said that he was going to kill Yasuko and Tommy, my [wife and] son, as well as me. I didn't take it seriously but the ambassador did. The last month when I really could have been helping a lot of Hmong get out and escape, I was back in Vientiane. Anyone that did get into Vientiane, of course, I gave them enough money, [to get] them across [to] Thailand.

Because of that bullet letter, I wasn't really up where I should have been the last month. One morning, about three in the morning, my good friend who was a CIA officer called me and said, "This is the morning, Steve. It's all going down the tubes today, so do what you have to do." I was already in KM6 and my family was there, so we just made sure everything was safe. The students were demonstrating and the government fell. It then became the Communist revolutionary government. We were there after the government fell, and we pretty much couldn't leave the compound. We had plenty of food. [After a week] the Communist government said, "OK, all the families can leave." We were able to get one suitcase and my wife and my son on an airplane and fly to Bangkok. [The twenty-six remaining men] were restricted to a compound and we thought something might happen where there'd be some kind of rapprochement where we could go back to work. It never did occur, and so about ten days later, we were allowed to leave with one suitcase each. In those ten days, all the American families had left and were in this big compound that held 100 or 200 families. There were a lot of pets, dogs and cats. My boss, who was an MD, said, "We can't leave these pets here to suffer. No one's feeding them. If the Vietnamese come in they'll eat them. I want you and Don [Dugan] to kill all the pets." That was one of the hardest things I've ever done.

NHIA THONG LOR In 1975 we had friends. They lived in Vientiane. They crossed the Mekong River to Thailand. At that time they could come back and forth easily, so they told us that was the only way we c[ould] go to Thailand. We [couldn't stay] in Laos like that because we c[ouldn't] really live in the village. We lived in the jungle.

We had a soldier [give us] a compass and the direction to go. [Some families] cut the bamboo [and made] a raft, [but] that is not easy. It is difficult to bring the bamboo. Later on we use[d] only two [pieces of] bamboo: one on each arm, [and we] swam. We [were] still [together] as a family. [I brought] seven people in the family from Laos to Thailand.

When we came to Thailand, the soldiers lived on the river. They knew that at that time there was a lot of fighting in Laos. They knew that people crossed the river. They tried to help bring people to the refugee camp. At that time, the United States had a program to have refugees [in] two refugee camps, one in Nong Khai and the other one in Ban Vinai. The Hmong people lived the most in Ban Vinai. Most Laotians lived in Nong Khai refugee camp. When I first came to Thailand, I came to Nong Khai refugee camp and then they transferred me to Ban Vinai.

STEVEN SCHOFIELD [The Hmong] went into camps in Thailand, and those who had worked for the U.S. government were vetted. If they wanted to come to the U.S., they were allowed to come. Unlike the Vietnamese boat people or any other refugees, the Hmong that are here are those who fought or worked for the U.S. government. They fought in that war and they were brought here, and they've done remarkably well.

NHIA THONG LOR I lived in Thailand only six months. I [didn't] live longer like other famil[ies] because I came to Nong Khai [because of an] American I knew very well in Vientiane. His name is Jerry Daniel[s]. He was the one in charge of looking for the people who served for the United States at the time. He tried to help if they wanted to come to United States. He saw me and knew me right away. He asked, "You want to go to United States?" and I said, "Yes." He did the paperwork right away and after they transferred my family to Ban Vinai refugee camp and had a last interview, they sent me to Bangkok for almost a month, and then on November 27, 1979, I came to America.

STEVEN SCHOFIELD As soon as I got back from Laos, I was fired. We got out and met up with our families in Bangkok. Yasuko, our son, Tom, and I went to Okinawa for a couple of days. I got back to Washington and they gave me a pink slip right way. I said, "Ten years of government service. Can't you find something for me?" The basic story was, "Well, we had 5,000 USAID employees in Vietnam, 700 in Cambodia, and 1,500 in Laos, and you're the last one back and there's nothing left." I was out of a job with a wife, family, no house, no car, no nothing. Just my one suitcase. It certainly wasn't as bad a situation as the Hmong were faced with, but it was difficult. So I went back to Chicago and went to school and I finished my degree. I started working in marketing and sales.

NHIA THONG LOR [It was] very difficult when I first came to America. I came to Denver in December. There was very heavy snow. They bought a coat for each [of us]. They said, "Put your coat on or you [will] be cold." I didn't speak any English, only sign by hand when I first came to Denver. I had my wife's brother-in-law. He was a high school student. He was our sponsor for our family to come to America. He had no car, no home. He had his uncle. We stayed with his uncle's family for maybe a couple months, and then I had to go. At that time they rented an apartment for us. We had no car to go

DAN SCHAEFER
6TH DISTRICT, COLORADO

2353 RAYBURN BUILDING
WASHINGTON, D.C. 20515
(202) 225-7882

3615 SOUTH HURON STREET, #101
ENGLEWOOD, COLORADO 80110
(303) 762-8890
FAX: (303) 762-8899

COMMITTEE ON COMMERCE
SUBCOMMITTEES:
ENERGY AND POWER
CHAIRMAN
TELECOMMUNICATIONS AND FINANCE
COMMITTEE ON VETERANS' AFFAIRS
SUBCOMMITTEE:
EDUCATION, TRAINING, EMPLOYMENT
AND HOUSING

**Congress of the United States
House of Representatives
Washington, D.C.**

July 22, 1995

On behalf of a grateful people of the United States of
America and the citizens of Colorado, we award today

THE DEFENDERS OF FREEDOM CITATION

to

Lieutenant Nhia Thong Lor

In honor of dedicated service and support of the American
Armed Forces of the United States of America during the Vietnam
War. This citation is in recognition of outstanding performance
of duty in action against enemy forces of Military Region II, in
his native country of Laos. He successfully executed primary
missions for air support and combat logistic support for United
States Military forces to include the rescuing of American air
personnel during the battles in the theater of operations. THE
DEFENDERS OF FREEDOM CITATION further commemorates the Lao-Hmong
of Military Region II, in Laos, during the Vietnam War.

I commend you for your bravery and loyalty to the United
States of America.

DAN SCHAEFER
Member of Congress
Sixth District of Colorado

Twenty years after the Secret War ended, Charles Lor received this official recognition from the United States. *Nhia Thong Lor*

shopping. We walked to the grocery store, and after we bought food we carried each bag home. It was very, very cold, our ears and our hands. We go like this. [Rubs hands together.] It was very cold and sometimes you sat down by the heat and you thought about your country and your homeland. You were homesick, you know.

I thought, "How can I live like this for [the rest of] my life in this country. No car. No job. No English." We cried a lot. Later on my brother-in-law had an American sponsor. They helped a lot, tried to find [us] jobs. My first job in this country, I worked in a hotel cleaning and sweeping. I washed windows and sheets. I didn't know how to ride a bus. They only taught you a couple times before you got out. [There was] a string. You pulled the string to let the bus driver know to stop. One time, I didn't see the place I [needed to] get out and I didn't know how to pull the string. It took me the whole day back and forth. [Laughs.] It was really difficult.

I remember one day my supervisor told me to go get a broom and dustpan, but I didn't know what she needed. I was gone maybe five, ten minutes. I didn't know what she needed, what she wanted. I came back. I tried to talk to her to point for me. She got mad at me. She used her finger to point at my head. After that I took the broom and the dustpan to finish the job. It was break time. I went to sit by the window. I watched the cars go back and forth in the street. I cried and cried until [break] was over. She came out and saw me crying. She came to hug me. I think she said something to apologize, but I didn't know what she was saying.

After that, I can tell that she was nice. She wanted me to do something. She wanted to make sure I knew what to do. After that, a friend of mine sent me to the job service to register for English as a Second Language. I took the class and picked up English a little bit. The job service, they sent me to school for a machine shop. I worked and went to school. I finished my class in the machine shop in two years. My teacher had a friend [with] a little shop. My teacher sent me to work with his friend. When I finished my school, they hired me to work full-time. I worked on machines for over twenty-five years, all my life.

I lived in Denver for four years and worked in the machine shop for four years. [Then] I moved to Milwaukee. I worked in Milwaukee until 2005 and then I moved to Madison. I bought the Asian grocery store on Fish Hatchery Road and I own the grocery right now. I don't see my wife because we try to work different shifts to help our kids in school. I work second shift and my wife works really early. Our lives are very difficult, but now it's OK. That's why we decided to buy the grocery store. We can see our kids more than before. I have six kids. Three boys, three girls. They're all grown up. My oldest son was born in 1980. He lives in St. Paul, Minnesota. He has his own dental [practice]. My second son lives with me in Madison, here. He's a mechanic with a Honda dealership. My third son works with a mortgage company in Milwaukee. Last year his company moved him to Florida. I have three girls and one is still in high school. There's another one in college.

I still question why I [joined the Army]. At that time I knew because I had to protect my family, my village. I wanted to do something to protect family and country. That's why I joined the Army. I don't know for other people, but for me.

15 ★ Hanoi Hilton

"What will my total days in North Vietnam be? As of today, February 27, 1973, it is 2,395 days — it is only a matter of time — our standard cliché. How I hate it…"— Fred Flom's POW diary

Though the total number of prisoners of war (POWs) during the Vietnam War — less than eight hundred — was small compared to other wars, Vietnam POWs captured American attention at a level not seen in other conflicts.[1] Along with becoming an emotional issue for Americans at home, POWs played a prominent public role because multiple parties — the U.S. government, the North Vietnamese, and antiwar activists — used them to advocate for their wartime goals. President Nixon, for example, raised the visibility of POWs to encourage the American people to remain committed to Vietnam, while antiwar groups used POWs as a rationale for ending the war. The North Vietnamese also worked to keep U.S. POWs visible, hoping to foster goodwill by releasing a few directly into the hands of antiwar activists visiting North Vietnam between 1967 and 1969.[2] The prominence of POW family groups, particularly the National League of Families of American Prisoners and Missing in Southeast Asia, also helped to keep the POW issue at the forefront of the American mind.

The first American POWs of the war were captured in South Vietnam in June 1954 and held by the Viet Minh for ten weeks. North Vietnam took its first prisoner on August 5, 1964, after shooting down a plane in the aftermath of the Gulf of Tonkin Incident. As the war escalated in the 1960s and the United States started running regular bombing missions over North Vietnam, the North Vietnamese captured a growing number of U.S. aviators, the majority of them officers. Many of the POWs held by North Vietnam were subject to a "systematic program of torture" as the North Vietnamese hoped to gain both intelligence and propaganda material.[3] Subject to isolation, inhumane treatment, and excruciating pain, POWs found it nearly impossible to satisfy both the North Vietnamese and the U.S. conduct guidelines for

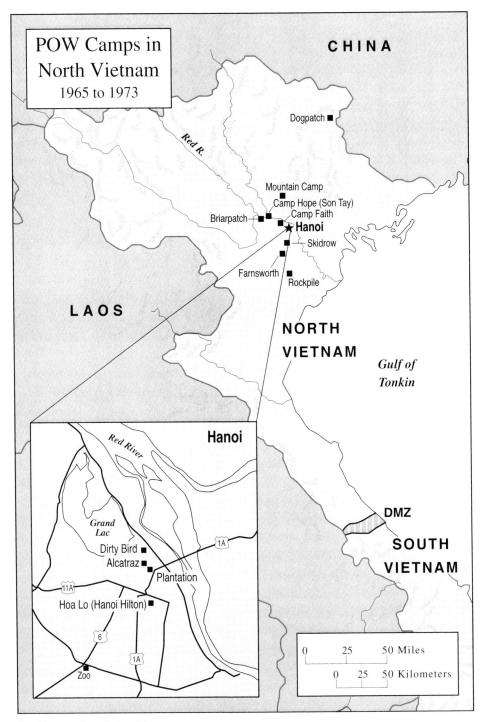

POW Camps in
North Vietnam
1965 to 1973

CHINA

Dogpatch ■

Red R.

Mountain Camp ■
Camp Hope (Son Tay) ■
Camp Faith
Briarpatch ■ ■ ★ Hanoi
■ Skidrow
■
Farnsworth ■
Rockpile

LAOS

NORTH
VIETNAM

Gulf of
Tonkin

Hanoi

Red River

Grand
Lac
Dirty Bird ■
Alcatraz ■
Plantation

11A

Hoa Lo (Hanoi Hilton) ■

6

1A

Zoo ■

1A

DMZ

SOUTH
VIETNAM

| 0 | 25 | 50 Miles |

| 0 | 25 | 50 Kilometers |

Patti Isaacs, Parrot Graphics

prisoners of war. Though many men sought simply to share as little information as possible, some were tortured into involuntary confessions and a few utilized North Vietnam's desire for propaganda to seek an earlier release, a choice looked down on by other POWs.[4] Despite the widespread use of solitary confinement, POWs relied heavily on one another, communicating via a tap code, sharing jokes and stories to sustain each other through the long months and years in prison camps. In November 1970 the United States staged an attempted rescue of POWs believed to be held at Son Tay prison camp outside Hanoi. The attempt failed as the prisoners had already been moved elsewhere. In response to the raid, the North Vietnamese moved most prisoners to Hoa Lo prison in Hanoi, also known as the Hanoi Hilton. Ironically, North Vietnam's decision to concentrate American POWs in one location helped to boost many POWs' morale through the final years of captivity.

As part of the 1973 peace agreement, U.S. POWs were released in stages alongside the withdrawal of U.S. troops from South Vietnam. The first group of POWs left Hanoi on February 12, 1973, and by March 29, all 591 prisoners had left North Vietnam. As noted by David L. Anderson, after two decades of war and more than 58,000 deaths, "the safe return of POWs . . . provided a rare opportunity for celebration at the military bases and towns that received them."[5] Unlike the hostile response many soldiers faced upon returning to the United States, the American people greeted POWs as heroes.

The 1973 return of these POWs, however, did not resolve the issue of U.S. soldiers missing in action (MIAs) or U.S. fears that some POWs had not been returned. Accounting for these soldiers and their remains was a prominent American concern in the 1970s, '80s, and '90s, preventing the restoration of official relations between the United States and Vietnam until 1995, after the Vietnamese pledged to assist more fully with the issue.

The oral histories shared in this chapter come from two POWs, Don Heiliger and Fred Flom. Heiliger's telling of almost six years of imprisonment is excerpted from an oral interview conducted in 2008. Fred Flom's comes from a cigarette paper diary that he kept during his last six weeks of captivity at Hoa Lo prison (Hanoi Hilton), after he learned he would be returning home following six and a half years as a POW. Excerpts of Flom's diary are reproduced here without edits.

Fred Flom, Menasha (Air Force, 23rd Tactical Fighter Wing)
Don Heiliger, Madison (Air Force, 333rd Tactical Fighter Squadron)

Fred Flom climbs into a F-105D Thunderchief before a training mission in Fort Worth Texas, 1976, three years after his return to the United States.
Fred Flom

FRED FLOM I am presently on the threshold of a kaleidoscope of emotional and physical excitement as I prepare to enter the real world after six and a half years of physical and mental deprivation. I eagerly anticipate every aspect of life that awaits me. I hope that all of my senses can continuously react with maximum efficiency so as not to deprive me of any of the excitement that awaits me. I fear, however, that my senses may be somewhat numbed by over-stimulation and some weeks or months from now, I'll glance back over my shoulder asking myself "what happened."

I intend to maintain a continuing diary for at least one year beginning with the day of release. This will be an attempt not so much to put down my activities of the day but more to capture my thoughts and feelings so as to follow my adjustment to freedom and society. I have given much thought over the past years to my personal psychology, my goals and philosophy of life, and my association with my wife and family. I feel I am ready and will have few problems, however there still exists that unknown element. The readjustment will be real. I am well aware that my family and friends as well as society has changed greatly but I await the challenge with great anticipation.

The mind is so forgetful; particularly in regards to thoughts and feelings. Thus a diary. As an introduction, I would like to put down an autobiographical sketch of the past six and a half years before my memory of these experiences fades too much. I do not seek sympathy or excuses, but merely relate the facts for personal future reflection.

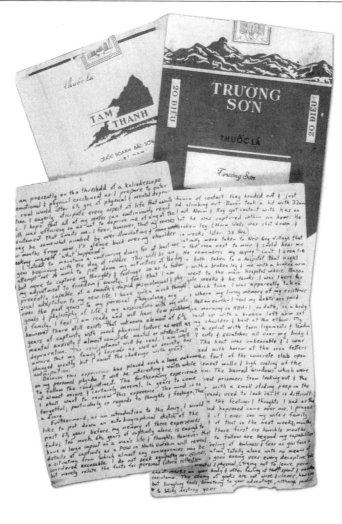

Fred Flom's diary, written on the back of Vietnamese cigarette papers. *Fred Flom, Photo by Joel Heiman*

DON HEILIGER I was "prompted" [into the service] by the good graces of the U.S. government and the University of Wisconsin. When I went to college it was required that all Land Grant schools not only offer but insist that anyone that hadn't already been in the service go into ROTC. I chose the Air Force. It was pretty exciting for a nineteen-year-old guy. I decided to go on to advanced ROTC. I expected to go on to pilot training. When I took the scores, they said I didn't have the ability to become a pilot. I wanted to prove them wrong, which I did. They allowed me to go into navigator training. When I graduated from the University of Wisconsin in 1958, I entered navigator training and I did all my navigator time, about two thousand–some hours, as an instructor.

Don Heiliger kneels in front of an F-105D Thunderchief at Takhli Air Base, Thailand, in spring of 1967. *Don Heiliger*

I graduated [from pilot training] in March 1965. I went on to 105 training at [Nellis] Air Force Base in [Las Vegas, Nevada]. When we graduated, Vietnam was well [under way]. I flew the Thud with the 333rd Fighter Squadron. I flew about thirty-three missions in sixty days. I moved to another squadron because they took guys that had been there a long time, and sent them down. The rule was once you flew one hundred missions, you were going home. The Thud averaged eighty-one missions. Some guys got shot down the first mission. Some people made it to their one hundred. But the average for a Thud driver was eighty-one missions. It's not a good figure.

Our targets were always military, usually bridges, railroad yards, things like that. We couldn't hit any of the airports or any of the big bridges. They wouldn't allow us to do that. I think we flew good missions. We were pretty accurate. When [my backseater] Ben and I flew, we tried our best to hit exactly what we were supposed to. [Three] nights before we were shot down, my best friend didn't come back. I was pretty sure about where he was going because I watched him do his flight planning. I flew the mission the next night [on] the same route basically. I scared myself to death because we got into clouds. It was all weather. There was nothing to see. That's why you have radar. I looked out the side once and we did have just a little bit of visibility off to the side. I thought I was touching a hill with my wing. I suspect Pete didn't have that luck. He bought it a couple nights before I was shot down. I will never know. His body came back a year and a half after I came home, and I went to his funeral down in Texas. Until Pete got it [three] nights before we did, it was pretty lively all the time. It felt [like] you were all by yourself. It's dark out there. Nobody is going to hit you. When one guy doesn't come back you start being a little more serious about it. We might have been the first ones shot down if Pete hit the ground. We are never sure on that one.

FRED FLOM I was shot down on 8 August, 1966. I apparently had amnesia and remember absolutely nothing about the event. The last thing I remember was being on an R and R in Bangkok. The first thing I remember was waking up one morning in Heartbreak Hotel, cell No. 1, no date, in a body cast from my waist up with a broken left arm set out parallel to my shoulder and bent at the elbow. My right arm was in a splint with torn ligaments and tendons. There were small cuts and scratches all over my body and blood everywhere. The heat was unbearable and I was starving as I gazed with horror at the leg irons at the foot of the concrete slab upon which I lay, the cement walls, the barred windows which were boarded up to prevent prisoners from looking out, and the heavy locked door with a small sliding peep in the middle which the guards used to look in. I prayed, "Oh God, if I ever see my wife and family again..."

DON HEILIGER It was on the 15th of May [, 1967]. It was a night mission. We had time on target of 9:10, 9:20, something like that. We were hitting a marshalling yard about thirty miles northeast of Hanoi near Kep Airfield. We felt pretty comfortable about it. We were out over the water most of the way instead of coming over land like Pete. Once we got over North Vietnam, we were probably at somewhere about one thousand feet. That's pretty low. We came in the final thirty miles. We found our initial point to hit the target. Then our vector [gear] showed that they were locked in on us. We put everything we had to jam them. We knew that wasn't completely effective. We got down to about eight hundred feet coming about five hundred knots[, and suddenly were hit]. All the lights started coming on right away. We got our bombs off, and then immediately started to climb. There is an old adage: "The air above you doesn't do any good if you are bailing out." You want a lot of air below you. We climbed and it was my decision to go back the way we came in. We didn't know how bad we were hit at this point except that we had all these lights on showing our engine was on fire. We started climbing. We got to five thousand and then ten thousand. By that time we were watching the fire creeping forward on the airplane. [The] 105 is a good plane. It doesn't blow up. I am not a sport parachutist, and as long as the engine was going, I was staying with the airplane. We were climbing

Don Heiliger, front, and Ben Pollard climbing into Pollard's plane in May 1967, approximately two weeks before their capture.
Don Heiliger

and trying to make it back to the Gulf of Tonkin because Tonkin is filled with our Navy's ships and the chance of getting picked up was pretty good.

We got to about fifteen thousand feet and the fire was creeping closer. It wasn't blowing up the airplane but it was not a good condition. I got to eighteen thousand feet and we lost all our instruments. The intercom works off the battery, thank goodness, so Ben and I could talk. It would be horrible if we couldn't: me not knowing what he is thinking, or vice versa. We had standby gauges that also worked off the battery. I don't think we had lights. I had my flashlight out. I was holding it in my teeth, I know that. I could see the standby gauges. Ben said, "The fire's gotten to my cockpit. I have to get out!" He is thirty-three inches behind me. That's close. Again, I am not going to leave. He said, "Don, I have to go." I said, "OK, bye!" He said, "Sayonara," and ejected. And so I know where the fire is, anyway. I got to about twenty-three thousand feet and the fire got to my cockpit.

You pull up on the handles. That arms the system. You squeeze the triggers. It blows the canopy. Point three seconds later you shoot out. One second after that, there is a lap belt that blows your [seat belt] cartridge. That kicks the seat back and you are left floating. Anytime below 14,500 feet or below, the parachute will open automatically. You can pull the ripcord anytime you want. I wasn't going to chance it and I pulled. It was probably way too fast. I probably lost some panels in the chute. I floated down. It is about a thousand-feet-per-minute rate of descent. As I got closer to the ground, I could see I was not going to land in a clearing. They teach you before you enter trees, cross your legs. We've had three kids since then, so I guess it was successful. The parachute got caught up in a tree, and all that stuff below me got caught up in another tree. It was kind of like being in the center of a hammock. That was fine. I carried about three hundred feet of let-down nylon tape with me exactly for that reason. You don't fool around. I've lost a couple of friends that bailed out. They didn't make it down because they fell getting out. It was really dark but I was going to sit that way until I could see light. I was losing feeling in one leg because of that pulling. So I said, "OK, I am going to have to get rid of all the stuff hanging below me." The emergency disconnect didn't go. I pulled out my hunting knife. I gave a good tug of my parachute and it gave way at the same minute. I could have been two hundred feet up there, but I was only ten or fifteen feet in the air. I came crashing to the ground. I didn't even cut myself with the knife.

I moved away from that area. I was scratching to find my way because there was absolutely no light. It was ten o'clock so I waited until the next morning. As soon as I saw light, I started moving away from that area. I climbed the first hill I came to. About four in the afternoon, I heard rumblings coming up that hill. Sure enough there were probably about forty-five villagers [with] everything from sticks to a couple with automatics. I hid myself the best I could with a bunch of rocks. This little head popped over the top of them. I can't imagine who was more afraid, him or me. He screamed something. I said, "OK, I have a decision. Real quick. Do I shoot?" I had fifty rounds. I could maybe last a short time. I elected to give myself up. I broke my weapon so they couldn't use it. They came up. They actually treated me pretty well. They put me in a room. There was a calendar with Ho Chi Minh's picture on it, so [I] suspected then that I was in North Vietnam, and not in China.

FRED FLOM The experiences to follow are beyond my capabilities of description. The feeling of loneliness and fear as you face a completely adverse situation, totally alone with no means of defense or recourse as your enemy uses every deceptive trick at his disposal, mental and physical, (trying not to leave permanent marks on your body and often failing at that) to totally destroy your spirit and resistance.

I would not see or have contact with a fellow American POW for the next month, nor the opportunity to talk to one for the next six months[,] only the unfriendly faces of gook officers and guards. All I had was a mat, mosquito net, blanket, set of pajama-like clothes, shorts and T-shirt, cup and water jug, and a bucket for a toilet. Washing was very infrequent and shaving even more so (sometimes more than a month at first). Two meals a day: a plate of rice, bowl of water and grass soup — very thin, and a small side dish of pumpkin.

I began quizzes [interrogations] immediately and learned quickly to hate and fear the sound of keys. There were many questions and name, rank, serial no. did not work. Several beatings convinced me it would be best to answer some: where born, hometown, what did my father do, squadron, base? I lied about most of them but found they accepted lies and were happy whereas silence only got more beatings. I recall that I was truly afraid for my life that first month. I was often threatened with my life and I almost believed it. I really wasn't aware of my value and indeed was scared they might kill me but it would take more than threats.

DON HEILIGER They took everything away from me except my underwear and my boots. We walked down to that little village. I think it was the same one I had been watching all day long. They put me into the hut where I saw a picture of Ho Chi Minh on the wall. They were very friendly. I was right near the Chinese border in the part that didn't see any action from the war. I think that is the reason they were friendlier than if I had been shot down on the border between North and South Vietnam where our guys were killed regularly. They gave me some sticky rice and bread. I told them I hurt my knee badly on the fall, so they brought in some medic and he tried to wrap it up. They did their best to accommodate me. They talked to me in their pointy English from a book they had. We were able to converse very minimally. I thought, "Hey, this is not too bad. General Westmorland says we will be out of here in six months. This little village isn't a bad place to spend my time." About an hour or two after I showed up, a couple of Communist cadres showed up. This is the first military people I had seen with uniforms. Paramilitary. They had a bullhorn microphone. They gathered the people from this village. By this time there were a couple other villages looking at

[me], this curiosity they had. They pulled all these people out right outside this little hut that I was in and got them all in a big semicircle. They started getting these people all revved up with this bullhorn, getting them really mad. They pulled me into the center of the circle. I hoped they had some crowd control because they didn't look like they were happy with me at all.

I didn't understand any Vietnamese at that point. Whatever they said, the crowd went absolutely still. There were eighteen little old ladies in the circle, wearing black, with no teeth because they chew betel nuts and it gets rid [of] most of the teeth. Roughly half of Vietnam was Christian because the French had been in there for almost a century about eighty years before this. They crossed themselves like they'd just given me my last rites. I thought, "This does not look good." They took me inside the hut and threw me up against the wall. They brought in two heavies with automatic weapons and leveled them at me. I said, "This is it. Just get it over with. I said my prayers and said them again. It went on for probably forty-five, fifty minutes. Finally this kind of head guy I had been talking pointy English with, he came in and dismissed these two [other] guys. He came up to me in enough English, "No die tonight. Tomorrow." I wasn't too much happier. It was like a last-minute pardon by the governor, but only for a day. That night when everybody went to bed, I started aching and screaming that my pains were bad. I wanted to get out of there. I kept yelling "Hanoi." I knew we had prisoners in Hanoi. I had seen pictures of them. I thought, I want to get to Hanoi, where I get to [be with] these other people. I am sure they had it all planned. In the middle of the night, maybe two or three in the morning, they gave me back my boots that they had taken them away from me. They started moving me down that mountain from that village, walking blindfolded most of the time. Every time they would stop, they would hit me with sticks and rocks. We got to the bottom right at about sunrise. In a clearing there was a jeep waiting. Evidently they had some manner of communication to say that, you'd better wait for this guy. They threw me in the back of the jeep. [They] made sure I was still blindfolded.

We went on that way for about a half a day. They stopped the jeep and opened the back. They shoved [someone] in there. It was Ben! He was delirious. He had hit his head badly on some rocks on landing. He was out of it most of the time we were together. They were trying to keep us quiet. I tried to do what I could for him, but it was pretty hard because he wasn't doing well. We rode the rest of the way into Hanoi. When we arrived, they took Ben out and then they took me. We were put into what we called Little

Nellis. So many of our pilots had gone through Nellis [in Las Vegas]. All the rooms were named after all those good casinos in Las Vegas: the Stardust, the Hacienda, the Riviera. They took us in there and that was the last time I saw Ben for five years.

The fun began when we got to Hanoi. That's when the torture started. By the Code of Conduct, you are only required to give your name, rank, serial number, and date of birth. Four items. That's good for a while, but it doesn't last for long. They want more, obviously. [When] you say you can't, in comes the heavy stuff, all the kinds of torture you can think of, most of it very crude. The main thing they did was to cut your circulation at your wrists. You can take that for a little while and you got no more feeling in your hands. You don't know how long you can last before it becomes permanent. We didn't know if anybody had said anything. You were under this mental restriction not to do anything more than name, rank, serial number, and date of birth. They put a lot of pressure on you. You had to have a second line of resistance.

FRED FLOM   What the Vietnamese wanted now was a war crimes confession. I could not give them that. I was beaten, put in stress positions, and shown confessions they had tortured from Kasler, Risner, and Denton. Finally I was beaten till my cast was completely broken and they worked over my broken arm[,] which they had now rebroken. I couldn't go on. I wrote a paper in which I said I was sorry I bombed North Vietnam and I would never do it again (half of which was true). They seemed satisfied and that night or the next I was taken back to the hospital and my arm was reset and put in another cast of the same type. That was on 9 September. That night I was moved to the Zoo or Camp America and put in cell 3 of the Barn. This cell was much bigger with 2 wooden pallets on concrete for beds and no windows. The heat coupled with the huge heavy cast covering my entire upper body and not being able to wash added considerably to my misery. Here, I made my first contact with another American via the tap code. (A means by which we could tap thru the wall to other POWs. The gooks were fanatical about preventing us from seeing or communicating with other POWs.)

I had moved to cell 7 of the [B]arn after a couple of weeks next to Bunny Talley. It was the end cell, very small with one bed and no windows. We would communicate via tap and were both optimistic. Bunny bet we'd be home by Christmas (he owes me a night's drinking at [the] first bar we get to). I thought by April. On 19 Oct they moved me down to the Carriage

House, a big old building that looked like a 2 car garage where they had been keeping some cows. They moved the cows out and me in. A two-month torture session began and I knew I was in hell. I had been saving a banana I got a few days before and a piece of candy from Sept 2 (Gook's Independence Day) to celebrate Julie's birthday[,] but I never saw them again.

I had been told to write a confession of crimes, a biography, and other information. I continually refused and now the real pressure was coming. Up to now all they had done at this camp was make me stand against the wall with my arms up for most of the day, after each quiz. When I got to the Carriage House, they beat me around then put my ankles in leg irons. I was sitting on a stool in front of a table with some paper and a pen on it. They tied the bar of the leg irons to the legs of the table holding my feet well off the floor and set the stool such that most of my weight was forcing my ankle into the irons. I was left in that position for 15 hours and harassed by the guards all night. My ankles bled and swelled such that the next day they had to pound the irons off. They then got a larger pair and had to pound them on. I was then tied to a stool with leg irons on and my free arm behind my back and beaten for long periods, with rest intervals, by the guards all day. I bled from my nose, mouth, eyes, and ears. That night they brought in a pallet, tied me to the pallet with leg irons[,] and left me alone. I was so tired I could hardly see, yet I couldn't sleep. That night I had diarrhea and shit my pants. The next day I was beaten for that. For the next three weeks, they left me tied to this pallet in leg irons in the middle of the floor of this big old bldg. Sometimes the guard would set the food out of my reach. A lizard fell from a rafter, landing two feet from my head and I watched it decay and rot. One night a rat or mole ran up my pants leg and was in my crotch before I woke up (I think it was a mole because it was so slow).

DON HEILIGER I know we have had people die up there. They are bigger heroes than me or some of the guys who came out. Some of them never gave anything. You were in a position where your hands were tied and these heavy bars were cutting off the circulation in your legs. You were screaming and they'd stick a rag in your mouth. They'd walk away. You lost your physical faculties, and you threw up. If they walked away and you threw up, [it's] over. How many of our guys didn't come back from that, I don't know. The second line of resistance they teach you is before you lose your mental faculties, do anything to get rid of the pain. As soon as they find you in another lie, they put it back on, but you gain time. I said, "I can outwait

Don Heiliger's "music appreciation course," smuggled out by a fellow POW and presented to Don after their release, was written on toilet paper strips with ink made from antifungal medicine. *Don Heiliger*

them." When I was shot down it was the second heaviest month in the Vietnam War of airplanes being shot down. They had a lot of guys to work on. They had Ben to work on over me because he was a rank higher. You can give rank. They knew he was a major. He was supposed to be in the front. That's true. Ben should have been in the front.

One of the things [I did] to take the pain off was I said, "OK, what do you guys want to learn about electricity?" I gave them a full college semester of electricity. I figured this is something you could get out of a book. This type of stuff fascinated them. I would save a week doing this kind of stuff. The main thing they wanted to do was to prove to you that they could make you go beyond the four items, that they could make you talk. That's all they cared about. The burden of this is just immense: thinking you are the only guy who went beyond those four things until you meet the other guy. I was put in with Bill Baugh and John Dramesi. I moved in with them at another camp away from the Hanoi Hilton. It was an old French film studio we called The Zoo. All three of us were Air Force captains. I was lucky to move in with Bill and John because [they knew] the tap code. Bill and John knew it by the time I was with them. Bill was shot down in December, and John in April.

[They were] nice guys to live with. You were in that room twenty-four hours a day. You talk about your wives, your children, tell jokes, tell stories. Then you go further into those things. You either retell the jokes, retell the stories, or you go further into your life. Seeing as you always want to tell them something new, you do go further into your life that after several months in of living with John and Bill I don't think there was much I didn't know about them and vice versa. It was embarrassing sometimes to meet some of the wives when you got out because there was so very little you didn't know. We would open up completely. You lose the façade. We get up in the morning, we look in the mirror, we dress a certain way. We do things so we can present ourselves to other people. When you are with those people all the time, you don't. It is kind of neat to say you have friends that are about as pure as can be.

There were a lot of interrogations. A lot of tough ones. People beating you up regularly. Good guards. Bad guards. You got two meals a day: a bowl of soup, a very thin vegetable of some sort. They would take the water off of it and serve it as a side dish with [maybe] a little bit of rice or a little piece of bread. That was it, twice a day. After Ho Chi Minh died, they added a breakfast to the other two meals. That could be a bowl of sugar or a banana. We got cigarettes a couple time a day. We communicated regularly in the tap code. We say, one-one is an "A," dot-dot-dot is a "B" and so forth. I was lucky. I had probably a total of seventy days by myself. [They were] in spurts, though, not at one time. Everybody knew what it was like to be by themselves. You wanted to make sure the solos were kept in communication. We'd even tell our jokes through our tap code. Everything we knew about each other, we would try to pass on through that system. We were pretty quiet about it. We did not tap if [the guards] were around because if they found [you] communicating, you would be brutally beaten just like when you were first shot down.

FRED FLOM In May of '69 I had my first indications of intestinal problems. It began with diarrhea and was followed by 4 weeks of constipation. Up to this time I was exercising a lot and in as good a shape as could be expected under the existing conditions. I had trouble eating, much pain in my lower abdomen (left side) and began losing weight. That winter and spring my intestinal problem continued to get worse. I was very weak, dizzy every time I got up and weighed about 105 pounds. Finally in May '70, the gooks took action. They moved me and Jeff to a special room out back that had big windows with plenty of fresh air. They gave me special food and medical care as well as letting us out in the fresh air and sunshine. The day they moved us out there, they gave me my first letter and picture of [my wife] Ginny. What a boost to morale. Also, I finally learned Erik's name (He was 4 yrs. 8 mos.). This, in total, I feel was the beginning of a long recovery.

DON HEILIGER After the first year, they moved Bill, John, and me across the way. We saw them building something. They were building nine-person units like a little condo area. They moved seventy-two of us over to occupy eight of them. You moved in now with nine people. Wow. From two people plus one to nine. New stories, new jokes, everything. One night in May, it was about a year after we were together, the second-year anniversary of me being shot down. It was a very stormy night, and Ed [Atterberry] and John [Dramesi] felt this was the night they should go, but our room commander said no way. They felt they should have the right to go. The guy who was the senior person of our eight rooms, Connie Troutman was next to us. So they got up in the ceiling, went over to the next one, and talked with Connie directly and said, "We want to go." Connie's rules were something like, "I can't allow you, but I can't stop you. If you want to go, go." They left a little after midnight. We all knew they were not going to go very far. They didn't have a plan really. It was to get out and find the river and float down until they got to the Gulf of Tonkin. We knew it wouldn't be hard to get out of the room. They had loosened the tiles in the roof. They were gone until about five o'clock the next morning. We could see the trail of stuff they left behind them all the way to the wall when we got up the next morning. We had mosquito net [to keep out] mosquitoes and the rats. We put that back up for them so it looked like nine people in the room. [The guards] didn't know until they opened up the door. They said, "Where are they?" I said, "They left." I was the room responsible. By that time, they had been captured anyway and brought back to that camp by five or six in the morning, but they started working on the rest of us very bad. It was a very bad couple of weeks. I don't [want] to ever go through that again. That was worse than when we were shot down. [I got] busted eardrums.

It was very bad. But like everything else, you pick up and go on. When they got done with us, the seven of us that were remaining, they started working on the heads of the other seven rooms. They took the senior guys who they thought were responsible for the escape. They didn't even know there was an escape going on. When Guarino went in for interrogation, they beat him to the point where he almost died. He slit his wrists but he didn't die. Luckily. He couldn't take it anymore. What do you do when you can't give them an answer? The seven of us survived. They brought John and Ed back. They put them through one heck of an interrogation, torture and all that stuff. Ed died three days later from the interrogation.

We lived another year in a room of nine. They brought in two [new] guys. They shuffled up our rooms a little bit. We were like that for the next year or so. There were a lot of interrogations. Do you not say something and let them torture and beat you around or do you give them just enough to make them mad at you but not to the point of torture? They will put you on your knees on cement, hands up, for days. You can't last very long on your knees, and when your knees give out you can't hold like that. Luckily, you have friends [helping] you. When the guards are gone, you are off of it and as soon as the guards [are] around, you are back on. You throw water in your face to look like you are sweating more.

FRED FLOM   At the end of June or early July 1970, I felt better, was able to eat somewhat better (although it still gave me a sick feeling) and I began putting on some weight, about 125 pounds by then. On July 14 the entire camp

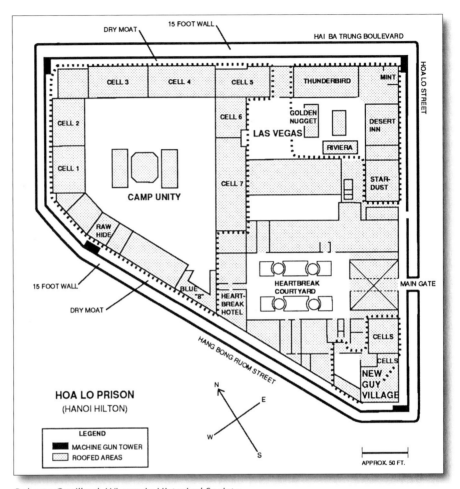

Roberta Couillard, Wisconsin Historical Society

of Son Tay moved to Camp Faith. This was truly a "good deal" camp by our standards. It appeared to have been recently built for the POW's. Cells with open windows and spacious cells. Half the camp was outside at the same time (3 hrs. per day) and eventually even permitted to talk to those who were still locked in. This kind of living was unknown to us. There were 57 men in our compound. This POW life, however, was short lived, as the night of 24 Nov, 1970 everyone from Camp Faith was very unexpectedly moved to the big prison at Hoa Lo. The move was completely spontaneous and came as a result of the Son Tay raid on the night of the 21st and early morning of 22 Nov. (If only we had still been at Son Tay — what a glorious way to leave.) When we learned about that raid later we almost cried.

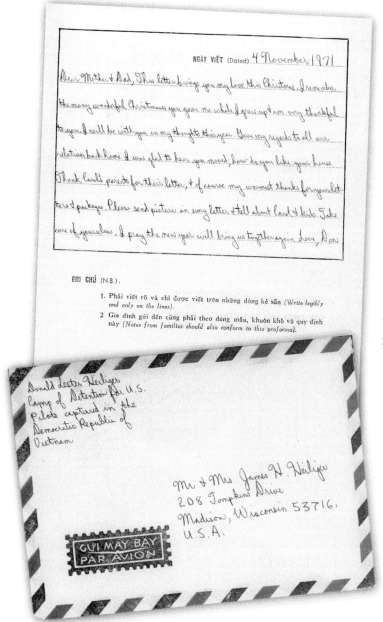

NGÀY VIẾT (Dated) 4 November 1971

Dear Mother & Dad, This letter brings you my love this Christmas. I remember the many wonderful Christmases you gave me while I grew up. I am very thankful to you. I will be with you in my thoughts this year. Give my regards to all our relatives back home. I was glad to hear you moved; how do you like your house. Thank Carol's parents for their letter, & of course my warmest thanks for your letters & packages. Please send pictures in every letter & tell about Carol & kids. Take care of yourselves. I pray the new year will bring us together again. Love, Don

CHI CHÚ (N.B.):

1. Phải viết rõ và chỉ được viết trên những dòng kẻ sẵn *(Write legibly and only on the lines).*

2. Gia đình gửi đến cũng phải theo đúng mẫu, khuôn khổ và quy định này *(Notes from families should also conform to this proforma).*

Donald Lester Heiliger Camp of Detention for U.S. Pilots captured in the Democratic Republic of Vietnam

Mr. & Mrs. James H. Heiliger 208 Tompkins Drive Madison, Wisconsin 53716, U.S.A.

GUI MAY BAY PAR AVION

Don Heiliger wrote this letter home to his parents in November 1971. *Courtesy of the Wisconsin Veterans Museum*

DON HEILIGER We were into a third year. Around that time they moved a lot of us to a camp outside of Hanoi. In our room there were twenty [of us]. Wow. We went from nine to twenty. There were new stories. We were like that over the summer of 1970. It was probably in November of 1970, about a month or so after the Son Tay Raid, they took everybody who was outside of Hanoi and moved them into the Hanoi Hilton. We moved into fifty-man rooms. People who had been solo for four years were finally with somebody. They couldn't keep them separate. What a time. Going from nine to twenty to fifty people. Wow! New stories, new people.

In the spring of '72, the bombings started heavily again. [The end] was getting close. Before we'd heard nothing. We thought, "Wait, is this war still on? Why aren't we home?" The bombing started heavily again and at that time they were starting to do [as] much in every city. I think our captors] were afraid. It was getting near. They were bombing closer to Hanoi, even bringing B-52s up closer, which was unheard of. [The North Vietnamese] took 208 of us and moved us up in a camp near China. It was just made for us. It was out in the boonies, up in the mountains, and I don't think we could have taken too many more steps and we'd have been in China. We sat up there from May until the next January. The Vietnamese said, "You're going to stay up here until the war is over." That's probably the only time they ever told us [the] truth. Around November to Christmas of '72, the bombing reached Hanoi, with the B-52s. We'd become a political football back here with the negotiations. They moved about half of us. By that time we were 350 and they moved about 208 of us near [the] China border. We felt it was because they wanted to make sure they were serious [about] hitting Hanoi. Maybe they'd wipe out the prison camp. They wanted some bargaining chips left.

FRED FLOM On 13 May, 1972, 209 men left Hoa Lo and headed for a camp in the mountains near the Chinese border. Our hands were tied and we were blindfolded at first. There were about 12 POWs per truck in the convoy. This trip was about as miserable as you could possibly imagine. The road was unbelievably rough and we bounced around in the back of the truck like a sack of potatoes. To make it worse we got hardly any food and water and we spent half of one day parked with the sun beating down on the covered trucks. We arrived at the new camp (Dog Patch) on 15 May and you can't imagine how we dreaded the thought of another trip like that and how happy we were to have finally arrived. However, we felt that when we finally went back to Hanoi, we would be on our way home and we could go through anything for that.

On Oct 25, 1972 they had a big camp wide shuffle, as if the big boys had said — that's not what we had in mind. They arranged everyone by date of shoot down. I felt pretty good about being in a group with some very early shoot downs and even then was getting ideas I might [be] able to hang on their shirttails and go out in the first group. We were damned optimistic and then on Oct 31 when we heard the peace proposal we thought: "that's it, man, we're going home" until they read the last few sentences. I felt it was only a matter of time, though.

On 2 Dec we saw some movies and half the camp was together at the same time. I met and talked to a lot of people and didn't see any of the movie. 9 Dec, magazines showed up for the first time. These were the first American magazines I had laid eyes on in almost six and a half years. *Sport*, *Pro Football*, *Sports Illustrated*, and some car mags. Great, even though they were 2 years old. On Christmas day half the camp was allowed outside together. This was another real thrill. Something had to be happening.

On 18 Jan, 1973 the camp filled up with trucks and I knew it was over. We'd go back to Hanoi and be home within 60 to 90 days. (Oh Ginny here I come). The next day almost everyone in the bldg was packed and ready to go by mid morning and definitely by mid afternoon. We sat around and waited till about 2 am on the 20th when we loaded up and moved out. We arrived at Hoa Lo that same evening (about a 16 hour trip). As we came in we waved and yelled at the guys we had left last May. All the fences and blinds were down. It was just one big courtyard now. I moved into cellblock 4 with forty men. The end was finally here.

DON HEILIGER On the 20th of January, the trucks rolled into our camp. We knew things were over from the Voice of Vietnam pretty much. When they rolled up we said, "This is it, guys." We passed the word around all the buildings. We're going. The next morning the Vietnamese came. They were surprised. We had our bedrolls all ready to walk out of the door into their truck. The ride down was much better than the ride up. It was a horrible ride when we moved up as far as their treatment. The ride down was much better. We got down to the camp. They divided us all up by order of shoot down. That was our rule for going home. We had twelve people who came home early. Eleven of them were traitors to us, to our organization. They were not in it and never will be because they accepted favors to get out. They rolled the trucks in there, and they moved us all back to Hanoi. A couple days later on the fifth day after the negotiations were signed, which was the 27th of January, '73, five days later, they brought us all into the courtyard. They had us kind of open up in a formation, as much as we could do. They lined us up and they read the Geneva Accords, which [guaranteed] us release within 60 days in four equal groups.

FRED FLOM On 29 Jan, '73, the gooks read us the peace treaty and we learned it had been signed the 27th of Jan. A couple days later we got copies of the agreements. On 4 Feb the entire camp got out together both morning and afternoon. This is the way we should have been living all along. It was great being together and talking to everyone, but at the same time, we were anxious for them to leave so we could start our countdown. The gooks, typically, would tell us nothing as to the date the first group would leave or how big it would be. Each day there were many rumors and much speculation. Finally, Sunday night they shaved and bathed, got their traveling clothes and Monday morning 12 Feb. '73 before we got out the first group had left — 116 strong.

The camp seemed almost lonely with half the men gone when we got out Monday morning, but now we could finally begin our countdown — 15 days as we had it figured. These last days were really going slowly. There were many people with whom I could talk, but it was difficult to put aside the anticipation and expectations of the imminent release. I kept going over my expected relationship with Ginny, future plans, and philosophies of life and living that would be new to her. For the most part my mind was just caged on the all-important point that soon I was going home and would be with Ginny again and would be free.

On 17 Feb, we had a special "go home" meal. It was a last minute deal and appeared as though the gooks would be releasing 20 men the next morning. Man what frustration, wondering if you might be picked with the top 20 to go home within hours. Speculating on what kind of release it was, how those 20 men had been picked, and what the gooks were trying to pull. The excitement had made the past few days pass more quickly, but I was glad it was over. Now I could get back to our countdown. I expect the release to be the morning of 27 Feb, 15 days after the first group. Of course the gooks won't tell us anything.

DON HEILIGER The first group left on the 12th of February. Just after they left, they grabbed twenty of us, me included, and they said, "There's been another partial release arranged, and you're in the next group." We said, "No. Only one of those twenty is amongst the next twenty on order of shoot down. We're not going." We sat that way for the whole week. They even brought in another firing squad. [Laughs.] "They're going to shoot us? One week before we're going to go home? Come on." We laughed at that one. Finally, the day before we left, a plane came in. A lieutenant colonel or colonel [on the plane] grabbed one of our senior guys, Norm Gaddis who is now a general, but was a colonel at the time. He went to talk with the negotiators. He came back to our room of twenty. He said, "Look, guys. I know that this is irregular. My understanding is it's perfectly OK with the U.S. I know you're refusing to go home, so I have only one [thing to do]. I'm ordering you out of Hanoi." He did and that's how I left. I had talked with some of my friends. I said, "Bill, I don't want to go early. What will all the people think?" He said, "Don, the guys who know you up here know what you've done. What are you worried about?" I said, "You're right." He made me feel better. We arrived back in the Philippines. They announced our group. It was unbelievable. The whole airfield was filled [with] people. For our group of twenty. Spike Nasmith had a sister who was an airline stewardess. She had arranged a couple stewardesses to come and meet him. They made him escape from the hospital. For two days, they didn't know where he was. The people were sweating. They couldn't let anything happen to us.

We were like gold to the hospital crew and they couldn't let anybody disappear. [Laughs.] They were afraid that something might go wrong. He came back in time.

FRED FLOM Today is Wednesday, 21 Feb, 1973. I have been writing this for the past 2 days during the siesta period. A final countdown to something you have eagerly anticipated for 6½ long cruel years is slower than you might think. It is worse than the long hours of a Christmas Eve for a small six-year-old boy who is awaiting the joys of opening presents on Christmas morning. Only 5 more days and I will be on the threshold of a new life. The expectations of new relationships with a wonderful wife and family in a manner few people have so vividly lived. My excitement and anticipation are real. The thoughts of dreams and plans finally being fulfilled are fantastic and satisfying. It's beautiful! I'll try to savor and absorb every moment. Ginny, I love you so very, very much.

It is now the morning of 27 Feb. Yesterday afternoon we had our "go home" special meal and some men got back their rings and special effects. I slept better last night than I thought I would. I guess because I was emotionally exhausted. Right now everyone is putting their stuff in order and throwing out all kinds of crap. We expect to leave sometime this morning. The first group left very early, but I guess the gooks discovered they didn't need so much time. This is going to be an exciting day and I'm super-anxious for things to get going. Ginny darling, our new life is about to begin. "My head is bloody, but unbowed." If I could ever forgive these gooks for the inhumane living conditions, and physical torture for confessions, military information, good treatment statements, and propaganda; it will be even more difficult to find forgiveness for the mental deprivation they forced on us. Except for our last few months, we had a complete lack of contact with the outside world and educational materials. I can understand why they might not want us to have any contact with the outside world, but why couldn't they give us something to occupy our minds. The resentment and bitterness I feel toward the gooks for this aspect of our treatment is deep and undoubtedly enduring. They completely starved our minds and for apparently no other reason than an attempt to keep our morale as low as possible.

Great Scot, what happened? I was programmed to leave, and now it is Tuesday noon. I guess it's a fitting finale to this continued frustrating existence. But is it a finale? How long will it take them to settle their differences?

When will we finally go — tonight, tomorrow, in a week, a month? Just another indication of what a POW's life is like. Nothing is ever certain, and you never know what is coming, or what will happen next. It is deathly quiet in the cell now. No one is saying anything. Last night there was a continuous roar of conversation. Everyone was expectant. Now we are all disappointed, and wondering — wondering how long it will be when we will go, what will happen. There is nothing left to do but wait, once again as we have had to do for over six years we must wait and wonder. What will my total days in North Vietnam be? As of today, February 27, 1973, it is 2,395 days — it is only a matter of time — our standard cliché. How I hate it . . .

It is now Tuesday, 6 March, about 5 PM. This is a new phase — "Freedom Phase." I am still standing in the threshold of my new life looking with awe, anticipation, and excitement at everything that is before me. It's wonderful. There is no way possible for me to express in words the emotions I have felt the past 3 days. It has been continuous excitement, things happening, and no time to take a breath. This is the first opportunity I have had to get at this, so we will have to go back to Sunday.

It was a dreary morning, rain and mist with low ceiling and visibility. There was some talk an aircraft could not get in. We sat around and the minutes dragged, everyone anxious and wondering. By 9:00 the weather was looking better and we were sure they could get in. The minutes were agonizingly slow, creeping to 10 and then 11. What a battle time can be. Nothing was happening — we were sure, but yet, — complications?? We had been put back in our rooms about 9:30 or 10:00. About 11:00 something finally happened — people, people, — photographers, newsmen, military, poured into our compound. They came right to our door and we saw it was the ICC [International Control Commission]. After a long hassle the gooks finally got rid of the newsmen and photographers and the ICC came in. (We would not permit the gooks a big propaganda show, and they were upset but had to comply). The ICC made a brief pass around the cell shaking hands with us and saying a few brief words. It was worth a few tears. "We're here to take you home." "You're heroes." "The whole world is waiting for you." This was our first real indication of what was coming, although the new shoot downs had said we were heroes and wouldn't believe it. Of course we thought they were probably just trying to make us feel better.

The ICC left the compound by about 11:30 and almost immediately the gooks told us to get ready to go. It was almost a rush now. We lined up in the compound, 106 of us, and they called off our names in order of capture.

While we were putting on the "traveling" clothes the excitement continually rose (and it hasn't dropped off yet). The bus trip to the airport was very interesting from the standpoint that it was the first time we have ever been able to look around outside prison walls. We had always been blindfolded. We saw some bomb damage, but more than that we saw what were once beautiful buildings. Completely run down and dirty filth and squalor those people live in.

DON HEILIGER My first wife divorced me while I was there. You can't do that, but she did. She went to Juarez, Mexico. It's illegal to do that, because of the Soldiers and Sailors [Civil] Relief Act of 1947. One of the things it did was [say] you cannot take civil action against any serviceman who's overseas in

Don Heiliger shakes hands with U.S. officers just moments after his release at Gia Lam airport, North Vietnam, February 18, 1973. Vietnamese officials can be glimpsed in the background.
Don Heiliger

the line of duty. Divorce is a civil action, so she could not get a divorce here. I am not the only one. There were a couple others who that happened to. That's why I didn't get any packages or letters. She took my information and threw it away. She told my kids I was dead. I had three kids from before. I don't know how she explained it to them when I came home.

We came home. It was delightful. We came through Hawaii then through San Francisco where they split us up. They could've come to St. Louis or Dayton from Madison. My folks were at the airport at Dayton. Dayton was where my kids were living with my former wife. She was at the airport but she didn't come out of the car to meet me, nor did the kids. That was kind of an emotional time with what had gone on. I got a lot of briefings on what had gone on. I was coming back to three kids who were now — When I was gone, they were eight, six, and four years old. [It] was six years later. My folks expected me to grab those kids because of what my wife had done. I said, "I haven't even seen them yet. I don't know how they're living. What kind of care they've had." I found out that they had had good care from their stepdad. I told my folks and my wife's folks, who were just as much against her as, as my folks were, "I don't know if I could've given them [such] good care." I quickly met Cher [my second wife] again, who I had known since she was a little kid in our church. I think we all came out pretty good. The Navy did a great job in following their pilots. They still are. They said, "What do you want to do? We're going to give you two things: your first promotion and your choice of assignment." I knew I would make lieutenant colonel. I said, "The only thing I want is education. I haven't had books for so long. Send me someplace. I want to compete. If I'm going to compete, I want to compete on what I can get up here." [Gestures to his head.]

FRED FLOM When we came out of the prison there were thousands of gooks lining the street. They were not antagonistic, but not friendly either. The bus trip was fairly quick, but not as fast as my heart. We got to the airport about 12:45. They gave us some beer and cookies, but that only took about five minutes. We came around the corner in the bus and saw that C-141[.] It was beautiful!! We got off the bus, lined up — marched 50 ft forward and before I knew it we were going thru the change-over 1 at a time, but quickly: FREDRIC R. FLOM 1/LT USAF a handshake and salute with Gen Ogan and a few steps the same with Col Lowry and an escort officer was taking me to the aircraft. I almost wanted to run. Americans beautiful Americans!! I was greeted by a flight stewardess with a kiss and into the aircraft. Shaking hands with everyone — and before I knew it the rest were aboard and the engines starting — taxi — takeoff — wheels in well and a sigh of relief and a big beautiful yell for freedom. It was all so fast so smooth, so beautiful, so great, and so much before me.

Epilogue:
The Road Home

"I'm blessed and I'm lucky even to sit with you and wear this blue ribbon. I wear it for the guys that aren't here. I wear it for you. I'm just a caretaker. That's all I am. I'm just a soldier trying to do a job."— Gary Wetzel

"Vietnam killed me. It just didn't get me right away."— Cletus "Ed" Hardy, *1948–2008*

In accordance with the January 27, 1973, signing of the "Agreement Ending the War and Restoring Peace in Vietnam," the final 23,000 U.S. troops left South Vietnam by March 29 of that year, leaving behind only a small Marine contingent at the U.S. embassy in Saigon. Yet the departure of U.S. troops did not mean the end to war in Vietnam. The peace agreement left North Vietnamese forces in South Vietnam, and the North and South continued to fight each other in a brutal "cease-fire war" that killed an estimated 56,500 ARVN (Army of the Republic of Vietnam) troops, 100,000 NVA/NLF (North Vietnamese Army/National Liberation Front) allies, and 15,000 civilians between 1973 and 1974.[1] As a series of South Vietnamese cities fell to Communist forces, North Vietnam gained the upper hand, and on the morning of April 30, 1975, the president of South Vietnam, Duong Van Minh, ordered a cease-fire and the surrender of South Vietnam. In an operation marked by confusion and desperation, helicopters evacuated remaining U.S. personnel and a limited number of South Vietnamese supporters from the rooftops of Saigon. Only a few hours later, North Vietnamese tanks crashed through the gates of the Saigon presidential palace and the war was over.

The war left Vietnam itself destroyed, heavily damaging infrastructure and farmlands and leaving behind a large wounded and refugee population.

The departure of the United States, which had long sustained the economy of South Vietnam, caused widespread unemployment, economic stagnation, and poverty, which also contributed to the fall of the South. In 1976, the former North Vietnamese government renamed the united country the Socialist Republic of Vietnam and sent thousands of former South Vietnamese government and military officials to reeducation camps, some never to return. In the aftermath of the war, the United States did not extend any foreign aid to Vietnam. The official relationship between the two countries was restored only in 1995 as Vietnam pledged to assist the United States in searching for any remains of U.S. soldiers still in Vietnam.

Though the United States was spared the devastation suffered by Vietnam, it too was fundamentally altered by the war. The combined blows of Vietnam and the Watergate scandal changed many Americans' attitudes toward their own government and the presidency, replacing faith with distrust. In the words of Marilyn Young, "a fundamental axiom of U.S. foreign policy had been that this nation is always on the side of freedom and justice," but after Vietnam "axiomatic American goodness was brought into question."[2] In 1973, Congress passed the War Powers Act over President Nixon's veto, limiting the amount of time U.S. forces could be deployed without congressional approval. The United States had spent more than $150 billion on the war, which contributed to the deficits and economic stagnation of the 1970s.[3] A nation that had seemed so confident with the election of John F. Kennedy in 1960 by 1976 suffered, in the words of President Jimmy Carter, from a "profound moral crisis."[4]

Many of the 2.6 million Americans who served in Vietnam — including those whose stories are told here — struggled greatly in the aftermath of the war.[5] As veteran Charlie Wolden states, "When you come home...you are different. You are changed. Your beliefs have changed." There was little recognition, appreciation, or support from the government as veterans returned home; the majority of Americans simply no longer wanted to think about Vietnam. Many veterans felt both stigmatized and ignored as they faced the experiences, injuries, and psychological effects of a war that differed drastically from their expectations. As veteran and author Tim O'Brien wrote, "A true war story is never moral.... If at the end of a war story you feel uplifted, or if you feel that some small bit of rectitude has been salvaged from the larger waste, then you have been made a victim of a very old and terrible lie."[6]

At least 60,000 veterans have committed suicide since the war, more than were killed in the war itself.[7] As of 1990, between one-quarter and one-third of homeless men were Vietnam-era veterans.[8] A study conducted between 1986 and 1988 found that after returning from Vietnam, 31 percent of male veterans and 27 percent of female veterans suffered from post-traumatic stress disorder, first identified by the American Psychiatric Association in 1980.[9] Countless others experience continued health problems from exposure to chemical herbicides like Agent Orange, and in 1984, Congress passed legislation requiring Veterans Affairs to both treat and compensate victims of Agent Orange. To cope with memories from the war and advocate for support, Vietnam veterans have relied on each other, creating their own veterans organizations such as the Vietnam Veterans of America, founded in 1978. The construction of the Vietnam Veterans Memorial in Washington, D.C., in 1982 created a national space for veterans — and all Americans — to come together and mourn the losses of Vietnam.

The United States paid a heavy price in Vietnam, yet only recently has American society come to appreciate the service and sacrifices made by this generation of young Americans. In the eyes of U.S. policy, Vietnam was a limited war in a faraway land, but for the Vietnamese the war was total. In 1985, veteran William Ehrhart returned to Vietnam. Speaking with a former Vietnamese general, Ehrhart asked, "Would it have mattered if we had done things differently?" "No," the general replied. "Probably not. History was not on your side. We were fighting for our homeland. What were you fighting for?"[10]

Gary Wetzel, Oak Creek (Army, 11th Air Assault Division)
Cletus "Ed" Hardy, Fennimore (Army, 101st Airborne Division)
Charlie Wolden, Amnicon Falls State Park (Marines, First Marine Division)
Sam King, Plum Tree, NC (Marines, Fifth Marine Division)

GARY WETZEL [After being wounded] I was evacuated to the 93rd Evac hospital. I was so messed up that I had to wait until I was stabilized and got some strength back before I could go from point A to point B. They did the best they could, trying to treat the wounds and keep infection down. I spent [about a month] in Japan. It was a bitch every day, but that's life. You deal with it. Did it hurt? Yeah, it hurt, but that's part of healing. You come back

The President of the United States

in the name of

The Congress

takes pleasure in presenting the

Congressional Medal of Honor

to

WETZEL, GARY GEORGE

Rank and organization: Specialist Fourth Class (then Pfc.), U.S. Army, 173d Assault Helicopter Company. *Place and date:* Near Ap Dong An, Republic of Vietnam, 8 January 1968. *Entered service at:* Milwaukee, Wis. *Born:* 29 September 1947, South Milwaukee, Wis. *Citation:* Sp4c. Wetzel, 173d Assault Helicopter Company, distinguished himself by conspicuous gallantry and intrepidity at the risk of his life, above and beyond the call of duty. Sp4c. Wetzel was serving as door gunner aboard a helicopter which was part of an insertion force trapped in a landing zone by intense and deadly hostile fire. Sp4c. Wetzel was going to the aid of his aircraft commander when he was blown into a rice paddy and critically wounded by 2 enemy rockets that exploded just inches from his location. Although bleeding profusely due to the loss of his left arm and severe wounds in his right arm, chest, and left leg, Sp4c. Wetzel staggered back to his original position in his gun-well and took the enemy forces under fire. His machinegun was the only weapon placing effective fire on the enemy at that time. Through a resolve that overcame the shock and intolerable pain of his injuries, Sp4c. Wetzel remained at his position until he had eliminated the automatic weapons emplacement that had been inflicting heavy casualties on the American troops and preventing them from moving against this strong enemy force. Refusing to attend his own extensive wounds, he attempted to return to the aid of his aircraft commander but passed out from loss of blood. Regaining consciousness, he persisted in his efforts to drag himself to the aid of his fellow crewman. After an agonizing effort, he came to the side of the crew chief who was attempting to drag the wounded aircraft commander to the safety of a nearby dike. Unswerving in his devotion to his fellow man, Sp4c. Wetzel assisted his crew chief even though he lost consciousness once again during this action. Sp4c. Wetzel displayed extraordinary heroism in his efforts to aid his fellow crewmen. His gallant actions were in keeping with the highest traditions of the U.S. Army and reflect great credit upon himself and the Armed Forces of his country.

Gary Wetzel's official citation for the Congressional Medal of Honor. *Gary Wetzel* and adjust. [When you left] you had a full body and you come back and [part of] it's gone. Your friends accepted you, but still you were different. You're in the crowd, but you're not there. That took a while.

I accepted the loss of the arm right away. [I realized] it's not going to grow back. Try and make the best of it. Try and adjust the best way [you] can. [When you lose] a limb, it takes about three years environmentally. Instead of doing things, or thinking "Oops," or grabbing or reaching for things, you figure out different ways. You [have to] try not to be so damn stubborn and [not] be afraid to ask for help. There are things you cannot do, and that's life.

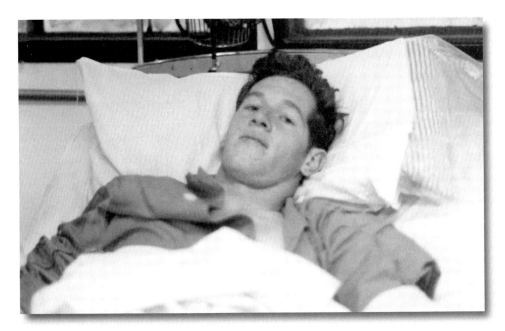

Gary Wetzel recovers from his wounds at the 93rd Evacuation Hospital in Vietnam.
Gary Wetzel

ED HARDY I didn't question much. At eighteen years old you don't. I talked about the jungle, the canopy. You couldn't penetrate it for medevacs or reconnaissance. A lot of mornings we'd need to see where we were going. In those days, 123s and 130s [airplanes] would come over and they would spray a defoliant we all know now as Agent Orange. It was a dioxin. They'd hit early in the morning when the winds were calm so they wouldn't get too much drift. That went on at seven o'clock in the morning. By eleven o'clock you could start to see the sun out through the jungle pretty good; the canopy would be gone. If you ever got up around the Ho Chi Minh Trail from the air, it looked like a forest fire had gone through there. I don't know

After surviving Hamburger Hill—one of the bloodiest battles of the war—Ed Hardy returned to the United States. *Ed Hardy*

if there's anything growing there to this day. I can remember thinking, "What the hell is this stuff?" I know what it is now. That was the part of Vietnam that killed me and I didn't even know what it was doing. It got me. It took quite a while to do it, but I guess I don't have any regrets.

We [vets] were having a lot of health problems already by 1980. I was living in San Diego, California, and I could not get my shit together for anything. I was sick. Civilian doctors would say, "You've got something in your blood." "You've got to get it taken care of." "Were you in Vietnam?" "You've got to go to the VA." [The VA said,] "No, that stuff will never hurt you." They denied it up until five years ago. I think most of my brothers from Vietnam will tell you the same thing. We go running off to these wars in the name of freedom for the oppressed. What are we doing to these young veterans?

Whole strips of land were decimated by Agent Orange, as seen in this aerial shot. *Jim Kurtz*

CHARLIE WOLDEN The Marines go to Okinawa and they go through about a three-day processing. I left Vietnam on Christmas Day, 1968. I was scared to death. I was scared to death the airplane was going to crash. I was feeling tremendously sad at leaving these guys. I was also eager to get home. I had an SKS [rifle] that I got a fifty-dollar export tag for so I could bring it home. I put it in the armory in Okinawa. We were up [at] seven o'clock in the morning, getting all of our stuff. I was supposed to get on a flight in Okinawa at nine o'clock. I go over to the armory and they don't have my SKS. I'm raising all kinds of hell: "Where's my SKS?" "Don't have it. Don't know anything about it." People on the bus are hollering, "Wolden, get on the bus. We want to get home." I wouldn't get on the bus. I got bumped from the flight. I went back over there. I said, "Where's my SKS?" They said, "I thought you were going home?" I said, "I got bumped and I might get bumped tonight. I have to get my rifle." My platoon commander when I was first in Vietnam, Lieutenant O'Brien, was platoon commander and company commander for Delta Company. He said. "I'll get it. I'll get it." He came out with my rifle. I wasn't about to let that thing go. It wasn't normal. I didn't know what "normal" was. I had a new normal.

I was taking my war souvenir home. I shot it about twenty times before I got home. It was all beat up. It was a wreck. It was probably from the French War. But it was a souvenir and it was given to me by Huey Mahoney, a good friend to me. Huey committed suicide when he got back. He gave me that rifle and I wanted to bring it home. I walked into the San Francisco airport with my SKS slung [over my shoulder]. I'm there in the airport, sleeping on the plastic chairs you sit on. I'm trying to get comfortable and I've got my SKS on the ground. This very large black man comes by and says, "Mister...mister...um...how about we put a box on that thing and get it on the airplane?" I was telling him, "I can't just let you have it." He said, "People are wondering." I said, "Look, do you have a driver's license? Let me see your driver's license." I took down his name and his driver's license number and I said, "You're going to be personally responsible if this thing doesn't show up in Duluth." [Laughs.]

My sister met me and I made her stop at the Red Owl store in Superior. Fifty bucks was a lot of money back then and I spent [that much] on four big shopping bags full of anything that I could send back to Vietnam. The first thing I did when I got home was I got a box from my mom and bundled it up and sent my platoon some food. My girlfriend came out and sat on my lap and told me that she'd been seeing this other guy and that she was sorry. I was broken-hearted. I drank a lot.

A March, 1966 demonstration outside the gates of the Badger Army Ammunitions Plant near Madison. *WHi Image ID 54591*

ED HARDY They spit at us. It was tough. I was just going, "What in the hell happened?" We landed in Oakland and they kept us on the plane for a while. I remember it was rainy and misty. There was a construction fence that guided you around and took you into a building. That's where you got your first steak and where they processed you out of the service. A lot of

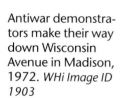

Antiwar demonstrators make their way down Wisconsin Avenue in Madison, 1972. *WHi Image ID 1903*

guys, they were going home. They weren't just getting out of Vietnam. They were going home. When we came around the corner there were MPs [military police] lined all the way around with weapons and their backs to us. They stood shoulder to shoulder and their reason for doing that was to keep us away from the people that were spitting over the top of them, on us. Oh God, they called us "baby killers," everything in the world. You hadn't been home for a year and you came home and your buddy that had a flat top when you had left now has wire-rimmed glasses and hair down to his ass. He'd changed a lot. Everything changed an awful lot.

SAM KING I thought, "I'm crazy. I'm insane. What's wrong with me? The world's changing and I'm battling it. I don't want this. Socially, I just don't fit in." There were times when I just had to be by myself for days. It was just hell. I'd wake up in the middle of the night screaming, sweat pouring off, crying for no reason. [I'd] drive down the road and just start bawling. I just hurt. I felt betrayed. I felt guilt for leaving my friends behind. I felt betrayed by the people of the United States for not accepting us. I was so mad I almost threw my beer bottle through the TV the night I watched the last helicopter lift off from the embassy in Saigon. We just left those people. We just left those people and it's a terrible thing. I reckon it really didn't matter to most people except us guys and a few supporters.

GARY WETZEL I had a good friend who got killed. He was a crew chief in another ship. They hit an LZ [landing zone] and he got shot through the head and was alive for a while, but he died. It just tears you apart, rips you apart. When Timmy died, I had him right [near me]. He kept telling me, "Tell Jane I love her." I'd said, "We'll get out of this shit, pal. Tell your own old lady you love her." But he died. My best friend. The rest of my life I will have good friends but [never] my best friend.

I found out later from my crew chief that when I put Timmy on the helicopter he was alive. He died en route to the hospital. I wished I would have stayed with him when he died [so] he didn't die alone. When I first talked to his mother, I said, "He kept saying, 'Tell Janie I love her.'" I got a phone call when I was in the hospital. I wheeled up in my wheelchair and I get the phone and it's his mother. "Hi, Gary." His grandmother, his father, and Janie [were on the phone]. I said, "Wait on. Hold on a minute." I had to stand up for this one and I wasn't walking yet. I locked the chair and I hugged the wall. I said, "Janie?" "Yeah, Gary." I said, "Timmy says…" I started babbling.

By the fourth or fifth time I got it out and said, "Timmy says I'm supposed to tell you that he loved you." We were bawling.

CHARLIE WOLDEN I love vets. I love combat vets. I understand them. I really do. I learn from all of them. When you come home...you are different. You are changed. Your beliefs have changed. Your maturity level in many ways is far more advanced than other people. I felt really comfortable around Korean War vets when I got home. I didn't want to associate with Vietnam vets. I wanted to keep Vietnam vets far away from me because they were going to remind me of something. I didn't want it. It was over, done with. You were very alone. I think Vietnam vets like to be alone. They have a tremendous need to be loved and wanted and needed, but they also want to be alone. The most successful Vietnam vets usually own their own businesses. They've got someone like their wife or a good secretary to take care of the details because the details they don't care about. The details are going to stress them out. Running the business, that is an adventure. That keeps the adrenaline rush going. When you don't have that you are liable to go into a depression. Most of the Vietnam vets we are seeing right now are having a hell of a time retiring. They're workaholics or alcoholics or both.

SAM KING I'd take wild chances because the ultimate high is adrenaline and the ultimate adrenaline you get is in war, when you're fighting for your life. You seek to find that thrill again. I never could. I did it through drugs. I did it through taking wild chances. In a car I did things that I'm lucky I lived through. I'd go out in the woods for three or four days at a time with just a knife, a match, and fishing line and just try to survive. I didn't have to do that, but I was trying to get a thrill. I carried on like that for many, many years. I didn't know at the time what was going on.

I got a job working on the Alaska pipeline. I moved to Alaska, and I gutted salmon in a fishing cannery. I actually worked at Prudhoe Bay on the western side of the field. I worked for different contractor companies doing cleanups, doing maintenance, [and] hauling. That was pretty exciting. I did that for about ten years. I was still going at it hard, drinking. I went through a second marriage, the one that I never should have started, but that's the way it goes too. It blew up there.

ED HARDY We all came home and depending on what your buddies were doing, you either took an acid trip or smoked pot and drank beer and self-medicated for a lot of years. Whenever we got uncomfortable with some-thing, we moved on. If you ever look at any real combat vet out of Nam, you find out he's never stayed in one place for very long. He's always moved on. It's just one of those things that I don't think is explainable. You're just not comfortable anywhere for very long, so you go someplace else.

My mother was telling me when I first came home how scared they were. They just didn't know what the hell was going to happen. I would tear out of bed at night and go flying outside and just [be] gone. The nightmares, the cold sweats, they're still there to this day. I know they'll never go away. They medicate for it. The VA tries to do something for it. In Tomah they have a fairly good PTSD program. Some of them just break down to guys sitting around and telling war stories and some of them are actually trying to do some good.

CHARLIE WOLDEN I became a therapist, and I had a Gulf War vet, right after the Gulf War. I had a situation with myself during a session. People think it's weird but it was an out-of-body experience. I said, "I've got to get on top of my own stuff if I'm going to be a vet counselor." I went to see a private psy-chiatrist down in Minneapolis. I saw him and I saw his male nurse. They just had me start from day one, to just line it up. I saturated myself with it. They have a new therapy out called exposure therapy. It worked. I started challenging some of my thoughts about things. I changed some of my be-liefs. [I realized] I wasn't really a coward. My definition of being a hero as a child was, "You're John Wayne. You're fearless." Hell, I was terrified over there. My definition [now] is overcoming your fear to do your job. I don't think much of the word "hero" any way you look at it.

GARY WETZEL I worked at Ladish. It was the first week in November. On my twenty-first birthday I'd bought a brand-new Corvette. A colonel, a major, and a first sergeant [showed up] at work at Ladish in Cudahy. They called up to my office, "Hey, Gary, some military people want to see you." I go down there and they introduce themselves and [tell me] I'm going on a trip. I said, "I'm not going anywhere." They knew where I was going, but they weren't at liberty to tell me. "You've got to." "No, I'm not going anywhere." [They gave me] the number for this liaison. A day or two later I go down there. I introduce myself and this colonel's all ecstatic but still wasn't at liberty to say where I was going or why. Finally, I called my congressman in D.C. [He says,] "Gary, I'm looking forward to meeting with you. You're going on to

In November 1968, Lyndon B. Johnson awarded Gary Wetzel the Congressional Medal of Honor, citing "extraordinary heroism in his efforts to aid his fellow crewman."
Gary Wetzel

get the big one." That was a trip. Whoever thinks they're going to get [the Medal of Honor]? I was flattered and honored to go to the White House and meet the president.

I grew up with nine brothers and sisters. [We'd say,] "When you're done with that butter knife, let me use it." Down in D.C., I had to watch other people eating to see where I started. Different world. We're in the White House. We're having coffee and crumpets with fancy silverware. The president comes in and sits right next to me, puts his hand on my knee. "How are you doing, son?" "Fine, Mr. President." [The president of the United States] is the next thing to God. We chatted a little bit. Then [there was] the ceremonial stuff. The president walks in front of us. We all walk in the White House and here are nine thousand people. Its like, "Wow, what a trip."

SAM KING It's changed over the last few years. We're actually popular now. I imagine in the last six or eight years I've had more people come up to me and say, "Thank you for serving," and ask about it. That never happened before. Never, never. We could pick each other out of a crowd. Combat veterans especially. You just know that look, especially if someone mentions Vietnam; you can just see it in the eyes. We have pretty much stuck together. That's how Vietnam Veterans in America got formed, which I'm a member of. That was a good thing. It gave us support amongst each other.

My dad had never talked to me about World War II. I knew he was a platoon sergeant. I knew he was all through the South Pacific with Sixth Marines. I came back and we talked about it some, but he hurt me. I love my dad. We weren't super close, but I loved him and I miss him. He said, "The only difference was you lost your war." Our relationship was never the same again. He was a very conservative Presbyterian man. I was going against everything he thought he'd ever taught me anyhow, but that hurt. It still

Sam King, left, and a buddy rest after a long day. *Sam King*

hurts. I'll never forget. After that I don't think we talked about the subject more than in passing ever again.

CHARLIE WOLDEN I sat over in Vietnam with a fantasy. [I thought,] "We'll win this war when we get a bulldozer five miles wide and a mile high to push these mountains into the flat area. We'll drop leaflets and tell the people to swim like hell. We'll just bulldoze it over and then we'll plant corn." This other guy would say, "It'd be a good place to put catfish ponds in too. We could have the corn and feed the catfish." It's very common to make up stories about what you'd do if you'd had the power. It served a purpose to get us through it, to emotionally and physically survive it. We had a saying, "Don't mean a goddamn thing." Suck it up. Don't put a meaning on it. If you put a meaning on it, you start feeling. We called it "the Nam." "Hey, I'm in the Nam. The Bush." Then there was "the World." This was the surreal world.

Control is a big issue for combat vets because we didn't have control. We didn't have control of anything except for what we had in our hands. We didn't have control over whether the helicopters were going to come for us. We didn't have control over what the weather was going to do or when a rat was going to come crawl up our legs. We didn't have control of when that mortar round was going to drop. It was random. We may have had to go up that hill but what made us go up those hills like that? Fear of shame. Fear of being shamed.

GARY WETZEL They read out the citations. When they're reading the citations, the memories come back of what happened. It's like, "Aw, jeez." All the killing. All the death. The guys who got hurt, and here I am. Why am I here? I was there for those guys. That's the meaning behind that. I try and live up to it. There was a time when you thought about giving [the medal] back or leaving it down at the Wall. I think your buddies wouldn't want that to happen. You try and make the best of it and stand [for what it] represents. It's very precious. It is forty years later and I'm still honored that I have that privilege. From a private to a four-star general, there's no rank because you all [the Medal of Honor recipients] have the blue ribbon. All different walks of life, all different types of ethnicity, but it is a bond. We're all one. We try and do good things. There are only ninety-seven living worldwide. When I first got involved in the society back forty years ago, there were 384 living recipients, the good bulk of which were from World War II and some World War I vets. Still, when I get together in a room with these guys I'm still in awe. It's so special to be amongst these people. They are a good bunch of folks.

SAM KING [One day] I went into this jewelry store to pick up a Marine Corps ring I had ordered, and the lady waiting on me was this pretty blonde from Wisconsin. We ended up going out together and that was twenty-four years ago. I've been married twenty-three years this coming August. She saved my life. She jerked me out, [saying,] "You want to be married to me, you're going to have to quit some of this stuff." We moved back here, my wife and me, and started to work. I was really having problems. I was short-tempered. I was just getting really angry. I was not sleeping. I was just impossible to live with. My wife finally told me one night after I woke up crying from this terrible dream, "You have to go to the VA." She kept on me. I finally went over to the VA Hospital in the [Twin] Cities and they sent me over to the Post-Traumatic Stress clinic. I went in and I met this guy. We talked and he asked me questions. It got so bad. I got angry. I stormed out. He wanted to put me in a therapy group. That was the last thing [I wanted], but I promised my wife. I didn't last long in that group. It didn't go well, but I got my doctor. Her name is Dr. Ames. She was really good. I started opening up to her and she helped me.

I had an incident. I was going to the VA Hospital in my pickup truck and a guy cut me off on [Interstate] 94. When I came to my senses we were on the other side of the [Twin] Cities. I was running almost a hundred miles an hour trying to chase this guy down. I freaked out. I went to the VA and I told my psychiatrist that things like that were happening. I was blacking out. She put me in the hospital. I stayed in the hospital for a good period of time on the psych ward. I was definitely in trouble. I got on medication, got in some combat groups that were really good. I stayed in-patient and when I came out I went to therapy on a regular basis. A few months later, I had another episode where I was homicidal or suicidal. I wanted to kill myself or somebody else. I went back in. I came out of that a little better. They got me to see Charlie [Wolden]. That was the best thing that ever happened to me. I was seeing Charlie regularly every week, working with him. [There were] long, terrible crying sessions, but Charlie was right there. We developed this group which Dan Hinkle and a number of others ran. Groups like that usually don't last very long. We were together over a year. That helped me a lot. I ended up getting reevaluated through the VA, and they made me 100 percent [disabled] between wounds and PTSD.

ED HARDY Around 2002, I started having quite a few health problems. They cut a big growth out. It wasn't malignant but it had dioxin in it. The damn thing weighed over a pound. It was blocking my airway off. I had to have an airway put in to keep breathing. I got through that one and it wasn't even six months before one popped up on the other side. They had to open me up and go in down through my throat. They shrunk it and pulled it out.

In 2005 during a routine lung X-ray they said, "You've got a spot in your right lung. You should get it looked at." I went down to Madison and had a CT scan. They kept dinking around. They said, "Well, you need to get this." "We can't tell what it is." "You need to get this done." "You need to get that done." They kept testing and testing and testing. Finally in August 2006, they said, "That spot has got problems. It's growing fast. It's got to come out. We're going to have to take the lower right lobe of your right lung." So they did.

I did chemotherapy in 2007 and I was feeling pretty good. Not quite a year ago now, I started getting pains in my stomach. They sent me down to Milwaukee and did a PET scan and said, "Well, it's malignant. It looks like it's moving around a little bit. We got to figure out what we're going to do." Since then it's taken my body over. It's in my bones. There are some days it feels like it's going to be today. There's nothing to do about it.

I've lived a good life, with no regrets. I've got a little boy. He's sharp as hell and we're pretty good buddies. That's going to be tough. I've had a lot of friends who have been right there for me. Hopefully they're going to be around to help him along if he needs something, Financially he's going to be fine, but money isn't everything either. How long do I have? I have to go on to hospice care. Yesterday they had to up the drugs by another 25 percent, and that's been three times in a month. The pain is just unbelievable. Vietnam killed me. It just didn't get me right away.

CHARLIE WOLDEN The National Center for PTSD has a written document. It is very poignant. It says something like this: "[One of] the largest contributing factors to mental health problems amongst combat veterans is the gross inconsistency between their naïve belief system going into war and the harsh reality of it. On the high side, it will destroy your preexisting belief system. On the low side, it will seriously challenge it. Either way, the soldiers who get through it will adopt the ethos of the Army and of that of the soldier: 'I'll die for you. You die for me. We're in this together. We're going to do it and get home.'" You adopt the belief system.

SAM KING I have my days. May is the anniversary of when I was wounded and when I lost my friends in one swoop. It's a rough time of the year for me. My problem is that I can bunker up, as we vets call it. I lock myself in the house and just sit and think. If I do that then the depression sets in. Things go downhill from there. It's a constant battle every day of my life. To think that something that happened so long ago could have so much influence over not only my life but my family's lives. They live with it too. My kids and my wife went through some really tough times with me.

I have thoughts about Vietnam a dozen times [a day]. Something brings it, some smell. When it gets real warm and rainy it all floods back. I fish a lot and I'll walk a trail along the river. The grasses are hanging off both sides of the trail. I don't even realize it but I'm on point. I still go down at the sound of a backfire, or if somebody drops something. It's embarrassing but it happens. I can't go into a restaurant and sit with my back to other people. If there is any way, I have to have a booth or my back against the wall. I know where every exit is and I look to pick the people out who I think could be trouble. It's never gone away. Not long ago, I was hearing voices. Voices of people I knew in Vietnam. I was hearing them. I wasn't imagining them. To me they were as real as [I'm] here talking.

GARY WETZEL People say, "Weren't you scared?" You're scared, but you're doing your job. You try not to let it get into what you want to try to do or accomplish. Here I am just blown to smithereens and shot and stabbed and bayoneted. You still function. Should I have been dead, medically? Probably, that's what they tell me. I think the big guy was looking down, "Keep the redhead alive." Here I am. I'm blessed and I'm lucky even to sit with you and wear this blue ribbon. I wear it for the guys that aren't here. I wear it for you. I'm just a caretaker. That's all I am. I'm just a soldier trying to do a job.

I went down to the Wall. It starts down here [gestures] and you're looking at the names. You're walking and looking at the names up here [gestures]. You're [also] looking at yourself in the black granite. You're walking with your brothers. That's respect. That's love. That's what it's all about. I touched [Timmy's] name. I just dropped. I said what I had to say and stood up. I saluted him. If my name was there, [like it] should have been, it would be an honor to have my brothers come down and say, "Gar'? Not a bad guy."

The cost of war.
Courtesy of the 101st Airborne Division

SAM KING Do I regret joining the Marines and going to Vietnam and fighting? No. If I had done it for political reasons, maybe yes, [but] I didn't do it for political reasons. I did it because it was a family tradition and it was a male rite of passage in my family. If you had the chance, you went to war. It changed the family's whole outlook about what kind of guy you were. I had five first cousins who were all over in different places about the same time.

Do I think that anything good came out of it? Yeah. Militarily we won the battles. We just couldn't win the political war. It bothers me a lot today. I hate to see that we may repeat [it]. You're doomed to repeat the history you don't remember. I just worry about it. When this [Iraq] war broke out, Vietnam veterans were the first to say, "These guys and girls are not going to come home to the same bullshit we did. We'll see to it ourselves that they'll come home as the heroes they rightly are."

ED HARDY I'm not a big reunion guy. I don't do it. I kind of wish I had, but I thought, "Well, what the hell? I just haven't stayed in touch like that." Those cold nights when the bullets were just flying all over hell and you thought you just weren't going to make it through the night; when the sun came up in the morning and you looked at your buddy, you thought, "By God, you're my best friend. We're never going to part, are we? We'll never let go. We'll always stay in touch." We never called each other after we got home. He went his way and I went mine. We all did it. Every one of us did it that same way. I think that comes back too. You just don't want to make that friend again. If you make friends, it hurts when you lose them. It's that kind of a thing.

I kind of feel that way with Noah, my little boy. What a loss. I've got the time and the money to enjoy him. He's going to be five in November. It'd be the greatest thing in the world if I could see him go to his first day of kindergarten. It doesn't look good. They're resilient. They bounce back at that age. We're getting him ready for it. He knows something's up but to have your little boy wake up in the morning and say, "How you feeling today, Daddy? You're going to get better today?" What do you say?

Appendix I
WISCONSIN VETERAN BIOGRAPHIES

Martin T. Acker
Army, 101st Airborne Division
Middleton*

In 1967, Marty Acker enlisted in the Army and became part of the 101st Airborne Division. Acker spent two years in Vietnam as a specialist fourth class. He and his wife Margaret have two children, Nick and Meggie, and live in Verona.

Marvin S. Acker
Army, 101st Airborne Division
Middleton

Marvin Acker served for three years in the Army's 101st Airborne Division. During his tenure in Vietnam, Acker earned two Purple Hearts, Parachutist Wings, and a Bronze Star. He worked as a real estate broker and builder after returning home and lives in De Forest.

George F. Banda
Army, 101st Airborne Division
Milwaukee

Drafted into the Army, George Banda served almost two years in the 101st Airborne Division, surviving the Fire Base Henderson

George Banda
James Gill/Wisconsin Public Television

attack. He earned numerous awards including the Silver Star for Gallantry and two Bronze Stars with Combat "V" for valor and meritori-

---

* Residency at time of service is listed for all veterans.

ous service. Banda is retired from his position in rescue and firefighting at General Mitchell Airport and lives in Milwaukee with his wife, Lorraine. He is affiliated with several veterans' associations including Disabled American Veterans, American GI Forum, and the American Legion.

John C. Brogan
Army, MAAG–Cambodia
De Pere

John Brogan enlisted in the Army on February 24, 1954. After working in Washington, D.C., for several months, Brogan volunteered to serve as part of the Military Assistance Advisory Group sent to Cambodia during the early years of U.S. involvement. He currently lives in Green Bay with his wife, Gisela. The couple have one daughter, Anja.

Joseph F. Campbell
Army, First Logistical Command
St. Charles, IL

Joseph Campbell spent three years in the Army after enlisting on December 30, 1965. He served two tours of duty in Bad Kreuznach, Germany, before deploying for a year in Vietnam. After the service, Campbell returned to the United States and worked as a salesman. He is now president of Machinery and Welder Corporation in West Allis. Campbell is the father of five children, Joseph Jr., Amanda, James, Edmund, and Peter. He is the national director for the Lao Hmong American Coalition and co-founder of Being There–Reaching Out, Inc., a volunteer organization that supports families of fallen Wisconsin military.

John M. Dederich
Marines, Third Marine Division
De Pere

John Dederich served for three years as a lance corporal in Vietnam. After his tour, he became manager of the Brown County Arena, settling in De Pere with his wife, Karen, and their three children. As president of Friends of Brown County Veterans, Dederich played an integral role in the financing and construction of the Brown County Veterans Museum.

Michael J. Demske
Navy, Coastal Division 11
De Pere

Mike Demske served in the Navy as a gunner's mate third class for nearly four years. He was awarded a Bronze Star with Combat "V" for valor, a Navy Commendation Medal, and two Purple Hearts. Demske is currently affiliated with Vietnam Veterans of America and is a past president of the Wisconsin State Council. He works as the Manitowoc County Planning and Park Commission director and lives in Manitowoc. He has one son, Scott.

Ted F. Fetting
Army, Ninth Infantry Division
Greenwood

After being drafted by the Army in May of 1967, Ted Fetting served as a private first class and specialist fourth class in Vietnam. After the service he held various positions with the Wisconsin Department of Veterans' Affairs. Fetting has also been director of the Milwaukee County Veteran Services, a real estate broker, farmer, and auctioneer. He has two children, Nick and Katie, and lives in Wauwatosa.

Fredric R. Flom
Air Force, 23rd Tactical Fighter Wing
Menasha

Fred Flom spent nearly seven years as a POW after his aircraft was shot down on August 8, 1966, over North Vietnam. Flom recorded his experiences on the back of Vietnamese cigarette wrappers during his final weeks in prison. In March 1973 he was released and returned to his wife, Carolyn, and children, Julie and Erik. Flom served a total of twenty-seven years with the Air Force, retiring as a colonel. He now works as a pilot for American Airlines and lives in Waupaca.

Cletus "Ed" Hardy
Army, 101st Airborne Division
Fennimore

Ed Hardy enlisted in the Army on September 19, 1967, and served two tours of duty in Vietnam. He earned a Silver Star for bravery in combat after surviving the battle of Hamburger Hill. After the war Hardy owned a commercial insurance brokerage and later a construction company in Hillsboro. He also served as a volunteer firefighter and was a member of Veterans of Foreign Wars. On April 30, 2008, Ed Hardy succumbed to cancer. He is survived by three children, Justina, Renée, and Noah.

Roger Harrison
Army, 101st Airborne Division
Racine

On September 30, 1968, Roger Harrison enlisted in the Army, serving in the 101st Airborne Division for one year, eight months, and nine days. After the service he settled in Racine with his wife, Marine. The couple raised three children, Thomas, Shawn, and David. Harrison worked at American Motors/ Chrysler Motors for thirty-six years. He is currently retired but is an active member of Vietnam Veterans of America and Veterans of Foreign Wars.

Donald R. Heiliger
Air Force, 333rd Tactical Fighter Squadron
Madison

Don Heiliger received an Air Force ROTC commission from the University of Wisconsin– Madison in 1958. After graduating first in his flight school class in 1965, he served as navigator-instructor. On May 15, 1967, Heiliger was shot down during a night mission over North Vietnam and spent nearly six years as a POW. After Vietnam, he served as an Air Force attaché in Uruguay, Chile, and Israel, retiring after nearly thirty years of service with the rank of colonel. Heiliger also spent twelve years on the Dane County Board of Supervisors. A past chairman of the Wisconsin Board of Veterans Affairs, he now lives in McFarland. In addition to three children from a previous marriage, Heiliger has three sons, Don Jr. and twins Dan and Dave, with his wife, Cheryl.

Daniel R. Hinkle
Army, Fourth Infantry Division
Bruce

In May 1965, Dan Hinkle enlisted in the Army. While in Vietnam he held the ranks of second and first lieutenant. Hinkle served

Dan Hinkle
James Gill/Wisconsin Public Television

twenty-two years in the army and lives in Bruce. He and his wife, Catherine, have four sons.

Michael H. Hoks
Navy, River Assault Division 112
Menasha

Michael Hoks served in the Navy's River Assault Division 112 for almost three years. He was awarded numerous honors for his service in Vietnam, including the Purple Heart and the Navy Commendation Medal with a Combat "V" for valor. After the war, Hoks worked in sales and paper machine operations. A member of the Mohican Veterans, the Military Order of the Purple Heart, and the War

Eagle Society, he and his wife, Peggy, live in New London. Hoks has one son, two daughters, two stepdaughters, and a grandson.

Bruce A. Jensen
Navy, River Assault Division 111
Milwaukee

After enlisting in the Navy on November 25, 1965, Bruce Jensen joined the Mobile Riverine Force. Serving as gunner's mate third class, he earned a Navy Commendation Medal and a Navy Achievement Medal with Combat "V" for valor. After returning from Vietnam, Jensen served as a Milwaukee police officer. He has volunteered with the Milwaukee Irish Fest

Bruce and Wayne Jensen
James Gill/Wisconsin Public Television

for twenty-five years, and joined the United States LST Association. He and his wife Patricia raised two sons and live in West Allis.

Wayne W. Jensen
Navy, Coastal Division 12
Milwaukee

After serving almost thirty years in the military, Wayne Jensen retired as a master sergeant. During his time in Vietnam, Jensen held the ranks of petty officer third class and gunner's mate, earning several awards. After the war he spent thirty-five years as a Milwaukee police officer. He and his wife, Donna, have two daughters, Wendy and Sheila.

Donald G. Jones
Army, Military Intelligence Corps
Madison

During his twelve and a half years in the military Don Jones was a member of the Army's Military Intelligence Corps. Jones held the rank of captain while in Vietnam, earning a Bronze Star and the Pentagon's Meritorious Service Medal. Jones has worked as the executive director of several organizations related to the war on poverty and is the event coordinator for the LZ Lambeau Welcome Home Weekend. Jones is the father of two and lives in Madison.

David F. Kies
Army, 173rd Airborne Brigade
Platteville

Drafted on October 5, 1965, Dave Kies served for twenty months, receiving an "early out" due to injuries. He was awarded a Purple Heart and a Bronze Star. Settled in Verona, Kies has

Dave Kies
James Gill/Wisconsin Public Television

worked as a used-car salesman and a Lands' End illustrator. He has five children with his wife, Anne. Affiliated with Veterans of Foreign Wars and the American Legion, he also volunteers to speak at schools and the Wisconsin Veterans' Museum.

Samuel E. King
Marines, Fifth Marine Division
Plum Tree, NC

Sam King enlisted in the Marines in February, 1969. After four years in Vietnam he returned to the United States and worked in construction, farming, and mental health care. When

King was fifty-four he graduated from the University of Wisconsin–Stout. He and his wife, Kaye, have four children, Samuel, Aaron, Zehe, and Orrie. They make their home in New Richmond.

James A. Kurtz
Army, First Infantry Division
Madison

Jim Kurtz was commissioned from the Army ROTC program at the University of Wisconsin–Madison in 1962. Having earned a Bronze Star and three Air Medals, he left the service in June 1967 and worked as an attorney on the Wisconsin Legislative Council and as chief

legal counsel for the Department of Natural Resources. Now retired, Kurtz volunteers as an oral historian for the Wisconsin Veterans' Museum and is a member of Veterans of Foreign Wars. He and his wife, Becki, have three children and live in Middleton.

Lance Larson
Marines, Third Marine Division
Appleton

After enlisting on February 9, 1967, Lance Larson spent nearly four years in the Marines as a radio operator. He was present for the entirety of the Khe Sanh siege in 1968. After the service Larson worked for the United

Jim Kurtz
James Gill/Wisconsin Public Television

Lance Larson
James Gill/Wisconsin Public Television

States Postal Service and had two sons, Leif and Kyle, with his wife, Janis. Larson lives in Appleton and is the author of three books.

Charles R. Lieb
Army, 101st Airborne Division
Minneapolis, MN

Charlie Lieb spent eleven years in the Army after graduating from the United States Military Academy on June 5, 1968. After Vietnam, he earned two master's degrees and taught courses for the ROTC at San Jose State University. Having retired from the service in 1979 as a major, Lieb worked for the FMC Corporation for several years and later became president of PDQ Manufacturing. He and his wife, Janet, raised three children, Matthew, Brandon, and Kristine, and live in Green Bay. An active volunteer in his community, he currently serves on the Green Bay Packers Board of Directors.

Nhia Thong "Charles" Lor
Military Region II Special Guerilla Unit
Long Cheng, Laos

A native of Laos, Nhia Thong "Charles" Lor was exposed to war at an early age. By the time he was twelve he had become a soldier, and at thirteen he was fighting on the front lines. After years of struggle and hardship in the Laos jungles, Lor and his family immigrated to the United States on November 27, 1979. He and his wife started their family soon after. The couple raised six children in Milwaukee where he worked in a machine shop for twenty-five years. Active in several veteran organizations such as Lao Veterans of America and the color guard of Vietnam Vet-

Nhia Thong Lor
James Gill/Wisconsin Public Television

erans of America, Lor is a past president of the Hmong American Coalition Wisconsin Chapter. He and his wife own and operate an Asian market in Madison.

Linda McClenahan
Army, Women's Army Corps
Berkeley, CA

On August 27, 1967, Linda McClenahan enlisted in the Army and joined the Women's Army Corps as a communications clerk, working one year in Vietnam and four as an Army reservist. After the service McClenahan worked as a communications manager, high school teacher, and varsity softball coach in

Linda McClenahan
James Gill/Wisconsin Public Television

Larry Miller
James Gill/Wisconsin Public Television

San Francisco. She also earned a B.A. in business and a master's degree in guidance and counseling. McClenahan is now a sister in the Order of St. Dominic in Racine where she works as a trauma counselor for veterans.

Kenneth W. McGwin

Navy, Seventh Fleet Amphibious Force
Montello

When Ken McGwin was drafted in 1967, he joined the Navy, spending four years as a fireman and a machinist's mate third class. After the war he spent two years in the reserves and the next thirty as a dairy farmer. McGwin has

worked as a power plant engineer for the past nine years and lives in Montello. He has two children, Sam and Maggie, with his wife, Julie.

John E. Mielke

Army, Medical Corps
Appleton

John Mielke volunteered for service in 1961, and served for two years as a Captain in the Army Medical Corps. He and his wife, Sally, reside in Appleton and raised six children: John Jr., Douglas, Donald, Ellen, Rebecca, and Martin.

Bill Moore
James Gill/Wisconsin Public Television

Daniel Pierce
James Gill/Wisconsin Public Television

Larry D. Miller

Marines, Third Marine Division
Rice Lake

Larry Miller spent two years in Vietnam as a corporal in the Marines. He is now a member of the Disabled American Veterans and is coordinator for a Marine Corps Toys for Tots. Miller was also roofer and business owner after the service. Married to Francine, the couple raised three children and live in Rice Lake.

William R. Moore

Navy, Seventh Fleet
Greenfield

On August 8, 1961, Bill Moore enlisted in the Navy. Assigned to the submarine force, he

served for six years as a second and third class electronics technician. After Vietnam he married his wife, Barbara Jean, and they started a family together. Ten years after his first term was complete he joined the 128th Air Refueling Group at Mitchell Field, serving twenty additional years and retiring as a master sergeant. He has two daughters, Michelle and Sheila, and two sons, Tom and Jim, both nuclear submariners.

Daniel P. Pierce

Marines, First and Third Marine Division
Stone Lake

Daniel Pierce joined the Marines in 1965, serving for three and a half years. He was promoted several times during his tour, holding the ranks of private first class, lance corporal, corporal, and sergeant. Pierce lives in Stone Lake and has two children, Jennifer and Joshua, with his late wife.

Roy T. Rogers
Marines, Fourth Marine Division
Neenah

Roy Rogers enlisted as a Marine in 1963 while still in high school. He served as a lance corporal, earning a Purple Heart, Good Conduct Medal, and the National Defense Service Medal, among others. Married to Darlene, the couple raised three sons, Brian, Alan, and Cory. Rogers also spent thirty-two years as a letter carrier for the Menasha Post Office. He has dedicated the last forty-five years to volunteering with numerous organizations, serving in administrative positions for the Military Order of the Purple Heart and Veterans of Foreign Wars.

James C. Rose
Army, 94th Infantry Division
White Lake

After enlisting in April of 1962, James Rose served thirteen years in the Army. During the Vietnam War he held the rank of staff sergeant. Rose lives in White Lake and has three children, Timm, Mark, and James Jr., with his wife, Jane.

Daniel D. Schaller
Navy, Fleet Air Reconnaisance Squadron 1
La Crosse

Dan Schaller served for four and a half years as an electronics technician third class after enlisting on February 26, 1962. During his tour of duty Schaller was awarded several Air Medals and Expeditionary Medals. Once back in the United States, he worked as an electronics technician, electrical support engineer, and plant engineer. Schaller is a member of Veterans of Foreign Wars and the American Legion. Married to Sonja, the couple have one daughter, Pamela, and live in La Crosse.

Steven R. Schofield
Army, First Special Forces Group and Studies
and Observations Group
Chicago

Steven Schofield traveled through Taiwan, Japan, the Philippines, and Vietnam during his three years with the Army First Special Forces Group. In 1969 he joined the Agency for International Development as a public health advisor and began operating as part of the Secret War in Laos. Schofield remained there until 1975 when the Laotian government fell. One of the last twenty-six Americans to leave Laos, Schofield returned to Chicago with his wife, Yasuko, and son, Thomas, and began working in marketing and sales. An advocate for the Hmong of Wisconsin and member of the Special Forces Association, Schofield lives in Newton.

Aloysius N. Sobkowiak
Marines, First Marine Division
Onalaska

Following the family tradition of Marine service, Al Sobkowiak joined the Marines in 1951 with only an eighth-grade education. In service for more than twenty years, he held every rank from Private to Captain. After retiring from the Marines Sobkowiak worked as a fraud investigator in San Diego, California. At the age of forty-one he attended high school for the first time and now holds a masters degree in public administration. Sobkowiak lives in Onalaska with his wife, Mary. The couple have four children.

Ray W. Stubbe
Marines, Chaplain Corps
Milwaukee

Ray Stubbe spent twenty-one years on active duty and eight in the reserves as a Navy chaplain. While in Vietnam Stubbe went out on multiple patrols and missions with

Rev. Ray Stubbe
James Gill/Wisconsin Public Television

his congregation of Marines. He was present during the siege of Khe Sanh. After the service Stubbe worked as a Lutheran pastor and has authored several books about the Vietnam War, including *Valley of Decision: The Siege of Khe Sanh* and *Inside Force Recon*. Stubbe lives in Wauwatosa.

Andrew W. Thundercloud, Jr.
Marines, First Marine Air Wing
Tomah

Andrew Thundercloud continued his family's military tradition when he enlisted on January 25, 1963. Thundercloud flew several hundred missions as a medical corpsman, caring for wounded soldiers as they were airlifted from the battle zone. In 1968 he returned to civilian life, working as a physician's assistant. Thundercloud has five children and lives in Tomah. A member of the Ho-Chunk Nation, he is also affiliated with Veterans of Foreign Wars, the Winnebago Veterans Association, and Vietnam Veterans of America.

Roger L. Treece
Navy, Fleet Air Reconnaisance Squadron 1
Cleveland, WI

Roger Treece spent three years in the Navy after enlisting before his eighteenth birthday. Part of the Fleet Air Reconnaissance Squadron I, Treece flew missions over North Vietnam to track enemy positions. He and his wife, Elayne, live in Cleveland and raised three children, Roger Jr., William, and George. Treece worked as a plastics engineer for many years and is currently the commander of the Manitowoc County Chapter of Disabled American Veterans.

Don Weber
James Gill/Wisconsin Public Television

Donald J. Weber
Marines, Fourth Marine Division
La Crosse

Don Weber enlisted on October 10, 1966, serving a total of four years. During his time in Vietnam, Weber provided security for construction battalions. He has been honored with a Presidential Unit Citation, two Bronze Stars, and a Purple Heart. An entrepreneur, Weber is now the chairman and CEO of Logistics Health in La Crosse. He serves on the Board of Directors for the Boys & Girls Club and the Family & Children's Center; he is also a member of American Legion. He and his wife, Roxanne, have four children, Elizabeth, Nicholas, August, and Maxwell.

Gary G. Wetzel
Army, 11th Air Assault Division
Oak Creek

In November 1968, Lyndon B. Johnson awarded Gary Wetzel the Congressional Medal of Honor, citing "extraordinary heroism in his efforts to aid his fellow crewman." Wetzel served two and a half years in the 173rd Assault Helicopter Company (Robin Hoods) after enlisting on February 15, 1966. He lives in South Milwaukee with his wife, Kathy.

Will Williams
Army, 27th Infantry Division
Crystal Springs, MS

Will Williams served two tours of duty in Vietnam, earning two Bronze Stars and a Purple Heart. When he returned to the United States he held a variety of jobs, ranging from miner to construction worker, and retired as a postal employee. Now a peace advocate, Williams volunteers with Veterans for Peace, the Madison Area Peace Coalition, and is a founding member of T.A.M.E.: Truth and Alternatives to Military through Education. Williams has been honored for his work with the Reverend Dr. Martin Luther King, Jr. Humanitarian Award; he was also named a Wisconsin Peacemaker of the Year in 2009. He and his wife, Dorothy, live in De Forest; they have one daughter, Letha.

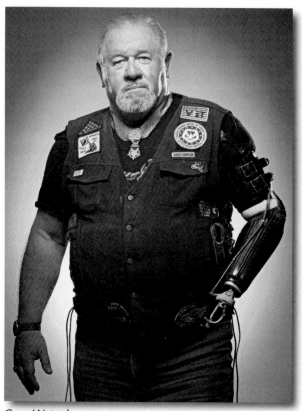

Gary Wetzel
James Gill/Wisconsin Public Television

Will Williams
James Gill/Wisconsin Public Television

Charles B. Wolden

Marines, First Marine Division
Amnicon Falls State Park

Charlie Wolden enlisted in the Marines on July 6, 1967, and served four years in Vietnam. Shortly after returning to the United States he enlisted in the Air Force as a B-52 pilot. Wolden was awarded the Purple Heart for wounds inflicted during the battle of Hue and an Air Medal for flying a classified mission to Egypt. Since leaving the military he has worked as a mental health therapist and as a team leader for the Milwaukee Vet Center. Wolden is the father of four and lives in Frederic with his wife, Janet. In 2001 he was named the Wisconsin Veteran Advocate of the Year by the Sheboygan County Veterans Service Officer Association.

APPENDIX II
THE HONOR ROLL

Military Personnel from Wisconsin who Died (Including Missing and Captured Declared Dead) as a Result of the Vietnam War, 1957–1995*

HDC = hostile, died while captured
HDM = hostile, died while missing
HDW= hostile, died of wounds
HK = hostile, killed

NHI = nonhostile, died of illness or injury
NDM = nonhostile, died while missing
NHO = nonhostile, died of other causes
† Body not recovered

AIR FORCE

NAME	RANK	HOMETOWN	TYPE	DATE OF DEATH‡
Robert L. Baldwin	Major	Tomah	HK	March 31, 1967
John L. Banks III§	First Lieutenant	Superior	NHO	March 29, 1966
Robert H. Barr	Lieutenant Colonel	Pewaukee	NHO	July 28, 1969
Walter C. Booth	Captain	Waukesha	HK	March 26, 1969
Gary E. Brunner	Captain	Racine	HDM	June 23, 1969
Robert I. Bush	Captain	Racine	HK	June 9, 1966
Clyde D. Dawson	Major	Fond du Lac	HK	March 23, 1966
John A. De Bock	Major	Beloit	NHO	August 3, 1967
William J. Deuster Jr.§	Airman Second Class	Green Bay	NHI	April 27, 1967
Lawrence C. Dobrenz	Airman First Class	Medford	NHI	October 24, 1966

* Sources: Southeast Asia Combat Area Casualties Current File (CACCF), as of November 1997 (electronic record), Records of the Office of the Secretary of Defense, Record Group 330, The National Archives at College Park and the Highground Vietnam Memorial Project, Inc., Neillsville, Wisconsin, www.thehighground.org. Names marked with a § are added from the list maintained by the Highground. In addition, the Highground lists these names (unverified in the National Archives) among the Wisconsin fallen: Carl F. Burdick, Paul R. Grazier, Lonnie W. Hoglund, William O. Johnson, Richard W. Krenz, Jon Thomas, and Francis W. Rasmussen.
‡ For persons who died while missing or captured, the date of casualty is the date died or declared dead (e.g., date of a finding of death), not the date declared missing or captured.

AIR FORCE

NAME	RANK	HOMETOWN	TYPE	DATE OF DEATH
Donald W. Downing	Lieutenant Colonel	Janesville	HDM	April 28, 1978
Walter F. Draeger Jr.	Captain	Deerfield	HK	April 4, 1965
Charles R. Fellenz	Chief Master Sergeant	Marshfield	HDM	June 29, 1978
Neil N. Greinke	First Lieutenant	Franklin	HDM	September 11, 1969
Robert Greskowiak	Captain	Greenfield	NHO	May 15, 1965
Patrick J. Hayes	Captain	Milwaukee	HDM	December 1, 1969
Duane A. Helmick	Captain	Milwaukee	NHO	May 5, 1968
Thomas M. Hergert§	Colonel	Milwaukee	HDM	March 8, 1964
Richard L. Hogle	Technical Sergeant	Manitowoc	NHO	June 13, 1966
Raymond C. Jajtner	Master Sergeant	Menomonee Falls	HDM	May 18, 1966
Leland C. Johnson	Airman First Class	Greenfield	NHO	October 10, 1969
James A. Ketterer	Captain	Milwaukee	HDM	July 19, 1976
Gary E. Knappenberger§	Staff Sergeant	Janesville	NHO	July 25, 1969
John M. Koenig§	Sergeant	Sun Prairie	NHO	February 1, 1970
Dean R. Krueger	First Lieutenant	Reedsville	HK	March 26, 1971
Roy R. Kubley	Captain	Glidden	HK	January 31, 1967
Lloyd A. McGrew	Major	La Crosse	NHO	July 17, 1970
Charles E. McLeish	Captain	Monona	HK	August 21, 1970
Todd M. Melton	Staff Sergeant	Milwaukee	HDM	February 5, 1973
John D. Morris	Staff Sergeant	Waukesha	HK	December 25, 1967
Leon C. Polaski	Sergeant	West Allis	NHI	January 29, 1970
John M. Rydlewicz	First Lieutenant	Milwaukee	HDM	August 12, 1971
Lance P. Sijan	Captain	Milwaukee	HDC	January 22, 1968
Wilbur A. Skaar	Major	Chippewa Falls	HK	May 17, 1968
James L. Smith	Captain	Larsen	HDM	December 28, 1970
James A. Steger	Staff Sergeant	Marshfield	NHI	November 30, 1967
Herbert J. Stober	Sergeant	Rochester	NHO	March 19, 1969
Thomas H. Trebatoski	Airman First Class	Stevens Point	NHI	October 3, 1966
Donald A. Watson	First Lieutenant	Tripoli	HK	July 31, 1965
Hayden E. Weaver	Airman First Class	Wyoming	NDM	May 16, 1965
Robert F. Wilke	Colonel	Milwaukee	HDM	May 5, 1978

ARMY

NAME	RANK	HOMETOWN	TYPE	DATE OF DEATH
Paul D. Abbott	Private First Class	Siren	HK	October 28, 1967
Roger C. Ackerman	Staff Sergeant	Lowell	HK	May 7, 1968
Clarence C. Adams	Sergeant	Milwaukee	HK	February 11, 1969
Dennis J. Adamski	Specialist Fourth Class	Appleton	HDM	June 19, 1967
Timothy C. Agard	Specialist Fourth Class	Janesville	HDW	February 19, 1968

ARMY

NAME	RANK	HOMETOWN	TYPE	DATE OF DEATH
Donald W. Allen Jr.	Specialist Fourth Class	Waterford	HK	February 2, 1968
Robert R. Allmers	Specialist Fourth Class	Oshkosh	NHO	December 10, 1969
Dale E. Anderson	Specialist Fourth Class	New Lisbon	HK	February 21, 1968
Erling A. Anderson	Private First Class	Eau Claire	HK	June 22, 1967
Gerald R. Anderson	Specialist Fourth Class	Kenosha	HK	February 4, 1968
Thomas L. Anderson	Specialist Fourth Class	La Crosse	HK	December 21, 1969
William J. Anderson	Private First Class	Superior	HDW	February 5, 1968
William Anderson Jr.	Specialist Fourth Class	Milwaukee	HDM	August 26, 1970
Timothy G. Arens	Corporal	Appleton	HK	October 1, 1968
Kenneth W. Arnold§	Corporal	Racine	HK	May 9, 1968
Jerry A. Ashburn	First Lieutenant	Port Edwards	HDW	June 17, 1969
James L. Asher	Corporal	Elmwood	HK	June 11, 1969
Roger C. Atkinson	Specialist Fourth Class	Madison	HK	February 26, 1968
Dennis L. Babcock	Private	Mauston	HK	May 28, 1969
Dwight F. Babel	Private First Class	Kenosha	HK	September 5, 1969
Lyman C. Bach	Staff Sergeant	Medford	HK	June 2, 1969
Russell L. Bahrke Jr.	Corporal	Suring	HK	August 13, 1970
Robert V. Bair	Specialist Fourth Class	Rochester	HK†	February 2, 1967
David J. Baitinger	Private	Winneconne	NHO	October 17, 1969
William D. Bakken	Private First Class	West Allis	HK†	February 12, 1969
Orval A. Baldwin	Warrant Officer	Hillsboro	NHO	October 5, 1969
Richard J. Balthazar	Corporal	Eland	HDM	August 22, 1967
Richard M. Banaszynski	Specialist Fourth Class	Pulaski	HK	October 25, 1968
Gerald J. Bannach	Sergeant First Class	Stevens Point	NHI	September 24, 1966
David G. Barnes	Specialist Fourth Class	Marinette	HK	May 5, 1968
Richard D. Bartholomew Jr.	Specialist Fourth Class	Wausau	HK	February 12, 1969
Gregory J. Bartkowski	Private First Class	Milwaukee	HK	October 30, 1968
Leonard W. Bauer	Specialist Fourth Class	Durand	HK	April 18, 1970
Robert L. Baumgart	Specialist Fourth Class	Mishicot	HK	May 6, 1968
Orland O. Bearwald	Private First Class	Oshkosh	HDW†	September 8, 1965
Jeffrey L. Beaty	Specialist Fourth Class	Blair	HK	February 16, 1967
Wayne R. Bebo§	Specialist Fourth Class	Marinette	HK	May 7, 1970
Robert M. Beck	Specialist Fourth Class	Aniwa	NHO	April 4, 1969
John P. Becker	First Lieutenant	Kenosha	HK	May 2, 1970
Thomas L. Becker	Sergeant	Janesville	HK	November 6, 1968
Joseph L. Begotka	Sergeant	Green Bay	HK	January 27, 1968
Gerald D. Behlke	Private First Class	Strum	HDW	May 22, 1967
Richard C. Behnke	Captain	Jefferson	HK	March 31, 1969
William C. Behrens	Sergeant	Two Rivers	HK	January 31, 1968
Mark S. Behrent	Private First Class	Appleton	NHI	June 16, 1970

ARMY

NAME	RANK	HOMETOWN	TYPE	DATE OF DEATH
John W. Beitlich	Specialist Fourth Class	Onalaska	HDW	October 26, 1969
William M. Bellile	Sergeant	New London	HK	June 9, 1969
Leslie Bellrichard§	Private First Class	Janesville	HK	May 20, 1967
Dennis M. Belonger	Private First Class	Manitowoc	HK	July 19, 1969
Robert J. Benedict	Private First Class	Little Saumico	HK	March 8, 1969
James M. Benicek	Warrant Officer	Racine	HK	September 29, 1970
Gerald A. Benson	Private First Class	Darlington	HDW	December 19, 1968
James D. Benway	Private First Class	Madison	HDW	July 9, 1966
Charles S. Beranek	First Lieutenant	Mosinee	HK	June 14, 1968
Dean M. Beranek	Sergeant	Rice Lake	HK	July 23, 1967
Raymond R. Berger	Specialist Fourth Class	Sheboygan	NHO	October 23, 1970
Larry W. Berkholtz	Sergeant	Sullivan	NHO	October 1, 1970
Dennis L. Bertschinger	Specialist Fourth Class	Milwaukee	HK	March 28, 1967
Reiner W. Bierowski	Sergeant	Milwaukee	HK	June 20, 1966
Kris Bilmer	Private First Class	Albany	HDW	June 25, 1969
Edward O. Bilsie§	Staff Sergeant	Madison	NHM	November 30, 1967
Paul L. Binder	Private First Class	Port Washington	NHO	January 16, 1970
Nolan W. Black	Chief Warrant Officer	Beloit	HK	October 30, 1969
Ronald P. Blaese	Private First Class	Combined Locks	HDM	July 23, 1967
John A. Blanco Jr.§	First Lieutenant	Winneconne	NHO	December 17, 1968
Robert G. Blank	Private First Class	Neenah	HK	December 21, 1968
Ralph L. Blauvelt§	Private First Class	Watertown	HDW	January 31, 1969
James N. Blavat	Sergeant	Green Bay	HK	April 14, 1969
Ronald R. Blohm	Warrant Officer	Eau Claire	HK	September 10, 1968
Ronald F. Boeing	Warrant Officer	Richland Center	HK	September 7, 1972
Robert J. Bohmer	Specialist Fourth Class	Milwaukee	HK	May 23, 1967
Michael D. Bohrman	Sergeant	Delafield	HK	June 2, 1970
Dean L. Bonneau	Warrant Officer	Oshkosh	NHO	May 4, 1970
David R. Borzych	Sergeant	Pulaski	HK	April 5, 1970
Richard L. Bowers	Major	Lake Mills	HDC	September 29, 1978
John M. Bozinski	Warrant Officer	Superior	HK	August 15, 1969
Gary L. Bradee§	Sergeant	Wauwatosa	HDW	May 7, 1969
James D. Bradle	Specialist Fifth Class	Laona	NHO	August 11, 1970
Thomas G. Brandes	Private First Class	Silver Lake	HK	November 17, 1965
Bernard G. Brantmeier	Specialist Fourth Class	Kewaunee	HK	June 25, 1970
Wayne A. Bratz	Sergeant	Valders	HK	March 11, 1969
Michael W. Braun	Staff Sergeant	Milwaukee	HK	May 26, 1968
Edward J. Brefczynski	Master Sergeant	Two Rivers	HK	February 10, 1968
Kenneth W. Brenwall	Specialist Fourth Class	Milwaukee	HDW	March 22, 1967
Anthony J. Breuer	Private First Class	La Crosse	HDW	March 2, 1968

ARMY

NAME	RANK	HOMETOWN	TYPE	DATE OF DEATH
Gerald R. Brines	Private First Class	Shullsburg	HDW	July 17, 1967
Gary M. Brixen	Staff Sergeant	Osseo	HK	November 21, 1967
Thomas E. Broome	Private First Class	Sun Prarie	HK	June 28, 1967
Edwin F. Brown	Sergeant	Beloit	HDM	January 10, 1968
Michael J. Brunner	Specialist Fourth Class	Marshfield	HK	January 9, 1968
Gary H. Brux	Captain	Greenwood	HK	October 6, 1966
Jerrald J. Bulin	Specialist Fourth Class	Beloit	HK	January 30, 1969
David J. Bulkley	Specialist Fourth Class	Chilton	HK	September 8, 1968
Thomas E. Bumgarner§	Staff Sergeant	Neenah	HDW	May 14, 1969
Mark Burchard§	Private First Class	Janesville	HK	November 17, 1969
Richard Burbach	First Lieutenant	West Allis	HK	February 7, 1968
Eugene L. Burbey	Private First Class	Kenosha	NHI	September 22, 1969
Robert Burgert	Sergeant	Milwaukee	NHO	February 13, 1963
Wynne L. Burlingame	Specialist Fourth Class	Milwaukee	HK†	June 7, 1968
Daniel L. Burr	Sergeant	Milwaukee	HK	March 17, 1968
John A. Buschke	Sergeant	West Allis	HK	February 23, 1969
Roger L. Buss	Specialist Fourth Class	Cottage Grove	HDM	January 24, 1965
Lawrence J. Butler	Specialist Fourth Class	Hayward	HDW	April 4, 1969
Dennis A. Calton	First Lieutenant	Baraboo	HK	March 11, 1971
Gerald C. Capelle	Captain	Fond du Lac	HK	April 1, 1965
Peter J. Carlson	Second Lieutenant	La Crosse	HK	May 11, 1967
Richard A. Carlson§	Private First Class	Plum City	HK	January 19, 1968
George J. Carr	Specialist Fourth Class	New Berlin	NHO	May 29, 1967
Patrick J. Carroll	Private First Class	Maiden Rock	HK	November 13, 1968
Richard K. Carter	Sergeant	Milwaukee	HK	November 19, 1967
Frederick R. Casper	First Lieutenant	Fond du Lac	HK	May 9, 1968
Robert P. Caspersen II	Specialist Fourth Class	Madison	HK	November 15, 1967
Dennis D. Chamberlin	Specialist Fourth Class	Elkhorn	HK	June 26, 1970
George A. Chapman	Specialist Fourth Class	Milwaukee	HK	August 26, 1971
Walter A. Chatos Jr.	Specialist Fifth Class	Oconomowoc	NDM	April 16, 1967
Mark A. Chmiel	Private First Class	Milwaukee	HK	January 23, 1967
Donald A. Christ	Private First Class	Milwaukee	HK	October 30, 1966
Paul E. Christjohn	Private First Class	Oneida	NHI	September 9, 1968
Raymond J. Churchill	Sergeant	Lyndon Station	HDW	August 4, 1966
Phillip H. Clark	Private First Class	Wisconsin Rapids	HK	March 4, 1966
Kenneth J. Cotter	Private First Class	Milwaukee	HK	April 6, 1970
Thomas L. Cottrell	Specialist Fourth Class	Milwaukee	HK	March 29, 1969
Dean D. Crane	Specialist Fourth Class	Neshkoro	HDM	June 21, 1967
Robert L. Crawley	Specialist Fourth Class	Baraboo	HDM	January 8, 1968
Carl L. Crowley	Private	Milwaukee	NHO	November 4, 1969

ARMY

NAME	RANK	HOMETOWN	TYPE	DATE OF DEATH
Thomas M. Curtis	Private	West Allis	HK	November 2, 1969
Leroy W. Cwikla	Private First Class	Lublin	HK	March 26, 1967
John R. D'Agostino Jr.	Sergeant	Green Bay	NHO	April 30, 1968
Timothy A. Dahl	Specialist Fourth Class	Menasha	NHO	September 30, 1969
George C. Dahlman	Specialist Fifth Class	Milwaukee	HK	April 18, 1969
Ralph A. Dahm	Specialist Fourth Class	Iron Ridge	HK	February 8, 1968
George F. Dailey	Captain	Fort Atkinson	HK	May 12, 1966
Dean L. Dalberg	Private First Class	Viola	HK	March 5, 1968
Thomas W. Damm	Chief Warrant Officer	Fond du Lac	HK	July 7, 1970
Lee R. Danielson	Sergeant	Cadott	HK	January 12, 1968
David B. Dann	First Lieutenant	Milwaukee	HK	November 8, 1966
Charles L. Davidson	Platoon Sergeant	La Crosse	HK	March 9, 1966
Thomas F. Dazey Jr.	Specialist Fourth Class	Neenah	HK	April 9, 1968
Elliott L. De Cora	Private First Class	Wyeville	HK	August 16, 1968
Jerome A. De Galley	Corporal	Milwaukee	HDW	March 31, 1969
Jack P. De Lange	Specialist Fifth Class	Elkhorn	HK	March 5, 1969
Jerald S. De Long	Corporal	De Soto	HDM	October 12, 1970
Charles R. De Windt	Private First Class	Lena	NHI	November 27, 1969
Glenn F. Dean	Sergeant	West Bend	HDW	August 27, 1968
Franklin D. Defenbaugh	Chief Warrant Officer	Superior	NHO	November 29, 1970
Adrian L. Del Camp	Major	Milwaukee	HK	March 4, 1968
Arthur G. Denton	Sergeant First Class	West Allis	NHO	August 18, 1971
James R. Devney	Private First Class	Eau Claire	HK	July 19, 1969
Llewellyn P. Dickenson	Specialist Fourth Class	Neopit	HK	May 3, 1969
James N. Diedrich	Private First Class	Hilbert	HK	February 18, 1970
Thomas E. Dobrinska	Second Lieutenant	Antigo	HDW	February 10, 1968
Jerome N. Doll	Corporal	Port Washington	HK	May 31, 1969
Eugene D. Dollar	Specialist Fourth Class	Milwaukee	NDM	January 25, 1966
David J. Donahoe	Corporal	Darlington	HK	October 28, 1967
Gary R. Dopp	Private First Class	Almond	HDM	September 25, 1966
Robert G. Drapp	Sergeant	Milwaukee	HDM	November 16, 1970
Terrance L. Drea	Specialist Fourth Class	Cazenovia	NHO	January 21, 1970
David L. Drought	Sergeant	Janesville	HK	December 31, 1967
Franklin R. Du Long	Staff Sergeant	Waukesha County	HK	April 28, 1968
Henry R. Duellman	Specialist Fourth Class	Tomahawk	NHI	February 10, 1969
Roy W. Dunbar Jr.	First Lieutenant	Elkhorn	HK	May 16, 1969
Delferd B. Dunifer	Specialist Fourth Class	West Allis	HK	February 2, 1968
Leonard E. Dutcher	Sergeant	Melrose	HK[†]	June 2, 1968
Dale D. Dwyer	Major	Milwaukee	NHO	June 18, 1967
Phillip J. Eberhardt	Corporal	Pewaukee	HDM	January 8, 1968

ARMY

NAME	RANK	HOMETOWN	TYPE	DATE OF DEATH
Roy L. Edelstein	Private First Class	Superior	HK	August 14, 1968
Edward V. Eiden Jr.	Sergeant	Winneconne	HK	April 11, 1969
Dennis Eitel	Sergeant	Phillips	HK	July 20, 1969
Allen N. Engel	Private First Class	Mount Calvary	HDM	June 19, 1967
Otto R. Ensslin	Corporal	Waukesha	NHO	April 22, 1967
Dale A. Erdman	Sergeant	Augusta	HK	April 7, 1970
Marvin l. Erickson	Private First Class	Ashland	HK	January 22, 1969
Robert D. Erickson	Specialist Fourth Class	Superior	HK	January 13, 1967
Loren L. Ertel	Specialist Fourth Class	Plymouth	HK	October 10, 1967
Charles L. Eschbach[§]	Platoon Sergeant	West Allis	NDM	January 25, 1966
Robert C. Essmann	Corporal	Fond du Lac	HK	June 6, 1969
William A. Evans	Sergeant	Milwaukee	HDM	March 2, 1969
Joseph N. Eveland	Specialist Fourth Class	Black Earth	HK	December 16, 1969
Thomas W. Faber	Private First Class	Wilson	HDW	June 25, 1969
Dale A. Fahrni	Private First Class	Spring Green	HDW	May 7, 1969
Fred A. Fedder	Warrant Officer	Waukesha	NHI[†]	August 9, 1969
Lloyd A. Feder	Corporal	Green Lake	HK	January 5, 1969
Peter M. Feierabend	Private First Class	Milwaukee	HK	February 16, 1964
Richard C. Ferdig	Specialist Fourth Class	Frederic	HK	August 4, 1967
Ted S. Ferguson	Corporal	Milwaukee	HK	July 22, 1968
Gary J. Fiedler	Private First Class	Racine	NHO	April 5, 1971
James R. Fischer	Sergeant	Oshkosh	HK	July 23, 1967
David B. Fitzgerald	Master Sergeant	Milwaukee	HK	April 5, 1971
John D. Fitzpatrick	Private First Class	Franklin	HK	November 19, 1966
Roger J. Flynn	Private First Class	Milwaukee	HK	December 18, 1969
Thomas H. Foley	Warrant Officer	Milwaukee	NHO	December 2, 1971
Gary L. Folz	Corporal	Wisconsin Rapids	HK	December 11, 1969
Joseph P. Foran	Specialist Fourth Class	Milwaukee	HK	February 16, 1967
Patrick J. Foran[§]	First Lieutenant	Milwaukee	HK	February 6, 1967
Kendall T. Fortney	Specialist Fourth Class	Stoughton	HK	March 6, 1968
William J. Franks[§]	Private First Class	Kenosha	HK	February 25, 1967
Paul R. Frazier	Sergeant	Milwaukee	HK	September 3, 1968
Ralph Fredenberg	Specialist Fourth Class	Shawano	HDM	April 24, 1968
Eugene M. Fricke	Specialist Fourth Class	Sheboygan	HDW[†]	May 6, 1971
Johnnie C. Fuller[§]	Staff Sergeant	Milwaukee	HK	May 18, 1967
James M. Gahagan	Sergeant	Cleveland	HK	January 17, 1969
Steven Gallegos[§]	Specialist Fourth Class	Kenosha	HDW	January 1, 1969
Jerry A. Garrick[§]	Staff Sergeant	Burlington	HK	March 30, 1969
Kenneth J. Garski	Sergeant	Stevens Point	HK	March 28, 1970
Gerald A. Gauthier	Sergeant	Manitowoc	HDW	January 20, 1970

ARMY

NAME	RANK	HOMETOWN	TYPE	DATE OF DEATH
Harry E. Geary	Corporal	Beloit	HK	June 3, 1967
Gary B. Gehrke	Specialist Sixth Class	Woodruff	HDW†	January 21, 1969
Randall H. Geis	Specialist Fifth Class	Milwaukee	NHO	July 27, 1971
Francis G. Gercz Jr.	Major	Milwaukee	HK	January 25, 1968
Paul E. Gerlach	Private First Class	Madison	HK	January 30, 1968
James A. Gerou	Private First Class	Milwaukee	HK	April 17, 1968
Allen R. Gibney	Specialist Fourth Class	Kenosha	HK	May 9, 1968
Michael E. Giese	Corporal	Milwaukee	HK	April 4, 1971
Wallace L. Giesen	Private First Class	La Crosse	HK	February 7, 1968
Terry A. Gilbertson	Staff Sergeant	Boscobel	HK	February 28, 1968
Jerry C. Gillett	Specialist Fourth Class	Cornell	HDW†	June 4, 1970
John R. Gmack	Corporal	Green Bay	NHO	May 28, 1970
Willard A. Godfrey	Specialist Fifth Class	Milton Junction	NDM	February 7, 1967
Ronald D. Golden	Specialist Fourth Class	Superior	HK	August 20, 1968
Roger D. Goldsmith	Specialist Fourth Class	Black River Falls	HK	July 23, 1967
Frank Gomez	Sergeant First Class	Milwaukee	HK	August 23, 1968
Wilfredo L. Gonzalez	Specialist Fifth Class	Milwaukee	HK	October 5, 1968
Kenneth G. Goodness	Private First Class	Nekoosa	HK	August 14, 1969
Richard J. Gorges	Private First Class	New London	HDW	February 13, 1970
Gregg M. Goslin	Specialist Fourth Class	Spooner	HK	November 12, 1967
Kenneth J. Grassl	Private First Class	Appleton	HK	January 29, 1968
Robert W. Grebby	Chief Warrant Officer	Walworth	HK	September 21, 1970
Dennis J. Green	Specialist Fourth Class	West De Pere	HK	August 8, 1969
Bruce J. Greenwood	Corporal	Maribel	HK	September 4, 1968
Roger W. Greetan	Private First Class	Oconto Falls	HK	July 18, 1967
Lon P. Gregorash	Specialist Fourth Class	Port Washington	HK	June 18, 1971
Thomas A. Greisen	Specialist Fourth Class	Madison	HK	June 4, 1969
Leon G. Greshamer	Second Lieutenant	New London	HK	February 8, 1968
Carl W. Grimes	Private First Class	Fond du Lac	HK	May 5, 1964
Dennis A. Groff	Private First Class	Kenosha	HK	February 28, 1969
John A. Gross	First Lieutenant	Menomonee Falls	HK	July 27, 1971
Allen F. Grotzke	Specialist Fourth Class	Portage	HK	November 15, 1969
Michael A. Gruber	Private First Class	Milwaukee	HK	December 5, 1965
Jerome E. Grunewald	Private First Class	Sheboygan	HK	June 4, 1968
Gustave F. Gudleske	Captain	Rhinelander	NHI	August 1, 1967
Bruce J. Guex	Corporal	Shawano	HK†	March 6, 1969
Leonard G. Guilette	Specialist Fifth Class	Casco	NHO	October 11, 1970
James J. Gunderson	Sergeant	Superior	HK	November 15, 1969
Melvin W. Gunderson	Private First Class	Cable	HDW	May 9, 1967
Dennis R. Gustafson	Corporal	Wentworth	HK	May 4, 1969

ARMY

NAME	RANK	HOMETOWN	TYPE	DATE OF DEATH
Ronald L. Gutke	Corporal	Almond	NHO	September 19, 1969
Maurice J. Haas	Sergeant	Cassville	HDW	August 30, 1968
Russell C. Haas	Specialist Fourth Class	La Crosse	HK	March 2, 1968
James R. Hagen	Lieutenant Colonel	Stanley	HK	December 24, 1964
Ronald F. Hagen	Master Sergeant	Nekoosa	HK	September 17, 1969
Gerald C. Hague	Private First Class	Maiden Rock	HDW	May 20, 1967
Peter O. Hajman	Sergeant	Milwaukee	HK	November 12, 1969
Carl R. Hallberg	Private First Class	Delavan	HK	May 18, 1967
Alvin L. Halverson	Staff Sergeant	Janesville	NHI	February 10, 1970
Gary J. Halverson	Specialist Fourth Class	New Richmond	HK	September 11, 1968
Harry B. Hambleton III	First Lieutenant	Elm Grove	HDW	September 15, 1968
Lyle C. Hansbrough	Specialist Fourth Class	Madison	HK	March 17, 1969
Stanley R. Hansen	Specialist Fifth Class	West Bend	HK	May 21, 1970
William H. Hanson	First Lieutenant	Park Falls	HK	September 12, 1968
William H. Harff Jr.	Specialist Fourth Class	Kenosha	HK	April 28, 1968
Bruce B. Hartman	Specialist Fourth Class	Prescott	HDW	January 9, 1969
Ronald J. Hasko	Private First Class	Wausau	HK	March 27, 1968
Glenn S. Haukeness Jr.	Chief Warrant Officer	Strum	HK	June 19, 1969
Ronald J. Haupt	Specialist Fourth Class	Marshfield	NHO	July 7, 1969
Jerry L. Hauschultz	Sergeant	Marion	HK	December 5, 1969
Gerald R. Hauswirth	First Lieutenant	Greendale	HK	March 14, 1970
Andrew L. Heider	Private First Class	Neenah	HK	May 13, 1968
William S. Heider	Specialist Fourth Class	Waukesha	HK	August 16, 1969
Ronald M. Heinecke	Specialist Fourth Class	Theresa	HK	August 18, 1968
Gregory A. Heinrich	Private First Class	West Allis	HK	May 4, 1969
Donald E. Heinz	Private First Class	Manitowoc	NHO	July 5, 1967
David P. Hellenbrand	Specialist Fourth Class	Janesville	HK	December 1, 1968
Kenneth L. Henke	Specialist Fourth Class	Berlin	HK	November 8, 1969
Vernon L. Henke	Private First Class	La Valle	HK	May 19, 1967
Arthur R. Henning	Corporal	Lake Tomahawk	HK	May 5, 1968
Richard J. Hentz	Specialist Fifth Class	Oshkosh	HDM	March 4, 1971
Robert H. Hering	Captain	Burlington	HK	August 19, 1968
Michael E. Hermsen	Specialist Fourth Class	De Pere	HK	March 22, 1969
Joseph J. Hernandez Jr.	Sergeant	Milwaukee	HDW	November 19, 1968
Frank V. Herrera	Sergeant	Green Bay	HK†	April 4, 1968
Everett Herritz§	Master Sergeant	North Freedom	HDW	July 15, 1967
James W. Hessing	Corporal	Bayfield	HK	May 23, 1970
Jerry W. Heuer	Private First Class	Sparta	HK	April 15, 1968
Raleigh L. Hewitt II	Warrant Officer	Kenosha	HDW	November 14, 1967
Donald A. Hierlmeier	Private First Class	Milwaukee	HK	February 16, 1968

ARMY

NAME	RANK	HOMETOWN	TYPE	DATE OF DEATH
James G. Hildebrandt	Staff Sergeant	Middleton	HK	July 18, 1968
William R. Hill	Captain	Kenosha	HK	April 16, 1967
Harry A. Hipke	Private First Class	Gleason	HK	September 9, 1965
Michael A. Hodge	Private First Class	Sparta	HK	February 6, 1968
Leroy D. Hoffman	Private First Class	Athens	HK	November 22, 1968
Alfred J. Holtz Jr.	Staff Sergeant	Milwaukee	HK	July 2, 1968
William J. Hondel	Second Lieutenant	West Allis	HK	March 13, 1968
Alec H. Horn	Private First Class	New Berlin	HK	January 16, 1969
Ruben L. Horton	Private First Class	Milwaukee	HK	May 27, 1968
Danny W. Houle	Private First Class	Hiles	HK	April 12, 1969
Gene J. H	Specialist Fifth Class	Neenah	HK	April 2, 1968
Charles F. Hughes	Captain	Hayward	HK	July 4, 1969
James K. Hughes§	Specialist Fifth Class	Milwaukee	HK	March 16, 1966
John R. Hulbert	Private First Class	Menomonie	HDM†	January 8, 1968
Wilhelm S. Hurkmans Jr.	Private First Class	Rhinelander	HK	July 22, 1968
John C. Imrie	Specialist Fourth Class	Johnson Creek	HK	August 18, 1967
Gary A. Isaacson	Private First Class	Amery	HK	June 22, 1966
Richard T. Jackson	Sergeant	Green Bay	HDM	January 6, 1968
Todd R. Jackson	Corporal	Manitowoc	HK	January 30, 1968
Harvey G. Jacobson	Corporal	Menasha	NHO	December 18, 1970
Mark N. Jacobson	First Lieutenant	La Crosse	HK†	January 27, 1969
Richard E. Jaeck	First Lieutenant	Cudahy	HK	March 14, 1964
William R. Janka	Specialist Fourth Class	New Berlin	HDM	March 5, 1967
Charles J. Janke	Specialist Fourth Class	Grantsburg	HK	November 12, 1965
Keith B. Janke	Staff Sergeant	Ashland	HK	May 28, 1969
Robert A. Jardine Jr.	Specialist Fourth Class	Port Wing	NHO	March 19, 1970
Daniel M. Java	Platoon Sergeant	Frederic	HDW	December 4, 1966
John A. Jelich	Chief Warrant Officer	Stevens Point	HK	April 1, 1972
Larry S. Jensen	Specialist Fourth Class	Milwaukee	HK	April 15, 1967
Charles A. Johnson	Corporal	Racine	HDW	September 11, 1967
Charles L. Johnson	First Lieutenant	Marshfield	HDW	June 23, 1967
Randolph L. Johnson	Sergeant First Class	Milwaukee	HDM	September 13, 1979
Ronald P. Johnson	Specialist Fourth Class	Arcadia	NHO	November 20, 1965
Ross A. Johnson Jr.	Private	Milwaukee	NHI	January 2, 1969
Timothy H. Johnson	Private First Class	Milwaukee	HK	November 6, 1965
Richard J. Johnston§	Specialist Fourth Class	Peshtigo	HK	June 22, 1967
Jeffrey R. Jordan	Private First Class	Pewaukee	HK	March 19, 1968
Richard H. Junk	Sergeant	Cassville	HK	May 20, 1968
Philip A. Kalhagen	Staff Sergeant	Madison	HK	June 19, 1970
Dale R. Karpenske	Sergeant First Class	Amery	NHO	March 9, 1968

ARMY

NAME	RANK	HOMETOWN	TYPE	DATE OF DEATH
Daniel M. Kasten	Specialist Fourth Class	Ripon	HK	May 7, 1967
Barry C. Kellenbenz	Second Lieutenant	Manitowoc	HK	January 19, 1969
Kenneth L. Keller	Specialist Fourth Class	Albany	NHO	May 25, 1970
Michael J. Kelley	Specialist Fifth Class	Menomonee Falls	HDW	March 25, 1968
Eric S. Kelly	Specialist Fourth Class	La Crosse	HK	August 12, 1971
Timothy J. Kennedy	Specialist Fourth Class	Burlington	HK	December 26, 1967
Harry Kerkstra§	Specialist Fourth Class	Williams Bay	HK	May 13, 1969
James E. Kesselhon	Corporal	Sun Prairie	HK	March 21, 1968
John M. Kessinger	Major	Janesville	HK	July 2, 1967
Ronald L. Kielpikowski	First Lieutenant	Green Bay	NHI	February 28, 1969
Patrick J. Kihl	Staff Sergeant	Milwaukee	HK	January 8, 1971
David R. Kink	Warrant Officer	Middleton	HDW	August 3, 1969
Andrew G. Kirchmayer	Captain	Fort Atkinson	HK	November 18, 1969
Norman C. Kissinger	Private First Class	Milwaukee	HK	February 9, 1968
Jeffrey J. Klaves	Specialist Fourth Class	Wauwatosa	HK	April 29, 1970
Thomas J. Klemp	Specialist Fourth Class	Reedsburg	NHO	November 6, 1966
Kenneth T. Kleppin	Specialist Fifth Class	Milwaukee	HK	January 8, 1970
Mark E. Klever	Corporal	Milwaukee	HK	June 6, 1970
Dennis L. Klimpke	Specialist Fourth Class	Colby	HK	April 15, 1968
John T. Kloc	Private	Franklin	NHO	May 10, 1967
David W. Kmetz	Specialist Fourth Class	Washburn	HK	March 11, 1968
John R. Knorr	Specialist Fourth Class	Manitowoc	HK	May 5, 1968
David W. Knouse	Private First Class	Gratiot	HK	March 3, 1968
Bruce N. Knox	Corporal	Madison	HK	February 4, 1968
James R. Knox	Specialist Fourth Class	Newton	HK	January 21, 1969
Felix D. Knutson§	Sergeant First Class	Nelsonville	HK	September 4, 1969
Darryl J. Koch	Private First Class	Hartland	HDW	April 15, 1967
Brian R. Koehn	Sergeant	Campbellsport	HK	January 4, 1971
Terrence E. Kohlbeck	Sergeant	Stratford	HK	May 6, 1968
Victor J. Kohlbeck	Sergeant First Class	Manitowoc	HDW	February 20, 1966
Nick Kokalis	Specialist Fourth Class	Milwaukee	HK	October 28, 1967
Roger J. Kopke	Staff Sergeant	Green Bay	HDW	October 30, 1969
David S. Kossowski	Specialist Fifth Class	Stevens Point	NHI†	July 30, 1968
Roger J. Kostka	Specialist Fourth Class	Algoma	NHO	June 1, 1970
Marvin D. Kostroski	Private First Class	Schofield	HK	August 26, 1966
William M. Kotnik	Sergeant	Sheboygan	NHO	October 17, 1970
John T. Krebs Jr.	Second Lieutenant	Browntown	HK	June 8, 1970
John W. Kreckel	Staff Sergeant	Milwaukee	HK	July 22, 1970
Joseph Kresic Jr.	Private First Class	Neshkoro	HK	November 30, 1968
Robert A. Kreuziger	Private First Class	Juneau	HK	April 6, 1966

ARMY

NAME	RANK	HOMETOWN	TYPE	DATE OF DEATH
Dennis J. Kromrey	Private First Class	Osceola	HK	February 26, 1968
Charles W. Krueger	Private First Class	Menasha	HK	May 31, 1967
Duncan F. Krueger	Private First Class	West Allis	HK	November 17, 1965
Wayne D. Krueger	Private First Class	Wausau	HK	March 26, 1968
Raymond H. Krug Jr.	Warrant Officer	Milwaukee	NHO	May 14, 1970
Leo F. Krumbine	Private First Class	Milwaukee	HK	February 22, 1966
Joseph B. Kube	Captain	Warrens	HDW	April 3, 1968
William R. Kuczewski	Private First Class	Milwaukee	HK	November 15, 1968
Paul D. Kuehl	Private First Class	Hartford	NHO	March 28, 1968
Gerald L. Kuhnly	Specialist Fifth Class	Siren	HDW	December 28, 1965
James P. Kurth	Specialist Fourth Class	Darlington	HK	March 20, 1970
Sidney A. Kurz	Sergeant	Milwaukee	HDW	October 18, 1970
Rex A. La Duke	Private First Class	Kimberly	HDM	June 7, 1967
Larry G. Lacaeyse	Private First Class	Reeseville	HK	March 5, 1969
Thomas A. Lahner	Specialist Fourth Class	Eau Claire	NHO	May 10, 1972
Larry R. Lalan	Specialist Fourth Class	Weyerhauser	HK	November 10, 1968
William O. Lang	Corporal	New Holstein	HK	September 8, 1968
Karl F. Lange	Lieutenant Colonel	West Allis	NHO	December 9, 1969
Michael W. Langer	Corporal	Milwaukee	HK	March 5, 1968
Thomas C. Larsen	Specialist Fourth Class	Oneida	NHO	September 8, 1970
James E. Larson	Sergeant	Mauston	HK	October 17, 1967
Randolph L. Larson	Specialist Fourth Class	Milwaukee	HDW	August 11, 1969
Donald R. Last	Specialist Fourth Class	Oshkosh	HK	July 10, 1967
Rodney J. Lawson	Flight Sergeant	Augusta	HK	March 12, 1968
James A. Leahy	Specialist Fourth Class	Madison	HK	August 8, 1968
Peter G. Lechnir	Specialist Fourth Class	Milwaukee	HDW	February 15, 1973
Terrance E. Ledden	Warrant Officer	Fond du Lac	HK	September 5, 1969
Michael T. Ledebur	Private First Class	Milwaukee	HK	August 2, 1966
Russell O. Ledegar	Private First Class	La Crosse	NDM	March 16, 1967
Donald H. Lederhaus	Private First Class	Milwaukee	HK†	December 27, 1966
James L. Ledin	Private First Class	Mellen	HK	July 15, 1966
Wayne R. Lefeber	Specialist Fifth Class	Milwaukee	HK	April 9, 1968
John E. Leis	Specialist Fourth Class	La Crosse	HK	June 20, 1971
Bruce C. Leising	Private First Class	Wauwatosa	HK†	November 6, 1967
James W. Lenz	Private First Class	Milwaukee	NHO	June 23, 1970
Richard J. Leonard	Specialist Fifth Class	Milwaukee	NHI	August 6, 1970
Donald C. Lepak	Sergeant	Amherst	HK	November 30, 1968
James T. Liebnitz	Specialist Fourth Class	Milwaukee	HK	February 27, 1969
James J. Lind	Sergeant	Oshkosh	HDW	January 5, 1968
Lee Roy E. Linton	Staff Sergeant	Reeseville	HK	November 29, 1970

ARMY

NAME	RANK	HOMETOWN	TYPE	DATE OF DEATH
Gary Loduha	Specialist Fourth Class	Milwaukee	HK	April 23, 1968
Kent W. Longmire	Sergeant	Walworth	HK	April 20, 1970
Manuel T. Lopez	Sergeant First Class	Oshkosh	HK	June 27, 1968
Terry W. Lorenz	Private First Class	La Crosse	HK	June 16, 1966
Jerome D. Lubeno	Sergeant	Trevor	HK	June 14, 1969
Leo J. Ludvigsen Jr.	Staff Sergeant	Sheldon	HK	May 2, 1970
John A. Luke	Specialist Fourth Class	Rapid Woods	HK	March 6, 1971
Clayton J. Luther	Private First Class	Baraboo	HDW	July 29, 1966
Michael J. Lutzke	Private First Class	Milwaukee	HDW	February 26, 1967
James E. Lynn	Sergeant First Class	Kenosha	HK	December 15, 1967
Patrick N. Lyons	Private First Class	Manitowoc	HK	February 28, 1967
David T. Maddux	Captain	Racine	HK	August 9, 1970
Vincent L. Mager	Specialist Fourth Class	Hales Corners	HK	November 27, 1968
Ronald J. Mahoney	Private First Class	Chili	HK	December 8, 1966
Robert J. Mann	Specialist Fourth Class	Brookfield	HK	January 8, 1967
Dennis R. Manske	Corporal	Pine River	HK	June 12, 1967
Paul E. Manske	Private First Class	Oshkosh	HK	May 13, 1967
James W. Manthei	Warrant Officer	Kewaskum	HK	March 21, 1971
Terry L. Manz	First Lieutenant	Milwaukee	NDM	January 28, 1967
Anthony G. Markevitch Jr.	Sergeant	Onalaska	HK	April 16, 1969
Terry L. Martin	Corporal	Milwaukee	HK	January 20, 1969
William P. Martin	Sergeant	Beloit	HK	April 2, 1967
William J. Martinez	Specialist Fourth Class	Milwaukee	HK	July 19, 1970
Dennis R. Mason	Specialist Fourth Class	Argyle	HK	May 28, 1968
Joel A. Matusek	Second Lieutenant	Kenosha	HK	November 27, 1967
Thomas E. Matush	Private First Class	Madison	HDM	January 12, 1967
Bernard R. Mazursky	Specialist Fourth Class	Madison	HK	May 4, 1968
James A. McCalvy	Private First Class	Milwaukee	HK	November 20, 1966
William G. McCann	First Lieutenant	Grantsburg	HK	October 21, 1966
Robert A. McCartney	Sergeant	Janesville	HK	April 15, 1967
Scott S. McCloskey[§]	Private First Class	Clintonville	HK	May 4, 1967
James P. McConnell	Specialist Fourth Class	Beloit	HK	December 26, 1968
Dennis L. McCormick	Private First Class	Waukesha	HK	August 19, 1968
Darrell E. McGee	Specialist Fifth Class	Berlin	HK	July 4, 1969
Daniel J. McGilvary Jr.	Specialist Fourth Class	Milwaukee	HK	February 7, 1967
Timothy A. McGurty	Corporal	Milwaukee	HK	May 23, 1968
Richard C. McKee Jr.	Private First Class	Green Bay	HDM	March 5, 1967
Robert P. McMaster	Sergeant	Green Bay	HDM	August 26, 1970
Randall A. Mee	Specialist Fourth Class	Tomah	HK	May 19, 1969
Richard A. Mehne	Private First Class	Oshkosh	HK	November 8, 1967

ARMY

NAME	RANK	HOMETOWN	TYPE	DATE OF DEATH
Thomas L. Meidam	Specialist Fourth Class	West Allis	NHI	August 4, 1967
William F. Meinecke	Private First Class	Milwaukee	HK	November 7, 1968
Bernard P. Meinen Jr.	Specialist Fourth Class	Chippewa Falls	HDW	December 20, 1967
Kenneth R. Mengel	Private First Class	St. Cloud	HK	June 12, 1968
David B. Merrill	Private First Class	Beaver Dam	HK	January 9, 1967
Douglas C. Merrill§	Private First Class	Rice Lake	HK	August 18, 1969
Nathaniel Merriweather	Sergeant	Milwaukee	HDW	April 5, 1966
Michael S. Mesich	First Lieutenant	Milwaukee	HK	May 21, 1970
Leo R. Meyer	Specialist Fourth Class	Fond du Lac	HK	October 5, 1968
Victor B. Meyers	Sergeant	Superior	HK	August 9, 1968
Terry F. Mezera	Warrant Officer	Eau Claire	HK	January 16, 1971
Lloyd D. Michael§	Lieutenant Colonel	Fond Du Lac	HDW	December 8, 1967
Steven Michalski	Corporal	Marinette	HK	April 5, 1969
Ronald A. Michaud	Private First Class	Niagara	HK	June 20, 1967
John A. Mietus	Private First Class	Eagle River	HK	May 22, 1967
Raymond E. Miladin	Private First Class	Kenosha	HK	November 9, 1967
John E. Milanowski	Sergeant	Milwaukee	HK	February 19, 1968
Andrew J. Miller	Sergeant	Sheboygan	HK	November 24, 1967
Keith N. Miller	Specialist Fourth Class	Racine	HK	April 8, 1969
Larry D. Milling	Specialist Fourth Class	Boyd	HK	April 6, 1969
James S. Mitchell	Chief Warrant Officer	Kenosha	NDM	July 23, 1968
Thomas C. Mitchell	Private First Class	Milwaukee	HK	November 15, 1966
William D. Mize§	Sergeant	Kimberly	HK	October 28, 1967
Phillip D. Monson	Sergeant	Gratiot	HDW	March 15, 1971
Andrew L. Moody Jr.	Sergeant	Germantown	HK	January 16, 1967
Gene C. Morack	Private First Class	New London	HK	May 13, 1968
Michael P. Moran	Private First Class	Milwaukee	HK	January 9, 1966
Larry H. Morgan	Specialist Fifth Class	Grand Marsh	NHI	June 6, 1968
Jerome D. Morneau	Corporal	Neillsville	HK	June 9, 1969
Carl P. Morrison§	Specialist Four	Milwaukee	HK	April 19, 1969
Edward A. Morrison	Private First Class	Kenosha	HDW	December 22, 1968
Larry C. Mosher	Sergeant	Gleason	HK	November 12, 1969
Wayne C. Mousel	Specialist Fourth Class	Eau Claire	HK	June 17, 1970
Robert J. Muellenbach	Staff Sergeant	Malone	HK	August 5, 1970
Joseph B. Mueller	Sergeant	West Bend	HK	March 21, 1970
Randy R. Mueller	Corporal	Milwaukee	HK	March 3, 1969
Robert G. Mueller	Private First Class	Hartford	HK	April 25, 1966
Tom R. Mueller	Sergeant	Seymour	HK	February 1, 1969
Russell W. Mulder	Sergeant	Adell	HK	October 24, 1970
Francis T. Mulvey	Corporal	Fennimore	HK	August 25, 1968

ARMY

NAME	RANK	HOMETOWN	TYPE	DATE OF DEATH
Thomas J. Murphy	Specialist Fourth Class	River Falls	HK	April 1, 1970
Timothy J. Murphy	Staff Sergeant	Green Bay	HK	October 17, 1968
George T. Murray	Platoon Sergeant	Stevens Point	NDM	June 17, 1967
Chester A. Myers Jr.	First Lieutenant	Eagle River	HK	March 10, 1967
Orlan M. Nelson	Sergeant First Class	Black River Falls	HK	February 23, 1969
John L. Nesovanovic	Warrant Officer	Milwaukee	NHO	October 2, 1970
Bruce P. Nettesheim	Sergeant	Sussex	HK	April 25, 1968
Earl J. Netzow	Specialist Fourth Class	Lake Mills	HDW	May 13, 1968
James R. Neubauer	Staff Sergeant	Columbia	HDW	February 4, 1966
Mark W. Neumann	Specialist Fourth Class	Madison	HK	August 25, 1967
Gregory E. Newman	Sergeant	Brown Deer	HK	March 23, 1969
Michael C. Newman[§]	Specialist Fourth Class	Madison	NDM	February 6, 1967
Jerry A. Nichols	Specialist Fifth Class	Portage	HK	June 26, 1969
Ronald R. Niles	First Lieutenant	Mauston	HK	July 31, 1969
Donald W. Noel	Specialist Fourth Class	La Crosse	HDW	April 26, 1969
Timothy J. Norman	Private First Class	Beloit	HK	February 19, 1970
John A. North	Private First Class	Germantown	HK	June 10, 1969
Wayne L. Noth	Specialist Fourth Class	Tomah	HK	June 17, 1969
George D. Novakovic	Specialist Fourth Class	Kenosha	HK	March 5, 1968
Duane A. Novobielski	Private First Class	Greenwood	NHO	October 4, 1967
Glenn E. Nowakowski	Warrant Officer	Oak Creek	HK	July 22, 1972
Larry H. Oertel	Specialist Fourth Class	Stratford	NHO	December 25, 1967
Paul A. Oestreicher	Specialist Fourth Class	La Crosse	HDM	October 6, 1967
Jerome E. Olmsted	First Lieutenant	Clintonville	NDM	November 30, 1967
Gregory J. Olsen	Corporal	Franklin	NHI	May 25, 1969
Craig S. Olson	Specialist Fourth Class	Osseo	HK	January 7, 1969
Duane V. Olson	Specialist Fourth Class	Arena	HDW	February 7, 1966
Rodney J. Olson	Private First Class	Eau Claire	HK	January 31, 1966
Thomas P. Olson[§]	Corporal	West Salem	HK	March 27, 1971
Charles F. Orlowski	Specialist Fourth Class	Milwaukee	HK	March 21, 1969
Robert E. Osuski	Staff Sergeant	Milwaukee	HK	February 24, 1968
Thomas W. Otte	Corporal	Kaukauna	HK	February 3, 1968
Philip M. Overbeck	First Lieutenant	Sturgeon Bay	HK	June 10, 1970
Harlan T. Pache	Private First Class	Arlington	HK	January 14, 1968
James H. Page	Specialist Fourth Class	Eagle River	HK	March 5, 1966
Paul J. Pamanet	Private First Class	Wausaukee	HK	November 21, 1968
Allen D. Papenfus	Private First Class	Appleton	NHO	March 15, 1967
Donald Paskowicz	Private First Class	Greendale	HK	July 15, 1967
Patrick J. Paulich	Private	Racine	HK	November 30, 1970
John P. Paulson Jr.	Specialist Fourth Class	Neenah	HK	December 11, 1967

ARMY

NAME	RANK	HOMETOWN	TYPE	DATE OF DEATH
Louis A. Pavlacky Jr.	Corporal	Delavan	HK	March 14, 1970
Richard C. Pawelke	Staff Sergeant	Milwaukee	HK	December 9, 1971
Terry J. Payne	Sergeant	La Crosse	HK	August 5, 1970
Gary L. Peat	Specialist Fourth Class	Rewey	HK	June 22, 1970
Marvin C. Pederson	Sergeant	Monroe	HK	January 6, 1969
Robert W. Peck§	Private First Class	Silver Lake	HDW	July 10, 1966
Roger A. Pederson	Specialist Fourth Class	Elk Mound	HK	March 29, 1971
Brian S. Perlewitz	Specialist Fourth Class	Milwaukee	HK	March 22, 1968
Terry L. Perz	Corporal	Green Bay	HK	December 16, 1969
David E. Peters	Warrant Officer	Milwaukee	HK	July 20, 1966
Lee R. Peters	Warrant Officer	Marshfield	NHO	July 30, 1970
Dennis N. Peterson	Specialist Fourth Class	Beldenville	HK	March 29, 1972
Lowell T. Peterson	Private First Class	Eau Claire	HK	March 7, 1968
Dan L. Pfister	Sergeant First Class	Sturgeon Bay	HK	June 18, 1968
Leon M. Phillips	Sergeant	De Pere	HK	March 9, 1968
Ronald E. Pickart	Warrant Officer	Fond du Lac	HK	January 8, 1970
William C. Pierson III	Chief Warrant Officer	Madison	HDM	October 16, 1978
Richard L. Pitzer	Corporal	Boscobel	HK	March 6, 1968
Murphy Pleasant Jr.	Private First Class	Milwaukee	NHO	January 2, 1969
Eugene J. Plier	Sergeant First Class	Sheboygan	HK	October 17, 1967
Ronald E. Pochron	Specialist Fifth Class	Pulaski	HK	October 1, 1968
Anthony J. Podebradsky	Sergeant	Lena	HK	February 15, 1968
John R. Poff	Corporal	Waukesha	HK	February 3, 1969
Peter P. Polak	Warrant Officer	Cable	NHO	February 21, 1969
Kurt F. Ponath	Private First Class	Cudahy	HK	September 12, 1968
David M. Price	Private First Class	Oconomowoc	HK	July 15, 1968
James A. Price	Private First Class	Peshtigo	HDM	January 2, 1968
Bernard A. Propson	Sergeant	Hilbert	HK	September 5, 1969
Marvin N. Propson	Specialist Fourth Class	Hilbert	HK	November 1, 1968
Robert Provenzano§	Specialist Fourth Class	Fort Atkinson	HK	January 18, 1967
Michael E. Prothero	Private First Class	Reedsburg	HDW	June 19, 1968
Richard B. Proveaux	Private	Milwaukee	HK	June 12, 1969
Thomas F. Przybelski	First Lieutenant	Green Bay	HDW	May 13, 1968
Robert A. Pulaski	Sergeant	Ladysmith	NHO	August 3, 1971
Terry L. Pundsack	Specialist Fourth Class	Milwaukee	HDM	September 25, 1966
Willy V. Quast	Staff Sergeant	Madison	HDM	January 7, 1967
Jeffery M. Quirk	Specialist Fourth Class	Manitowoc	HK	May 8, 1968
Robert R. Rades	Private First Class	Hawkins	HK	November 13, 1968
Leland E. Radley	Private First Class	Boscobel	HK†	August 25, 1968
Roger W. Raih	Private First Class	Manitowoc	HK	April 1, 1968

ARMY

NAME	RANK	HOMETOWN	TYPE	DATE OF DEATH
Steven P. Rance	Private First Class	Green Bay	HK	September 26, 1968
Dennis R. Rank	Specialist Fourth Class	Adams	NHI	May 11, 1969
Robert E. Ratajczak	Specialist Fourth Class	Oshkosh	NHO	March 16, 1971
Dale E. Rauber	Specialist Fourth Class	Cambridge	HK	February 21, 1969
John A. Rausch	Sergeant	Big Bend	HK	October 1, 1968
Bruce H. Rawling	Specialist Fourth Class	Prescott	HDW	January 23, 1969
James C. Reamer	Staff Sergeant	Milwaukee	HK	August 5, 1971
Dennis W. Reed	Private First Class	Milwaukee	HK	April 9, 1968
Jon E. Reed	Sergeant	Somerset	HK	September 6, 1970
Ronald H. Reilly	Sergeant First Class	Ripon	NHO	July 16, 1970
Robert H. Reinke	Corporal	Appleton	HK	March 21, 1967
Neil G. Reuter	Captain	Milwaukee	HK	July 5, 1966
Louis G. Rhoades	Corporal	De Pere	HDW	June 6, 1968
Jon W. Rich§	Sergeant	Peshtigo	HK	May 21, 1970
Duane L. Richard§	Specialist Fifth Class	Middleton	NHI	February 10, 1970
Dale W. Richardson	Major	Cashton	HDM	January 15, 1979
Edmond W. Richardson	Staff Sergeant	Potosi	HK	September 13, 1970
Donald J. Richter	Corporal	Sheboygan	HK	March 26, 1969
Roger A. Rickert	Corporal	Bowler	HK	September 27, 1968
Carl J. Riederer	Private First Class	Manitowoc	HK	February 23, 1969
James G. Riley	Specialist Fourth Class	Mauston	NHO	December 11, 1967
Severiano Rios	Corporal	Oak Creek	HK	April 2, 1970
James M. Risch	Private	Milwaukee	NHO	March 26, 1971
Roger L. Ritschard	Corporal	Monticello	HDW	November 22, 1970
Edward H. Rixmann	Private First Class	Star Prairie	HK	June 1, 1967
Jon P. Robbins§	Specialist Fifth Class	De Pere	HK	February 23, 1969
Kenneth D. Roberts	Staff Sergeant	Wausau	HK	February 5, 1967
Thomas J. Roberts	Corporal	Burlington	HK	August 22, 1970
Eugene F. Robinson§	First Sergeant	Appleton	HK	March 9, 1966
Lance A. Robinson	Corporal	Brookfield	HK	March 23, 1971
Timothy F. Robson	Corporal	Green Bay	HK	May 20, 1969
Jose M. Rocha	Corporal	Milwaukee	HK	February 7, 1971
John M. Roe	Private First Class	Milwaukee	HDM	November 16, 1970
William J. Roeglin	Sergeant	Greenfield	HK	November 3, 1969
Elwood J. Roehl	Specialist Fifth Class	Janesville	NHI	September 23, 1969
Douglas R. Roest	Sergeant	Kenosha	NHO	March 13, 1970
Paul F. Rogalske	Sergeant	Kewaunee	HK	May 1, 1970
John W. Rohr§	First Lieutenant	Middleton	HK	April 5, 1970
Robert J. Rosenow	Corporal	La Farge	HK†	May 29, 1969
Thomas A. Rosenow	Warrant Officer	Cashton	HK	August 10, 1969

ARMY

NAME	RANK	HOMETOWN	TYPE	DATE OF DEATH
Ronald A. Ross	Captain	Muskego	HK	October 31, 1969
Steven J. Roum	Private First Class	Cambridge	HK	January 27, 1969
Jerome M. Rouse	Corporal	Coleman	HK	November 2, 1970
Alan M. Royston	Specialist Fourth Class	Mazomanie	HK	February 24, 1969
Mark P. Rudolf	Sergeant	Milwaukee	HK	January 13, 1970
Carl D. Ruenger	Corporal	North Prairie	HK	April 27, 1970
John L. Rueth	Specialist Fourth Class	Loyal	HK	March 17, 1969
Franklin J. Runge	Specialist Fourth Class	Gillett	HK	March 12, 1969
Dennis D. Rutowski	Private First Class	Waterford	HK	November 8, 1965
Edward K. Ryan	Sergeant	Milwaukee	HK	September 13, 1968
John W. Sadler	Captain	New Lisbon	NHO	April 25, 1969
James A. Salamone	Specialist Fourth Class	Shorewood	NHI	March 31, 1969
Francis M. Samz	Specialist Fourth Class	Argonne	NHO	April 8, 1969
Ronald S. Sandel	Private First Class	Thorp	HK	October 9, 1967
Johnnie D. Sanderson	Private First Class	Burlington	HK	September 27, 1967
John V. Sartor	Private First Class	Kenosha	NHO	July 24, 1968
James A. Schachtner	Sergeant	Somerset	HK	June 29, 1970
David R. Schaefer	Sergeant	Sturgeon Bay	HK	May 1, 1969
Kenneth L. Schaefer	Private First Class	Beaver Dam	HK	July 3, 1966
Gerald R. Schiesl	Corporal	Manitowoc	HK	March 24, 1969
Jerrold J. Schliesman	Sergeant	Rio	HK	November 17, 1965
Floyd A. Schliewe	Specialist Fourth Class	Lebanon	NHO	October 20, 1970
William D. Schlutter	First Lieutenant	Sheboygan	NHO	March 17, 1971
David J. Schmidt	Specialist Fourth Class	Mukwonago	NHO	April 1, 1970
Larry R. Schmidt	Sergeant	Oconomowoc	HK	August 12, 1969
Lawrence E. Schmidt	Specialist Fourth Class	Waukesha	NHI	November 4, 1969
Peter A. Schmidt	Specialist Fourth Class	Milwaukee	HDM	August 15, 1970
Frederick Schmitt	Sergeant First Class	Kiel	HK	February 1, 1969
James K. Schmoll	Specialist Fourth Class	Shiocton	HK	February 20, 1971
William J. Schneider	Specialist Fourth Class	Janesville	HDW	December 1, 1966
Ray A. Schold	Specialist Fourth Class	Kenosha	NDM	September 3, 1967
Gary L. Schroeder	Private First Class	Appleton	NHO	October 20, 1970
Robert E. Schroeder Jr.	Corporal	Milwaukee	HK	November 2, 1969
James P. Schueller	First Lieutenant	Marshfield	NDM	June 17, 1967
Arnold R. Schuh	Private First Class	Kaukauna	HK	October 20, 1969
David M. Schuh	Sergeant	Elcho	HK	March 6, 1968
David C. Schultz	Private First Class	Milwaukee	HK	October 28, 1968
Michael W. Schumacher	Specialist Fourth Class	Janesville	HDW	February 11, 1969
Daniel C. Schuster	Chief Warrant Officer	Milwaukee	HK	July 3, 1968
Russell A. Schwartz	Specialist Fourth Class	Milwaukee	NHO	July 8, 1969

ARMY

NAME	RANK	HOMETOWN	TYPE	DATE OF DEATH
Bruce R. Scott	Private First Class	La Crosse	HK	July 11, 1967
Robert L.R. Seekamp	Private First Class	Kendall	HK	July 19, 1969
Joseph D. Seibert	Sergeant	Green Bay	HK	March 6, 1968
Gary D. Sengstock	Staff Sergeant	Marinette	HK	August 8, 1970
Donald J. Severson	Specialist Fourth Class	Superior	HK	July 22, 1970
Thomas E. Severson	Specialist Fourth Class	New Richmond	HK†	March 10, 1970
Kris E. Shaw§	Specialist Fourth Class	Albany	HK	July 29, 1969
Thomas Shaw	Specialist Fourth Class	Milwaukee	HK	November 15, 1966
Thomas F. Shaw	First Lieutenant	Fond du Lac	NHO	April 27, 1972
John C. Shellum	Specialist Fourth Class	Superior	HK	April 18, 1969
Ronald D. Shepherd	Specialist Fourth Class	Watertown	HDM	July 5, 1967
Dennis W. Shew	Specialist Fourth Class	Madison	NHO	September 11, 1969
Barry J. Short	Platoon Sergeant	Milwaukee	HK	April 30, 1967
Dennis L. Siegel	Private First Class	Marion	HK	February 23, 1968
Daniel Sikorski	Specialist Fourth Class	Milwaukee	HK	October 17, 1967
Alan E. Singer	Sergeant	Shawano	HK	May 4, 1969
Robert A. Singerhouse	Private	New Richmond	HK	December 3, 1965
Monte T. Sloan§	Captain	Superior	HDW	December 10, 1966
Daniel R. Smeester	Corporal	Green Bay	HK	July 1, 1967
Donald L. Smith	Staff Sergeant	Fennimore	HK	December 21, 1967
Fred D. Smith	Sergeant	Wittenberg	HK	March 30, 1969
Jack R. Smith	Warrant Officer	Mequon	HDM	May 14, 1970
Kenneth E. Smith	Specialist Fifth Class	Woodville	HK	May 15, 1970
Larry A. Smith	Sergeant	Fort Atkinson	HK	April 16, 1969
Lloyd S. Smith	First Lieutenant	Portage	HDM	November 10, 1966
Lynn H. Smith	First Lieutenant	Cudahy	HK	February 1, 1968
William T. Smith	Staff Sergeant	Marshfield	HK	April 2, 1970
David G. Smithwick	Specialist Fourth Class	De Pere	NHO	October 30, 1971
Arden G. Sonnenberg	Private First Class	Kenosha	HK	August 25, 1968
Gene B. Spencer	Private First Class	Walworth	HDW	June 23, 1966
Winfield A. Spoehr Jr.	Corporal	New London	HK	December 19, 1967
James R. Springer	Private First Class	Kenosha	HK	November 7, 1968
James V. Spurley Jr.	Sergeant	Madison	HK	May 12, 1969
Curtis J. Steckbauer	Captain	Manitowoc	NHO	July 1, 1963
Dennis E. Stecker	Specialist Fourth Class	Manitowoc	HK	November 17, 1970
William J. Stedl	Specialist Fourth Class	Greenleaf	HDW	March 10, 1969
Philip C. Stein	Sergeant	Milwaukee	HK	April 4, 1969
Richard W. Stein	Specialist Fourth Class	Brookfield	HK	October 26, 1967
George C. Steinberg	Captain	Milwaukee	HK	April 11, 1966
Terry M. Steiner	Sergeant	North Fond du Lac	NHO	March 11, 1970

ARMY

NAME	RANK	HOMETOWN	TYPE	DATE OF DEATH
Merlin C. Stelpflug	Corporal	Dickeyville	HDW	September 21, 1967
Vernon G. Stich	Specialist Fourth Class	Madison	NHO	August 7, 1967
Steven M. Sticks	Private First Class	Okauchee	HK	July 4, 1969
Gregory W. Stoddart	Specialist Fifth Class	Oshkosh	NHO	April 6, 1970
James A. Stoeberl	Specialist Fifth Class	Almena	NDM	October 7, 1967
Michael H. Stoflet	Private First Class	Elkhorn	HK	November 1, 1966
Donald R. Stoltz	Specialist Fourth Class	Milwaukee	HK	December 4, 1968
Dennis M. Stoppleworth	Private	Middleton	NHO	June 20, 1970
Gerald S. Stozek	Specialist Fourth Class	Fond du Lac	HDW	September 28, 1968
John G. Strachota	Specialist Fourth Class	Milwaukee	HK	November 13, 1970
Kenneth L. Strittmater	Private First Class	La Crosse	HDW	March 2, 1969
William H. Stroud	Private First Class	Milwaukee	NHO	October 14, 1970
Thomas J. Sturgal	Sergeant	Ashland	HK	March 22, 1968
Frederic C. Styer	Specialist Fourth Class	Menomonie	HK	May 28, 1967
Frederick V. Suchomel	Specialist Fourth Class	Sun Prairie	NHO	April 15, 1969
Clarence M. Suchon	Corporal	Stevens Point	HK	March 22, 1971
Donald A. Sudbrink	Specialist Fourth Class	Hartland	NHO	January 1, 1970
Stanley J. Sukowatey	Private First Class	Waunakee	HK	May 13, 1968
John F. Sullivan	Corporal	Franklin	HK	August 18, 1968
Terrence L. Sund	Specialist Fourth Class	Menomonee Falls	HDM	December 6, 1967
Larry I. Sutton	Specialist Fourth Class	Danbury	HK	July 23, 1967
Gene S. Swager	Specialist Fourth Class	Balsam Lake	HK	April 15, 1970
Larry W. Swiggum	Specialist Fourth Class	Genoa	HDW	August 7, 1968
Robert T. Szymanski	Sergeant	Milwaukee	HDM	November 20, 1967
K. J. Taschek Jr.	Specialist Fourth Class	Darlington	HK	March 20, 1969
Leonard J. Tauschek	Private First Class	Beloit	HK	September 7, 1967
Andrew J. Taylor	Sergeant First Class	Milwaukee	HK	May 2, 1970
Larry L. Techmeir	Sergeant	Stanley	HK	July 14, 1969
Joseph A. Teresinski	Specialist Fourth Class	Oneida	HK	February 6, 1971
David L. Tessmer	Corporal	Wausau	HK	May 27, 1969
Thomas E. Thayer[§]	Sergeant Major	Eland	HK	November 8, 1965
William A. Theisen	Sergeant	Deerbrook	HDW	December 24, 1969
Le Roy E. Thelen	Sergeant	Glenbeulah	HK	July 9, 1970
Ronald C. Thiex	Specialist Fourth Class	Bowler	HK	March 3, 1969
Scott L. Thiry	Private First Class	Milwaukee	HK	October 31, 1967
Charles J. Thoma	Major	Madison	HDW	January 12, 1967
Leonard D. Thompson	Specialist Fourth Class	Madison	HK	April 25, 1967
Stuart H. Thomson	Sergeant First Class	Milwaukee	HDM	January 29, 1968
David W. Timm	Chief Warrant Officer	Brodhead	NHO	April 5, 1968
Richard R. Timmons	Corporal	Fond du Lac	NHO	July 16, 1970

ARMY

NAME	RANK	HOMETOWN	TYPE	DATE OF DEATH
Paul H. Tober	Specialist Fourth Class	Tigerton	HK	February 23, 1969
Thomas J. Tomczak	Sergeant	New Berlin	HK	July 23, 1968
Victor D. Tomczyk	Private First Class	Dorchester	HDM	January 2, 1968
Barrent O. Torgerson	Specialist Fifth Class	Turtle Lake	NHO	October 28, 1969
Gearwin P. Tousey	Private First Class	Green Bay	HK	February 25, 1968
Thomas C. Treible	Corporal	West Allis	HK	May 19, 1969
Albert R. Trudeau	Warrant Officer	Milwaukee	NDM	October 26, 1971
Pekka Trunkhahn	Specialist Fourth Class	Kenosha	NHO	May 16, 1966
Byron C. Tucker	Warrant Officer	Sparta	NHO	August 15, 1968
Dennis Tuinstra	Private First Class	Racine	HK	June 2, 1969
Michael B. Turner	Corporal	La Crosse	HK	May 11, 1968
Jayson F. Ulrich	Sergeant	Milwaukee	HK	August 17, 1969
Michael J. Unsinn	Specialist Fifth Class	Green Bay	HK	January 3, 1969
Stanley F. Urbas	Specialist Fourth Class	West Allis	NHO	January 26, 1969
Thomas H. Utegaard	Sergeant	Eau Claire	HK	June 13, 1969
Robert E. Uthemann	Staff Sergeant	Milwaukee	HK	June 4, 1970
Thomas E. Vail	Specialist Fourth Class	Janesville	NHO	July 19, 1970
Francis P. Valdez	Specialist Fifth Class	Oshkosh	HK	June 7, 1970
Rudolph G. Valenta	Specialist Fourth Class	Milwaukee	NHI	October 8, 1971
David F. Van Den Heuvel	Private First Class	West De Pere	HK	March 2, 1969
Allen L. Van Keuren	Staff Sergeant	Elkhorn	HK	December 14, 1967
Murray W. Van Lone Sr.	Staff Sergeant	Kenosha	HK	January 20, 1968
William W. Van Mater	Sergeant	Friendship	HK	September 22, 1968
James L. Vanbendegom	Staff Sergeant	Kenosha	HDC	July 31, 1967
Charles G. Vander Heyden	Sergeant	Oshkosh	HK	August 21, 1968
Paul W. Vanderboom Jr.	Specialist Fourth Class	Fond du Lac	HK	August 18, 1969
Cornelis A. Vandersterren	Corporal	Waukesha	HK	September 13, 1968
Peter M. Vanderweg	Sergeant	Oak Creek	HK	July 25, 1970
Glen O. Venet	Specialist Fourth Class	Kenosha	HK	February 28, 1969
Michael J. Verhaeghe	Specialist Fourth Class	Racine	NHO	April 9, 1969
Edward Veser	Sergeant	Milwaukee	HK	May 6, 1970
James M. Vielbaum	Private First Class	Hartford	HK	January 31, 1968
Lawrence S. Vogel§	Private First Class	Beloit	HK	January 27, 1967
Ralph L. Vogeli	Sergeant First Class	Cambria	HK	January 6, 1969
Valentine B. Vollmer	Specialist Fourth Class	Clintonville	HK	February 16, 1968
Dennis R. Wagie	Sergeant	Dousman	NHO	May 2, 1969
Michael J. Wagner	Private First Class	Watertown	HK	February 22, 1970
Philip R. Wagner	Sergeant	Manitowoc	NHO	September 28, 1971
Randall W. Wagner	Corporal	Egg Harbor	HK	November 27, 1968
Paul W. Wahler Jr.	First Lieutenant	Racine	NHO	November 18, 1967

ARMY

NAME	RANK	HOMETOWN	TYPE	DATE OF DEATH
Gary A. Waldorf	Private First Class	Green Bay	HK	September 11, 1968
Eugene K. Wallace§	Staff Sergeant	Chippewa Falls	HK	June 18, 1969
Thomas D. Walker	Private First Class	Elkhorn	HK	December 26, 1968
Leon A. Wangerin	Specialist Fourth Class	Milwaukee	HK	May 20, 1967
James C. Ward	Private First Class	Milwaukee	HK	October 11, 1965
Richard J. Warden	Warrant Officer	Sheboygan	HK	July 4, 1970
Walter R. Waschick	Private First Class	Merrill	HK	February 9, 1968
Steven E. Wasson	Corporal	Spring Valley	HK	May 5, 1970
David J. Watson	Specialist Fourth Class	Oshkosh	NHI	November 9, 1971
Johnny L. Webb	Private First Class	Milwaukee	HK	June 11, 1970
Douglas R. Weiher	Specialist Fourth Class	Milwaukee	HK	April 12, 1968
Dennis E. Weinberg	Private	Milwaukee	HK	November 24, 1966
Thomas R. Weiss	Specialist Fourth Class	Glenbeulah	NHO	October 20, 1970
Larry M. Welsh	Private First Class	Muscoda	HK	July 15, 1968
Gary L. Westphal	Sergeant	Bonduel	HDW	June 13, 1971
Scott B. Westphal	Specialist Fourth Class	Menasha	HK	February 21, 1972
Michael L. White	Private First Class	New Berlin	NDM	March 13, 1968
Randall J. Wicklace§	Specialist Fourth Class	Turtle Lake	HK	January 16, 1969
David John W. Widder	Captain	Sheboygan	HK	March 24, 1965
Anthony J. Wieckowicz	Specialist Fourth Class	Conrath	HK	January 23, 1969
Lloyd G. Wiegel	Private First Class	Shullsburg	HK	May 19, 1966
John G. Willems	Specialist Fourth Class	Hilbert	HK	September 3, 1969
Terry J. Williams	Specialist Fourth Class	Oconomowoc	HK	January 31, 1968
Larry A. Williamson	Specialist Fourth Class	Racine	HK	May 21, 1967
Lawrence J. Wissell§	Captain	Lake Geneva	HK	December 21, 1968
Arthur E. Wojahn	Specialist Fourth Class	La Crosse	HK	September 5, 1969
Jeremy R. Wojtkiewicz	First Lieutenant	Weyerhauser	HDW	January 17, 1969
Aaron L. Wood	Private First Class	Waukesha	HK	May 17, 1968
Dennis M. Wood	Staff Sergeant	Beloit	HK	December 11, 1968
Durel S. Woods§	Corporal	Milwaukee	HK	July 19, 1969
Randall A. Woolcott	Private First Class	Milwaukee	HK	February 12, 1968
Larry R. Woolridge	Private First Class	Dousman	HK	November 15, 1968
James K. Wozniak	Corporal	Armstrong Creek	NHO	September 1, 1969
David J. Woznicki	Specialist Fourth Class	Hatley	HDM	December 7, 1967
Vincent Wright	Private First Class	Milwaukee	NHO	June 17, 1971
Clinton C. Wusterbarth	Corporal	Manitowoc	HK	March 18, 1968
Glen H. Young	Private First Class	Brodhead	HK	October 28, 1966
John E. Young	Specialist Fourth Class	Oconto	HK	November 7, 1967
Michael E. Young	Specialist Fourth Class	Racine	NHO	November 11, 1969
Thaddeus Zajac	Specialist Fourth Class	Milwaukee	HK	September 27, 1965

ARMY

NAME	RANK	HOMETOWN	TYPE	DATE OF DEATH
Thomas H. Zehner	Private First Class	Bruce	NHO	February 20, 1967
James G. Zeimet	Warrant Officer	Brookfield	HK	September 4, 1968
Robert E. Zeske	Private First Class	Milwaukee	HK	May 25, 1968
Robert G. Zink	Private First Class	Stevens Point	HK	June 19, 1968
Frank Zydzik Jr.	Specialist Fourth Class	Phillips	HK	January 7, 1970

MARINES

NAME	RANK	HOMETOWN	TYPE	DATE OF DEATH
Lee C. Adams	Private First Class	Milwaukee	HK	April 19, 1968
Vincent J. Agius	Lance Corporal	Janesville	HDW	April 17, 1967
James J. Ahrens	Private First Class	Green Bay	HK	June 19, 1969
Terry L. Albright	Private First Class	Greenfield	NHO	October 7, 1969
Merlin R. Allen	Lance Corporal	Bayfield	HK	June 30, 1967
Roscoe Ammerman	Staff Sergeant	Madison	HK	October 3, 1965
Jack W. Anderson Jr.	Private First Class	Milwaukee	HK	September 3, 1967
Marlyn R. Anderson[§]	Corporal	Menomonie	HK	Febuary 11, 1968
Ralph T. Anderson[§]	Lance Corporal	Janesville	HK	May 2, 1968
Richard L. Anderson	Private First Class	Oshkosh	NHO	April 25, 1969
Dennis L. Antoine	Corporal	Franklin	HK	July 21, 1967
Thomas L. Armitage	Private First Class	Medina	HK	February 12, 1969
Robert D. Arnold	Private First Class	Galesville	HK	April 18, 1966
Robin L. Arnold[§]	Lance Corporal	Wisconsin Rapids	HK	July 24, 1966
James M. Arries	Private First Class	Elk Mound	HK	April 1, 1967
John J. Arteaga	Lance Corporal	Milwaukee	NHO	September 10, 1970
Nikola Babich	Lance Corporal	Milwaukee	HK	May 27, 1968
David L. Banks	Private First Class	Superior	NHI	April 21, 1969
Michael J. Banovez Jr.	Corporal	Madison	HK	July 18, 1966
Albin A. Baranczyk	Corporal	Menasha	HK	May 17, 1966
Michael P. Bartelme	Lance Corporal	Watertown	HK	May 2, 1967
Robert J. Beck	Lance Corporal	Oshkosh	HK	September 18, 1968
Terrence D. Beck	Lance Corporal	Fort Atkinson	HK	December 20, 1967
Willie Bedford	Private	Milwaukee	NHO	May 3, 1970
Edward A. Beilfuss Jr.	Private First Class	Milwaukee	HK	November 1, 1967
Larry W. Bender	Corporal	Stoughton	HK	May 31, 1968
David G. Bendorf	Lance Corporal	Livingston	HK	May 20, 1967
Frederick L. Benishek	Corporal	Antigo	HK	June 7, 1969
Allan F. Berweger	Private First Class	Ashland	HK	May 10, 1967
Patrick W. Best	Private First Class	West Allis	HK	May 13, 1969
Norman K. Billipp	Major	Milwaukee	HDM	July 16, 1976

MARINES

NAME	RANK	HOMETOWN	TYPE	DATE OF DEATH
Glen A. Bjerke	Corporal	Edgerton	NHO	August 2, 1967
Thomas J. Blackman	Private First Class	Racine	HK	May 10, 1968
Thomas J. Blaha	Private	Madison	HK	February 8, 1968
Gordon H. Blexrude	Sergeant	Eau Claire	NHO	August 24, 1965
James L. Boehler	Private First Class	Racine	HDW	August 21, 1967
Terri M. Boettger	Sergeant	Milwaukee	HK	December 16, 1967
James E. Brannon	Private First Class	Milwaukee	HK	March 25, 1969
Frederick H. Brodhagen	Private First Class	Greendale	HK†	March 24, 1967
Dennis L. Brown	Lance Corporal	Milwaukee	NHO	June 29, 1968
Richard J. Brunke	Private First Class	Milwaukee	NHO	December 14, 1965
Frederick W. Bungartz	Private First Class	Chippewa Falls	HK	February 14, 1968
Thomas R. Burns	Lance Corporal	Fremont	HK	May 26, 1967
Anthony G. Calverley	Lance Corporal	Racine	HK	July 15, 1966
Giovanni H. Campbell	Private First Class	Milwaukee	HK	June 12, 1969
Francis J. Capezio	Private First Class	Pell Lake	HK	March 6, 1968
Thomas J. Carstens	Corporal	Hartland	HK	August 14, 1967
Richard R. Cerra	Private	Bruce	HK	August 7, 1968
John T. Chapman	Captain	River Falls	NHO	January 8, 1968
Andrew J. Chicantek	Lance Corporal	Greenfield	HK	May 29, 1968
Benjamin A. Chitko	Gunnery Sergeant	Pembine	HK	September 16, 1966
Wayne C. Chitwood	Corporal	Necedah	HK	January 24, 1968
David F. Cleereman	Lance Corporal	Green Bay	HDW	January 29, 1969
Robert L. Cloutier	Private First Class	Somerset	HK†	May 21, 1966
Patrick A. Connelly	Private First Class	Green Bay	HK	June 19, 1968
James A. Corey	Lance Corporal	Kimberly	NHI	March 2, 1968
Bruce W. Crabb	Private First Class	Milwaukee	HK	September 11, 1968
David A. Cramer	Private First Class	Burlington	HK	February 22, 1968
Thomas H. Crook	Private First Class	West Bend	HK	February 23, 1969
William L. Cunningham	Private First Class	Antigo	HK	March 1, 1968
James S. Dahl	Private First Class	Milwaukee	NHO	May 14, 1968
Michael J. Davidson	Private First Class	Cassville	HK	May 12, 1967
Jerry F. De Gray	Lance Corporal	Milwaukee	HDW	October 17, 1967
David W. De Laat	Lance Corporal	Burlington	HDW	June 11, 1970
Albert Dean	Private First Class	Milwaukee	HK	May 14, 1966
Allan Decker§	Lance Corporal	Delavan	HK	August 25, 1968
Vasilios Demetris§	Second Lieutenant	Fennimore	HK	February 24, 1969
Raymond R. Demoe	Private First Class	Elk Mound	HK	March 25, 1967
Paul D. Derby	Captain	Menomonie	HK	November 17, 1968
Charles F. Deuel	Private First Class	Palmyra	HK	March 1, 1968
Stephen K. Dibb	Sergeant	Milwaukee	HK	July 21, 1966

MARINES

NAME	RANK	HOMETOWN	TYPE	DATE OF DEATH
Robert J. Diedrich	Lance Corporal	Random Lake	HK	April 30, 1968
Donald G. Dingeldein	Private First Class	Waukesha	NHO	September 14, 1966
James T. Dobish	Private First Class	Oshkosh	HK	May 20, 1967
David G. Dobosz	Private First Class	Clear Lake	HK	June 20, 1970
James M. Donstad	Private First Class	Edgerton	NHO	February 4, 1969
Jean P. Dowling	Lance Corporal	Madison	HDM	January 29, 1966
Allen W. Dumke	Corporal	West Allis	HK	October 20, 1969
Mark R. Dziedzic	Private First Class	Oak Creek	HK	March 16, 1968
Roger A. Ellis	Private First Class	Holmen	NHO	December 26, 1967
Michael L. Ewing[§]	Private	Readstown	HK	June 11, 1968
William H. Farvour	Corporal	Green Bay	HK[†]	February 16, 1969
Arleigh F. Felch	Sergeant	Sheboygan	HDW	August 5, 1967
Edwin J. Fickler	Captain	Kewaskum	HDM	February 4, 1974
Richard W. Fischer	Gunnery Sergeant	Madison	HDM	December 8, 1978
La Voughn H. Folkers	Sergeant	Racine	HK	February 28, 1967
David J. Frischmann	Lance Corporal	Waukesha	HK	February 1, 1967
William Fuchs Jr.	Private First Class	Milwaukee	HK	February 28, 1966
Eugene O. Fuller	Private First Class	Wyocena	HK	September 9, 1968
Daniel F. Gallagher	Lance Corporal	Blanchardville	NHO	September 10, 1970
John P. Gannon	Lance Corporal	Plymouth	HK	June 27, 1967
Paul S. Gee	Captain	Manitowish Waters	HDM	August 5, 1974
Larry F. Geiger	Private First Class	Milwaukee	HK	April 26, 1967
Thomas A. Gerg	Private First Class	Brookfield	HK[†]	January 12, 1967
Ricky M. Gilbertson	Private First Class	Milwaukee	HK	May 3, 1967
Gary L. Gillard[§]	Staff Sergeant	Racine	HDW	May 15, 1969
Thomas A. Goebel[§]	Sergeant	Blanchardville	NHO	October 26, 1970
Glenn R. Gradecki	Corporal	Milwaukee	NHI	December 29, 1969
John P. Gray	Lance Corporal	Brillion	HK	May 31, 1968
Ben J. Greene[§]	Sergeant	Tomahawk	HDW	May 7, 1968
Michael J. Gregorius	Lance Corporal	Appleton	HK	August 12, 1969
Donald L. Grieger	Private First Class	Milwaukee	NHI	December 2, 1969
Ronald L. Grenier	Private First Class	Brill	HK	August 2, 1968
William T. Grudzinski	Lance Corporal	Edgerton	HK	October 21, 1966
Edward R. Grusczynski	Lance Corporal	Denmark	HK	August 25, 1969
Thomas C. Guden	Private First Class	Berlin	HDW	June 25, 1967
Paul J. Guelig	Private First Class	Glenbeulah	HK	April 24, 1970
Michael M. Gukich	Lance Corporal	North Prairie	NHO	May 8, 1967
Kenneth W. Haakenson	Private First Class	Racine	HK	March 13, 1968
Kenneth D. Haas	Lance Corporal	Stanley	HK	August 5, 1967
James F. Hackett Jr.	Lance Corporal	Milwaukee	HK	January 28, 1970

MARINES

NAME	RANK	HOMETOWN	TYPE	DATE OF DEATH
Blake H. Halfman	Lance Corporal	Fond du Lac	HK	February 17, 1968
James L. Hamlet	Private First Class	New Richmond	HDW	June 10, 1967
James P. Harteau	Private First Class	Waukesha	HK	April 6, 1966
Dennis M. Harter	Lance Corporal	Wabeno	NHI	August 3, 1969
Michael A. Harvey	Private	Milwaukee	HDW	March 1, 1969
Kenneth B. Hawley	Corporal	Oshkosh	HK	August 12, 1966
Wayne M. Hayes	First Lieutenant	Menomonie	HDW	July 6, 1967
Carl W. Heiden	Lance Corporal	Milwaukee	HK	September 24, 1967
Paul W. Heinz	Private First Class	Brown Deer	HK	March 1, 1968
Robert A. Heiser	Private First Class	Rib Lake	HK	August 22, 1967
Laurence J. Herfel	Lance Corporal	Madison	HK	February 24, 1968
Raymond T. Heyne	Lance Corporal	Mason	HK	May 10, 1968
John J. Hickey	Lance Corporal	Green Bay	HDW	April 25, 1969
Charles H. Hill	Corporal	Fond du Lac	HK	June 22, 1966
Timothy L. Hren	Corporal	Milwaukee	HK	July 8, 1968
Charles F. Huff[§]	Lance Corporal	Fort Atkinson	HK	June 3, 1968
Vernon D. Jacobs	Private First Class	Galesville	HK	March 17, 1969
Ronald E. Jahnke	Private First Class	Menasha	HK	January 8, 1966
Clayton D. Jenkins	Lance Corporal	Pembine	HK	June 3, 1969
Alan T. Jensen	Sergeant	Hales Corners	HK	October 17, 1967
Donald P. Johnson	Lance Corporal	Gilman	HK	March 13, 1967
Kent L. Johnstone	Corporal	Amery	HK	February 4, 1967
Allen J. Kakuk	Private First Class	Two Rivers	HDW	August 9, 1966
Dennis W. Keefe	Lance Corporal	Wauwatosa	HK	July 19, 1968
Randall W. Kelpine	Corporal	Milwaukee	HK	May 26, 1968
Philip J. Kimpel	Private First Class	Fond du Lac	NHO[†]	March 11, 1967
Eli J. King[§]	Lance Corporal	Milwaukee	HK	June 22, 1967
John W. Kirchner	Private First Class	La Crosse	HK	May 27, 1969
Ronald F. Kitzke	Lance Corporal	Wauwatosa	HK	December 27, 1967
Earl W. Knutson Jr.	Private First Class	Clinton	NHO	December 25, 1966
Douglas L. Kramer	Private First Class	Milwaukee	HK	March 6, 1967
Eugene R. Kritz	Sergeant	Milwaukee	HK	April 11, 1967
Gerald Kropidlowski	Lance Corporal	Stevens Point	HK	November 2, 1967
John E. Krzmarcik	Private First Class	Wausau	HK	June 7, 1969
Walter L. Lamarr	Private First Class	Sturtevant	HK	February 25, 1969
Christian A. Langenfeld	Private First Class	Oshkosh	HK	January 27, 1968
Michael D. Laux	Corporal	Appleton	HK	March 25, 1966
Charles R. Le Bosquet	Corporal	Madison	HK	August 21, 1969
David L. Leet	Captain	Kenosha	HDM	April 13, 1975
Roman H. Leicht	Private First Class	Sheboygan	HK	March 29, 1969

MARINES

NAME	RANK	HOMETOWN	TYPE	DATE OF DEATH
Mario R. Leon	Private First Class	Milwaukee	HK	March 29, 1969
Raymond R. Lewis	Corporal	Milwaukee	HK	February 18, 1968
Michael E. Lex	Lance Corporal	Menomonee Falls	NHO	April 16, 1969
William B. Libersky	Lance Corporal	Bloomer	HDW	January 11, 1970
Kenneth G. Liebhaber	Private First Class	Neenah	HK	February 17, 1969
Theodore P. Linski	Lance Corporal	Milwaukee	NHO	July 27, 1967
Jerome W. Litke	Private First Class	Milwaukee	HK	June 4, 1966
Robert O. Long§	Private First Class	Beloit	HK	August 18, 1965
Lawrence A. Luciani	Lance Corporal	Kenosha	NHO	December 29, 1969
Terry B. Lund	Lance Corporal	Kenosha	NHI	December 31, 1969
Eugene K. Lupe	Private First Class	Green Bay	HK†	May 18, 1968
Robert S. Lutz	Private First Class	Oconomowoc	HK	February 6, 1968
Thomas V. Madison	Lance Corporal	Delavan	HK	July 23, 1966
Michael P. Malueg	Private First Class	Antigo	HK	March 6, 1969
John K. Marshall	Lance Corporal	Green Bay	HK	November 17, 1968
Dennis R. Martin	Lance Corporal	Muskego	NHO	August 24, 1965
Vernal G. Martin	Private	Marshfield	HK	August 8, 1966
Howard V. Matson Jr.	Lance Corporal	Brookfield	HK	December 4, 1966
Richard E. Matyas	Private First Class	New London	HDW	March 10, 1969
Patrick R. McClure	Private First Class	Racine	HK	May 11, 1969
Richard W. McKenzie§	Lance Corporal	Pound	HK	February 25, 1968
Jeffery E. Mead	Lance Corporal	Janesville	HK	March 12, 1968
Michael O. Mellon	Corporal	New Berlin	HDW	August 26, 1968
John C. Mercier	Lance Corporal	Racine	HK	December 8, 1966
Edward K. Meyer§	Private First Class	Whitewater	HK	May 15, 1967
James F. Meyer Jr.	Private First Class	Oak Creek	HK	February 17, 1968
Daniel L. Meysembourg	Private First Class	Madison	HK	March 11, 1968
John M. Mihalovich	Corporal	Milwaukee	HDW	March 25, 1968
Gary R. Miracle	Lance Corporal	Wausau	HK	February 23, 1969
Harold J. Moe	Captain	Eau Claire	HK	September 26, 1967
Randy W. Molkentine	Corporal	Milwaukee	NHI	March 5, 1969
Kevin W. Moore	Private First Class	Milwaukee	HK	March 31, 1968
James M. Moriarty	Private	Appleton	HK	August 22, 1968
Marco F. Mueller	Lance Corporal	Port Washington	HK	May 15, 1968
Michael L. Mulcahy	Private First Class	Stoughton	HK	September 13, 1967
Nicholas L. Natzke	Sergeant	Merrill	HK†	September 22, 1967
Randall K. Nauertz	Corporal	Altoona	NHI	December 2, 1968
Vernon L. Nelson	Corporal	Glenwood City	NHO	January 21, 1969
Terry J. Neumeier	Corporal	Kewaunee	HK	August 30, 1965
Larry J. Nicholson	Private First Class	Hartford	HK	June 6, 1969

MARINES

NAME	RANK	HOMETOWN	TYPE	DATE OF DEATH
Gilbert R. Nickerson	Private First Class	Racine	HK	August 18, 1965
Russell C. Nicolai	Corporal	Milwaukee	NHI	July 6, 1969
Michael C. Nielsen	Lance Corporal	Beloit	HK	July 26, 1969
George E. Norbut§	Lance Corporal	Eau Claire	HK	September 2, 1967
Leonard M. Nowak	Private First Class	Luxemburg	HK	May 28, 1968
Richard J. O Hare	Private First Class	Racine	HK	March 6, 1968
Carl E. Oldfield	Private First Class	Janesville	NHO	October 25, 1969
Gary W. Olson	Corporal	Milwaukee	HK	March 15, 1967
Daniel J. Orlikowski	Private First Class	Athens	HK	March 7, 1967
Steven R. Ott	Lance Corporal	Black River Falls	NHO	August 16, 1970
Martin J. Pamonicutt	Private First Class	Neopit	HK	June 23, 1969
Daniel G. Patrick	Private First Class	Salem	HK	April 5, 1967
William A. Patterson	Private First Class	Superior	HK	June 9, 1968
Bradley A. Pearson	Private First Class	Clear Lake	HK	July 20, 1966
Richard E. Perez	Lance Corporal	Washington Island	HK	September 6, 1969
Steven O. Perlewitz	Corporal	Algoma	HK	February 26, 1967
Joseph J. Peterlich	Lance Corporal	Antigo	HK	May 19, 1968
Carl E. Peterson	Colonel	Kenwaunee	HK	February 10, 1968
Darwin S. Peterson	Private First Class	Pleasant Prairie	HK	March 13, 1970
John A. Peterson	Lance Corporal	Deerbrook	HK	February 23, 1969
Timm C. Peterson	Lance Corporal	Clayton	HK	January 10, 1967
William E. Pierson	Lance Corporal	Brookfield	HK	December 15, 1967
James D. Plecity	Corporal	Madison	HK	December 6, 1967
Frank M. Pokey Jr.	Corporal	Milwaukee	HK	March 16, 1967
Jesus Quesada	Private First Class	Milwaukee	HK	January 28, 1969
David P. Quinlan	Lance Corporal	Milwaukee	HK	July 29, 1969
Kenneth W. Radonski	Private First Class	Milwaukee	HK	February 17, 1968
Ronald J. Ray	Lance Corporal	Greenleaf	HK	August 12, 1969
James R. Rice	Private First Class	Cudahy	HK	August 12, 1969
Melvin L. Rimel§	Gunnery Sergeant	Milton Junction	HK	January 21, 1968
James M. Ringle	Private	Wausau	NHO	March 31, 1967
K B. Rische Jr.	Corporal	Milwaukee	HK	June 3, 1967
Gerald A. Robinson	Lance Corporal	Kenauee	HK	May 16, 1967
Royce E. Roe	Private First Class	Pewaukee	HK	February 25, 1969
John C. Romanshek	Corporal	Milwaukee	HK	December 6, 1967
Gerald J. Rossow	Lance Corporal	La Crosse	HK	August 25, 1969
Robert P. Ruminski	Lance Corporal	Two Rivers	HK	April 1, 1967
Charles G. Rush Jr.§	Gunnery Sergeant	Sun Prairie	HDW	April 21, 1969
Jack R. Rush	Lance Corporal	Algoma	HK	July 2, 1967
Roberto Sanchez	Lance Corporal	Racine	HK	May 2, 1968

MARINES

NAME	RANK	HOMETOWN	TYPE	DATE OF DEATH
Roy A. Schaefer Jr.	Private First Class	Fond du Lac	HK	March 5, 1967
Gerold Schaeffer	Private First Class	West Bend	HK	June 10, 1966
Dale A. Schepp	Lance Corporal	Wausau	NHI	December 9, 1969
David L. Schettl	Lance Corporal	Manitowoc	HK	May 17, 1968
Robert J. Schley	Corporal	Oregon	HK	April 30, 1967
John S. Schmid	First Lieutenant	Salem	HK	December 28, 1965
Ronald K. Schmid	Lance Corporal	Juda	HK	December 28, 1966
Harry W. Schneider	Corporal	Janesville	HK	February 16, 1968
Jerome A. Schuett	Private	Reedsburg	HK	February 13, 1968
Gerald W. Schultz	Private First Class	Beloit	NHO	March 3, 1969
John R. Schurrer	Corporal	Milwaukee	HK	June 18, 1968
Dale W. Schwefel	Private First Class	Watertown	HK	February 2, 1969
Richard W. Schwendler	Corporal	Milwaukee	HK	November 16, 1965
James M. Scriver	Lance Corporal	Kenosha	HK	September 9, 1970
Michael Sears	Corporal	Milwaukee	HK	March 6, 1968
Dennis L. Senz	Lance Corporal	Tomah	HK	December 18, 1967
James M. Shepard Jr.	Corporal	Marshall	HK	June 27, 1967
Paul Shireman Jr.§	Private First Class	Camp Douglas	HK	July 29, 1968
David A. Siemanowski	Private First Class	Milwaukee	HK	March 26, 1966
Gary W. Smith	Private First Class	Fort Atkinson	HK	February 24, 1969
Timothy J. Smith	Private First Class	Lake Geneva	HK	September 9, 1968
Duwayne Soulier	Private First Class	Milwaukee	NHO	May 1, 1967
John C. Stecker	Corporal	Milwaukee	HK	May 19, 1967
Arthur C. Stephens Jr.	Lieutenant Colonel	Milwaukee	NHO	May 16, 1971
Gordon W. Stoflet	Lance Corporal	Madison	HDW	June 29, 1967
Ronald J. Streckert	Private First Class	Chilieutenanton	HK†	December 28, 1967
Frank J. Strnad§	Lance Corporal	Junction City	HDW	June 22, 1968
Gridley B. Strong§	Private First Class	Beloit	HK	April 21, 1968
Howard D. Strouse	Master Sergeant	Superior	NHO	October 6, 1966
Mikal J. Sullivan	Lance Corporal	West De Pere	HK	June 6, 1968
Emil J. Tadevich Jr.§	Corporal	Ashland	HK	December 31, 1965
Dale F. Tegelman	Lance Corporal	Manitowoc	NHO	July 17, 1967
Ernest W. Tews	Lance Corporal	Beloit	NHO	April 30, 1969
Clayton J. Theyerl	Private First Class	Racine	HK	February 25, 1968
Larry E. Thomas	Private First Class	Pittsville	HK	May 14, 1969
Wayne R. Thomas	Lance Corporal	Milwaukee	HK	June 17, 1969
William P. Thomas	Private First Class	Belmont	HK	May 2, 1969
Kenneth E. Thresher	Lance Corporal	Milwaukee	HK	December 23, 1967
Larry D. Traaseth	Lance Corporal	Eau Claire	NHI	December 18, 1967
Curtis L. Tremaine	Private First Class	Oconomowoc	HDW	June 3, 1967

MARINES

NAME	RANK	HOMETOWN	TYPE	DATE OF DEATH
Charles J. Treweek	Corporal	St. Francis	HK	May 27, 1968
James N. Tycz	Sergeant	Milwaukee	HK	May 10, 1967
Joseph R. Vandehei	Corporal	Green Bay	HK	March 19, 1969
James L. Van Bendegom§	Staff Sergent	Kenosha	HDC	July 31, 1967
Dan A. Vanerem	Lance Corporal	Green Bay	HK	January 5, 1969
John P. Vis	Private First Class	Brookfield	NHO	September 18, 1967
Gerald A. Vizer	Private First Class	Eau Claire	NHO	May 30, 1967
Duane A. Vogel	Corporal	Sheboygan	HK	December 23, 1966
Donald C. Voltner	Private First Class	St. Francis	HK†	February 28, 1969
Robert T. Walsh	Staff Sergeant	La Crosse	HK	August 10, 1966
Gary T. Walz	Lance Corporal	Prairie Du Chien	HDW	May 12, 1969
Allan C. Ward	Corporal	Deerfield	HK†	April 30, 1968
James W. Washkuhn	Lance Corporal	New Berlin	NHO	November 8, 1966
Albert C. Watson Jr.	Lance Corporal	Mauston	HDW	October 31, 1967
James T. Webber	Private First Class	Eau Claire	HK	June 28, 1970
Karl E. Weber	Private First Class	Two Rivers	HK	November 14, 1968
Robert L. Weeden	Lance Corporal	Waukesha	HK	May 2, 1968
Dennis D. Wehrs	Lance Corporal	La Crosse	HK	May 25, 1968
Stephen J. Westphal	Private First Class	Ixonia	HDW	April 13, 1968
Rickey J. Whitehead	Private First Class	Kenosha	HK	February 26, 1969
David J. Wilcox	Lance Corporal	Portage	HK	November 22, 1968
Gordon W. Will	Private First Class	Waupaca	HK	October 19, 1967
Michael J. Wilson	Private First Class	Sussex	HDW	October 14, 1968
Scott T. Wimmer	Private First Class	Milwaukee	NHO	October 14, 1968
Robert J. Wisch	Private First Class	Milwaukee	NHI	October 10, 1967
Edward Witek§	Sergeant	Lublin	HK	January 18, 1970
Ralph M. Wixson	Private First Class	Janesville	HK	May 16, 1967
Robert C. Wolf	Corporal	Milwaukee	HK	January 7, 1968
Curtis S. Woods	Private First Class	La Crosse	HK	April 12, 1969
Theodore R. Woods Jr.	Corporal	Milwaukee	HDW	March 21, 1967
Richard T. Wucinski	Private First Class	Milwaukee	HK	January 23, 1967
William F. Zahn Jr.	Private First Class	Milwaukee	HK	June 7, 1969
Henry J. Zeichert	Lance Corporal	Cochrane	HK†	September 10, 1965
Steven L. Zobel	Lance Corporal	Oshkosh	NHO	May 21, 1968
Dennis J. Zwirchitz	Private First Class	Abbotsford	HK	March 16, 1968
David L. Zywicke	Lance Corporal	Manitowoc	HK	December 7, 1967

NAVY

NAME	RANK	HOMETOWN	TYPE	DATE OF DEATH
John L. Abrams	Lieutenant	Menomonie	HK	July 13, 1968
Michael J. Allard	Lieutenant	Schofield	HK	August 30, 1967
William G. Andrus	Hospital Corpsman Third Class	Milwaukee	NHO	September 16, 1967
William T. Arnold	Lieutenant Commander	West Allis	HDM*	May 18, 1978
Dan M. Bennett	Hospital Corpsman Third Class	Madison	HK	December 12, 1968
William A. Beyer	Hospitalman	Platteville	HK	February 1, 1967
Lester O. Biehl Jr.	Constructionman	Sheboygan	NHO	September 2, 1965
David J. Bredesen	Hospital Corpsman Third Class	Whitelaw	HK	May 15, 1969
John M. Bronkema	Disbursing Clerk Second Class	Shell Lake	NHO	March 9, 1967
Raymond L. Cork Jr.	Commisseryman Third Class	Racine	HK	December 4, 1967
Tom J. Cress	Lieutenant	Milwaukee	HDW	January 6, 1961
Kent A. Cunningham	Hospitalman	Appleton	HK	November 1, 1968
Douglas J. Daane	Hospital Corpsman Third Class	Oostburg	HK	June 1, 1970
Robert J. Davies	Airman	Rhinelander	NDM	July 29, 1967
Richard L. Davis	Constructionman	New London	HK	August 26, 1968
Robert H. Decker	Hospital Corpsman Third Class	Marshfield	HK	October 18, 1967
Luis Delgado-Class§	Hospitalman	St. Francis	NHO	May 20, 1968
Bruno W. Demata	Seaman	Milwaukee	HDM	February 27, 1969
Richard A. Dexter	Hospital Corpsman Third Class	Rutland	HDW	July 2, 1968
John J. Fiedler	Aviation Structural Mechanic First Class	Janesville	NDM	July 29, 1967
Richard C. Fina	Hospitalman	Hudson	HK	May 24, 1968
Terrence J. Freund	Radioman Second Class	Sheboygan	HK	October 26, 1966
Donald L. Gallagher	Chief Aviation Ordnanceman	Sheboygan	NDM	February 6, 1968
Dell C. Geise	Hospitalman	Burlington	HK	January 26, 1967
Alexander Giejc	Hospitalman	Milwaukee	HDW	February 16, 1968
William R. Glueckstein	Hospitalman	Brookfield	HK	January 29, 1966
William D. Gorsuch	Aviation Boatswain's Mate Third Class	Cambria	NHO	October 2, 1969
Harvey D. Gray	Hospital Corpsman Third Class	Plainfield	HK†	May 5, 1968
Jimmy R. Harries	Fireman	Spencer	HK	June 25, 1968
Jack H. Harris	Commander	Schofield	NHO	October 26, 1966

NAVY

NAME	RANK	HOMETOWN	TYPE	DATE OF DEATH
John F. Hartzheim	Aviation Electronics Technician Second Class	Appleton	HDM	February 27, 1968
Robert L. Hasz	Airman	Baraboo	NDM	July 29, 1967
Lloyd G. Howie	Lieutenant Junior Grade	Oconomowoc	NDM	May 15, 1970
James B. Hudis	Lieutenant Junior Grade	Brookfield	NHO	October 26, 1966
Roy A. Huss	Lieutenant Junior Grade	Eau Claire	NDM	February 6, 1968
Richard Jensen	Hospitalman	Brillion	HDW	November 23, 1965
Gary A. Johnson	Hospital Corpsman Third Class	Madison	HK	April 30, 1969
Robert W. Joosten	Hospitalman	Little Chute	HK	July 16, 1967
Larry D. Judkins	Hospitalman	Appleton	HK	February 10, 1967
Joseph P. Jurgella	Quartermaster First Class	Stevens Point	NHO	October 25, 1970
Kenneth H. Kanaman	Hospital Corpsman Third Class	New London	HK	March 3, 1970
James T. Kearns	Lieutenant Commander	Port Washington	HK	September 14, 1965
Donald A. Kirkham	Hospitalman	Brookfield	HK	February 1, 1968
James D. La Haye	Commander	Green Bay	HK	May 8, 1965
Steven J. Layton	Hospital Corpsman Third Class	Racine	HK	May 1, 1968
Larry J. Leindecker	Seaman	Antigo	HK	April 30, 1968
James R. Loy	Hospitalman	Green Bay	HK	January 11, 1968
Lin A. Mahner	Hospitalman First Class	Medford	HDW	May 25, 1969
Charles W. Marik§	Lieutenant Commander	Dousman	HDM	May 16, 1973
Thomas J. Meenan	Radioman Second Class	Menomonee Falls	HK	June 6, 1968
Loren R. Millard	Hospital Corpsman Third Class	Marshfield	HK	June 6, 1968
Thomas P. Moore§	Hospital Corpsman Second Class	Racine	HK	January 3, 1968
Richard A. Moran§	Lieutenant Commander	Wauwatosa	NHO	August 7, 1966
William H. Murphy III	Lieutenant Junior Grade	Madison	HK	November 19, 1967
Gordon L. Nagel	Boatswain's Mate Second Class	Wauseka	NHO	October 5, 1969
Jerald L. Pinneker	Lieutenant Junior Grade	Milwaukee	HK	March 20, 1966
Richard D. Pliner	Chief Yoeman	Elroy	NHI	June 6, 1970
Eric R. Radtke	Hospitalman	Menomonee Falls	HK	September 10, 1967
Ronald R. Reinke	Hospital Corpsman Third Class	Middleton	HK	September 6, 1967
Rodney H. Rickli	Seaman	Fond du Lac	HK	February 15, 1967
Raymond D. Robinson	Aviation Structural Mechanic Third Class	Kenosha	HK	July 13, 1968

NAVY

NAME	RANK	HOMETOWN	TYPE	DATE OF DEATH
Richard A. Roesler	Hospitalman Second Class	Rhinelander	HK	June 4, 1968
William J. Rohan	Hospital Corpsman Third Class	Racine	HK	September 16, 1966
John R. Ruoho	Machinery Repairman First Class	Florence	NHI	December 3, 1967
Thomas A. Sagen	Guided Missile Group Third Class	Two Rivers	NHI	August 24, 1965
Dennis R. Schmidt	Airman	Appleton	NHO	November 28, 1967
David F. Schuette	Storekeeper Third Class	Green Bay	NHO	February 10, 1970
Richard C. Simon	Boatswain's Mate Third Class	Ellsworth	HK	November 3, 1968
Steven J. Smith	Hospital Corpsman Third Class	Viroqua	HDW	April 6, 1969
Thomas H. Smith	Quartermaster Second Class	Markesan	HK	November 1, 1968
Lawrence N. Stangel	Constructionman	Green Bay	HK	January 31, 1968
Richard W. Stindl	Gunner's Mate Third Class	Beloit	HK	May 15, 1969
Steven P. Swatek	Hospitalman	Peshtigo	HK	March 1, 1968
Blaine H. Walsh	Seaman	Thiensville	NHI	November 27, 1969
Nicholas G. Walz	Engineman Third Class	Steuben	HK	December 23, 1967
Daniel L. Westlie	Engineman Third Class	Augusta	NHO	January 10, 1969

Notes

Chapter One: Advise and Assist

1. Kathryn C. Statler, *Replacing France: The Origins of American Intervention in Vietnam* (Lexington: University Press of Kentucky, 2007), 27.
2. David L. Anderson, *Trapped by Success: The Eisenhower Administration and Vietnam, 1953–1961* (New York: Columbia University Press, 1991), 18.
3. Ibid., 134.
4. Ibid., 64.
5. Statler, *Replacing France*, 196.

Chapter Two: Naval Presence

1. Fredrik Logevall, *Choosing War: The Lost Chance for Peace and the Escalation of War in Vietnam* (Berkeley: University of California Press, 1999), 164, 189.
2. Ibid., 179.
3. Ibid., 117.
4. Ibid., 199.
5. Edward J. Marolda, *By Sea, Air, and Land: An Illustrated History of the U.S. Navy and the War in Southeast Asia* (Washington, DC: Naval Historical Center, 1994), xiii–xiv.

Chapter Three: Send in the Marines

1. Marilyn Young, *The Vietnam Wars, 1945–1990* (New York: HarperPerennial, 1991), 135.
2. Ibid., 139.
3. Fredrik Logevall, *Choosing War: The Lost Chance for Peace and the Escalation of War in Vietnam* (Berkeley: University of California Press, 1999), 213–214.
4. Young, *The Vietnam Wars*, 137.
5. Ibid., 147.

Chapter Four: Elusive Enemy

1. James William Gibson, *The Perfect War: Technowar in Vietnam* (Boston: Atlantic Monthly Press, 1986), 94.
2. Marilyn Young, *The Vietnam Wars, 1945–1990* (New York: HarperPerennial, 1991), 160.

3. Ibid.

4. Robert D. Schulzinger, *A Time for War: The United States and Vietnam, 1941–1975* (New York: Oxford University Press, 1997), 182.

Chapter Five: All Hell Broke Loose

1. Marilyn Young, *The Vietnam Wars, 1945–1990* (New York: HarperPerennial, 1991), 177.

2. John Prados and Ray W. Stubbe, *Valley of Decision: The Siege of Khe Sanh* (Annapolis, MD: Naval Institute Press, 2004), 41.

3. Young, *The Vietnam Wars*, 186.

Chapter Six: Khe Sanh

1. James H. Willbanks, *The Tet Offensive: A Concise History* (New York: Columbia University Press, 2007), 19.

2. Ibid.

3. Robert D. Schulzinger, *A Time for War: The United States and Vietnam, 1941–1975* (New York: Oxford University Press, 1997), 261.

4. Willbanks, *The Tet Offensive*, 24.

5. Ibid., 25.

6. Estimates of the number of NVA troops surrounding Khe Sanh range from 20,000 to 40,000. See Spencer Tucker, *Vietnam* (Lexington: University Press of Kentucky, 1999), 141 and Willbanks, *The Tet Offensive*, 22–23.

7. Willbanks, *The Tet Offensive*, 61; Tucker, *Vietnam*, 141–142.

8. Willbanks, *The Tet Offensive*, 25, 61.

9. Schulzinger, *A Time for War*, 260.

10. George R. Vickers, "U.S. Military Strategy and the Vietnam War," in Jayne Susan Werner and Luu Doan Huynh, eds., *The Vietnam War: Vietnamese and American Perspectives* (Armonk, New York: M.E. Sharpe, 1994), 119. As highlighted by Ray Stubbe, U.S. casualty rates are also difficult to assess, due to the various roles (including air support, air strikes, and relief efforts) that U.S. forces played in the battle. U.S. casualty rates also do not include South Vietnamese killed and wounded. See also Tucker, *Vietnam*, 142.

Chapter Seven: Tet

1. James William Gibson, *The Perfect War: Technowar in Vietnam* (Boston: Atlantic Monthly Press, 1986), 162.

2. Robert D. Schulzinger, *A Time for War: The United States and Vietnam, 1941–1975* (New York: Oxford University Press, 1997), 260.

3. Ibid., 261.

4. Lloyd C. Gardner, *Pay Any Price: Lyndon Johnson and the Wars for Vietnam* (Chicago: Elephant Paperbacks, 1997), 424.

5. Marilyn Young, *The Vietnam Wars, 1945–1990* (New York: HarperPerennial, 1991), 226.

Chapter Eight: Battle of Hue

1. James H. Willbanks, *The Tet Offensive: A Concise History* (New York: Columbia University Press, 2007), 43.

2. Ibid., 44.

3. Ibid., 47.

4. Marilyn Young, *The Vietnam Wars, 1945–1990* (New York: HarperPerennial, 1991), 219.

5. David F. Schmitz, *The Tet Offensive: Politics, War and Public Opinion* (Lanham: Rowman & Littlefield, 2005), 99.

6. Willbanks, *The Tet Offensive*, 52–53.

7. Schmitz, *The Tet Offensive*, 99; Willbanks, *The Tet Offensive*, 54.

8. Willbanks, *The Tet Offensive*, 54.

Chapter Nine: Brown Water Navy

1. Edward J. Marolda, *By Sea, Air, and Land: An Illustrated History of the U.S. Navy and the War in Southeast Asia* (Washington, DC: Naval Historical Center, 1994), 163.

2. Ibid.

3. Ibid., 209.

4. Ibid., 268.

5. Ibid., 269.

Chapter Ten: Brother Duty

1. David L. Anderson, *The Columbia Guide to the Vietnam War* (New York: Columbia University Press, 2002), 58.

2. Ibid., 59.

3. Loren Baritz, *Backfire: A History of How American Culture Led Us into Vietnam and Made Us Fight the Way We Did* (New York: William Morrow, 1985), 302. Most historians estimate that between 10 and 20 percent of U.S. soldiers sent to Vietnam served in combat units. See also James E. Westheider, *Vietnam War* (Westport, CT: Greenwood Publishing Group, 2007), 78; and D. Michael Shafer, "The Vietnam Combat Experience: The Human Legacy," in D. Michael Shafer, ed., *The Legacy: The Vietnam War in the American Imagination* (Boston: Beacon Press, 1990), 82.

4. Baritz, *Backfire*, 292.

5. Westheider, *Vietnam War*, 79.

6. Shafer, "The Vietnam Combat Experience," 87.

7. Baritz, *Backfire*, 292.

8. Anderson, *The Columbia Guide to the Vietnam War*, 58.

9. Shafer, "The Vietnam Combat Experience," 89.

Chapter Eleven: Hamburger Hill

1. Andrew Weist, *Vietnam's Forgotten Army: Heroism and Betrayal in the ARVN* (New York: NYU Press, 2007), 157.

2. Ibid., 159.

3. Ibid., 159, 160.

4. Ibid., 164.

5. "The Battle for Hamburger Hill," *Time*, May 30, 1969.

6. Rick Perlstein, *Nixonland: The Rise of a President and the Fracturing of America* (New York: Scribner, 2008), 387.

7. "The Battle for Hamburger Hill," *Time*, May 30, 1969.

8. Perlstein, *Nixonland*, 387.

9. Weist, *Vietnam's Forgotten Army*, 175.

Chapter Twelve: The Price

1. John T. Greenwood and F. Clifton Berry, *Medics at War: Military Medicine from Colonial Times to the 21st Century* (Annapolis: Naval Institute Press, 2005), 140.

2. Ibid., 148.

3. Jan K. Herman, *Navy Medicine in Vietnam: Oral Histories from Dien Bien Phu to the Fall of Saigon* (Jefferson: McFarland, 2008), 1.

4. Greenwood and Berry, *Medics at War*, 140.

5. Ibid.; Herman, *Navy Medicine in Vietnam*, 2.

6. James E. Westheider, *Vietnam War* (Westport, CT: Greenwood Publishing Group, 2007), 72.

7. Bettie J. Morden, *The Women's Army Corps, 1945–1978* (Washington, DC: Center of Military History, 1990), 222–223.

8. Ibid., 246–249.

9. Westheider, *Vietnam War*, 90.

10. U.S. National Archives, "Statistical Information About Casualties of the Vietnam War," www.archives.gov/research/vietnam-war/casualty-statistics.html.

11. Robert D. Schulzinger, *Time for Peace: The Legacy of the Vietnam War* (New York: Oxford University Press, 2006), xv.

Chapter Thirteen: Firebases

1. Robert D. Schulzinger, *A Time for War: The United States and Vietnam, 1941–1975* (New York: Oxford University Press, 1997), 275.

2. Marilyn Young, *The Vietnam Wars: 1945–1990* (New York: HarperCollins, 1991), 240; Rick Perlstein, *Nixonland: The Rise of a President and the Fracturing of America* (New York: Scribner, 2008), 477.

3. Schulzinger, *A Time for War*, 282.

4. Young, *The Vietnam Wars*, 237.

5. Ibid., 248.

6. Andrew Wiest, *Vietnam's Forgotten Army: Heroism and Betrayal in the ARVN* (New York: NYU Press, 2007), 182.

7. Young, *The Vietnam Wars*, 280.

Chapter Fourteen: Secret War

1. David L. Anderson, *The Vietnam War* (New York: Palgrave Macmillan, 2005), 97.

2. Marilyn Young, *The Vietnam Wars, 1945–1990* (New York: HarperPerennial, 1991), 234.

3. Ibid., 235.

4. Ibid.

5. Ibid.

6. Ibid.

7. Anderson, *The Vietnam War*, 116.

8. Mark Atwood Lawrence, *The Vietnam War: A Concise International History* (New York: Oxford University Press, 2008), 170.

Chapter Fifteen: Hanoi Hilton

1. Stuart Rochester and Frederick Kiley, *Honor Bound: American Prisoners of War in Southeast Asia, 1961–1973* (Annapolis: Naval Institute Press, 2007), ix.

2. Michael J. Allen, "Help Us Tell the Truth About Vietnam: POW/MIA Politics and the End of the American War," in Mark Philip Bradley and Marilyn B. Young, eds., *Making Sense of the Vietnam Wars: Local, National and Transnational Perspectives* (New York: Oxford University Press, 2008), 252, 268.

3. Rochester and Kiley, *Honor Bound*, 144.

4. Ibid.

5. David L. Anderson, *The Vietnam War* (New York: Palgrave Macmillan, 2005), 109.

Epilogue: The Road Home

1. Marilyn Young, *The Vietnam Wars, 1945–1990* (New York: HarperPerennial, 1991), 290.

2. Ibid., 314.

3. Mark Atwood Lawrence, *The Vietnam War: A Concise International History* (New York: Oxford University Press, 2008), 171.

4. Ibid., 172.

5. Ibid.

6. Tim O'Brien, *The Things They Carried* (Boston: Houghton Mifflin, 1990), 76 as cited in Young, *The Vietnam Wars*, 329.

7. Young, *The Vietnam Wars*, 324.

8. Ibid., 321.

9. James E. Westheider, *Vietnam War* (Westport, CT: Greenwood Publishing Group, 2007), 164–165.

10. Young, *The Vietnam Wars*, 327.

List of Participants

The following veterans took part in the Wisconsin Vietnam War Stories Project, which is a partnership of the Wisconsin Historical Society and Wisconsin Public Television, in association with the Wisconsin Department of Veterans Affairs. We thank you for your participation and service.

Martin Acker
Marvin Acker
Dennis Aldrich
Mike Allen
Thomas Baertsch
George Banda
Rick Berry
Mike Berzinsky
Jack Boers
Ray Boland
Doug Bradley
John Brogan
Keith Brunette
Joe Campbell
Steve Charles
Theodore Christjohn
John Couper
Robert Curry
James Daley
John Dederich
Mike Demske
Kerry Denson
Teddy Duckworth
Rick Erck
Michael Falbo
Ted Fetting

Glenn Fieber
Peter Finnegan
Fred Flom
Mark Foreman
Marv Freedman
Joel Garb
Dave Gehr
Sue Haack
Cletus "Ed" Hardy
Roger Harrison
Don Heiliger
Daniel Hinkle
Michael Hoks
Leon House
Bob Hunt
Gene Hunter
Bill Hustad
Lou Janowski
Bruce Jensen
Wayne Jensen
Fred Johnson
Don Jones
David Kies
Sam King
Charles Kocourek
Jim Kurtz

Lance Larson
David Lee
Charlie Lieb
Nhia Thong "Charles" Lor
Mick Lyons
Steve Manthei
Robert Maves
Jim Mayr
Linda McClenahan
Ken McGwin
John Mielke
George Miller
Larry Miller
Bill Moore
Cletus Ninham
John Nusbaum
James Overman
Owen Mike
Lowell Peterson
Bob Piaro
John Pieper
Daniel Pierce
Steve Piotrowski
John Plaster
Alice Plautz

Steve Plue
William Rettenmund
Roy Rogers
Jeremy Rockman
James Rose
Dan Schaller
Tom Schober
Steven Schofield
Bill Schuler
James Seaton
Marty Severson
Tom Sharratt

Howard Sherpe
Al Sobkowiak
Everett Soetenga
Robert Spencer
Harry Steindorf
Ike Stefanski
David Stone
Ray Stubbe
Andy Thundercloud
Roger Treece
Dave Van Dyke
Greg Walsko

Mike Weaver
Don Weber
Robert Webster
Henry Weege
Gary Wetzel
Alvin Whitaker
Daniel White
Sandy Wilcox
Miles Wilkens
Will Williams
Charlie Wolden

Index

About the Authors

In addition to this volume, Sarah Larsen is co-author of *Wisconsin Korean War Stories* (WHS Press, 2008), the companion volume to the Wisconsin Public Television documentary of the same name. A graduate of the University of Wisconsin–Madison, Larsen worked on the production of *Wisconsin Korean War Stories* and *Wisconsin World War II Stories: Legacy* with the History Unit of Wisconsin Public Television. While working on that project she compiled the first searchable, electronic list of Wisconsin soldiers killed while serving in the Second World War. For this volume, Larsen transformed the raw transcripts of veteran interviews into a comprehensive, book-length format. She lives with her family in Madison.

Jennifer M. Miller has worked as a teacher and lecturer for the University of Wisconsin–Madison History Department from which she received her master's degree in 2005. An expert in U.S. foreign relations with East Asia during the Cold War, she is writing a PhD dissertation on U.S.–Japanese relations during the 1950s. She is a member of the Society for Historians of American Foreign Relations and has been published in *Reviews in History*. Miller co-authored *Wisconsin Korean War Stories* with Sarah Larsen and is author of the historical chapter introductions for this book. The recipient of a Fulbright Fellowship, she is currently living in Tokyo for research.